International Management

MGT400

David Ahlstrom | Garry D. Bruton

CENGAGE
Learning

Australia • Brazil • Japan • Korea • Mexico • Singapore • Spain • United Kingdom • United States

CENGAGE
Learning

International Management: MGT400

David Ahlstrom | Garry D. Bruton

Executive Editors:
 Maureen Staudt
 Michael Stranz

Senior Project Development Manager:
 Linda DeStefano

Marketing Specialist:
 Sara Mercurio
 Lindsay Shapiro

Senior Production / Manufacturing Manager:
 Donna M. Brown

PreMedia Supervisor:
 Joel Brennecke

Rights & Permissions Specialist:
 Kalina Hintz
 Todd Osborne

Cover Image:
 Getty Images*

* Unless otherwise noted, all cover images used by Custom Solutions, a part of Cengage Learning, have been supplied courtesy of Getty Images with the exception of the Earthview cover image, which has been supplied by the National Aeronautics and Space Administration (NASA).

For product information and technology assistance, contact us at
Cengage Learning Customer & Sales Support, 1-800-354-9706

For permission to use material from this text or product, submit all requests online at **cengage.com/permissions**
Further permissions questions can be emailed to
permissionrequest@cengage.com

ISBN-13: 978-1-111-00366-1

ISBN-10: 1-111-00366-1

Cengage Learning
5191 Natorp Boulevard
Mason, Ohio 45040
USA

Cengage Learning is a leading provider of customized learning solutions with office locations around the globe, including Singapore, the United Kingdom, Australia, Mexico, Brazil, and Japan. Locate your local office at: **international.cengage.com/region**

Cengage Learning products are represented in Canada by Nelson Education, Ltd.

For your lifelong learning solutions, visit **www.cengage.com/custom**

Visit our corporate website at **www.cengage.com**

Printed in the United States of America

Table of Contents

(*Note – this is a "custom" textbook that has been designed specifically for this course in a joint effort between your instructor and the publisher. Please note that some chapters have been removed intentionally and some pages may be black & white as dictated by the changes.)

2

CULTURE AND INTERNATIONAL MANAGEMENT

Overview

One of the key challenges in doing business internationally is the considerable differences in culture around the world. When we talk about culture we are discussing those subtle but profound things that shape differences in values and behavior in societies. Cultural differences can be seen in a wide range of everyday things, such as how close individuals stand when talking (North Americans stand about one arm's length apart when talking, but people in other countries tend to stand much closer together), the nature of communication between individuals (for example, in Russia, China, and Japan there is a great hesitancy to say no directly in response to a request, while in Anglo countries such as Australia and the United States there is no similar hesitancy), and how influential each country's legal system is (in China the legal system has great flexibility in how different laws are interpreted and enforced, while common-law countries, such as the United Kingdom or the United States, rely on a large body of case law and commentary). To understand why management can differ in diverse areas of the world it is vital to understand culture and its consequences. This chapter will examine culture—a topic that provides important foundational material for much of what we will examine later in the book. The topics covered in this chapter include:

* Learning about different cultures that exist around the world.
* Conceptual models for better understanding the world's cultures.
* Understanding the impact of environmental factors on culture.
* Identifying distinctive management styles that exist in different countries.

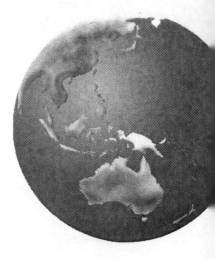

CULTURAL CONFUSION: AN ACCENTURE MANAGER IN INDIA

A senior information technology manager working for Accenture from the United Kingdom was running a major IT and support operation in India. Accenture is a major consulting firm and the support operation was on behalf of a large consumer electronics firm. The manager was concerned that the Indian IT support employees were not being helpful to the customers calling from the U.S., the United Kingdom, and other Commonwealth countries. He knew about the lack of assistance to those customers because there were many complaints. These problems had reached a crisis point, and the client was asking Accenture to considering canceling the contract.

The manager had carefully instructed his Indian employees on how to help the customers who were calling. The Indian employees he found were easily trained and very attentive. Indian culture was very hierarchical with the group playing a very strong role. As the employees were trained in the various regional accents they expected to hear in the United Kingdom and elsewhere, they learned the material quickly. The employees were even taught how to use similar spoken inflections. The manager was therefore surprised when the customers were still unhappy and giving their customer service very low ratings.

Customers reported that the Indian employees answered their questions too narrowly and literally, and they made little effort to supply extra information that the customer needed but did not know how to ask for. This puzzled the Indian employees who felt they were answering the questions asked—what more could the customers want? The employees also felt that some customer requests were difficult to figure out: customers used slang that the Indian employees did not understand, and they insisted on urgent action that the Indian staff had trouble understanding—how could the customers be in such a rush at midnight to fix a computer problem? The British site manager decided that he needed to conduct more training, especially something management scientists were calling "empathy training" to help employees better understand the customers and their needs, particularly the urgency to get a computer fixed.

To illustrate the difficulty faced at the firm, one customer was making a second call about the printer on his home network not printing. The Indian employee did a nice job diagnosing the problem in the second call, figuring out that it was a simple communication problem of some kind, perhaps with the mechanical AB switch the customer had set up with his PC to switch between the printer and another device. The employee had become convinced that it was a hardware problem and that the customer had to contact the computer store that sold him the switch and cable. The customer was not happy with that, because in a prior call, the Indian support staff had told him how to set up the printer and advised him to buy the switch in the first place. Now the customer felt that the support center was not being helpful about the resulting problem. He did not believe the switch was broken. He asked to speak to the manager, and since the United Kingdom manager was unavailable at that time, he took the call. After questioning the customer, the manager discovered that the customer had purchased the wrong type of AB switch— the switch purchased was designed to attach two PCs to one printer, rather than attaching two printers to one PC, which is what the customer actually wanted (the two types of switches are generally not substitutable for each other). The customer was understandably irate, and asked, "Why didn't the staff warn me that there are *two types* of AB switches? That is an easy mistake to make if you don't know these devices well!" The support staff had initially been too casual in instructing the customer, and had not reminded the customer to be careful not to buy the wrong type of switch.

The British manager angrily told his staff later that one simple reminder to the customer in the original call would have avoided this problem, and later, one additional question would have identified the problem, rather than telling the customer that they could not help and to simply contact the vendor the next morning.

Similar problems occurred when customers were instructed to buy a certain type of DVD player but were not warned about possible compatibility problems between regions; nor were customers warned about the differences between different types of PAL (British and South American) television systems. In all these cases, irate customers were understandably upset that their time was wasted, especially when a simple reminder from the support staff could have avoided these unnecessary problems. "How can I get the staff to think just a little outside of their job descriptions to let the customer know what to do and what to watch out for?" the British manager wondered.

The manager, based on his cultural expectations, assumed his employees would take the initiative and go beyond the instructions of the job, putting themselves in the customer's place. He did not reason that many of the Indian employees would be uncomfortable doing this. The cultural impact of strong hierarchical and group orientation provides many benefits, but the negative is that the employees did not want to be accused of not following their supervisor's instructions and answering customer queries to the letter. Moreover, they believed that their bosses were paid to make decisions outside of the prescribed steps, not them. The switch problem was held up by the British manager as an example of how to think beyond the customer's stated problem—not how to set up an A-B switch per se, but how to solve

(Continued)

his networking problem. Customers, the boss explained, are not always able to state their problems clearly, and, it takes asking many questions to find out what a customer's problem really is. Moreover, it is important to take the time to find this out, and put oneself in the customer's shoes.

Once the manager instructed his employees that they should ask questions beyond the basic diagnostic requirements, he even recommended two more specific questions to be sure the employees did not miss anything: "What is your situation now?" and "What are you trying to accomplish

with this hardware/software?" With this help, the employees became less anxious about looking beyond their literal job requirements. This small training step overcame a cultural difference which had the potential to derail the success of the entire business operation.

Culture
Acquired knowledge people use to interpret experience and actions. This knowledge then influences values, attitudes, and behaviors.

Understanding culture is fundamental to understanding many of the differences in business around the world. A firm operating in a single country only has to contend with the culture of that country. As a result, most managers do not find much difficulty in adjusting to regional variations within their own countries.[i] However, as business expands to different countries, the culture in each of those diverse regions must be taken into account; managers and companies that ignore cultural differences do so at their peril. The Daimler Chrysler merger will be discussed later in this text, and this short case will show that cultural differences can lead to significant difficulties in international business.

In broad terms, **culture** is the acquired knowledge people use to interpret experience and actions. This knowledge, in turn, influences the values, attitudes, and behaviors of those people. Culture, thus, is connected to the knowledge, beliefs, customs, and habits acquired by members of a society. The impact of culture on international business depends on in which regions of the world a firm is active. For example, someone from the United States would have little difficulty doing business in Canada, the United Kingdom, or Australia. However, that same person might find a very different cultural environment in countries such as India or China or even Germany. Cultural differences affect a wide range of issues: they can create a great deal of misunderstanding and strife for a manager and damage an organization's reputation in a foreign country for years. For example, early in its economic reform, China asked a number of major multinational enterprises to help modernize its industry. At the time of the request, China's market was not seen as the dynamic, growing market it is today. Thus, many firms declined, expecting to be able to pursue such opportunities later if the market proved to be more attractive. However, the officials that had invited these firms felt a loss of "face" (a cultural characteristic we will examine in detail later but that can be described as respect) when their offer was refused. As a result, when these multinational enterprises later decided that it was time to enter the China market, they were surprised when the Chinese government officials were not supportive. A lack of understanding of the cultural impact of saying no, a rational economic choice at the time, has hampered these firms' ability to enter the China market. What seemed like a rational business choice to the managers violated cultural norms in China, and hindered their later efforts to enter the growing Chinese market.

This chapter focuses on national cultures and how they impact management in different countries. There are many cultures, just as there are many languages, and it is impossible to learn about every one in detail. There are, however, some basic frameworks that help to describe and summarize national cultures that are useful in a wide range of settings. These frameworks can help students and business people to understand the similarities and differences in the national cultures of the world. It is possible to see clusters of cultures in various regions of the world. In addition, there are certain cultural protocols or etiquettes that are relevant to a variety of situations. The understanding of these broad differences will allow you to understand culture's consequences on managing internationally in a multitude of diverse settings.

PIZZA HUT AND THE ROLE OF LOCAL TASTE

An illustration of the difficulties culture can represent to a firm is the dilemma that market strategists at Pizza Hut faced in the mid-1980s. Pizza Hut, which was bought by Pepsi in the late 1970s, was encouraged by Pepsi management to "go international." At that time, Pizza Hut already had a number of overseas operations, mostly in Western European and Latin American countries. In particular, management wanted Pizza Hut to expand to new markets, such as China, where economic reforms had caused a takeoff of annual GDP growth to about 10 percent per year throughout the 1980s. The China experts warned Pizza Hut that Chinese people would not eat pizza because they do not like cheese, or cannot digest it, and tomatoes are not part of Chinese cuisine. "The Chinese consumer will reject your product, so don't bother," one well-known management academic told Pizza Hut during her presentation to their top management. "It is against Chinese culture to eat pizza," she added.

Pizza Hut was not so sure about that. Top management recalled that Kentucky Fried Chicken (KFC) was told something quite similar about the Hong Kong and Mainland China markets, that is, that Chinese cuisine already had so many types of chicken dishes that people would not like the southern U.S.–style fried chicken. In response, KFC modified their recipes slightly while introducing some side items that fit with local tastes (and price points), and KFC was able become the most successful fast food restaurant in China. Most importantly, KFC noticed that the Chinese urban consumer was becoming more mobile, and had disposable income to spend on the one child the government would let families have (China's one-child policy started in 1979).

Pizza Hut cut down on cheese and tomato sauce, and added local toppings such as soy sauce chicken, tuna fish, corn, and crab sticks. They even introduced new pizzas, such as the Thousand Island dressing pizza, which didn't use tomato sauce, and the Homemade Sweet & Creamy Pizza, which look like small apple turnovers, with a topping of sweetened condensed milk. In reporting to top management, the head of global business development reminded management that culture and tradition were not the only forces working on consumers in a given society. Local tastes are important; not only do they change, but so-called nontraditional products can be repackaged to fit local tastes and a country's changing socio-economic environment.

Ahlstrom, D. (2009). But Asians don't do that: The limits of culture as a predictive analytical device. *The Chinese University of Hong Kong, Faculty of Business Working Paper Series*, 2008–2009.

This chapter will initially illustrate the depth of impact culture has on society and then define the concept exactly. This discussion will include the range of impacts culture can have and the common mistakes firms make in dealing with culture. We will then examine different frameworks that can be used to better understand culture in a given situation. Figure 2-1 summarizes the flow of this chapter. There can be subcultures in a country, for example in Spain there are subcultures, such as the Basque and Catalonians. But here we will focus on countries' primary cultures because they will allow us to better contrast cultures around the world.

CULTURE DEFINED

Anthropology is the study of human culture and customs (*anthropos* in Greek means humankind, and *-logy* refers to the study of something). Though people often think of the study and application of "culture" in terms of rainforest tribes, all societies have a culture that is relevant to business and affects the workplace and general commercial environment.

| FIGURE 2-1 | Chapter 2 Conceptual Flow |

To illustrate the power of culture, consider that Hispanic people from Central America and the Caribbean started moving to the United States and Canada in large numbers after World War II. These new immigrants continued to exhibit cultural patterns in terms of beliefs and behaviors consistent with the Latin American culture. However, their children and grandchildren picked up cultural patterns consistent with North American culture very quickly, including the use of English. As a result, after two or three generations in the United States, the descendants of Hispanic immigrants have largely become indistinguishable from the general population. Spanish is no longer their primary language, the population is only slightly more likely to be Catholic, and children are just as likely to marry someone who is not Hispanic.[ii] Some of the most distinguishable aspects of U.S. culture include its high trust (in a high trust society, people will typically trust someone until that person proves untrustworthy), reliance on an abstract rule of law, the importance of punctuality, and a strong "can-do" spirit. These aspects of the culture, and even regional English usage patterns, are readily accepted by all immigrant groups within two to three generations after arriving.

In broad terms, culture can be defined as the acquired, collective knowledge of a group that they use to interpret experiences. This knowledge in turn translates into values that guide behaviors. Thus, culture includes the knowledge, beliefs, customs, and other capabilities and habits acquired by members of a society. Culture is not genetically-based or encoded but is learned by people and encouraged by societies and governments.[iii] When you talk about culture and its effects, you are primarily talking about learned behaviors of a wide range of people in a given society. Culture is not set in stone, and will change as the society undergoes change and new traditions are introduced and inculcated.[iv] However, such changes are typically slow and occur over a period of time.

HOW CULTURE IS TRANSMITTED

Culture is transmitted through its people in a variety of ways—both formal and informal.[v] Informal transmission happens every day as individuals interact with each other, watch television, or read books. Formal transmission can occur through efforts to socialize an individual, such as in schools and government.[vi] For example, Japan has a strong and distinct culture. In this society parents and grandparents consciously spend considerable effort educating children about Japan and its culture. Young Japanese children are taught at a very young age about the hierarchy in society and how they should behave. This is illustrated by the concept of *giri*, which loosely translates to the right way to behave, though it often refers directly to the rather formalized system of gift giving and exchange relations in Japanese society (when gifts are given, to whom, and how much they should cost). People from western societies are often surprised at the degree to which this formal (though largely unwritten) system of gift giving is refined in Japan. Even those who are visiting Japan for an extended stay for the first time are influenced by *giri* and the extent to which Japanese people give gifts. To violate one's *giri* obligation is to make a major social blunder—much more so than an etiquette misstep in the United States or United Kingdom.[vii] Japan has a group-oriented culture where participation in, and consistency with, the group (whatever that group may be) is extremely important. Part of fulfilling one's *giri* can involve giving the correct gifts at the correct time, making sure they are properly wrapped, and that they are in the right price range. Thus, if a manager is given a gift by an employee, protocol dictates that the manager (a person with a higher status in this situation) should give a gift that is (at least slightly) higher in value than what he or she received. Failing to understand and act appropriately on *giri* is a serious

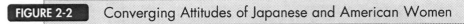

FIGURE 2-2 Converging Attitudes of Japanese and American Women

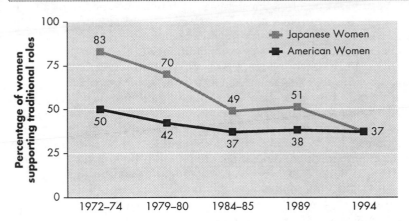

social offense that carries the stiffest of Japanese penalties: shame and perhaps even exclusion from the group.[viii] In contrast, if one fails to bring a gift or violates some other social norm in North America, such as not saying "Good morning" to coworkers, people may be offended, but it is unlikely to create major problems.

However, even an old, well-established culture like Japan's does change. For example, male and female roles have historically been very clear in Japan, considered to be a society dominated by men and masculine values.[ix] Women were thought to hold (and be accepting of) a subordinate role in Japanese society. However, recent studies show that Japanese women now have very similar attitudes to American women in terms of women's roles. These merging values can be seen in Figure 2-2.

One outcome of this shift in culture is that marriage and birth rates are dropping significantly in Japan. Historically, a Japanese woman worked until she married, then she was expected to quit and become a homemaker. Japanese women's attitude toward work has changed in a manner consistent with the United States and Europe, where many more women want to work professionally and not fully devote themselves to raising children. And with this option of professional advancement and more educational and economic opportunities, many Japanese women have postponed marriage and opted for very small (or no) families.[x]

CULTURE'S IMPACT

The impact of culture on organizations is broad. For example, culture can affect all aspects of the management of a firm including, but not limited to, strategy, hiring, pay/promotion, organization, and evaluation of performance. This wide range of issues is addressed in the following chapters.

To illustrate the extent of the impact of culture, we initially examine cross-cultural communication. The nature of communication in an international firm will be further explored later in the text as will a variety of other issues including negotiations, human-resource management, leadership, decision making, and evaluation and control. In this section we use this examination of part of the communication concerns for an international firm to illustrate that culture can affect organizations in a wide variety of unexpected ways. Following the discussion of communication, we then examine the broad roots of what leads to cultural problems for managers. This will lead to a discussion of the major cultural mistakes that firms often make and how they can avoid them.

Communication

Communication is one of the most critical factors in the success of a business. A wide range of cultural issues affects communication in an international firm. For example, when people from North America ask a question, they expect the listener to understand the intent of the question and answer accordingly. But this is not always the case in other cultures (recall the opening vignette on the Accenture manager). As a result, managers from North America are surprised when they find out how literally a question can be answered in a setting like China, even when there are no significant language barriers. For example, Chinese employees typically work in enterprises organized around a hierarchical structure in which they are encouraged not to think independently but to follow orders precisely. This results in expatriate managers being driven to distraction by their employees answering questions with a brief exactness that can leave out important (and seemingly obvious) information.

Expatriate managers in China have observed that employees in China who have been trained in the more traditional, hierarchical organizations are more likely to answer questions quite literally and fail to think laterally about the intent of the questioner or about the actual problem.[xi] Imagine, for example, that you asked an employee of yours in China if a local bus will stop at a certain train station. It would not be uncommon for that employee to answer literally and simply say "no." Yet you must remember that the employee may be failing to tell you that the bus stops a few minutes' walk away from the station.[xii] The Chinese employee is answering literally that the bus does not stop in the train station's bus bay and may have failed to grasp the intent of your question, which was to find out if the bus stops in the *vicinity* of the train station, not if the bus stops literally in the train station's bus bay. For expatriates in China or other hierarchical countries where answering queries literally and doing exactly (and often only) what is being asked is customary, it is important to keep asking questions to be sure the intent of your question is understood. Imagine how such simple, cross-cultural communication misunderstandings can affect a firm considering that there are a multiplicity of situations that can occur in a business setting on a day to day basis. You can start to understand how frustrating an international assignment can be and how it is important to prepare yourself and train your coworkers and subordinates in handling these and other problems.

Culture has an impact on not only how communication takes place in an organization but also what is actually communicated.[xiii] In the United States and other Anglo countries, such as Australia and the United Kingdom, managers tend to be focused on work-related issues when they are in the workplace. Managers typically do not want to know (and often legally cannot ask) about issues outside the sphere of work such as the worker's children, divorces, illnesses in the family, and personal finances. However, in other cultures, the manager's role is similar to that of a father. In Latin American societies, such as Mexico, the manager is expected to want to know and be willing to help on many personal issues. The same involvement by the manager is true for Chinese organizations, except in Hong Kong, which is more similar to the United States.

The manner in which information is communicated is also impacted by culture. For example, in the U.S. communication in business tends to be direct. If a mistake is made, managers are taught to confront the person directly. Similar approaches are consistent with Northern European culture in general. However, in other societies such a direct confrontation is seen as rude. For example, in East Asia, such a confrontation causes the person who is confronted to lose **face**, or the respect of his peers. The result of such a confrontation is that the person confronted may leave the organization; not necessarily the outcome intended. In such a situation, confronting the person privately so that the person can keep the respect of others is very important. If the person has seniority in the company, it may be

Face
Respect of a person's peers; avoiding embarrassment.

COMMUNICATION: MONOCHRONIC AND POLYCHRONIC

Edward Hall expanded his framework on communication by including the notion of monochronic versus polychronic cultures. Monochronic societies tend to do things in a linear way, valuing punctuality and strict schedules. Most Northern European cultures, including the Anglo-American culture, are considered monochronic; Germany tends to be the archetype for this dimension with a strong emphasis on being on time for any meeting. In Latin America and the Middle East, people tend to be more polychronic: schedules are more fluid, and people tend to do more than one thing at a time.

Business people from a monochronic culture, such as the United Kingdom, can get frustrated when colleagues from polychronic cultures, such as Italy, do not show up on time for a social dinner. In the Italian business person's mind, when he said dinner was around 8:00 pm, he expected you to go there and talk to other friends or colleagues, and perhaps start dinner, and he would arrive when he could. One U.S. business person mentioned that if he wants his Italian or Latin American colleagues to arrive at an 8:00 pm, he will tell them that dinner will start about 7:30 pm, to provide some cushion for the lateness that is common in less than crucial meetings. However, sometimes you just have to wait for people.[xiv]

It's always good to be on time for social gatherings as well as business meetings in different countries, regardless of the type of culture. An individual may be from a polychronic culture, but it does not mean he or she will tolerate someone being late to their meeting. If the person is from a monochronic culture, he or she is likely to not see you if you are late.

CULTURE

necessary to speak to his or her assistant to present the negative information, rather than speaking directly to that senior person.

Communication can be verbal or non-verbal.[xv] Anthropologist Edward Hall highlighted this in his famous book and 1960 article with Mildred Reed Hall, "The Silent Language of Overseas Business."[xvi] The Halls argued that high-context and low-context cultures exist. Low-context cultures include most cultures of the developed west, such as the United States, the United Kingdom, and Europe. High-context cultures include those of East Asia, India, and Africa.

In high-context cultures, the context in which what is spoken plays a major role in communication and the behavior of individuals. The status of the person who is speaking, why the person is speaking (was it initiated by the speaker or was it in response to a question), and the other person's status all impact the nature of how something is to be communicated. In contrast, in low-context cultures, such as the United States, the information is very straightforward, and the context has less impact on how such information is likely to be spoken and interpreted.

Americans and British, for example, generally value direct and clear communication. Most people from Anglo countries would not add honorific terms to their communication, such as calling a customer "honorable customer." In East Asia and other developing regions, such as the Middle East, communication is much higher context and such honorific terms are commonly used. Nonverbal cues are quite important in high-context cultures. For example, in most East Asian cultures, nonverbal signals, such as silence, or indirect answers, such as "That will be very difficult" (usually a polite way of saying "no" in East Asia from Japan to Indonesia) are critical to understanding what is being communicated.

So, in high-context culture:

* communication is less direct
* speech is unhurried and drawn out
* greater emphasis is placed on the context or nonverbal cues and less emphasis is placed on the actual information
* interpretation is looser, which sometimes can be problematic for the listener because answers may be indirect and it takes experience on the part of the listener to interpret what was really said
* face is very important: direct, embarrassing questions or statements are to be avoided, or asked in a very discreet way, sometimes via an intermediary

In low-context culture:

* the primary interest is the information and the context is less important
* the listener wants to get lots of information
* lack of clarity or ambiguity is generally regarded as negative
* interpretation should be unequivocal
* direct and embarrassing questions are often asked; face-saving is not very important

Communication between individuals from low-context and high-context environments can be particularly problematic. Even when individuals are proficient in a foreign language, they tend to retain the speech patterns and local dialects of their home country and culture. In addition, individuals interpret communication on the basis of one's own cultural norms.[xvii]

Problems in Dealing with Culture

Parochialism
Belief that there is no other way of doing things except what is done in one's own culture.

Culture's influence is widespread and can often affect unexpected areas. One problem is **parochialism**, or the belief that the only way to do something is the way it's done in one's own culture. People who believe this are often simply unaware of other ways of doing things. However, such individuals' inability to recognize that they are treating other individuals with less than full respect can cause difficulties in the workplace.

Ethnocentrism
The ethnocentric view of culture holds that an individual or a firm will believe that their own way of doing things is the best, and will not seek to adapt to local cultural practices.

Ethnocentrism is related to parochialism in that it reflects a sense of superiority about a person's or firm's homeland. Ethnocentric people believe that their ways of doing things are the best, no matter what cultures are involved. With parochialism the person may not know that there are other ways of doing things, but with ethnocentrism they know there are other ways but still believe their way is the best. Both parochial and ethnocentric people tend to project their values onto others, and see foreign cultures as odd or of little or no value to them. Another potential problem in dealing with culture is **polycentrism**. Polycentrism is the opposite of ethnocentrism in that people seek to do things the way locals do—"When in Rome, do as the Romans do," as the old saying goes. Although this aphorism reflects a useful approach to doing business in foreign lands, it can sometimes become a problem. For example, if a manager is abroad for a long time, he or she may start to "go native" and no longer accept the views of the home office, choosing to adopt the culture and practices of the local setting. This can result in the local culture having the final say on things such as bribes and the status of women or minorities, which may be values inconsistent with the parent firm or even homeland laws. Polycentrism is a major source of ethical lapses at many firms.[xviii]

Polycentric
The polycentric view of culture holds that multinational enterprises (MNE) should treat each international subsidiary largely as a separate national entity. This means that the subsidiary should do things in a local manner, and MNE subsidiaries may come to differ from each other.

Common Culture Mistakes

International businesses can make many potential cultural mistakes. Even firms that are culturally savvy will occasionally make cultural missteps. For example, Coke is one of the world's most admired and widespread international companies. However, when the firm entered the China market, they chose some Chinese characters for Coca-Cola that when read in Chinese sounded like Coca-Cola. Unfortunately no one at Coca-Cola bothered to check the meaning of these characters, which actually meant "bite the wax tadpole." This was certainly not an attractive name for a beverage that at the time was unfamiliar to the general Chinese population. The firm had to backtrack and choose a new set of Chinese characters for Coca-Cola. The characters they settled on still sound like Coca-Cola, but the name's meaning now gives a good feeling. Firms that need to create product names using Chinese, or other foreign languages, should be certain to get help to avoid unexpected or embarrassing translations.

Protocol
Rules for how individuals in a business setting are to interact with each other.

Protocol is how individuals in a business setting should interact with one another. An example of protocol is understanding proper etiquette when a

McDONALD'S AND ADAPTING IN CHINA

McDonald's has been successful in the Mainland China market, due in no small part to its understanding that a restaurant meal for most people in China is a big treat, particularly for children. McDonald's came to China with the expectation of opening a fast food hamburger restaurant positioned similar to those in the U.S. and their successful franchises in Hong Kong. McDonald's learned early in the strategic planning process, and from its experiences with its first few restaurants, that it faced a very different environment in China. McDonald's in North America and Hong Kong provides a cheap meal, but McDonald's cannot ever be as cheap as the food stalls and other low-cost venues in China. Realizing this, McDonald's moved aggressively to position the restaurant as a fun, mid-range priced restaurant, with high quality. To provide that quality the firm actually has limited wait staff service in some locations.

McDonald's also decided to focus on a particular niche in the market: children. China has a one-child policy that limits an urban family that is not an ethnic minority to a single child. This child is typically given a great deal of attention by the parents and grandparents. As a result, in spite of China's modest per capita income, the combination of two parents and four grandparents can produce a reasonable level of purchasing power for each child. So McDonald's determined to focus on children by doing things like running special parties for children, and having the latest toys for children (McDonalds is one of the major toy retailers in China).

The firm convinced Chinese consumers that a trip to McDonalds is a special occasion, and McDonalds has created a more upscale environment in many of its Chinese restaurants than anywhere else in the world. They have also effectively reinforced this position, keeping it different from its low-priced image in the United States and in China's special administrative region of Hong Kong.

---

prospective client or business partner arrives from overseas. Does he or she expect to be met at the airport? Should you bring him or her to lunch, or arrange a banquet dinner in their honor? To Americans, these may seem like unimportant points, but to a business person from China or other East Asian countries, this is very important and signals your commitment and seriousness about their business.

Even sophisticated firms with in-house experts to advise on avoiding cultural gaffes will still make them, including protocol mistakes. For example, not long after the recent purchase of IBM's personal computer division by the Chinese computer firm Lenovo, one of the top Lenovo executives from China visited the U.S. to meet key officials of IBM. IBM did not send anyone to the airport to meet this senior executive. As a result, the Chinese executive felt slighted and this incident has had an impact on efforts to integrate the two firms. A similar situation occurred when a senior programmer from China, working temporarily in Canada in one of the early China–Canada "worker exchange programs," caused what became a difficult international incident for the Canadian government when she refused to hand over a significant amount of sensitive computer programming she had written for the firm, even threatening to return to China with it. Her reasoning was that she felt slighted by her Canadian host firm from the moment she had arrived in Canada. For example, although an executive from the firm did meet her at the Toronto airport in the morning, the executive who met her simply brought her to breakfast, and then left. She was, in her mind, never given a proper greeting or the expected Chinese-style banquet—standard for important foreign visitors. She felt she was treated like a student intern, not the foreign dignitary that she was (she had 20 years experience in the science and technology field). This and other related "face" issues conspired to create a small crisis in the firm and even an international incident. Not understanding the expected protocol is another potential mistake and, as with communication, minor missteps can create major problems for managers and their organizations.

Culture-based mistakes that firms make can include even simple issues, such as how individuals interact with each other in a society. In many Eastern cultures, it is more common for people of the same gender to hold hands or clasp arms in public than it is for people of the opposite gender to do so. In Hong Kong, foreign visitors may be surprised to see so many teenaged girls holding hands. Yet in Hong Kong and many societies in that region, such hand holding is simply a sign of friendship; while the same behavior in individuals of the opposite gender can be seen as too forward and is usually frowned upon, at least by the older generation. In contrast, in most European and North American countries it would be unusual for two individuals of the same sex to hold hands unless there was a sexual relationship between them.

A telecommunications company was trying to expand its operations in Saudi Arabia. The negotiations had been going very well between one of the top executives of the firm and a prince, who was a major shareholder in the local firm the telecommunications company wanted to partner with. The negotiations went so well, in fact, that when the two of them went for a walk, the prince took the American executive's hand in his. To the Saudi, this was a sign of the strength of their friendship and comfort level. However, for the American it was surprising and a source of discomfort. A mistake would have been the business person reacting either physically or verbally based on his misunderstanding of the prince's intent and cultural norms. It is important to observe the behavior of those in the country that you would like to understand, particularly in terms of protocol and communication.

Avoiding Cultural Problems

In the case of the telecommunications executive mentioned in the previous section, while he was surprised when the Saudi prince took his hand during their walk, he was able to react appropriately because his colleagues had prepared him for situations like this. Such training helped raise his cultural sensitivity. **Cultural sensitivity** is a state of heightened awareness for the values and frames of reference of the host culture. Managers must keep an open mind about other cultures, and be aware that they may be able to learn from them.[xix]

Cultural sensitivity
Heightened awareness for the values and frames-of-reference of the host culture.

ANALYZING CULTURE

Knowing that culture can significantly affect how an organization conducts international business and that a variety of potential mistakes can be made when conducting business is important. The manager needs to understand culture well enough so that he or she is prepared to be successful in international business and avoid cultural gaffes. This section presents a variety of well-known frameworks that are useful for understanding the many dimensions of culture. These frameworks in part have been taken from the fields of sociology and psychology. As a result, we label the first model sociology and the second psychology. The third framework is labeled as expansive because it builds on the psychological framework, making it even more expansive than its original form. The last framework, from the major GLOBE study on culture and leadership, is the most recent. It's based on the psychological model, but is useful in developing clusters of nations that share cultural characteristics. Each framework is useful in different settings and for different people.

Sociology Framework

Kluckhohn and Strodtbeck developed a framework called dimensions of value orientation.[xx] This framework examines six dimensions, four of which are especially helpful to international managers in understanding important values of different cultures. The six dimensions include:

- Time orientation (past, present, or future)
- Space orientation (private, mixed, or public)
- Activity orientation (being, thinking, or doing)
- Relationships among people (group, hierarchical, or individualistic)

* Relations to nature (subjugation, harmony, or mastery)
* Basic human nature (evil, mixed, or good)

The first dimension focuses on time orientation. Cultures place different emphasis on history and tradition. The U.S. is less oriented toward history and tradition, compared with countries in Asia or the Middle East. Americans typically are willing to throw out old ideas and try new things; the society places only limited emphasis on historical events (to illustrate this point, U.S. students should quickly write down who fought the U.S. in the War of 1812 and what major U.S. city was burned during that war).[1] Contrast the United States' lack of historical emphasis with a country such as Saudi Arabia, which sees itself as the historical seat of Islam where tradition is paramount. Saudi Arabia continues to wrestle with change, while ensuring changes are consistent with their culture and their perceived traditions and history of Islam. For example, Saudi Arabia permitted television only when calls to prayer could be televised.

A culture's time orientation can also be an area of concern in terms of punctuality. In the United States or Germany, if someone asks you to be somewhere at a given time, then they expect you to be there at that time. In other regions, such as South America, the start time for a dinner or reception could be anywhere from one to two hours after the appointed time. If you arrive on time you may be there by yourself for a bit. Locals know that the start time for a social event is flexible and won't arrive exactly at the appointed time. This can throw off people from North America or Northern Europe, who believe that 7:00 pm means 7:00 pm and certainly no later than 7:05 pm.

A second key dimension of concern is space orientation. This dimension is concerned with whether space is viewed as a public good. In many parts of the world, usually the more crowded places like Japan or Hong Kong, space is viewed as a public good. Such an orientation is demonstrated in an office environment where most everyone works in a common area with cubical dividers. To someone from Australia or the United States, where space orientation is much more private, such working arrangements could be uncomfortable. If an Australian or a North American is waiting in line, he usually will stand back about a foot behind the person in front of him, and even further back at an ATM. In Japan and China the person will stand much closer. This can be unsettling to Westerners, who do not want strangers standing so close to them. Similarly, in some countries in the Middle East, such as Israel, it is more common for people to stand quite near during a conversation, whereas most individuals from North America would prefer to stand at arm's length. How close people stand to each other is reflective of their judgment about what their personal space is. Judgments on such things can vary widely. In the Middle East, it is considered rude for a person to step back the distance of an arm's length during a conversation. If that happens, the Middle Easterner is likely to close the gap by moving close to the other person again. To most Westerners, this lack of space in a conversation is also unsettling, but it is likely that backing up will be misinterpreted by the Middle Easterner as a sign of rejection or even rudeness.

Activity orientation refers to how proactive individuals are in society. Individuals in many societies are deterministic and believe little can be done to change fate. Consider the political situation in Russia, a culture that is not proactive. Most Russian politicians are viewed by the public at large as ineffective and often corrupt. However, the same public feels that there is little that can be done to change politics and so they assert little effort to do so. In contrast, the Canadian public is focused on "doing." An active effort is taken on by many citizens to influence the actions of the country and to help point businesses in the direction they view as right. The challenge in this is not a lack of action but rather too many conflicting actions.

---

[1]The War of 1812 was fought between the United States and England and the major U.S. city burned was Washington, D.C. In many societies, this justifies long-term resentment and hostility. Yet the United States and England are now two of the closest allies in the world, despite having fought two major wars and having come close to hostilities again during the U.S. Civil War in 1861. Contrast the U.S.'s response to the War of 1812 to the ongoing hostilities in the Balkans in Eastern Europe, conflicts that have been going on for centuries.

Aspects of the sociology framework differ from country to country. In Japan and China, for example, people typically view themselves as part of a group, not as individuals.

Confucius
Chinese philosopher who lived from 551 to 479 BCE. He was from eastern China and was a well-known and well-traveled teacher and philosopher.

Another dimension to the sociology framework is the relationship among people. People can view themselves principally as part of a group, and identify with that group, or as individuals. As noted before, in Japan the focus is often on the group. For example, the classic Japanese phrase "A nail that sticks out needs to be hammered down" can mean those individuals who "stick out" need to be hammered down to conform to the group. Similarly, most Chinese people have a strong focus on the group and how they fit into the appropriate hierarchy.

To understand why Chinese people see themselves as part of a hierarchy, it is important to understand a little about Confucianism, the philosophy that forms the basis for many aspects of Chinese culture. **Confucius** (551–479 BCE) was born in eastern China and was a well-known teacher and philosopher. He lived at approximately the same time as Socrates, Buddha, and Plato. Confucius argued that a hierarchical ordering of relationships was the key to maintaining a healthy and stable society, that is, people should know their place. If people acted according to their station in life, social harmony, which was the ultimate goal of a society, would prevail. Confucius believed the hierarchy should put husbands above wives, parents over their children, elder siblings over younger siblings, and rulers over citizens. He argued the importance of reverence for age and learning. Today hierarchy is particularly important in China and Korea (two countries where Confucian influence is strong). This generally makes for a stable society, but does not lend itself to the building of a commercial system, though it has been argued that once a commercial system is in place, Confucianism's long-term thinking helps promote its development.[2]

To illustrate the differences in individual- and group-oriented cultures, consider how people from each group select a restaurant. In a group-oriented culture, such as China, individuals prefer to eat at crowded restaurants. In fact, if faced with the choice of eating at two similar restaurants, one with a long line and the other without a line, a Chinese person will most likely choose to eat at the busier restaurant. This contrasts

[2]Confucius argued that a "superior" person (literati) should stay away from the pursuit of wealth, though not necessarily from the wealth itself. Therefore, becoming a civil servant was preferred to becoming a business person and conferred a much higher status in the Confucian hierarchy. Today, entrepreneurship is viewed in different ways throughout East Asia. It's still common for successful entrepreneurs (more so than average citizens) in Hong Kong, Taiwan, China, and Singapore to hide their wealth and downplay their success. A rich entrepreneur in Hong Kong or Singapore, when asked about his or her business, will respond, "We are doing okay," even if they are actually doing very well.

with individual-oriented cultures, such as Canada or the United States, where individuals would more likely focus on finding a new restaurant that others do not know about, that offers something unique and is not so crowded. There is evidence that Americans today are even less likely to view themselves as group oriented or as part of a hierarchy than they were even 25 years ago.[xxi] The lack of understanding led to major problems at the opening of the U.S.–based Disney Corporation's new theme park in Hong Kong. Disney built food facilities that were not consistent with the demand of Chinese consumers, who like to eat meals only at certain times of the day (in Hong Kong, it often seems to visitors that all of the roughly seven million citizens of the territory are trying to get into the restaurants at 1:00 pm, the start of the lunch hour). This contrasts with Americans who do not mind eating lunch at different times. When Hong Kong Disneyland opened, many guests were unhappy that restaurants were not prepared for the crowds of people all insisting on having lunch at 1:00 pm.

The relationship to nature is a dimension in the sociology framework that has become increasingly important to business. The role of environment and how a society views it is critical. While Kluckhohn and Strodtbeck discuss the relationship to nature in three distinct views, it is more realistically a continuum. Few modern societies subjugate themselves to nature. But the level of harmony with or mastery of nature can vary widely. The Nordic countries, such as Finland and Sweden, place a very high priority on a clean environment and working with nature. The end result is low levels of pollution, recycling, and an active promotion of alternative energy sources. Contrast this to China, where the environment has traditionally received a much lower priority than economic development. The result is that more than 25 percent of China's citizens do not have clean water to drink and 16 of the world's 20 most polluted cities are in China.[3]

Kluckhohn and Strodtbeck's dimension of the basic nature of man is one that affects managers as they interact with workers. Does the culture view workers as employees wanting to do a good job or as people who must be closely monitored because they will most likely take advantage of the firm? The view in many cultures, such as that of Bhutan, is that workers want to perform well. Bhutan is a small Himalayan kingdom that believes that the quality of life and the happiness of its citizens are the key to the nation's success. In contrast, Chinese workers are typically treated harshly as they are viewed largely as replaceable and having a strong inclination to take advantage of their employers, given the chance.

Psychological Framework

Another valuable cultural framework was created by organizational psychologist Geert Hofstede.[xxii] His initial data were gathered from two surveys with over 116,000 respondents from over 70 countries around the world—making it the largest organizationally based study ever conducted. The individuals in these studies all worked in the local subsidiaries of IBM and as a result, they formed a narrow but well-matched sample. That is, they were similar in most respects except for their nationality (and national culture). What accounts for systematic and consistent differences between national groups within an otherwise homogenous multinational population is the different nationalities.

Hofstede identified four dimensions along which cultures can be distinguished: power distance, individualism collectivism, uncertainty avoidance, and masculinity femininity (sometimes called production orientation). Later, Hofstede developed a fifth dimension, Confucian dynamism, or long-term orientation, which will be discussed last.

---

[3]China's protection of the environment is likely to improve with economic growth. Some see the effort and performance on behalf of the environment for the 2008 Beijing Olympics as a herald of China's level of commitment to improve the environment.

Power Distance Power distance is the extent to which less-powerful members of institutions and organizations accept the unequal distribution of power and submit to authority. Managers from western countries may assume that employees want responsibility and will take it if given a chance. However, in high power-distance countries, people are more likely to obey the orders of their superiors and often do not value being "empowered"—they may feel uncomfortable with making decisions that they feel should be made by their boss. Because bosses behave one way and employees another in your own country, does not mean that this will be the case in a foreign country.

The effect of this dimension can be measured in a number of ways. For example, organizations in low power-distance countries generally will be decentralized and have flatter organizational structures. These organizations also will have a smaller proportion of supervisory personnel, and the lower strata of the work force will consist of highly qualified people. By contrast, organizations in high power-distance countries will tend to be more centralized and have tall organizational structures.

Americans have a fairly low power distance. They prefer to do things for themselves rather than seek outside help and are generally egalitarian; bosses are often called by their first names and meetings are informal. Foreigners visiting the United States regularly comment that it is difficult to tell the wealthy from the poor in appearance, conversation, and behavior. In Sweden and other Nordic countries in Europe, people are even more egalitarian.

Indeed, in many societies, lower-level employees tend to follow orders as a matter of procedure. In societies with high power distance, however, enterprises are organized with assumptions of hierarchy and obedience; examples include Latin America, South Korea, China, and India. In India, because power distance is

VOLVO FORD MERGER: SUCCESSFUL CULTURAL INTEGRATION

Cultural similarities in the Nordic countries and North America can be seen in the 1999 Ford Motor Company acquisition of Volvo's automobile operations.[4] The merger has been far more successful than that of the Daimler Chrysler merger, which is discussed in a later vignette. In fact, the Volvo Ford merger has been cited as one of the two most successful mergers that has occurred in the automobile industry in recent years. Some of its success can be traced to the formation of 19 teams to search for synergies in every possible area of the two firms quickly after the merger. However, the merger has also been aided by the cultural closeness of the two countries involved, Sweden and the United States.

Cultural differences abound between the two nations. The Swedes are more commonly focused on group decision making than are the Americans. This approach is in part due to the fact that the Swedes tend to be more egalitarian than Americans in decision making; what Hofstede refers to as power distance.[5] However, there are more similarities than differences in the two nations. Almost all Swedes speak English very well, so communication problems are minimized. The Swedes, like the Americans, focus on facts and figures to support their decision making. The creative process in decision making is also similar in the two nations, with greater value placed on knowledge and understanding than on the position of the person providing the data. A similar emphasis on the facts and figures to build knowledge and understanding means that individuals in the two nations evaluate problems similarly.

The result of the cultural similarities has been a largely smooth integration between the two firms despite the distance between the two countries. The smooth integration has allowed the full range of strategic and financial goals of the merger to be met.

Executive Planet. Business Etiquette. Sweden— Let's Make a Deal, Parts 1, 2, and 3 (see the Sweden entry in http://www.executiveplanet.com).

de Geer, H., Borglund, T., & Frostenson, M. (2003). Anglo-Saxification of Swedish business: Working paper within the project 'Scandinavian Heritage'. Business Ethics: A European Review, 12(2), 179–189.

Tierney, C. (2004). Ford purchase of Volvo is rare success story: Acquisition pays off with pooled strengths. The Detroit News. http://www.fordforums.com/f349/eu-ford-purchase-volvo-rare-success-story-64074/ (accessed September 28, 2008).

Wernle, B. (1999, September 13). Now the real work begins at Volvo. Automotive News Europe, Vol. 4, Issue 19.

[4]The truck operations went to another firm.
[5]Thus, the cultural differences in egalitarian decision making between the Germans and Swedes would be even greater than anything experienced by the Americans, despite the fact that both Germany and Sweden are in fairly close geographic proximity to each other in Europe.

FIGURE 2-3	Power Distance Index in Several Countries

Country			
Arab World	80	India	77
Argentina	49	Indonesia	78
Australia	36	Ireland	28
Brazil	69	Israel	13
Canada	39	Italy	50
Chile	63	Japan	54
China	80	Mexico	81
Denmark	18	Poland	68
East Africa	64	South Africa	49
El Salvador	66	South Korea	60
France	68	Spain	57
Germany	35	Sweden	31
Greece	60	Turkey	66
Hong Kong	68	United Kingdom	35

high, employees generally expect bosses to make nearly all of the decisions. In Confucianism-based countries, it is believed that correct answers exist and are to be found in books or from authorities, such as bosses, teachers, or sagely wisdom. Organizations in high power-distance countries will have a large proportion of supervisory personnel, and the people at the lower levels of the structure often will have low job qualifications. This latter structure encourages and promotes inequality among people at different levels. Figure 2-3 lists the power-distance societies.

Individualism Collectivism Individualism collectivism is the second dimension of Hofstede's framework. He defines high-individualistic societies as consisting of loosely linked individuals, who view themselves as largely independent of groups that make their own choices—the groups in which they are members, be it a church, a political party, a social organization, or group at work, do not make decisions for them. People in high-individualistic societies, such as those of Australia, Canada, and the United States, are motivated by their own preferences, needs, rights, and contracts and they tend to primarily look after themselves and do things by themselves. They are more likely to adopt new ideas, be inventive, and try new things.[xxiii]

Collectivism is the tendency of people to associate with groups where group members look after each other in exchange for group loyalty. They work together more readily and do not mind subordinating themselves to the goals of the group. Japan scores high on Hofstede's collective index. The roots of this tendency may come from Japan's historical dependency on rice farming. Rice farming under Japan's difficult and colder weather conditions required that a whole village work together to grow rice. Historians have argued that this collective organization of the village has carried over into today's Japanese companies.[xxiv] When Japanese business people introduce themselves, they normally include the name of the company they work for with their names. For example, a manager may say, "Hello, I am Mr. Hamada of Toyota," or "Ms. Saito of Sony." The

FIGURE 2-4   Individualism Collectivism in Several Countries

Country	
Arab World	68
Argentina	86
Australia	51
Brazil	76
Canada	48
Chile	86
China	40
Denmark	23
East Africa	52
El Salvador	94

France	86
Germany	65
Greece	112
Hong Kong	29
India	40
Indonesia	48
Ireland	35
Israel	81
Italy	75
Japan	92

Mexico	82
Poland	93
South Africa	49
South Korea	85
Spain	86
Sweden	29
Turkey	85
United Kingdom	35
United States	46
West Africa	54

identification with the group in Japan is so strong that companies influence even the clothes people wear outside of work and where they spend their leisure time.

The effects of individualism and collectivism can be measured in a number of specific ways. Hofstede found that, in general, wealthy countries tend to have higher individualism scores while poorer countries tend to have higher collectivism scores. The U.S., Canada, Australia, Denmark, and Sweden, among others, have high individualism and high GDPs. Conversely, Indonesia, Pakistan, and a number of South American countries have low individualism (high collectivism) and lower GDPs. Figure 2-4 lists various countries based on individualism.

CULTURE

EGALITARIANISM IN SWEDEN

While power distance in many Asian and Latin American countries is high, in the North American and the Nordic countries of Europe, power distance is low, particularly in staunchly egalitarian Sweden. The Nordic countries have a long history of egalitarianism, possibly because of their location in a challenging northern climate. In many respects, Sweden is a country of relatively small class differences. Many people even consider the very concept of social class outdated, because it has become notoriously hard to define. A Swedish manual laborer may well earn as much as a lower official, and his children can choose to study at the same university as those of the company president. All in all, the principle of equal opportunity has had a strong position in Swedish society, much due to the long predominance of the Social Democratic Party.

The ideal that each and every person has the same value is manifested in the Swedish forms of address. Just as in Anglo-Saxon countries, Swedes use only one form when speaking to a single person: *du* ("you"). This contrasts with the more polite forms of the pronoun present in more hierarchical countries, such as in Latin America, southern Europe and Japan. Irrespective of one's gender, age, or social class, *du* can always be used. Although Swedish contains a more polite form of you, *Ni* (derived from the German *Sie*), which was previously used between strangers and by children addressing adults, it is rarely used today, mostly by older people or when addressing more than one person.

A recent story about the King of Sweden is illustrative of Sweden's egalitarianism. When the King of Sweden went Christmas shopping for his family (an act that would be highly unusual in other monarchies), the salesperson demanded to see his "government issued picture identification (ID)" in order to allow him to use his credit card. The king could not produce any ID, and the (lowly) salesperson was not persuaded by other shoppers' argument of "This is our king. I can recognize him from TV," until the king searched the bottom of his pockets and discovered a coin with his face on it, truly a most authentic piece of government-issued picture identification.

Peng, M. W. (2006). *Global Strategy*. Mason, OH: Thomson/South-Western.

Uncertainty Avoidance Uncertainty avoidance is the extent to which the members of a culture feel threatened by uncertain or unknown situations or by ambiguity in a situation. Countries organized around high uncertainty avoidance have populations that tend to have a higher need for security and a strong belief in experts and their knowledge; examples include Germany, Japan, and Spain. People in cultures with low uncertainty avoidance are more willing to accept the risks that are associated with the unknown, and accept that life must go on in spite of this uncertainty. Examples include Denmark, the United Kingdom, the United States, and Canada.

Countries with low uncertainty avoidance are associated with willingness by their members to work in situations where they do not know people well, and do not require previously established relationships to conduct business. Although all cultures have a system of reciprocity and obligation, the high uncertainty-avoidance countries usually depend more on personal connections to conduct business than do the lower uncertainty-avoidance countries, which depend more on impersonal contracts.

The effect of uncertainty avoidance can be seen in other ways. Countries with high uncertainty avoidance cultures tend to have a high degree of structure in organizational activities, more written rules, less risk taking by managers, lower labor turnover, and less ambitious employees. Low uncertainty avoidance societies are exactly the opposite: they tend to have less structure in organizational activities, fewer written rules, more risk taking by managers, higher labor turnover, and more ambitious employees. The organization encourages personnel to use their own initiative and assume responsibility for their actions. Figure 2-5 provides an uncertainty avoidance index for several countries.

FIGURE 2-5   Uncertainty Avoidance in Several Countries

Country			
Arab World	38	Indonesia	14
Argentina	46	Ireland	70
Australia	90	Israel	54
Brazil	38	Italy	76
Canada	80	Japan	46
Chile	23	Mexico	30
China	20	Poland	60
Denmark	74	South Africa	65
East Africa	27	South Korea	18
El Salvador	19	Spain	51
France	71	Sweden	71
Germany	67	Turkey	37
Greece	35	United Kingdom	89
Hong Kong	25	United States	91
India	48	West Africa	20

FIGURE 2-6 Masculinity Index in Several Countries

Country					
Arab World	52	France	43		
Argentina	56	Germany	66	Poland	64
Australia	61	Greece	57	South Africa	63
Brazil	49	Hong Kong	57	South Korea	39
Canada	52	India	56	Spain	42
Chile	28	Indonesia	46	Sweden	5
China	66	Ireland	68	Turkey	45
Denmark	16	Israel	47	United Kingdom	66
East Africa	41	Italy	70	United States	62
El Salvador	40	Japan	95	West Africa	46
		Mexico	69		

Masculine Feminine This dimension refers to the distribution of roles between genders and the more dominant role in a given society. A country high on the masculine dimension places more value on success, money, and a more assertive outlook. Femininity or relational orientation is the term used by Hofstede to describe "a situation in which the dominant values in society are nurturing and caring, interpersonal harmony and relationships, with an emphasis on the quality of life." Figure 2-6 summarizes scores for countries using Hofstede's dimensions for masculinity.

Countries with a fairly high masculinity (low femininity) index, such as the Germanic countries and the U.S., place great importance on earnings, recognition, advancement, challenge, and production. Production is placed ahead of relationships and achievement is defined in terms of recognition and wealth. The workplace is often characterized by high job stress, and many managers believe that their employees dislike work and must be kept under control.

Cultures with a very high masculinity index, such as Japan, tend to favor large-scale enterprises, and economic growth is seen as more important than conservation of the environment. The school system is geared toward encouraging high performance. In Japan, young men are expected to have good careers and to stay with one company, and those who fail to do this often view themselves as failures. Fewer women hold higher-level jobs and often society expects them to devote themselves to their children's education, although as noted before, women's attitudes on this matter have changed (Figure 2-2). There is high job stress in the workplace, and worker satisfaction in Japan tends to be low.

Cultures that score lower on masculinity (higher on femininity) tend to favor small-scale enterprises, and they place greater importance on environmental conservation. The school system is designed to teach social adaptation. Some young men and women want careers; others do not. Many women hold high-level jobs, and they do not find it necessary to be assertive. Countries with a low masculinity index (higher femininity), such as Norway and Thailand, tend to place great importance on cooperation, a friendly atmosphere, and employment security. Individuals are encouraged to be group decision makers, and achievement is defined in terms of the social environment. Managers give their employees more credit for being responsible and allow them more freedom, which leads to higher

MANUFACTURING CHINA: MATTEL

The ability for Hofstede's model of culture to provide insight can be seen in a specific problem in Chinese manufacturing. China is one of the major manufacturing centers in the world, and there is much discussion in mature markets that Chinese goods will displace all manufacturing. What is not recognized commonly is that in some industries, almost all manufacturing is in fact done by Western companies and then the products exported to mature markets in North America and Europe. Thus, in high-technology domains close to 90 percent of Chinese exports are actually products manufactured by Western companies to export to their home markets.[xxv]

The other major type of Chinese manufacturers is original equipment suppliers. In this process, these firms take their designs and products to the Chinese manufacturers, who produce the product and charge the Western firm some percentage for doing so. The Chinese firms in this domain typically are in low value-added domains such as clothing and toys. In 2007, Mattel announced a recall of over 20 million toys. These toys were found to have dangerous problems, such as lead in the paint and magnets that could be swallowed.

The recall has its roots in cultural differences. Mattel is a Western company that is used to working in a fairly low power-distance typical in the U.S. and Europe. Thus, the employees are expected to be able to operate without direct supervision and not depend on a rulebook or their supervisors' orders to get things done. But in China, with its high power distance, most employees are more accustomed to being directed by a boss (or by a list of rules). Combine this with the collective orientation, and there is a strong tendency for the employee to do exactly what their employer is telling them to do. Thus, if the senior manager says to use paint with lead because it is cheaper, it is not common for the Chinese employees to question that instruction. However, Mattel, being accustomed to working with suppliers from the United States, assumed that Chinese suppliers would act the same way; Mattel did not believe it was necessary to monitor its Chinese suppliers as closely as it should have if it had understood the cultural differences. The behavior of the Chinese supplier may have also been further affected by the higher masculinity value in China that causes financial rewards to commonly outweigh all other forms of rewards, sometimes to the neglect of other values.

One other cultural difference in Chinese and U.S. firms can also be noted in this case. The Chinese manager tragically committed suicide when the recall occurred. Some may argue this is because of the loss of respect that such problems cause to the reputation of the firm and the manager. It is likely as significant as the fact that the death penalty can be given in cases where the government feels fraud and damage was caused to the national effort of economic development.

ETHICS

employee satisfaction. Typically, less job stress is found in the workplace, and industrial conflict is somewhat uncommon in these societies.

Confucian Dynamism Hofstede and colleagues later added a final fifth dimension, Confucian Dynamism, also known as long-term orientation. They sought to address why many Asian countries had undergone such rapid economic development. This dimension identifies if the culture of a region builds on Confucian teachings. It emphasizes thrift, perseverance, a sense of shame, and following a hierarchy. Hofstede argued that these concerns dominated in Asian countries, such as Taiwan, Hong Kong, and Japan, to a larger degree than in the West. Figure 2-7 shows several countries and their long-term (dynamism) orientation.

Integrating Hofstede's Dimensions

Learning about the cultural values of countries can be useful. However, learning about every culture is a very daunting task. Therefore, it is helpful to cluster together countries with broad similarities in their cultures. Such clustering can be seen if countries are aligned in terms of pairs of dimensions. To illustrate, Figure 2-8 plots 53 countries on the power distance and uncertainty avoidance pair of dimensions. There are 10 clusters of countries that are generated from the 53 individual countries; the countries in the cluster having greater similarity with each other than with the other countries. One cluster is composed of those nations with a common British heritage such as the United Kingdom, Australia, Canada, New Zealand, and the United States in the upper left-hand quadrant, which is characterized by small power

FIGURE 2-7   Dynamism in Several Countries

Country			Country	
Australia	31		Norway	20
Brazil	65		Pakistan	0
Canada	23		Philippines	19
China	118		Singapore	48
East Africa	25		South Korea	75
Germany	31		Sweden	33
Hong Kong	96		Taiwan	87
India	61		Thailand	56
Japan	80		United Kingdom	25
Netherlands	44		United States	29
New Zealand	30		West Africa	16

FIGURE 2-8   Power Distance, Uncertainty Avoidance, and Country Clusters

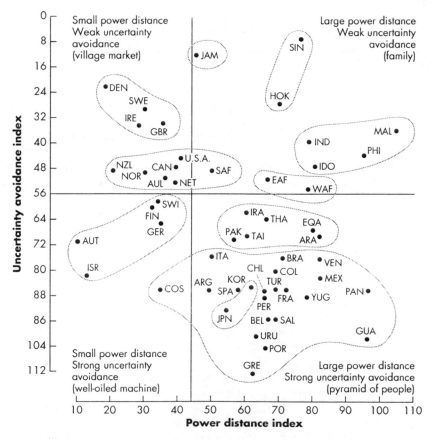

Source: G. Hofstede (1991) *Cultures and Organizations: Software of the Mind.* Maidenhead, UK: McGraw-Hill.

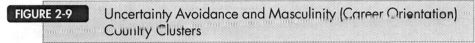

FIGURE 2-9 Uncertainty Avoidance and Masculinity (Career Orientation) Country Clusters

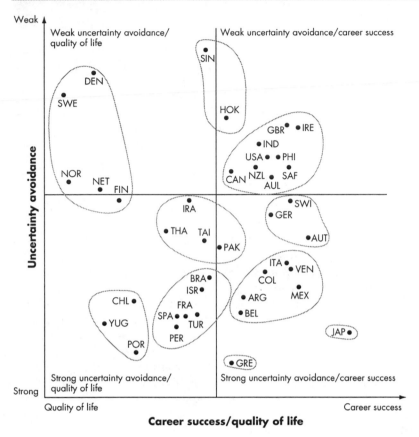

Source: G. Hofstede (1991) *Cultures and Organizations: Software of the Mind.* Maidenhead, UK: McGraw-Hill.

distance and weak uncertainty avoidance. These countries tend to be moderately unconcerned with power distance, and they are able to accept conditions of uncertainty. In contrast, many Latin American and southern European countries are characterized by large power distance and moderate uncertainty avoidance. One exception is Japan, which has a high uncertainty avoidance and a notable lack of interest in entrepreneurship among its people.

Another perspective can be seen in Figure 2-9, which maps the position of 53 countries in terms of the uncertainty avoidance and masculinity femininity, or production orientation combination. The most masculine country is Japan, followed by the Germanic countries (Austria, Switzerland, and Germany) and Latin American countries (Venezuela, Mexico, Argentina). Many countries in the Anglo-American cluster, including Ireland, Australia, the United Kingdom, and the U.S., have moderate degrees of masculinity. So do some of the former colonies of Anglo-American nations, including India, South Africa, and the Philippines. The Northern European cluster (Denmark, Sweden, Norway, and the Netherlands) has low masculinity, indicating that these countries place high value on quality of life, preservation of the environment, and the importance of relationships with people over money.

The clustering of these cultural factors into various two-dimensional graphs helps to show how nations can share similar cultural traits. Business people who are aware of the general cultural orientation of a nation in which they are working can more easily understand how to approach business in that nation.

Expansive Framework

Another helpful culture framework was developed by the Dutch researcher Fons Trompenaars, who expands on Hofstede's work. Trompenaars administered research questionnaires to over 15,000 managers from 28 countries, both developed and lesser-developed. Trompenaars used seven dimensions to differentiate national cultures, building on Hofstede's five dimensions. Trompenaars' seven dimensions include 1) individualism versus collectivism, 2) time orientation, 3) universalism versus particularism, 4) neutral versus affective, 5) specific versus diffuse, 6) achievement versus ascription, and 7) relationship to nature.

Two of Trompenaars' dimensions overlap with Hofstede—individualism versus collectivism and achievement versus ascription (similar to Hofstede's masculine feminine production orientation dimension). Some dimensions are similar to the sociology framework of Kluckhohn and Strodtbeck, including time orientation and relationship to nature. Trompenaars' view of time orientation is a little bit different, however, in that time is thought of as sequential versus synchronic in addition to past, present, and future orientations. In sequential cultures, such as the U.S. and Germany, schedules rule the business; things are usually done sequentially and not out of order, when possible. When a meeting is in progress, it is not considered polite to take phone calls, or do instant messaging, while in a synchronic (polychronic using Edward Hall's terms), such as in the Middle East and Hong Kong, it is quite common for people to take a phone call during a meeting. Though many from sequential cultures, such as Germany's, would consider this impolite, in a synchronic culture where people multitask even in meetings, it is not uncommon for that call to be answered and for the person to stop the meeting.

There are also unique aspects to this framework, such as Trompenaars' universalism versus particularism. (See In-class Exercise #1 at the end of this chapter.) In cultures emphasizing a universalistic orientation (such as the U.S., the United Kingdom, and Germany), people believe that absolute values, such as goodness or truth, are applicable to all situations. Judgments are more likely to be made without regard to the particular situation. In particularistic societies (China and much of Latin America) each situation must be judged separately. One outcome of this is that how people are treated can depend highly on their relationship with one another. Thus your friend might expect to get your business regardless of your needs and the value of his company's product because, after all, you are friends. Judgments in a particularistic society emphasize one's position in a hierarchy and one's loyalty, especially to family and friends.

Another unique cultural dimension from Trompenaars' model is neutral versus affective. Neutral cultures, such as those of Singapore and Japan, tend not to show emotion, particularly in public. In contrast, affective or the more emotional cultures (Brazil, Mexico, and Italy) do not discourage the expression of emotion. The specific versus diffuse dimension focuses on how a culture emphasizes notions of privacy and access to privacy. In specific cultures (for example, the United Kingdom), individuals have large public spaces and relatively small private spaces. Diffuse cultures (such as Southern Europe), on the other hand, make no clear distinction between public and private spaces.

Finally, the specific versus diffuse dimension is loosely related to Hofstede's power distance dimension, although it also has some unique aspects. A specific

DAIMLER CHRYSLER MERGER AND THE IMPACT OF CULTURE CLASH

In 1998, Daimler of Germany and Chrysler of the United States merged. The combination was intended to generate a company that would reach the critical mass necessary to compete on a global basis. The economies of scale in the auto industry are great. It is expected that worldwide the number of firms will decline dramatically over the next 50 years as the industry consolidates, seeking to reach the critical mass necessary to survive.

Contrary to expectations, the value of Daimler's stock declined with the announcement of the deal and would continue to decline until it was worth less than 50 percent of its original value. Daimler would ultimately have to sell Chrysler to private equity investors. Daimler purchased Chrysler for over $36 billion and would ultimately sell it for less than $5 billion. Combining two firms is always very difficult and, in this case, problems arose that could not be overcome.

Particularly problematic in integrating the two firms were their differences in culture. Some of these differences were firm specific. For example, the two firms focused on two different types of products. Daimler sold high-end, highly engineered automobiles. In contrast, Chrysler was a scrappy, cost-conscious company. The Germans were aware of this difference but they were never able to truly value the American brands. This had two results. First, the brands of the two firms were never integrated, which meant that brand management for this newly combined firm became confusing. Additionally, the two firms were never able to fully integrate their supply chains. The Daimler engineers felt using the Chrysler lower cost/lower quality inputs would damage their brand image, and Daimler did not want to share its parts with Chrysler. Chrysler would ultimately get some steering and suspension

components, a transmission, and a diesel engine from Daimler. But generally, there was little integration of the two firms, with both Daimler and Chrysler largely keeping their supply chains separate. Compare this to the previously discussed Ford Volvo merger, in which the input parts were fully integrated across the two firms. The separation of Daimler and Chrysler is clearly illustrated by the fact that there were corporate headquarters in both the United States and Germany. A single corporate headquarters was never created.

Another clear difference is the language difference. Almost all young Germans speak English. But Americans seldom learn German, and language-learning ability for individuals over 40 years old tends to be much less than for younger people. The result was that language difficulties would continue to plague the two firms working together. However, more critical to the failure were the differences in national cultures of Germans and Americans. German culture tends to be very hierarchical, while Americans, as noted earlier, are very egalitarian and prefer flat organizations. One impact of this was that the Germans felt Americans were too unstructured, while the Americans found the Germans too rigid. To illustrate, Germans typically take a problem, analyze it, discuss the potential solutions, pick one, and then move on. Americans use a much more interactive process. They not only have active discussions with large numbers of people, but they revisit issues as new information or insights become available. At Daimler Chrysler, the Germans felt that once the decision had been made, they would not revisit a problem. The Germans also felt very uncomfortable with the active give and take of the Americans. The Americans saw such interactions as healthy, but to the Germans, they were confrontational

and very uncomfortable. The result often was that the Americans would think a consensus had been reached when in fact the Germans just did not want to argue.

The means to analyze many of the problems at Daimler were also different. The Americans felt comfortable stopping at their bosses' or anyone else's office and discussing the issue at hand. They considered this creative. Germans, however, had a structured approach in which lower-level employees generated extensive analysis of the problem and then passed that analysis up the hierarchy until a decision was made. This approach resulted in the Germans having much larger staffs than the Americans.

This does not mean that Daimler did not realize they had a problem and try to address it. For example, to encourage communication among the various parties, the firm forced both firms to use IBM Lotus Suite, which allowed instant messaging among the parties, but this did not address the underlying differences. The outcome of these differences was that the synergy initially expected between Chrysler and Daimler was never been realized.

Corcoran, G. (2007, May 14). Was Chrysler buy a 'deal from Hell'? Mr. Bruner weighs in. *Wall Street Journal Online*. http://blogs.wsj.com/deals/2007/05/14/was-daimlers-buy-of-chrysler-a-deal-from-hell-robert-bruner-weighs-in/

Edmonson, G. & Welch, D. (2005, August 15). Dark days at Daimler. *BusinessWeek*, pp. 31–38.

Ostle, D. (1999, November 22). The culture clash at Daimler Chrysler was worse than expected. *Automotive News Europe*, Vol. 4, Issue 24.

Woods, L. (2007, May 18). How Daimler, Chrysler merger failed. *Pressbox*. http://www.pressbox.co.uk/detailed/Business/How_Daimler_Chrysler_Merger_Failed_122434.html.

culture might be more likely to assign decision responsibility to a boss, thus giving specific responsibility for outcomes, whether positive or negative. A more diffuse society will be more accepting of the diffuse assigning of responsibility.

The GLOBE Study

The GLOBE study is a recent, large scale research effort that involved over 150 researchers from 61 different countries. This research sought to examine the interrelationships between societal culture, organizational culture, and organizational leadership. The research team initially identified nine different cultural items. While Trompenaars built on Hofstede's work, the GLOBE study built not only on Hofstede's work but also on the work of Trompenaars, and Kluckhohn and Strodtbeck.

The first six items in the GLOBE study were based on Hofstede's earlier works. However, the GLOBE study made variations in some of Hofstede's variables. The uncertainty avoidance and power distance were largely the same as Hofstede's earlier work. However, the individual group orientation variable was split into two parts—societal collectivism and in-group collectivism.

* Societal collectivism is the degree to which organizational and societal practices encourage the collective distribution of resources and collective action.
* In-group collectivism is the degree to which individuals express pride, loyalty, and cohesiveness in their organization or family.

Similarly, the masculinity variable of Hofstede was split into two variables, referred to as gender egalitarianism and assertiveness.

* Gender egalitarianism refers to the degree to which an organization or society minimizes gender role differences and gender discrimination.
* Assertiveness is the degree to which individuals are confrontational.

The seventh cultural item is future orientation. It is drawn from Trompenaars and concerns the importance placed in the society on the delaying of gratification and the importance of planning. The eighth cultural dimension is humane orientation, and it is drawn from the work of Kluckhohn and Strodtbeck and concerns the degree to which individuals are rewarded for being fair, caring, and kind to others. The last dimension of the framework is performance orientation. This is the one element that is not based on the other culture frameworks, though it bears some resemblance to Hofstede's masculine feminine dimension. This dimension is most closely related, however, to David McClelland's need for achievement (discussed later in Chapter 7, Motivation). Performance orientation is concerned about the extent to which achievement is a motivator.

One contribution of the GLOBE study is that it has allowed the clustering of countries and cultures to be more specific than was possible with Hofstede's initial work. The result has been the recognition of a number of country clusters that share a similar cultural orientation. Using such clusters allows individuals to quickly gain insight into what the culture of a nation would be, based on its cluster. The following countries are seen as belonging to the same clusters:

* Latin Europe: Spain, Portugal, Italy, French Switzerland, France, and Israel
* Eastern Europe: Albany, Georgia, Greece, Hungary, Kazakhstan, Poland, Russia, and Slovenia
* Germanic Europe: Austria, Germany, the Netherlands, and Switzerland
* Anglo: Australia, Canada, the United Kingdom, Ireland, New Zealand, South Africa (white sample), and the United States
* Southern Asia: India, Indonesia, Iran, Malaysia, the Philippines, and Thailand
* Arabic: Egypt, Morocco, Turkey, Kuwait, and Qatar

The GLOBE study will be revisited again in Chapter 8, Leadership.

Culture Framework Integration

Each cultural framework has some overlap with each other, but they all also have characteristics that make them unique. It cannot be said that one framework is right and another is wrong. Instead, each framework takes a complex domain (culture) and breaks it down in a manner in which people can readily understand it. Once a business person, for example, begins to build a foundation of understanding their actions, she or he can be more directed and logical, and less likely to violate cultural norms.

If a business person is going to work in a new environment or if a firm is moving into a new market, then rather than relying on a single model of culture, typically multiple frameworks of culture should be employed, because the frameworks are not mutually exclusive. Thus, a business person or a business can gain different insights by using the various frameworks to identify elements that the frameworks see differently and those where there is agreement. The goal is to gain insights to help prepare the business person and firm to make directed and logical choices. However, it is important to note that each framework is merely a tool, and tools are only as useful as the skills of the person using them. Thus, frameworks should be employed as guidelines to help the manager, not as laws written in stone.

SUMMARY

Culture is fundamental to differences in business around the world. Managers can make numerous pitfalls associated with culture. However, managers who analyze culture in the different societies in which they operate are more likely to be successful. Four major frameworks can be used to help one understand cultural settings. These frameworks (Kluckhohn and Strodtbeck, Hofstede, Trompenaars, and GLOBE) each approach the domain of culture slightly differently, but they all have the potential to help a business person clearly understand the environment in which they are operating.

The related concept of values is also important to the international operation of a business. Values concern individual predispositions, while culture is concerned with entire societies. Both can and do change as society changes. Upcoming chapters will demonstrate how culture and values shape a wide range of managerial issues, including the strategy of the firm, human resource management, communication, decision making, leadership, and evaluation and control in the firm.

MANAGERIAL GUIDELINES

A number of managerial guidelines should be used to direct the actions of managers, based on culture and its role in the organization.

1. It is important to recognize that culture is pervasive in business. Businesses that operate in different countries must evaluate their actions in light of cultural differences.
2. Managers must evaluate the cultural differences that exist between themselves and others as they begin to conduct business across national borders.
3. The greater the cultural difference, the more crucial it is for the manager to understand that key cultural dimensions can influence how their communication and actions are perceived.
4. Sensitivity training is useful for preparing managers to address the cultural differences that can exist as they conduct business across national borders.
5. Do not project your own culture and value system onto others. Projection means that you assume other people think the way you do. In any cross-

cultural interaction, this is not a good assumption to make. This does not mean that you should abandon your own values when working in another culture. But do not assume that others share your values and preferences, and will act the way you would.

6. Managers, on the whole, must be prepared to overcome the bias of believing their culture or way of doing business is best. Business people should not violate their personal ethical standards or those of the company. For example, while it may be acceptable in some societies to discriminate against women or minorities, if you are from an advanced economy in Europe or North America, such behaviors are not typically acceptable either personally or legally. Local business partners may practice discrimination and encourage you to do the same, but being culturally accepting does not mean that you have to allow or participate in such actions that violate your or the company's ethics.

7. Communication is affected by culture; so not only what you say but how you say it is important. In many nonwestern countries, hierarchy is important, as is age; managers must be sensitive to protocol associated with age, status, and seniority.

8. Almost all business people understand that you may not know all the intricacies of their culture. As a result, it is typically acceptable to ask them what is appropriate in a given situation. The fact that you are trying to adapt to their culture and understand their language will be appreciated.

9. One way to learn about a culture is to carefully observe how the locals behave, particularly the leaders of a society (such as bosses, professionals, and politicians). How do they meet and great people? How do they ask people to do things and thank them for help? How do they relate to their peers, subordinates, and authority? When do they give gifts and what do they give? Table 2-1 summarizes some of the issues on which a manager should focus as she or he considers culture in different settings.

TABLE 2-1   Cultural Etiquette around the World

Etiquette	Specifics	Example
Greetings	How do people greet and address one another? What role do business cards play?	In Japan and China, business cards are very important. Give and receive them with two hands and read them when you receive them, and put them away carefully (never into a back pocket!). Bring large numbers of cards on any foreign business trip or try to create one if you do not have one, even if you are a student. Keep some in your travel bag so you do not forget to have some on hand. It is very embarrassing to travel to a meeting around East Asia having forgotten your business cards.
Degree of Formality	Do people in the firms I am visiting dress and interact formally or informally?	The U.S., Canada, Australia, and New Zealand are less formal than most countries. Though khaki pants are okay in these countries, they may be too informal for most business settings elsewhere. Usually, darker clothes and suits are necessary for most business settings worldwide. Work on a manufacturing or shop

		floor would be an exception. Bring more formal clothing just in case. In Singapore, Indonesia, Malaysia, the Philippines, and in other parts of Southeast Asia, ties are not commonly worn in business settings, although quality business attire is. Be sure to inquire about this with your host organization. Never, ever wear flip-flops or sandals in a business setting in foreign countries unless you are 100 percent certain such informality is acceptable.
Personal Inquiries	What kinds of questions are acceptable?	Be careful when asking questions about someone's spouse and family unless you are sure this topic is okay (in Islamic countries one should not ask about family). While most people from Western countries usually do not mind family questions, they do not like personal questions about their health, appearance, how much they earn, what they are eating for lunch, why they like cold drinks and not hot drinks, their marital status, and other personal details. Consider these topics *off limits* until you know that person well enough to ask such personal questions.
Gift Giving	Do business people exchange gifts? What gifts are appropriate? Are there taboos associated with gift giving?	Japan has a widely recognized system of gift giving often known as *giri*. *Giri* guides people in when to give gifts, to whom, and at what value. Ask people who know, or consult a book, such as *Kiss, Bow or Shake Hands* (Morrison, T. & Conaway, W.A., 2006) for information on this and other protocols worldwide. Gift giving is less formalized in China and other parts of East Asia, but is still important.
Touching	What are the attitudes toward body contact?	For most countries, shaking hands is okay, even in countries where the practice is not common, such as Japan. When meeting a businesswoman from a nonwestern country (for example, in India, East Asia, the Middle East, and Africa), it is usually best to wait until she extends her hand first to shake hands.
Eye Contact	Is direct eye contact polite? Is it expected?	Indian people will typically make direct eye contact and even stare at total strangers. This is not considered impolite in India, though in many countries it is considered rude and some people might consider it aggressive act, so staring is best avoided. In contrast, many East Asians will avoid direct eye contact, making some Westerns think they are not listening. Do not make that assumption. As always, check the norms of the country to which you are traveling.
Physical Distance	How close do people stand next to each other?	In some countries, such as the Middle East, businessmen (though not women) will stand or sit near to the person with whom they are talking, and at a proximity that most Westerners would feel uncomfortable with. North Americans, for example, will normally stand at arm's length, or even sometimes side by side when talking. If someone is standing too near, resist the inclination to back up, as the person will just close the distance again, and may feel that you are being rude.

TABLE 2-1   (Continued)

Etiquette	Specifics	Example
Emotions	Is it rude, embarrassing, or usual to display emotions?	Most U.S. business people avoid showing emotions, except for small talk and jokes. In Germany and Austria, it is generally considered a bit frivolous to start off a meeting with a joke. Most countries in East Asia have less small talk and jokes at business meetings, and lighten up at lunches and dinners instead. Southern Europeans and Latin Americans, on average, will normally express more emotion at meetings. Latin American business people, for example, may start describing you as "my good friend" even though you have just been introduced to them a few minutes earlier.
Silence	Is silence awkward? Expected? Insulting? Respectful?	Many less-expressive cultures do not mind some silence at a meeting. Do not feel that you need to fill in the silence with comments or questions. Feel free to take some healthy pauses in conversations to think or write something down.
Speaking Style	How do you address people? Is it proper to use first (given) names?	In Asia, you normally would not address people by their given names unless you know them or are a colleague at the same level or above in the organization. At meetings, the one running the meeting may be addressed more formally, such as "Mr. Chairman" or "Mr. Supervisor" though as always, watch for the norms within the organization. In Australia, the U.S., and Canada, first names are regularly used. Even a professor will commonly be called by his or her first name in Australia by students.
Eating	What are the proper manners for dining? Are certain foods taboo?	Most cultures are proud of their cuisines and special drinks. Make an effort to enjoy the food and drink with your host. Definitely do not criticize the food in the host country. Try not to be too picky about the food—this is a good way to insult your host and harm your chances of doing business in that country. On the other hand, do not assume that just because people do not want to go out for lunch, dinner, drinks, and so forth that they do not like you. While some cultures encourage a lot of after work socializing, such as in Japan or Latin America, others, such as in North America, do not.
Body Language	Are certain gestures or forms of body language rude?	If you are going to a new country for the first time to do business, buy a book such as *Kiss, Bow or Shake Hands* or check international business Web sites, such as www.executive planet.com, so you can learn which gestures or body language to avoid. For example, most East Asians would consider you impolite if you slumped low in your chair with your feet up, or clasped your hands behind your head and leaned way back in your chair when speaking or listening. They would wonder if you are paying attention to them. In Thailand and the Middle East, it is considered quite rude to show the bottom of your foot or shoe.

CULTURE AND DOING BUSINESS IN INDIA

India is the second most populous nation in the world with over a billion citizens. India encompasses over 3,250,000 square km in land mass, making it physically the seventh largest country in the world. There are 24 languages spoken in India by its one billion citizens. As a result, the language of business is often English because it is a common language spoken by all well-educated Indian people. In fact, it is estimated that for 90 million people in India, English is one of their three major spoken languages.

Business in India tends to be organized around family business groups. Business groups are a concept that will be discussed in greater detail later in the book, however, it is sufficient to say now that these are highly diversified entities in which a given family controls the business. As a result, it typically is helpful to have introductions to various firms with which you wish to do business. There are communities from different parts of India, with their own distinct dialects, that have a disproportionate impact on business in India. The most important communities include Marwari, Gujarati and Chettiar. People from these communities have controlling interests in some of the largest Indian business houses and commonly prefer to do business with individuals also originally from these regions. Another significant group in Bombay is a religious group known as the Zoroastrians. The small group practicing this religion has generated some of the most significant business groups in India. The religion has a three-fold path *"Good*

thoughts, good words, good deeds." As an outcome of this belief, they actively conduct many good works in India.

The negotiation process in India typically is a slow moving process because Indians prefer to build relationships before conducting business—an important part of their culture. The approach to time also tends to be quite lax. It is important to make appointments in advance and, for foreigners, it is important to be on time, even though their Indian host may not always be on time. Hierarchy also tends to be quite important in the culture, so paying appropriate respect to individuals, such as standing when senior members of the firm enter a room, is important. This same focus on hierarchy will typically result in final negotiations always needing the approval of the senior management of a firm. There is a cultural tendency not to say "no" directly because it may be seen as rude. As a result, phrases such as "we will need to consider this issue further" or "it may be difficult" may in fact mean no.

Other cultural difference need to be heeded as well. For example, pointing with your finger is considered rude; Indians prefer to point with the chin. Displays of public affection are not appreciated, so greetings that include hugs or kisses should not occur. While moderate aggressiveness is often revered in the Western workplace as a sign of confidence and ingenuity, in the Indian context it is seen as a sign of disrespect.

ADDITIONAL RESOURCES

Axtell, R. E. (1998). *Gestures: The Do's and Taboos of Body Language Around the World.* New York: John Wiley & Sons.

Baker, C. & Willis, P. (2004). *Cultural Studies: Theory and Practice* (2nd ed.). Thousand Oaks, CA: Sage Publications.

Martin, J. & Chaney, L. (2006). *Global Business Etiquette: A Guide to International Communication and Customs.* Westport, CT: Praeger Publishers.

Morrison, T. & Conaway, W.A. (2006). *Kiss, Bow, or Shake Hands (The Bestselling Guide to Doing Business in More Than 60 Countries).* Avon, MA: Adams Media.

EXERCISES

Opening Vignette Discussion Questions

1. How could the problems that arose in the opening vignette have been avoided?
2. If you were in charge of sensitivity training for Accenture, what do you think should be included in the training prior to sending someone to India?
3. Based on the vignette, discuss what the cultural characteristics of India, using the Hofstede model to describe these characteristics.

DISCUSSION QUESTIONS

1. Compare and contrast the differences and similarities in the various culture frameworks discussed in the chapter.
2. Is cultural convergence occurring in the world? That is, do you think that the various world cultures are coming closer together, or are they getting more different and prone to conflict? Why or why not?
3. If you were going to conduct cultural-sensitivity training for someone coming to your country, what do you think they would need to know to successfully navigate the culture?
4. What would be a common list of issues you should be taught about, if you were about to be sent to China to conduct business?

IN-CLASS EXERCISES

1. You are a manager responsible for marketing promotion in a widely dispersed multinational enterprise based in Canada. Some marketing people under you who are based around the world have gone to Mexico for a key meeting (you stay behind in Canada). After the meeting has gone on in Mexico City for a few days, you get a call from the Mexican marketing executive in charge of running the meeting and producing the worldwide promotion campaign proposal. She is quite upset with one of the colleagues from Taiwan. She tells you that they worked for several days planning a new company promotional campaign along with several colleagues from different countries in Latin America, Russia, Japan, and Taiwan, all of whom arrived in Mexico City right before the meeting started. The job proved quite challenging and took a few days to complete. She feels that the group is doing a nice job and should be rewarded. At the end of the first day, she said that she wanted to treat everyone to a nice dinner at a local five-star hotel, paying out of her own (not the group's) budget. However, the group member from Taiwan announced that he was quite tired and was not able to join the group for dinner or drinks after work. The Mexican executive said she was surprised and disappointed by his attitude. After all, she said, ". . . this is a chance for the working group, which may have to interact regularly in the future, to get to know each other. In fact, not only did the Taiwanese colleague say he did want not go to dinner that night, it turned out that he didn't want to go to dinner on any of the other nights either, saying it had been a very long trip from Asia, he wanted to go to bed early, and he didn't drink anyway." He even turned down a chance to go to a festival that was an annual custom in Mexico City.

   The Mexican executive was so upset about the Taiwanese colleague's refusal to join the group for their first dinner of the conference that she called you very late at night at home to tell you what happened. "The meeting is going well and our advertising plan looks fine. It is our colleague from Taiwan—how can he behave like this?" the Mexican executive asked. "This is really rude of him!" She guessed that it must be that he didn't like the group and maybe didn't like Mexican food. She suggested that you should send someone else from the Greater China group in the future, because this guy is hurting the camaraderie and morale of the group, which is serious when it comes to a creative effort, such as marketing and promotion. "These social events are important to company morale—we always do things this way in Latin America, and it works well," she tells you.

   You decide to contact the Taiwanese colleague by email to find out why he seems to be making the Mexican marketing executive so upset and is apparently hurting the morale of the group. The Taiwanese colleague emails back, saying that his Mexican host is overbearing and not listening to him when he says he is tired and needs to go back to the hotel and rest. "It's like talking to a brick wall," he tells you. "I just do not feel like going out to dinner—it was a long trip, I am not feeling that well, and besides, we are already working all day. I need to go back to the hotel and rest. I wouldn't mind seeing the city a little, but we are working all day—it's too much. If this were a sales situation it would be different, but working for nine hours on a tough plan is enough, I need to go to the gym early in the morning before we meet and then rest at night. I have told her this, and she just ignores me, saying I must not like her and our group. That's nonsense. Tell her to back off a little and give me some personal space."

As the marketing manager back at the home office, how would you handle this problem and smooth things out in your group? You do not want to lose the Taiwanese colleague—he understands the Greater China market well, which is central to your growth plans. The Mexican marketing executive is also valuable—she is a loyal employee and quite effective in her position in Mexico and all around Latin America. How can you fix this problem so they can work together? Just telling both of them to "listen better" is not adequate; you have to be more specific in your recommendations. Can you think of anything about culture and people's personal preferences that is likely to be influencing both of your subordinates' behavior and how to fix this problem?

2. You have been assigned to help prepare a key employee, Raymond, a chemical engineer from Mainland China, who will be moving to a rural region in North America to work in the fast-growing tar sands oil-extraction industry. That region has almost no Chinese people living there. Raymond will relocate his whole family and is expected to stay for three years; they will be one of the only Chinese families in the town. Raymond is a talented chemical engineer in his late thirties who is important to the firm's success in the North American market in the fast growing new oil-extraction industry.

Raymond has not spent any time in the West or much time working with people from outside of China. His wife is an accountant and they have two kids, a 14-year-old daughter and a 15-year-old son. Raymond speaks English pretty well. His family does not speak English well, but they understand some and should be able to get by okay.

Break into groups for the following activities. Complete Exercise A before reading Exercise B.

Exercise A: Your group should prepare a list to help with Raymond's training before he leaves. The list should tell him about what to expect—both at work and after work in his new North American community. Tell him about some of the cultural issues he may run into with his coworkers and customers in the chemical business, and how he should handle them. You also want to give some advice about living in such a place (say semi-rural [non-urban] United States or Canada).

Exercise B: After about two weeks on the job, Raymond calls you at company headquarters. He is upset about his new home, and his family is unhappy, and they don't want to stay. In particular, he has two questions for you:

i. No one came to greet him and his family at the airport upon their arrival in the U.S., so he had to find his own way to the company, which was a long ride from the airport through very unfamiliar roads in the countryside. Later, Raymond's managers invited him to a nice breakfast at a hotel overlooking the Rocky Mountains. They apologized for being very busy and having to catch a flight right after that. Raymond called you to talk about this behavior. "I feel insulted by my new colleagues," Raymond said. "Imagine only being invited to a breakfast meeting on my first visit here. And having to find my own way to the company! The company told me that I am a key employee here to do a big job, and yet no one greeted me at the airport. In China, this would never happen. A new employee and his family are treated to a nice banquet. That is how we always treat important visitors in China." I wonder why they did not do the same for us?"

Raymond is obviously angry about his initial treatment. As a manager in charge of these personnel moves you are worried, because first impressions tend to influence later experience. How can you explain this situation to him better? Are the Canadians just being rude?

ii. In his first week in the new town, Raymond's daughter went out to the local shopping mall with two new classmates. While walking around, her friends suddenly stepped into a food shop and bought some snacks to eat. They came out with the food and drink but did not buy anything for Raymond's daughter. She came home upset and wanted to know, "Why are the foreigners so unfriendly?" Raymond did not understand this either. "People should not buy something to eat only for themselves without offering anything to their friend," he told you. "What is wrong with these Canadians?" He wants to know what he should tell his daughter. What do you do as Raymond's boss? Would you tell Raymond to stop complaining about such trivial matters and just get his work done? Or is there anything else you could recommend?

3. Compare your answers given in Exercise A with those in Exercise B (both i and ii). Did you prepare Raymond for the problems that came up in Exercise B? Knowing about these problems, how could you have better prepared Raymond, as asked in Exercise A?

TAKE-HOME EXERCISES

1. Go to the Web site http://www.executiveplanet.com and select two different nations. Contrast the impact of culture on negotiations in those nations. Report your findings to the class.
2. Form a team and summarize what you believe the primary cultural aspects of your home country to be. Report your findings to the class.
3. In your view, how do foreign nationals misunderstand your country? Make a list of the most important of these. Are they cultural in nature? Historical? Political? Other? What types of training could a firm pursue to overcome these misunderstandings?
4. In 2005, a number of Chinese firms sought to buy U.S. firms. This includes the China National Offshore Oil Corporation purchase of Chevron, the Lenovo purchase of IBM's laptop business, and Haier's purchase of Maytag. Research one of these proposed acquisitions. Which ones were completed? What would be the cultural implications of each of the proposed acquisitions? In other words, would some of the mergers be expected to be more difficult because the nature of the integration that would be required, or the business involved?

SHORT CASE QUESTIONS

Daimer Chrysler Merger and the Impact of Culture Clash (p. 57)

1. What are some of the major differences you see in doing business in Germany if you are an American?
2. Renault Motors is a French firm that owns Nissan Automobile of Japan. Why do you think this merger worked when the Daimler Chrysler merger did not?
3. Think of ways that the Daimler Chrysler merger could have been encouraged to succeed.

7

MOTIVATION

Overview

Prior chapters addressed the overall elements of a firm, such as its industry and the culture in which it is was located. But now it is time to start to examine how a firm manages people in different settings. Important among these issues is motivation, which encourages people to reach high levels of work performance. Motivation is problematic in international settings because how people are motivated can vary by region of the world. For example, recall from Chapter 2 that culture affects basic issues, such as whether individuals place more emphasis on financial rewards or their lifestyle. This fundamental difference will in turn affect what motivates individuals.

This chapter will review the major theories of motivation, their implementation, and effect. These theories were primarily developed in North America and are reviewed from that setting. We then explore how motivation changes as we apply those ideas in a international setting. The theories will be separated based on whether they principally see motivation as something internal to the individual (content theories) or as part of process (process theories). This chapter examines:

* content (need) theories of motivation:

    Maslow's hierarchy of needs
    Alderfer's ERG
    Herzberg's extrinsic and intrinsic motivators
    McClelland's theory of learned needs

* process theories of motivation

    expectancy
    equity
    goal setting

VIRGIN ATLANTIC, RICHARD BRANSON, AND WHAT WORKERS WANT

Richard Branson did not graduate from a university. Yet today he is one of the richest people in the United Kingdom, and his business interests include over 250 different companies. Best known are his music retailer, Virgin Music; his telecommunications firm, Virgin Mobile; his insurance, financial planning, and credit card retailers, Virgin Money; and the second largest airline in the United Kingdom, Virgin Atlantic.

In each of these firms, Sir Branson (who was knighted by Queen Elizabeth II for his business accomplishments) has often overcome critics who said he could not be successful. A key part of the success is Branson himself; he is the quintessential entrepreneur and will do whatever is necessary to make each of his efforts successful. For example, Branson donned a wedding dress to promote the start of the bridal retailer Virgin Brides. However, another key success factor is his employees and their motivation in working for the companies.

Branson has always seen people as critical to his success. He stated:

Convention dictates that a company should look after shareholders first, its customers next and worry last about its employees. Virgin does the opposite. For us, employees matter most. It just seems common sense that if you start with a happy, well motivated work force you're much more likely to have happy customers. In due course the resulting profits will make your shareholders happy.[1]

One of the key ways that Branson has tried to motivate employees at his firms is to provide them with ample flexibility and make the work both challenging and interesting. Once he empowers employees, he also gives them room to fail. For example, an executive once made a bad choice and lost the firm a large amount of money. When the employee came to Branson's office he expected to be fired. Instead, Branson fired at the employee with a water pistol, then told him to get back to work. That day the executive, and the entire firm, learned to take risks and learn from them, because a failure did not necessarily mean termination.

Often it is assumed that employees are only motivated by money. However, this has not proven to be the case for Branson. His workers want interesting and challenging situations where they can make a visible contribution, an environment that Branson has tried to create for them. A body of research in the West supports the view that money is not a primary motivator for many employees. These studies from a variety of work settings, ranging from heavy manufacturing to computer engineering, consistently find that employees rank appreciation of work and being involved in work as the most important motivating factor.

It should be noted that in these surveys, when asked what they thought workers wanted, supervisors consistently ranked extrinsic motivators, such as salary and working conditions, among the highest motivators, and intrinsic motivators as lowest. Interestingly, in the same surveys, employees also indicated they thought coworkers were most interested in salary.

This situation reflects an extrinsic bias that can be traced to an attribution error. An **attribution error** occurs when people try to make sense out of events in their lives and make assumptions about the issues involved. For example, when asked to assess themselves on driving skill, nearly everyone says they are an above average driver. No one considers himself or herself a below average driver.[i] Thus, perhaps managers assume everyone is interested in money because they themselves are interested in money.

Managers need to be careful that they do not make a fundamental attribution error in assuming that all their employees only want more money. Richard Branson has found a way for his organizations to motivate people. It should be noted that, while Branson puts a premium on creating situations that empower managers, he also says often that he is in the business of creating millionaires. Thus, Branson does not hesitate to motivate individuals who are successful when they perform. Managers cannot assume that the method of motivation they have in their own countries, or motivation methods people like Branson have used, will work in other settings. It is doubtful that Branson's system will work in an African, Malaysian, or Kuwaiti firm because those countries have a different cultural setting. The system Branson created is unique to those entrepreneurial ventures and the cultures in which Branson operates those businesses. There are many ways to motivate employees and colleagues. Firms need to find those that offer the best opportunity for the firm in that setting.

Previous chapters looked at outside factors that affect a business internationally. We now begin to look internally at issues a firm must deal with as it manages in an international setting. The most difficult tasks in international management concern people. One of the key areas firms must focus on as they internationalize is motivating a wide range of people in different settings to do their work well. In

Attribution error
Occurs when people try to determine cause and effect in their lives and make incorrect assumptions about what actions led to particular situations.

[1]Broad, M. (2003, February 18). Richard Branson. *Personnel Today.*

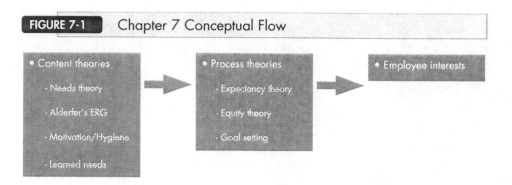

FIGURE 7-1   Chapter 7 Conceptual Flow

large measure, this difficulty comes from the fact that what motivates people in one region of the world may be much different in another region. For example, in many parts of Africa it is not uncommon for wages to be partly determined by the size of the employee's family, because motivation comes less from the level of the wage than the approval of the family, tribe, or village. Contrast this with North America, where salary is the primary motivator for performance and no one would even consider the size of someone's family to determine pay. An international firm with operations in both North America and Africa may find that transplanting its focus on pay as a motivator from North America to Africa may actually work to reduce motivation, because it may place the person receiving the monetary reward in conflict with his or her reference group at the company. Thus, culture is important in discussing motivation in international settings because employees in various cultural settings have different values that affect their needs and how they might be motivated. This chapter lays out the component parts of motivation and how motivation can differ in various international settings. Figure 7-1 summarizes the flow of the material we will examine in this chapter.

MOTIVATION COMPOSITION

Motivation
The driving force behind an individual's actions that energizes and directs goal-oriented behavior.

Motivation is an internal state or condition that *activates* a person's behavior and gives it direction toward accomplishing a task. Motivation energizes and directs goal-oriented behavior as well as the intensity and direction of behavior. Motivation is based on emotion, particularly on the search for positive emotional experiences and the avoidance of negative ones. Motivation is important because it determines an individual's effort toward performing a task. Thus, if an individual is motivated he or she will extend high levels of effort toward achieving the organization's goals. A person's level of effort will in turn be affected by the organization's capacity to satisfy that individual's needs and life interests, plus the person's ability to achieve the desired outcome.[2] Motivation can be represented by this conceptual expression:

$$\text{Motivation} = \text{Ability} \times \text{Values} \times \text{Life Interests and Goals}^{ii}$$

In Chapter 2 we discussed Hofstede's well-known model of cultural values, including power distance, uncertainty avoidance, masculinity, individualism, and long-term orientation. An individual's cultural values will affect what motivates

---

[2]Life interests (sometimes called job interests) represent work activities that one might prefer to do, such as working with numbers or doing influencing and selling. This topic is discussed later in the chapter.

that individual. For example, employees who are more individualistic may be motivated by a need to have jobs that allow them to express themselves or that provide them with some personal space. Employees higher on the collective scale would be more motivated by jobs that permit social interaction and working in teams. You will recall that Hofstede also discussed the masculine feminine dimension of culture. Cultures that had high masculine or production-orientation scores placed more emphasis on money and title, while those with a feminine or relational orientation were motivated more by lifestyle concerns, such as free time, holidays, and company social activities.

Thus, what motivates employees cannot be assumed without first asking questions.[iii] To illustrate some difficulties a firm may face, consider the hotel industry. Hotel employees in China are strongly motivated by bosses' public recognition of a job well done. In contrast, hotel staff in Australia stated they were motivated by a flexible work week. They did not mind working long hours sometimes, but they preferred options to work three days per week, so they could be off the other four days. In a collective-focused society, such as China's, peer pressure and peer recognition exercise strong influence on people, particularly in a work setting. In contrast, Australians typically value a work–life balance. That Chinese employees could be motivated by something as simple as recognition and praise in front of their coworkers came as a complete surprise to their Western managers, as well as the fact that the staff may become upset if supervisors fail to provide such public praise. Similarly, employees in parts of Asia may expect employee housing, which can be scarce and very expensive.[iv] Firms in Latin America have also reported that housing can be a useful motivator.[v]

One outcome of globalization and increasing cultural diversity in the workplace is that identifiying what motivates employees has become increasingly important. However, just as there are a number of motivators, there are also numerous different ways to classify and understand motivations. This chapter will look at a wide variety of these different perspectives on motivation. To do this we break the different views on motivation into categories. First, we look at the "content" theories of motivation. This perspective focuses on employees' needs, and there are four specific theories in this perspective. Next we will examine the process perspective of motivation. This perspective accepts the importance of needs yet focuses on the dynamics of motivation by which needs are examined and fulfilled; three specific theories will be examined. For each of these seven theories we initially look at the basic understanding of the theory that was primarily developed and tested in North America. We then examine the theories' implications and applications in international settings. Next, we address how an international firm can use these diverse theories in developing their own systems to motivate employees.

CONTENT (NEED) THEORIES OF MOTIVATION

Most motivation theories recognize that motivation begins with people's needs. **Needs** are things or conditions people have that can trigger behaviors to satisfy those needs. Unfulfilled needs create a tension that makes people want to find ways to satisfy those needs. The stronger a need is and the greater the person's awareness of it, the more motivated that person is to try to satisfy that particular need. This section examines four content theories of motivation that help global managers understand employee needs and how to better motivate their employees (and themselves). Figure 7-2 summarizes these theories and maps their component parts.

Needs
Represent things or conditions that people would like to have.

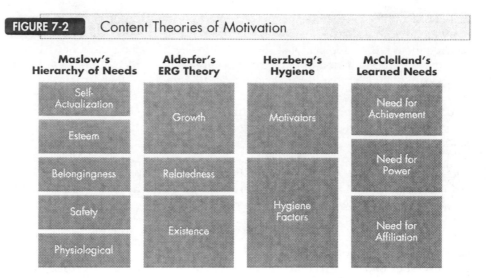

FIGURE 7-2 Content Theories of Motivation

Maslow's Hierarchy of Needs	Alderfer's ERG Theory	Herzberg's Hygiene	McClelland's Learned Needs
Self-Actualization	Growth	Motivators	Need for Achievement
Esteem			
Belongingness	Relatedness		Need for Power
Safety	Existence	Hygiene Factors	
Physiological			Need for Affiliation

Needs Theory

One of the best-known content theories of motivation is Maslow's hierarchy of needs. Outlined by psychologist Abraham Maslow in the 1950s, this theory condenses the innumerable human needs into a hierarchy of five basic needs. (Figure 7-3 summarizes Maslow's model.) At the bottom of the hierarchy are the physiological needs, which include the need to satisfy basic requirements for food, fresh air, clean water, and shelter. In an organizational setting, such a basic need could be represented by salary—employees have a need for a minimum level of basic salary, apart from the opportunity to earn more later. Next comes the safety need—the need for a secure and stable environment and the absence of illness and threats. In a work setting, this roughly corresponds to employee needs for good working conditions and job security. Maslow's third need level is belongingness. Belongingness includes the need for social interaction with other people and affection. In an organizational setting, this could include a job that provides some opportunities for teamwork and social activities. The next highest need is self esteem. Self-esteem can be attained both through personal achievement and via recognition from others. Some jobs provide esteem opportunities as a natural part of the job, such as those in the performing arts or the media, while other jobs have to create such opportunities, such as through employee recognition programs and awards. At the top of the hierarchy is self-actualization, which represents the need for self-fulfillment—a sense that a key goal has been accomplished. Many tasks have clear, built-in milestones that can help to fulfill this need, such as working toward a bachelors or masters degree, while other tasks must have intermediate objectives and final goals created for which employees can aim.

Maslow argued that a person's behavior is motivated primarily by the lowest unsatisfied need at that moment in time. Physiological needs are initially the most important and people are motivated to satisfy them first. Once these most basic needs are filled, the safety need emerges as the strongest motivator. As safety needs are satisfied, the belongingness need becomes most important. In international settings this theory has led firms to focus on the nature of the local economic setting as the principal indicator of an appropriate employee motivator. Thus, in a poor state like Bangladesh, money might be the principal motivator for most people. Only when a person satisfies a lower-level need does the next higher need, such as job security, become a primary motivator. In the economically advanced

FIGURE 7-3	Maslow's Hierarchy

Self Actualization – self-fulfillment
↑
Self Esteem – recognition
↑
Belongingness – social interaction
↑
Safety – stable environment
↑
Physiological Needs – food, shelter

countries of Europe, higher-level needs such as self-esteem and self-actualization would be expected to be more common, because food, housing, and employment are easily attained. This progression up the needs hierarchy is known as the satisfaction–progression process. Maslow's theory predicts that even if a person is unable to satisfy a higher need, he or she will be motivated by the possibility of fulfilling it until it is satisfied.

Maslow's hierarchy of needs is one of the best-known motivation theories. The model was helpful when initially proposed because it helped firms recognize that employees from different countries may be motivated by different needs. However, today the model is criticized for failing to explain the specifics of employee needs and neglecting job interests. For example, researchers have found that individual needs do not follow the same progression up the scale from lower to higher in the different parts of the world.[vi] Gratification of one need level does not necessarily lead to increased motivation coming from the need to satisfy the next item in the hierarchy, as proposed by Maslow. Moreover, not all people exhibit all five needs to the same extent. For example, some people may have very little in the way of social needs. They might like to work alone and prefer not going out to numerous company functions and lunches, and, in fact, may be annoyed (and thus demotivated) by repeated requests by colleagues or the company to attend social events or to socialize after work. This is usually quite acceptable in North American work settings where firms generally do not stress the social aspect of work. However, many South American cultures place great importance on social aspects and, as a result, employees are more likely to be motivated by a system that gives rewards based on social needs, such as having company dinners or weekend retreats. Most Japanese firms also expect employees to attend social functions and go out together after work to restaurants and bars, making it a little uncomfortable for employees who do not want to socialize so regularly. High social needs may also be important in motivating employees in Northern European countries, such as Denmark, Norway, and Sweden, that stress quality of life over masculine production orientation.[vii] This does not mean that all people in South America or Northern Europe emphasize such needs in the same way, but it is the way the society and its organizations tend to be ordered.

Maslow's model is helpful because it reminds managers who may be inclined to emphasize money as the sole motivator that there are different employee needs and that people are not motivated by the same things at the same time, with culture being a key factor in generating these different needs. A performance package based on bonuses and/or salary increases that is useful in the United States may not be the road to higher motivation and performance for some of its employees. This, in turn, suggests that managers in international firms should strive to find out what their employees really want and how to account for those needs in a motivation-and-reward system.

LINCOLN ELECTRIC IN MEXICO

Employees in countries outside of North America may have different needs than those of employees within North America. U.S. manufacturer Lincoln Electric is well known for its effective motivation-and-reward system based on **piecework**. With piecework, a worker is paid a fixed rate for each unit produced or action performed. Piecework can be very effective for manufacturing and is widely used in China and in high-production operations in East Asia. It is normally combined with a (low) base salary, similar to a salesperson's low base pay and commissions. In many of the world's more developed economies, piecework is staunchly resisted by workers and their unions. Yet Lincoln Electric has maintained a very disciplined and effective piecework system since its founding in the nineteenth century—a system that has been copied, at least in part, by many firms worldwide.

Lincoln Electric was founded in 1895 to make electric motors. The firm today is known as the world's leading manufacturer of welding equipment. Lincoln Electric has a long history of human resources innovation. The firm introduced its piecework system nearly a century ago, in which employees are paid largely for the number of welding devices and other units they can produce—a system that has worked well and continues through today. However, at the same time, the firm also introduced employee advisory committees. Each department in the firm created groups of employees to advise the firm, and these employees meet every two weeks. The creation of such labor groups was a radical innovation at the time. The firm later introduced other radical innovations, such as life

insurance for employees, stock ownership plans for employees, annual bonuses based on output for the year, and a strong no-layoff commitment.

All of these human resources innovations continue today. However, today additional incentives are included for minimizing defects and teamwork, but Lincoln Electric employees are largely on their own in figuring out how to produce as much as possible. For example, Lincoln Electric allows individual employees leeway in organizing their workspaces and scheduling their work hours, and the annual bonus for each employee can average over $24,000 per year.

Although Lincoln Electric has been very successful in the United States, it has had trouble implementing this system overseas. As the former CEO, Don Hastings, observed a few years ago in the *Harvard Business Review*:

"[Lincoln's] incentive system is transferable to some countries—especially in countries settled by immigrants, where hard work and upward mobility are ingrained parts of the culture. But in many other places, it won't easily take root. It is especially difficult to install it in a factory that has different work practices and traditions. For example, even though German factory workers are highly skilled, and in general, solid workers, they do not work nearly as hard or as long as the people in our Cleveland factory. In Germany, the average workweek is 35 hours. In contrast, the average factory workweek in Lincoln's U.S. plants is between 43 and 58 hours, and the company can ask people to work longer hours on short notice—a flexibility that is essential for the system to work.

The lack of flexibility was one reason why our [motivation and reward system] approach would not work in Europe."

The Lincoln Electric employee system worked very well with the culture of the U.S. But in Mexico the cultural factors, such as lower individualism and less commitment to production, did not fit well with Lincoln Electric's piece-rate pay system. In addition, the plant in Mexico was unionized and there was a predisposition against workers earning different amounts.

To successfully implement the system in Mexico, Lincoln Electric decided to introduce it gradually. Lincoln Electric allowed a few select workers to opt into the system, and as they began to do well, other workers requested to be allowed into the piecework system. Although cultural values were important in suggesting what motivation system would work, Lincoln Electric was able to overcome any possible hindrances. It effectively used a system of social learning to gradually influence all the workers to understand how the system benefited them. And benefit them it did. After about two years, all 175 workers in the plant had opted into the incentive system. Workers make more money than before and Lincoln Electric has its productive system in place. Culture is important in determining what companies can do, but sometimes it is possible to get something done in spite of local culture and traditions, though a system may have to be implemented carefully, as Lincoln Electric did in Mexico.

Hastings, D. (1999). Lincoln Electric's harsh lessons from international expansion. *Harvard Business Review* 77(3), 162–178.

Alderfer's ERG Theory

Piecework
A type of work in which a worker is paid a fixed "piece rate" for each unit produced or action performed.

The ERG theory was developed by psychologist Clayton Alderfer to overcome problems associated with Maslow's hierarchy of needs theory.[viii] The ERG theory groups human needs into three broad categories: existence, relatedness, and growth (notice that the theory's name is based on the first letter of each need). Existence needs include a person's physiological and physically related safety needs, such as the need for food, shelter, and safe working conditions. Relatedness needs include a person's need to interact with other people, receive public recognition, and feel secure around people (i.e., interpersonal safety). Growth needs consist of a person's self-esteem through personal achievement as well as the concept of self-actualization presented in Maslow's model. Alderfer's existence needs correspond to Maslow's physiological and safety needs; relatedness needs correspond to Maslow's belongingness needs; and growth needs correspond to Maslow's esteem and self-actualization needs.

The ERG theory argues that, different from Maslow, an employee's behavior is motivated simultaneously by more than one need level. A person might try to satisfy the growth needs of meeting a tough goal even though that person's relatedness needs are not fully satisfied. Unlike Maslow's model, the ERG theory includes a frustration–regression process whereby those who are unable to satisfy a higher need become frustrated and regress back to the next lower need level. For example, if existence and relatedness needs have been satisfied, but growth need fulfillment cannot be achieved, an individual will become frustrated and relatedness needs will again emerge as the dominant need and source of motivation.

The ERG theory explains the dynamics of human needs in organizations reasonably well because human needs cluster more neatly around the three categories proposed by Alderfer than the five categories in Maslow's hierarchy. The combined processes of satisfaction–progression and frustration–regression also provide a more accurate explanation of why employees need change over time. Internationally, the model also suggests how cultures with different values may be motivated by different needs. For example, some people from a collectivist society would be motivated by the need to be part of the group. People in such a society would prefer to work in firms that have social events and in which employees work in teams. Employees from a more collectivist society would also prefer that the firm provide lunches and tea breaks in which all employees can participate. Indeed, in many Asian countries it is common for all offices to close from about 1:00 pm to 2:00 pm so all employees can go to lunch together. This is also true in several European countries, as anyone knows who has tried to find open businesses or government offices during lunchtime. In some countries lunch breaks can go on for two to three hours. Employees from such countries may become demotivated by working alone and not having social opportunities at work. But collectivism is not the only cultural value that affects motivation. There are, in fact, a variety of cultural issues that have an impact on motivation. For example, in countries higher on Hofstede's dimension of uncertainty avoidance, security may be a more motivating factor than Maslow's highest need of self-actualization growth and thus be a more important need.[ix] Alderfer's model allows for greater flexibility than Maslow's because it also recognizes that people have different needs though they do not move up in a rigid hierarchy as Maslow suggested originally.

Thus, internationally, ERG theory allowed for more complex models of compensation to be developed, which resulted in the recognition that a mixture of needs must be addressed. For example, it suggests that firms in a poor nation, such as Bangladesh, focus on both wages and the need for relatedness as motivators. Maslow's hierarchy of needs and ERG theory are helpful in reminding managers of the various needs of their employees, but these models failed to address a number of specific work-related needs, such as the often-voiced need to be involved with company decisions and other nonmaterial or intrinsic needs.[x] Subsequent authors sought to address intrinsic needs' impact on motivation in particular.

Motivation—Hygiene Theory

Motivators

In Herzberg's motivation-hygiene theory, these are positive influencers, such as job involvement, that are intrinsic to a job and that can push employees to higher levels of performance.

Management scholar Frederick Herzberg found the basic need theories unsatisfying, and sought to examine extrinsic (external) as well as intrinsic (internal, task-related) **motivators**. In Herzberg's formulation, intrinsic motivators include 1) achievement, 2) recognition for achievement, 3) the work itself, 4) responsibility, and 5) growth or advancement. These are all intrinsic in that they are related to the task and the psychological state of the individual. Extrinsic factors include: 1) company policy and administration, 2) supervision, 3) interpersonal relationships, 4) working conditions, 5) salary, 6) status, and 7) security.[xi] Herzberg argued that intrinsic factors tend to be motivators. The more extrinsic, hygiene factors can serve to de-motivate, but not motivate. This model is useful because it breaks the concept of motivation into factors that motivate to take action, and factors that create dissatisfaction and might cause people to avoid doing certain things, but will not motivate them.[3] Thus, motivation is not just putting things in place to encourage behavior, it also is concerned with removing things that could discourage desired behaviors.

To clarify Herzberg's approach to motivation, consider why people may be motivated to travel to a certain city for a holiday. The city-state of Singapore has one of the highest per-capita incomes in the world. Singapore has tight controls over many aspects of life; for example, you cannot buy chewing gum without a doctor's prescription (to prevent people from dropping it on the street), there is little litter because of strict policing with high penalties if you are caught, and you can be fined if you do not flush a public toilet after use. Singapore is therefore well known for being very clean and orderly, but it was not always that way. People find many Asian cities to be cluttered and disorderly, and previously, Singapore was no exception. However, one of the first things that the ruling People's Action Party sought to do when Singapore gained its independence from Malaysia in the mid-1960s was to make Singapore much cleaner and more orderly than any other Asian city. The government believed that if Singapore remained dirty, international business people would be less likely to do business there or travel there for a holiday. As a result of this conscious effort, in the late 1970s Singapore became the cleanest city in Asia and one of the model cities for the world. Thus, the leadership was able to fix a hygiene factor by eliminating those things that would discourage people from traveling to the city.

While a *bad* hygiene factor may prevent (de-motivate) you from visiting a city, an absence of such factors is not enough to encourage (motivate) people to travel to a city for a holiday. Singapore has since recognized this and knows it has to produce specific reasons to motivate people to come there, as opposed to just removing reasons not to. Singapore has developed an amusement park on Sentosa Island, just off of its coast, and is bringing in gambling casinos and other attractions. Recognizing the interaction of both items—reasons to *do* things and taking away reasons to *not do* things—led Herzberg to argue it was necessary to have both motivators and hygiene factors (also called "dissatisfiers") to be successful.

However, while managers need to address both (extrinsic) motivators and (internal) hygiene factors, they will likely address these needs separately. Improving hygiene factors works to minimize job dissatisfaction and employee turnover but does not increase motivation. This separation of issues helps international firms that must address the needs of worldwide organizations. A hygiene factor such as working conditions expected in different settings can vary widely. For example, a furniture factory setting that dissatisfies employees in a rich European country, such as Norway, may gain a dramatically different response in Vietnam.

[3]Herzberg's data and research design have been questioned by organizational scholars in recent years, particularly in terms of the narrow sample used (engineers). Nevertheless, it is conceptually useful to discuss needs in terms of motivators and hygiene factors, that is, motivation versus dissatisfaction (demotivation).

Firms must recognize these differences and improve hygiene factors that potentially cause dissatisfaction in each setting.

When using the motivator-hygiene model, firms also cannot assume that intrinsic items, such as employee growth opportunities and interesting work, will have the same motivational effect internationally. For example, workers in some countries, such as Japan and Greece, are motivated more by job security than growth opportunities or interesting work.[xii] Though Herzberg's work has been criticized because of his methods, particularly using a sample of professionals, his theory does add to our understanding of the needs theories by being more specific about needs and arguing that fulfilling some needs will not necessarily motivate employees to perform better. Employees who are frustrated may say, "The company is just throwing money at the problem by offering me a raise and covering over the real issue," when in reality the firm needs to fix the situation, possibly by giving the employee more interesting work. Thus, extrinsic needs, such as working conditions and (sometimes) additional money, can actually de-motivate. Perhaps once people feel they are getting a reasonable salary, they would prefer improvements in an intrinsic need (such as more interesting work) rather than getting more money for a job they dislike. Recognition of these issues by international firms encouraged them to tailor their motivational systems to a much higher degree than had occurred previously.

Learned-Needs Theory

Harvard psychologist David McClelland studied school children from a very young age and followed them for many years. He found that some factors that motivate individuals are learned from childhood. Particularly, he identified three learned needs that shape their motivation: need for achievement, need for affiliation, and something not emphasized in the other major need theories—the need for power.[xiii] Each of these learned needs will be discussed in turn, with their implications for international business discussed at the end of the section.

Need for Achievement (nAch) One widely studied learned need is the need for achievement, or "nAch." People with a high nAch want to accomplish reasonably challenging goals through their own efforts. They prefer working alone rather than in teams and choose tasks with a moderate degree of difficulty—challenging but achievable. People with a high nAch typically prefer positive feedback and recognition for their successes. That positive feedback could be public recognition from the firm and peers, or it could be recognition from the boss.

McClelland argued that the need for achievement explained why some societies are able to produce more than others.[xiv] Successful entrepreneurs tend to have a high nAch, possibly because they establish challenging goals for themselves and are motivated by testing out different approaches to their goals and then meeting them. To the high nAch person, achieving by completing a task is more important than the financial reward. Corporate and team leaders should have a somewhat lower nAch because they must delegate work and build support through involvement, and thus are likely to have a higher need for power or "nPow." Morgan McCall of the Harvard Business School similarly studied individuals with high needs for achievement; he termed them corporate "high fliers."[xv] McCall found that many were not good team players, as they were motivated more by their own achievements, not the team's. These individuals did perform well in large companies where they were given considerable independence, as though they were running their own businesses. However, you may not want such an entrepreneur in a setting where significant administrative experience is needed. The understanding of nAch shapes which managers may work best in different settings. New markets such as China or Russia, when those

DOES NEED FOR ACHIEVEMENT VARY BY COUNTRY?

Because need for achievement (nAch) is thought to be a learned need, it may differ across cultures and countries. The United States, possibly drawing on the Protestant work ethic and a long tradition of immigration, has long been thought to inculcate high levels of nAch. Studies examined literature, such as the McDuffy Reader series, that was used to teach children in the U.S. in the 1800s and have found consistently high levels of nAch in the pages of those books. Recent studies have similarly measured higher-than-average levels of nAch in the U.S. Another study reported that nAch, as inferred from literature read primarily by preteens in the U.S., was positively related to the number of patents recorded in the U.S. between 1800 and 1950. Bradburn and Berlew similarly analyzed achievement motives in British school readers and showed a strong correlation of achievement themes with Britain's industrial growth.[xvi] Drawing on popular literature in Europe from the Middle Ages, researchers linked increases in apparent nAch to economic growth. Children's literature in China also showed a similar emphasis on encouraging achievement. The evidence is compelling: societies that encourage and reward high achievement have more entrepreneurship and higher sustained economic growth.[xvii] In contrast, societies that do not expect excellence, fail to encourage achievement, and reward idleness while failing to penalize destructive behavior, find that people tend to give them exactly what they are implicitly asking for.[xviii] Management scholars and psychologists from Maslow onward would agree this is not particularly surprising—organizations and societies do tend to get what they encourage and reward. There are still many employers, though, who continue to reward a less desired performance outcome while hoping that improved performance will somehow still occur. Research suggests that this type of hope for improvement is likely to be in vain.[xix] A central lesson in motivation is that you most often get the behavior that you reward.

countries were initially opening to investment and there were few organizational supports, would have been best served by an individual with high nAch and an entrepreneurial bent. However, as markets mature and firms grow, it may be better to put someone with administrative (and international) experience in charge. For example, if a manager has to operate a factory with large numbers of employees and deal with established relationships, a high nAch person may not be the right fit. A high need for affiliation or nAff manager may be needed in such a setting. The skills and interests behind factory management today are much different than what was needed earlier, so an individual with lower nAch fits better now.[xx]

McClelland found need achievement to be relatively common across cultures, although some societies did a better job in training its members to strive for achievement that others.[xxi] For example, in India, researchers found that entrepreneurs trained in the need for achievement performed better than those who were not trained.[xxii] Managers in New Zealand and in the United States showed similar results.[xxiii]

Need for Affiliation (nAff) Need for affiliation, or "nAff," refers to a desire for approval from others, and as a result, it means conforming to their wishes and expectations, and avoiding conflict. People with a strong nAff want to form positive relationships with others; this is much like Maslow's belongingness need and Alderfer's relatedness need. They try to build a favorable image of themselves and take steps to get others to like them. Moreover, high-nAff employees actively support others and try to smooth out conflicts that occur in meetings and other social settings. As with nAch, a key difference is that need for affiliation is learned rather than instinctive.

High-nAff employees tend to be more effective than those with a low nAff in coordinating roles, such as helping diverse departments work on joint projects. Because they are motivated more by relationships and gaining success through the group, they are typically more effective in sales positions in which the main task is cultivating long-term relationships with prospective customers. Generally, employees with high nAff prefer working with others rather than alone, tend to have better attendance records, and tend to be better at mediating conflicts.

Although people with a high nAff are more effective in many jobs requiring social interaction, they tend to be less effective at allocating scarce resources and

People with a strong nAff (need for affiliation) want to form positive relationships with others, which means they are often effective at selling and negotiating.

making other decisions that may require conflict or confrontation. For example, research has found that executives with a high nAff tend to be indecisive and are perceived as less fair in the distribution of resources. People in these decision-making positions must have a relatively low need for affiliation so that their choices and actions are not biased by a personal need for approval, but a manager may be able to use a person with high nAff by giving him or her the special role of challenging key ideas and new business plans for his or her department, sort of a devil's advocate role. Whereas the high nAff individual may not want to do this on his or her own accord, if given the official sanction, that person may be more likely to take on the task.

There is evidence that culture can encourage greater nAff values in given locations. For example, East Asian societies emphasize harmony. The Chinese have a saying that "harmony is the most valuable." The Japanese have a similar saying, as do the Koreans. This reflects the societal organization and influence of these cultures that encourage people to affiliate and create large social and work groups. The drive for group cohesiveness may override an individual's other learned needs.

The need for nAff can be seen in the way people in Chinese organizations might expect most everyone to go to lunch together. If you do not want to go to lunch with the group at 1:00 pm every day, then some people may wonder why you are upsetting the harmony of the group and its cohesiveness by not joining them. In such settings, it is commonly believed that workers who prefer not to eat with the group do not like their coworkers and are too individually minded. This can obviously be a source of frustration for someone with a low nAff, especially from a culture like that of the United States or Australia, which does not insist that people always do things together in large groups. Such an individual might wonder why his or her coworkers must always have lunch together or hang out together during non-work hours.

International firms relocating managers to a society with a high nAff must prepare that employee to understand that "work time" does not necessarily stop at the end of the day. If after-work drinks and dinner are part of the work ritual, then colleagues will expect the employee to participate. Those high-nAff colleagues will expect that the expatriate have the same nAff as they do, that is, they will project their high nAff onto others (though having read this textbook, the student should again remember that not everyone will have the same values and to avoid projection). Conversely, firms from societies that value large group activities should also realize that people from individualistic cultures may be uncomfortable in large groups and with the personal questions common in those settings. For many international firms from the West, integrating nAff individuals into their motivation-and-reward systems has been difficult. Increasingly, these firms are building sensitivity training for new expat and local managers into their culture to provide an understanding of nAff. However, efforts to deal with the issue beyond such sensitivity training have been limited.

Need for Power (nPow) Need for power, or "nPow," refers to a desire to exercise authority over people and resources. People with a high nPow are thus motivated by the opportunity to be in a position of authority. They frequently rely on persuasive communication (see Chapter 12), make more suggestions in meetings, and tend to publicly evaluate situations more frequently. Some people have a high need for personalized power. They enjoy power for its own sake and use it to advance their career and other personal interests. Power is a symbol of status and a tool to fulfill personal needs, rather than a delicate instrument to serve stakeholders. Others may have a high need for socialized power. These individuals want power as a means to help others, such as improving society or increasing organizational effectiveness.

Corporate and political leaders have a high nPow. However, McClelland argued that effective leaders should have a high need for socialized rather than personalized power. These leaders have a high degree of altruism and social responsibility and are concerned about the consequences of their actions on others. In other words, leaders must exercise their power within the framework of moral and ethical standards. The ethical guidance of their need for power results in trust and respect from employees, as well as a commitment to the manager's vision. Managers may be able to motivate someone with a high need for power by placing them in authority over some resources, such as giving a custodian responsibility for multiple floors and providing him or her some resources to get the jobs done efficiently.

Applying Learned-Needs Theory McClelland argued that achievement, affiliation, and power needs are learned rather than instinctive, and are thus inculcated by cultures and societies. Accordingly, he argued for developing training programs that strengthen these learned needs. McClelland developed an achievement-motivation program in which trainees practice writing achievement-oriented stories and engaging in achievement-oriented behaviors in business games. Trainees also complete a detailed achievement plan for the next two years and form a reference group with other trainees to maintain their new-found achievement motive style.

These programs have had some success. For example, need-achievement course participants in India subsequently started more new businesses, had greater community involvement, invested more in expanding their existing businesses, and employed twice as many people as non-participants. Similar achievement courses for North American small business owners have also reported increases in the profitability of the participants' businesses.[xxiv]

Integrating the Different Content (Needs) Related Theories One of the main points in content theories of motivation is that different people have various needs at different times. Consequently, corporate leaders should not be surprised if distributing the same reward results in different levels of need fulfillment. Rewards that motivate one person may have less effect on someone with different needs. A firm based in a South American culture with a high relational orientation may base its reward system heavily on social activities that the firm provides (e.g., employee luncheons, awards dinners, weekend activities, company retreats). If that firm were to come to a more individualistic society in North America and try to provide a similar motivation-and-reward system, the more individualistic employees in that culture would probably not be motivated by such rewards, and might actually try to avoid them. One American employee working for an Argentinean multinational organization commented, "They expect me to work all day, and then hang out with them [the Argentinean coworkers] at night also? If they want to give us some incentives to work hard, they should just give me a gift certificate for the restaurant—I'll go myself when I feel like going, or perhaps with a colleague but not with the whole department. That's just a pain." Thus, international firms need to offer a choice of rewards in different settings. Research on motivation and culture suggests that emerging economies more often have low individualism, higher uncertainty avoidance, high power distance, and a relatively low emphasis on production-orientation.[xxv] The needs of the extended family are also emphasized over individual needs in many East Asian countries, particularly in the more traditional companies. Activities, commerce, and worship center on the family and maintaining its integrity and prosperity. Businesses are often seen as a family asset and outsiders are not permitted much access to a key aspect of the family's prosperity. Under these circumstances, firms with an individualistic bent will be seen as troublesome for the family. Organizations in emerging markets are more likely to give group rewards and generally do not encourage risk taking.[xxvi] Firms may find it difficult to import a reward system relying heavily on individualism and low uncertainty avoidance to societies that value collectivism and risk avoidance.

Content theories of motivation also warn us against relying too heavily on financial rewards as a source of employee motivation. While money does motivate employees to some extent, there are other powerful sources of motivation, such as challenging assignments and interesting work, learning opportunities, some control over one's workspace and schedule, and praise from colleagues and supervisors. Such needs can be easily met by companies that understand money is not the only motivator, and that pay attention to more intrinsic forms of motivation—needs that do not cost a firm anything to meet, apart from more vigilant and mindful management.[xxvii]

PROCESS THEORIES OF MOTIVATION

Content theories explain the different needs people have in different situations, whereas process theories describe the processes through which need deficiencies are translated into behavior. Three of the most popular process-motivation theories are expectancy theory, equity theory, and goal setting. Figure 7-4 summarizes the process theories and their component parts.

Expectancy Theory

Expectancy theory is a process-motivation theory based on the idea that work effort is directed toward behaviors that people believe will lead to desired outcomes.[xxviii] Figure 7-5 summarizes the relationships in expectancy theory. As can be seen, an individual's effort level depends on three factors: effort-to-performance (E→P) expectancy, performance-to-outcome (P→O) expectancy, and outcome valences (V). Employee motivation is influenced by all three components of the expectancy theory model. If any component weakens, motivation weakens. Each component of the model will be examined in turn.

SEMCO: CREATIVE MOTIVATION IN BRAZIL

Once the various needs theories are understood, firms can use this knowledge to build an effective compensation system. For example, in some international settings, employees respond to pay for performance coupled with empowerment when properly implemented. Semco is a well-known Brazilian manufacturer. Its units include:

- the industrial machinery unit, now manufacturing mixing equipment
- Sembobac, a partnership with Baltimore Air Cooler, making cooling equipment
- Cushman and Wakefield SEMCO, a partnership with Rockefeller property company Cushman and Wakefield, managing properties in Brazil and Latin America
- Semco Johnson Controls, a partnership with Johnson Controls, managing large scale facilities such as airports and hospitals
- ERM, a partnership between Semco and Environmental Resources Management, one of the world's leading environmental consultants
- Semco Ventures, offering high-technology and Internet services

- SemcoHR, a human resources management firm
- Semco-RGIS, an inventory control firm

Semco has used profit sharing effectively to help build employee empowerment and engagement such that employees are interested in furthering their employer's interest. Brazilian employees have a fairly low individualism score and, as in most Latin American countries, are considered to be collectivist. This suggests that allowing a group of employees to earn a bonus and collaborate on its distribution will be effective if the nature of the job is such that work can be shared. Commented Semco president Ricardo Semler:

"Profit sharing won't motivate employees if they see it as just another management gimmick, if the company makes it difficult for them to see how their own work is related to profits and to understand how those profits are divided ... Twice a year, we calculate 23 percent of after-tax profit on each division income statement and give a check to three employees who've been elected by the workers

in their division. These three invest the money until the unit can meet and decide—by simple majority vote—what they want to do with it. In most units, that's turned out to be an equal distribution ... The guy who sweeps the floor gets just as much as the division partner.

One division chose to use the money as a fund to lend out for housing construction ... Some of [the division employees] have already received loans and have begun to build themselves houses ... Semco's experience has convinced me that profit sharing has an excellent chance of working when it crowns a broad program of employee participation, when the profit-sharing criteria are so clear and simple that the least-gifted employee can understand them, and perhaps most important, when employees have monthly access to the company vital statistics—costs, overhead, sales, payroll, taxes, profits."

Semlar, R. (1989, September–October). Managing without managers. *Harvard Business Review*, pp. 2–10.

E—P Expectancy The effort-to-performance (E→P) expectancy is an individual's perception that his or her effort will result in a particular level of performance. Expectancy is defined as a probability, and therefore ranges from 0.0 to 1.0. In some situations, employees may believe that they can unquestionably accomplish the task (a probability of 1.0). In other situations, they expect that even their highest level of effort will not result in the desired performance level (a probability of 0.0). For instance, unless you are an expert skier, you probably aren't motivated to try some of the black diamond ski runs at New Zealand's Mt. Hutt. The reason is a very low E→P expectancy. Even your best efforts will not get you down the hill feet first! In most cases, the E→P expectancy falls somewhere between these two extremes.

P—O Expectancy The performance-to-outcome (P→O) expectancy is the perceived probability that a specific behavior or performance level will lead to specific outcomes. This probability is developed from previous experience or social learning derived from watching others. For example, students learn from experience that missing classes either ruins their chance of a good grade or may have no effect at all. In extreme cases, employees may believe that accomplishing a particular task (performance) will definitely result in a particular outcome (a probability of

FIGURE 7-4 Process Theories of Motivation

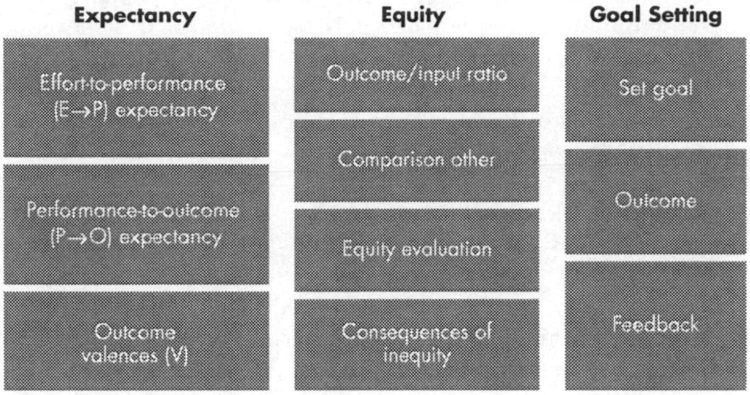

Expectancy	Equity	Goal Setting
Effort-to-performance (E→P) expectancy	Outcome/input ratio	Set goal
Performance-to-outcome (P→O) expectancy	Comparison other	Outcome
	Equity evaluation	
Outcome valences (V)	Consequences of inequity	Feedback

1.0), or they may believe that this outcome will have no effect on successful performance (a probability of 0.0). More often, the P→O expectancy falls somewhere between these two extremes.

One important issue in P→O expectancies is determining which outcomes are most important to us. We certainly don't evaluate the P→O expectancy for every possible outcome. There are too many of them. Instead, we only think about outcomes of interest to us at the time. One day, your motivation to complete a task may be fuelled mainly by the likelihood of getting off work early to meet friends. Other times, your motivation to complete the same task may be based more on the P→O expectancy of a promotion or pay increase. The point is that your motivation depends on the probability that a behavior or job performance level will result in the outcome that you anticipate.

Outcome Valences The third element in expectancy theory is the valence of each outcome considered. **Valence** refers to one's anticipated satisfaction or dissatisfaction with an outcome. The number may range from −100 to +100 to reflect the overall value placed on the outcome: a maximum positive valence of +100 would be highly desired, while the lowest valence of −100 would be something that a person would work hard to avoid and a valence of 0 would mean no motivation at all. If you have a strong relatedness (social) need, for example, then you would value group activities and other events that help to fulfill that need. Outcomes that move you further away from fulfilling your social need, such as working from

Valence
The anticipated satisfaction or dissatisfaction that an individual feels about an outcome.

FIGURE 7-5 Expectancy Theory of Motivation

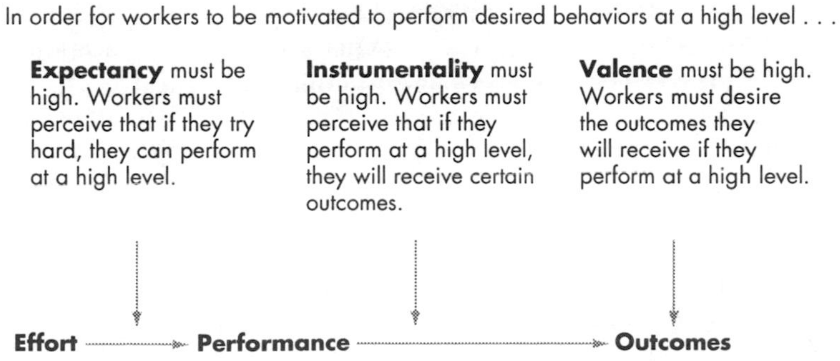

In order for workers to be motivated to perform desired behaviors at a high level . . .

Expectancy must be high. Workers must perceive that if they try hard, they can perform at a high level.

Instrumentality must be high. Workers must perceive that if they perform at a high level, they will receive certain outcomes.

Valence must be high. Workers must desire the outcomes they will receive if they perform at a high level.

Effort ⟶ Performance ⟶ Outcomes

home, will have a strong negative valence and you would work to avoid that undesirable outcome.

Notice that some outcomes directly fulfill personal needs, whereas other outcomes indirectly fulfill those needs. You might be motivated to achieve the highest sales in your company in a particular month because "it feels great." This is the direct outcome of growth-need fulfillment. At the same time, you might want to be the top salesperson because you will be mentioned in the company magazine, thereby indirectly fulfilling your social needs.

Expectancy Theory in Practice One of the appealing characteristics of expectancy theory is that it provides clear guidelines for increasing employee motivation by altering your E→P expectancies, P→O expectancies, and outcome valences. Because E→P expectancies are based on self-esteem and previous experience, employees should be given the necessary tools and competencies, clear role perceptions, and favorable situational factors to reach the desired levels of performance. This involves properly matching employees to jobs based on their abilities and their job interests, clearly communicating the tasks required for the job, and providing sufficient resources for them to accomplish those tasks.[xxix]

Even when employees have the capacity and resources to perform the work, they may have low E→P expectancies because of low self confidence. Counseling and coaching may help employees to develop confidence about the skills and knowledge they already have to perform the job. Similarly, E→P expectancies are learned, so positive feedback typically strengthens employee self confidence. Behavior modification and behavioral modeling also tend to increase E→P expectancies in many situations.

The most obvious ways to improve P→O expectancies are to measure employee performance accurately and distribute more valued rewards to those with higher job performance. Many organizations have difficulty putting this straightforward idea into practice. Some executives are reluctant to withhold bonuses for poor performance because they do not want to experience conflict with employees. Other firms fail to measure employee performance very well.

P→O expectancies are perceptions, so employees should believe that higher performance will result in higher rewards. Having a performance-based reward system is important, but this fact must be communicated. When rewards are distributed, employees should understand how their rewards have been based on past (recent) performance. More generally, companies need to regularly communicate the existence of a performance-based reward system through examples, anecdotes, and public recognition of employee performance.

Increasing outcome valences are affected by those things that are valued by employees. This brings us back to what we learned from the content theories of motivation—namely, that companies must pay attention to the needs and reward preferences of individual employees. Companies should develop more individualized reward systems so that employees who perform well are offered a choice of extrinsic rewards, including bonuses, additional vacation time, or opportunities to travel to conferences and training sessions. It is important not to neglect intrinsic motivators, such as career path and control over resources to accomplish a job, as possible reward outcomes that may be valued by the employee.

Expectancy theory also emphasizes the need to discover performance outcomes that have negative valences, thereby reducing the effectiveness of existing reward systems. For example, peer pressure may cause some employees to perform their jobs at the minimum standard even though formal rewards and the job itself otherwise motivates them to perform at higher levels.

For most employees, rewards such as bonuses, additional vacation time, and opportunities for career advancement are as important as a paycheck. Without a clear reward system, motivation and morale can suffer.

Expectancy Theory Internationally Expectancy theory offers one of the best models available for predicting work effort and motivation in different cultures. All three components of the model have received much support in past research, and there is particularly good evidence that P→O expectancies influence employee motivation. As suggested by the discussion above, in different countries employees may be motivated by much different outcome rewards. For example, in the United States, employees are more likely to have an individualistic orientation. Most Americans will have no expectations that the company should "take care of them." Thus, the outcomes are typically focused on monetary rewards. Asian firms that try to reward North American employees partly through company social activities such as lunches and dinner banquets as they would in Asia may be surprised to find that such "social rewards" are not motivating at all to many North Americans, who, on average, do not value group activities as highly as an Asian staff.

In more collectivist cultures, especially those with higher risk avoidance, employees may believe that being taken care of is an obligation of the company, and will be motivated by the offer of additional job security, perhaps in exchange for loyalty or accepting a lower salary. This used to be true in China until the economic reforms of the 1980s and 1990s dismantled the old "iron rice bowl" system that Chairman Mao and his followers promulgated after the end of the Chinese Civil War in 1949. (The **Iron Rice Bowl** was a concept that the state, through the state-owned enterprises, would meet all of the workers' needs, including food, schooling for children, healthcare, and even recreation and holiday facilities for workers.) Thus, historically Chinese workers were to give their firms (and the state) absolute loyalty in return for having their basic needs met.[4]

Similarly, Brazilians expect that an outcome of their performance will even include being helped with personal financial problems. The personnel departments of larger Brazilian firms typically provide a range of financial assistance to employees. To many Americans this may sound acceptable until they recognize that the firm will also ask a number of personal questions, including ones about home and life plans, which would seem highly intrusive to most North Americans.

Iron Rice Bowl
In China, the idea of the iron rice bowl is that the state meets all workers' needs. This means not only food, but schools for kids, hospitals, and even vacation locations for workers. These benefits were typically organized around the large state enterprises they served.

[4]This system was gradually dismantled starting with China's reforms in the late 1970s.

Brazilians accept that these questions are part of the firm's effort to make sure that employees are getting their health care and retirement plans in order.[xxx]

Equity Theory

Equity theory explains how people develop perceptions of fairness in the distribution and exchange of resources.[xxxi] As a process theory of motivation, it explains what employees are motivated to do when they feel inequitably treated. This theory is widely accepted in the media and popular culture, but research on equity theory is more cautious about its applicability. There are four main elements of equity theory: outcome/input ratio, comparison other, equity evaluation, and consequences of inequity. Each will briefly be examined in turn.

Outcome/Input Ratio

The outcome/input ratio is the value of the outcomes received divided by the value of inputs provided in an exchange relationship. Inputs include skills, effort, experience, amount of time worked, performance results, and other employee contributions to the organization. Outcomes are things that employees receive from an organization in exchange for inputs, such as pay, promotions, recognition or an office with a window. Employees receive many outcomes, so it isn't always easy to determine the overall values.

For example, a major European retailer opened a number of stores in China in the 1990s, and brought a large back-office operation there in 2000 to function as a regional Asia headquarters. At that time, they brought a number of expatriate staff from Europe and paid them salaries typical for Europe, plus additional hardship pay for relocating to China. The retailer also had a number of local Chinese managers who worked in the back office in positions comparable to the Europeans. Although they received comfortable pay by Chinese standards, substantial pay inequity existed between the Chinese managers and the Europeans. Although the firm ordered individuals not to talk about salary, this instruction was ignored, and the European salaries and benefits became known. When the large wage discrepancy between employees doing essentially the same work was discovered, the Chinese managers became quite dissatisfied. This puzzled the European management, because they knew that the Chinese managers' pay was at the top of the local pay scale for employees with comparable experience and skills. Why would they expect the same money, the Europeans asked? The heart of the difficulty can be seen in equity theory—workers performing basically the same activity but receiving much lower wages.

Both inputs and outcomes are weighted by their importance to the individual. These weights vary from one person to the next. To some people, seniority is a valuable input that deserves more outcomes from the organization. Others consider job effort and performance the most important contributions in the exchange relationship, and give seniority relatively little weight. Equity theory recognizes that people value outcomes differently because they have different needs and interests. For example, it accepts that some employees want time off with pay whereas others consider this a relatively insignificant reward for job performance.

As with expectancy theory, equity theory has been criticized for being too calculative and too material-achievement focused, and as such, being mostly relevant to Anglo-American settings. For example, in some cultures, equity in outcome is seen as more important than equality in the equity outcome/input ratio. That is, in many societies some feel that employees of about the same age and experience should be paid about the same, even if there are better performers in the group. If a high-performing employee were to stand out by virtue of a higher salary, then that individual would feel embarrassed. Multinational firms have found this to be common in Japan, though it has reportedly been changing with the younger generation now entering the workforce. Historically, Japanese employees valued salaries that were relatively equal, and did not feel comfortable or particularly motivated by being paid more, even if they were productive enough to justify the higher pay. Harmony or "fitting in" with colleagues was more valued than extra pay or promotion.[xxxii] In the outer resort islands of Hawaii, typically thought of as a more relaxed culture, hotel human resources executives have reported that if they pay out bonuses and extra money for working longer hours, the employees will respond by working less, not more. The employees feel that they only need to work to earn a certain amount of money for the week and after that, they can take it easy and take the rest of the week off. Thus, even in a country like the United States there are exceptions to equity theory reliance on the output/input ratio.

Comparison Other Equity theory states that we compare our situations with a "comparison other," but the theory does not identify the comparison other. It may be another person or group of people, or even yourself in the past. It may be someone in the same job, another job, or another organization. Most of the time, we tend to compare ourselves with others who are nearby, in similar positions, and with similar backgrounds. A luxury hotel chain in East Asia needed extra hotel workers for the extended Christmas–New Year–Chinese New Year holiday season, so they brought housekeepers from a sister hotel in Vietnam to its resorts in Thailand for short-term assignments. The hotel chain provided room and board along with the wage that was standard in Vietnam, and employees received more money than they would have otherwise. However, the Vietnamese hotel workers stopped comparing themselves to hotel workers back in Vietnam, and instead compared their compensation with the Thai hotel employees in the Thai resort who were getting paid about twice as much. The result was a difficult situation in which the guest workers were very unhappy about what they thought was inequitable pay. Management was confused because they thought they were paying a nice premium to bring the Vietnamese employees over to Thailand for the holiday season. Finally, the hotel workers tried to organize a union and management consented to increase their pay by about 25 percent. The Vietnamese employees still felt underpaid compared to the locals, but they felt more motivated than before.

People in more senior positions, CEOs for example, compare themselves more with counterparts in other organizations because they may not have a direct comparison within the company. Some research suggests that employees frequently collect information on several referents to form a "generalized" comparison other. For the most part, however, the comparison other varies from one person to the next and is not easily identifiable. As the world continues to globalize the comparisons are increasingly becoming more standardized for many professionals. Those professionals who feel that an organization does not match their comparison other may now not only change employers but even change the country in which they are employed.

Equity Evaluation We form an equity evaluation after determining our own outcome/input ratio and comparing this with the comparison other's ratio. Consider the European retailer situation again. The Chinese managers felt pay inequity because they believed the European managers were receiving higher outcomes (pay) for inputs that they believed were about the same. The over-reward inequity and under-reward inequity is illustrated in Figure 7-6.

In the equity condition, the Chinese managers would believe their outcome/input ratio to be similar to the European managers. In this particular case, expatriate managers are providing the same inputs as the local Chinese managers, so they may even feel motivated to improve their performance. Or, they may just feel that they are more experienced, thus more productive and effective in their jobs.

MOTIVATION IN RUSSIAN MANUFACTURERS

While expectancy theory is popular in the individualistically minded U.S. (with low uncertainty avoidance) international application can present challenges. Americans have a "calculative involvement" in their organizations, which employees can readily understand. This helps to explain the popularity in the U.S. of expectancy theories of motivation, which see employees as generally having a high need for achievement (nAch) and being motivated by consciously expected and well-calculated outcomes. In contrast, as in many developing countries, Russia is high on Hofstede's collectivism dimension and uncertainty avoidance.

Thus, security and social belonging will be highly valued needs in Russian society, particularly given the upheavals of recent years.

An examination of Russian manufacturing managers found that employees may respond positively to motivational approaches emphasizing group benefits that reinforce the importance of team contributions. Empowerment should be done sincerely, and must be backed up by actions that reinforce mutual trust. Employees should also have access to information about the business and its performance. Information about the employees' own departments or other sub-units is particularly

necessary, as this is the level of performance that they can affect.

Thus, in a country such as Russia, motivational approaches focused on the individual are not likely to be eliminated. However, to be successful, such motivation efforts should be tied to development and mastery of work-related skills. As with many developing countries, excellent educational opportunities that will be prized by the employees include overseas training.

Elenkov, D.S. (1998, Summer). Can American management concepts work in Russia? A cross-cultural comparative study. *California Management Review*, 40(4), 133–156.

The Chinese managers would feel inequity and ask for redress, or they would threaten to leave the field (quit) during the Chinese New Year season in January or February.

The equity theory model recognizes that an individual makes more complex equity evaluations when he or she and the comparison other have different outcomes and inputs. By comparing outcome/input ratios, the model states that equity occurs when the amount of inputs and outcomes are proportional. They do not necessarily have the same amount. For instance, we feel equitably treated when we work harder than the comparison other and receive proportionally higher rewards as a result.

FIGURE 7-6　Over-reward versus Under-reward Inequity

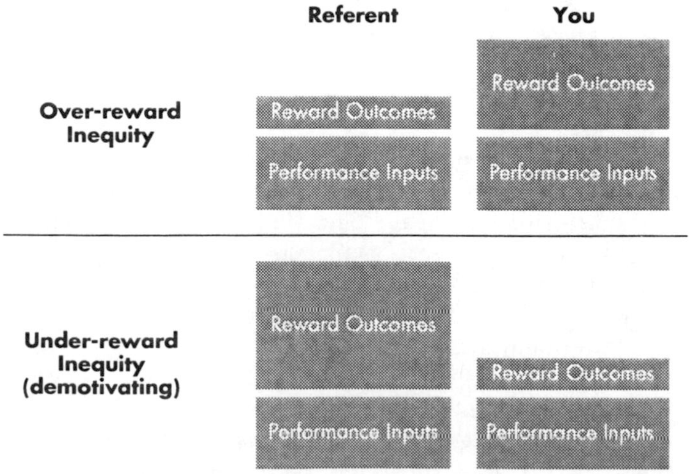

Consequences of Inequity The outcome of the evaluation that inequity exists is that employees will be motivated to take some action. This was seen in the prior example when the Chinese managers tried to reduce the perceived inequity by putting pressure on the European retail firm to increase their pay. There are five possible categories of actions that can be taken to reduce feelings of inequity.

Changing Inputs. Under-rewarded workers tend to reduce their effort and performance if these outcomes don't affect their salary and compensation. Overpaid workers sometimes increase their inputs by working harder and producing more. This effort to increase inputs is similar to the efficiency–wage hypothesis from Nobel Laureate Kenneth Arrow, who theorized that people who knew they were getting paid more than the going market rate would work harder to try to justify that additional pay.[xxxiii]

Changing Outcomes. Employees who feel they are in an under-rewarded situation might ask for more money to resolve the inequity. If they do not receive the pay raise they may take actions that change the perceived outcomes. For example, these employees may call in sick frequently, steal supplies, or misappropriate company money or facilities. Each of these outcomes provides more benefits to the employees. Outcomes change can also come from some action that hurts or harms a firm; such actions provide a psychological benefit to the employee. This situation is seen in the information technology industry when software engineers insert malicious lines of code into applications, or even bring codes home with them and withhold them from the company if they are unhappy. Numerous computer security incidents in Singapore, for example, were traced to employees who felt they were under compensated by their employers.[xxxiv]

Changing Perceptions. In an inequity situation that the employee cannot (or prefers not to) change, he or she may feel it necessary to distort inputs and outcomes to restore perceived equity. This is most common in an overpayment situation. Employees who believe they are overpaid may try to convince others that they are worth the money. They do this by emphasizing perceived inputs such as seniority, training, knowledge, teamwork, contribution, and so forth. In more extreme cases, they may try to take credit for their colleagues' or subordinates' work to boost their perceived contribution. In more hierarchical organizations, this problem of supervisors improperly taking credit for employee actions is something that managers must watch for carefully. It is important for managers not to isolate themselves and to stay in touch with employees throughout the reporting hierarchy.

Leaving the Field. Some people try to reduce inequity by getting away from the inequitable situation. Equity theory thus explains some instances of employee turnover and job transfer. For example, employee turnover in many large retail operations in Europe can be quite high, sometimes over 200 percent, and inequity is often credited by the individuals who leave.

Changing the Referent. If an employee who is feeling inequity cannot seem to alter the outcome/input ratio, he or she might justify the inequity by replacing the referent with someone having a more comparable outcome/input ratio. As was mentioned earlier, people sometimes rely on a generalized referent, so changing the referent to protect one's sense of self esteem is easy and common in the absence of other avenues to right the inequity. This outcome is particularly attractive to international firms. This approach can be used by firms as they help employees to establish what potential referents are obtaining. For example, the rapid economic growth of China has been generated in part through employees' willingness to work for 80 cents per hour, but that same, economic growth has now begun to push wages higher, particularly in South China. The government's control of information and media often results in widespread misperceptions of what wages and benefits other workers are receiving. To overcome misinformation, many firms in South China today are increasingly open about what they are paying and how their pay compares to other firms and industry averages. Firms are seeking to establish a more accurate referent point and comparison for the employee salaries.

Ethics and Equity Workplace inequity extends beyond employee motivation to the organization's ethical conduct. It particularly relates to the rule of distributive justice mentioned in Chapter 1. **Distributive justice** asserts that inequality is all right if employees have fair access to resources and opportunity in the firm so that any inequality is the result of effort. Thus, inequalities are ultimately in the best interest of the firm and its employees; talented workers are rewarded commensurate with their work and ability to improve the lot of the firm's stakeholders. Employees in difficult or more risky jobs could be expected to be paid more under distributive justice.

Applying the distributive justice rule is challenging because it is difficult to determine how far "the least well off" benefit is from those who receive higher rewards. Consider what former General Electric CEO Jack Welsh earned. GE rewarded Welsh with a $9 million annual pension, not to mention a number of other perks including a $15 million apartment. He was also given the use of a GE corporate jet and other company resources. Many critics felt Welsh's employment contract was overly lavish when it finally was made public during his divorce proceedings in 2002. (Welsh agreed to give up some of his benefits after they were made public.)

If Welsh had not stepped in as CEO, it is quite likely that GE would not have done as well as it did. The world of business also learned a lot from GE about restructuring and selecting and training top management. Welch is credited with boosting GE's market capitalization from $13.9 billion in 1981 to an estimated $490 billion by 2001—an increase of $476.1 billion. He and many other CEOs have argued that with market cap increases in the tens or hundreds of billions of dollars, giving a CEO a few hundred-million dollars is no big deal. However, it is important to remember that Jack Welsh did not do it all on his own; there are 300,000 employees at GE and decades of history that played a role in creating GE's market capitalization. GE has had a string of fine leaders over the twentieth century dating back to inventor Thomas Edison himself. Thus, the issue of whether Welsh's pension and other perks are unethical or otherwise problematic likely depends on a person's view of distributive justice.

Perceptions of equity change not only with the country and culture, but also with the times. As the world increasingly is open to more market opportunities, equity comparisons that account more fully for someone's productive input (and not just their salary) may become more accepted.[xxxv]

International Perspectives and Equity We've stressed how managers must be wary of projecting their views and values onto others. It cannot be assumed that everyone shares the same interpretation of equity or that people will get upset if someone is earning more money. Individuals vary in their equity sensitivity—that is, our outcome/input preferences and reaction to various outcome/input ratios. A simple test to determine your own equity sensitivity is at the end of this chapter (see In-class Exercises #1).

At one end of the equity sensitivity scale are the "Entitleds." The Entitleds feel comfortable in situations in which they receive proportionately more than others. Entitleds know how much everyone else is making, or want to find out. They are highly sensitive to anything they perceive as inequitable, and will regularly talk

Distributive justice

Asserts that inequality is acceptable if employees have fair access to resources and opportunities such that they recognize any inequality to be the result of their own effort and not because of favoritism by management.

MOTIVATION IN CHINA

At nine o'clock in the morning, a leadership and motivation workshop begins as Shanghai executives from one of mainland China's biggest computer firms start wrestling with a list of progressive management theories. Ten minutes later, a harried senior executive shuffles in. "Stop everything," someone shouts. The 60 participants are ordered to stand up and hold a minute's silence to focus their collective corporate thoughts on the error of the colleague that came in late. The offender—who is in China's top one per cent of earners—bows his head and walks to a corner of the room for his 10-minute dose of shame, while his colleagues go back to discussing the managerial benefits of lateral thinking over parallel thinking.

Such humiliation is common in Chinese companies for errors in performance. For example, other companies will make employees stand for five minutes, holding their mobile phone aloft if the offending article has rung during a meeting. It is humiliating—but humiliation is a particularly effective motivator in China, human resource managers say, and has long precedent in Chinese commercial culture over the past two centuries, although it runs counter to a lot of modern thinking both in China and the West.[xxxvi]

Many individuals not familiar with modern China will point to writers like Confucius to argue that managers in China practice a polite managerial method that focuses on saving face. However, modern China draws more on criticism and self-criticism as developed by Mao Zedong than from Confucius' teachings. Chinese society has transformed radically in recent years, but many managerial behaviors still relate to actions, such as the criticism sessions, organized by the Communists during Mao's reign.

For example, many Chinese universities still post notices on bulletin boards about students who are in breach of campus rules. Some universities will make violators address student gatherings to publicly denounce their own behavior and spell out their reformed ways. Dunce caps are foisted on underachievers in some primary schools, while in others, teachers make the children vote each week for the worst student in class. Staffs from restaurants, beauty salons, and department stores, among other enterprises, are typically made to line up every day outside the premises for a military-style drill. Model employees are commended and those who are thought to have let the team down are loudly chastised.

Recently, outside one of the many high-priced restaurants in Beijing, a young waitress trembled as her manager screamed at her for spilling something the previous evening. The young lady, who probably earns about 20 Yuan (U.S.$2.30) per day was near tears as her 40-odd colleagues and dozens of people waiting at a bus stop looked on. "She won't be spilling anything today," one onlooker said, nodding in approval.

While the leaders of many mainland (Chinese) companies dislike this approach, many others still use public humiliation because it is often perceived as having a more immediate impact than subtle methods of motivating staff. A human resources manager with a leading mainland domestic appliance firm said the firm had dabbled with the idea of introducing more sophisticated motivating techniques, but decided it was more effective to use its own version of the carrot-and-stick approach. "We don't dangle anything," she said. "We hit them with both the stick and the carrot."

Goff, P. (2003, April 21). Ritual humiliation. *South China Morning Post* (Hong Kong), p. 11.

CULTURE

about people who did not do anything for them, or organizations that mistreat them. Entitleds might accept having the same outcome/input ratio as others, but would prefer to receive more than others performing the same work. Or they may try very hard to work less while still getting paid—in fact they may spend all their time working less, or scheming to work less while maintaining their income. Those who have read the Pulitzer Prize–winning novel *The Good Earth* by Pearl S. Buck about village life in China in the early part of the twentieth century will recognize the Entitled character of the lazy uncle.[xxxvii] He spent most of his time pretending to work or saying that he was going off to work but seldom did, and somehow he ended up well off at the end of the story. For most of the book, the lazy uncle was the happiest character in the novel. Entitleds often talk about what other people get in terms of salary and benefits and whether they are worth it. They often feel that they are unappreciated and underpaid and are willing to share their feelings. Entitleds judge others on what they do for them.

At the other end of the scale are the "Benevolents." Benevolents are tolerant of situations in which they are under-rewarded. They might still prefer equal outcome/input ratios, but do not mind if others receive more than they do for the same inputs as long as they feel fairly treated. They usually like to see an equal workload, but are more accepting of unequal compensation. Benevolents rarely talk about what others are earning and about who "owes them." This group will be concerned about Entitleds who are not doing their fair share of work and seem to be getting a free ride, but they are not demotivated by inequity situations.

Somewhat in the middle is the third group—the "Equity Sensitives." Equity Sensitives want their outcome/input ratio to be equal to the outcome/input ratio of the referent other, and even small differences can create emotional tension and demotivation for them. Like Entitleds, they get upset and demotivated if they discover the comparison person is earning more money than they do. But unlike Entitleds, Equity Sensitives generally do not scheme to get out of work and get by with minimal input.

A company's motivation and reward system needs to account for such differences in people by checking the system, not just for pay equity but for a reasonable balance of workload and other inputs, as well as outcomes. Managers in particular need to identify Entitleds and let them know they are appreciated and that steps are being taken to reward them properly.

Are Entitleds, Equity Sensitives, and Benevolents equally spread around the world? Because equity sensitivity may be based partly on personality, it is possible that different equity-sensitivity behavior is as well distributed around the world as different personality types. However, these differences in distribution are likely due to differences in cultural values. For example, workers in China demonstrate a Benevolent equity orientation when they compare their salaries to what they earned before rather than to what others earn. This may be because of the strong collectivist and high power distance cultural values present in China.[xxxviii] Although there is a test instrument to assess where employees stand on this equity scale, you can easily determine this by listening to people talk about salaries and compensation, or their acceptance of workload, agreeableness toward taking on new tasks, or volunteering for work. Equity sensitivity usually is very evident, and managers need to pay attention to this and emphasize fairness for Equity Sensitives and growth opportunities for Benevolents who may want to work hard in order to learn.

Equity theory has received support in research and practice. Organizational behavior researchers have applied the equity theory model to explain why professional baseball players change teams, why employees steal from their employer, and why people become hostile at work. One of the clearest lessons from equity theory is that we need to continually treat people fairly in the distribution of organizational rewards. Recent research has shown that companies maintaining a reasonably equitable pay environment such that the top paid employee (such as the CEO) does not earn more than 50 times the lowest paid full-time employee outperform companies with more inequitable compensation.[xxxix]

Maintaining feelings of equity is not an easy task. For example, two large surveys, one in Australia and the other in the U.S., reported that about half of all employees feel underpaid. This was true even for over a third of those earning more than $100,000 annually. Major league baseball players in the U.S. reported feeling underpaid and unwanted even when earning millions of dollars per year.[xl] Why do so many people feel this inequity? One reason, as we discussed above, is that people have different levels of equity sensitivity, so they may react differently to the same situation. Some people (Benevolents) are generally content to compare themselves with themselves, so if they are doing better this year than last year, they will generally be motivated—at least inequity perceptions will not be a problem for them in this case. Others (Entitleds) are regularly talking about what everyone else earns, and how this or that company exploits its employees and customers. Employees also have differing opinions about which inputs should be rewarded; should age and seniority be rewarded, employee needs, competencies and skills, or pure performance output? Which outcomes are more valuable than others is another factor to consider in developing a motivation-reward system.

ESTONIAN PAY DISCRIMINATION

Estonia is a small Baltic nation that was formerly part of the Soviet Union. It is located across the Gulf of Finland from Finland. Estonia has done very well since its transition from communism. The Estonian and Finnish languages are very close to each other, and there was an easy and relatively quick movement of Finns into Estonia seeking low-cost highly trained individuals. Estonia has a strong technological foundation and is the home of the founders of Skype, which allows phone calls over the Internet. Estonia has also been blessed with good elected officials who have avoided the corruption that has typified so many transitional economies as they move from communism. The Estonian leaders have also been very innovative, with the nation being one of the first in the world to employ a flat tax where all people pay the same percentage on their income.

Estonia is unique in that approximately 40 percent of its population is ethnically Russian and not Estonian. Since Estonia achieved independence from the Soviet Union, there have been some difficulties in the treatment of the ethnic Russian minority. In general, Estonians feel great hostility to Russia and believe their country was forcefully incorporated into the repressive Soviet Union. As a result, after gaining statehood, Estonia quickly established the need to speak fluent Estonian as a requirement for citizenship, and a large number of individuals whose families lived in Estonia for many years are now officially stateless. This has made travel particularly hard. The official and only language used in schools is Estonian, and discrimination and the overall hostility to Russians has led to several instances of rioting by ethnic Russians.

Research shows that, while at the time of independence there was no discrimination in pay, ethnic Russians, even if they are fluent in Estonian, now receive substantially less pay than ethnic Estonians. The difficulty for international firms who move to Estonia is how to respond to this discrimination. Local Estonians expect to make more than ethnic Russians, so issues of expectancy and equity come into play. But if the firm supports such discrimination, is it acting ethically?

Kroncke, C., & Smith, K. (1999). The wage effects of ethnicity in Estonia. *Economics of Transition* 7(1), 179–199.

ETHICS

It will be difficult to please all types of employees, but firms have to try to regularly check systems for equity, and then tell their employees that they are doing this. Overall, trying to maintain feelings of equity in the workplace will probably always be challenging, but firms must be proactive about it.

Goal Setting

Another major process theory of motivation is the theory of goal setting. Edwin Locke, Gary Latham, and colleagues have done a great deal of work over the years on the importance of goal setting for motivation and performance. Organizations have discovered that goals can yield very effective results and prevent issues of demoralization. Vague statements such as "Do your best" or "Our work is really an art and not a science so we cannot have goals" have been shown by goal-setting research to be unhelpful—goals can be applied for most endeavors, including sports and education and even less-structured activities like research and development.[xli] Goals are identified by setting customer satisfaction objectives or improvements on other key measures, such as a reduction in crime rates for a police force or on-time performance and improved fuel usage for a city bus company.[xlii] Research has shown that organizations that set goals can enjoy higher performance from their employees. Goals are the immediate or ultimate objectives that employees are trying to accomplish from their work effort. Goal setting is the process of motivating employees and clarifying their role perceptions by establishing performance objectives. Goal setting potentially improves employee performance in two ways: first by adding to the intensity and persistence of effort, and then by giving employees clearer roles so that their effort can be directed toward behavior that will improve task performance.

Goal Setting in Practice Internationally Goals must have a measurable outcome and a time or date to determine if that goal has been reached. Failing to set a goal means that the considerable motivational potential of the goal setting will be lost.

Vague statements such as "Do your best" are not really goals and are worthless in motivational and performance terms. Instead, behavioral scholars have identified six conditions to maximize task effort and performance: specific goals, relevant goals, challenging goals, goal commitment, participation in goal formation (sometimes), and goal feedback. Additionally and perhaps most importantly, goals must be made *public*. That means for your goal to increase your motivation and ultimately your performance, you must be specific about the goal and the date by which you will accomplish it, and you must tell someone about it. Secretly set goals have little or no motivational or performance value. Employees put more effort into a task when they work toward specific goals rather than amorphous targets. Specific goals have measurable levels of change over a specific time, such as, "Reduce the defect rate by five percent over the next six months." Specific goals communicate more precise performance expectations, so employees can direct their effort more efficiently and reliably.

Many companies apply goal setting through a formal process known as management by objectives (MBO). There are a few variations of MBO programs, but they generally identify organizational objectives and goals. These goals then move down through the organization with each level determining what is necessary to achieve the larger goal. So, if a firm has decided to expand revenue by 10 percent, there must be a wide range of changes in behavior by various departments, from marketing to production. For the actual sales force, expanding revenue by 10 percent means that they will need to expand the number of cold calls, which are calls made to potential customers without a prior appointment. So one of the goals for the sales force may be to make 20 percent more cold calls this quarter. This goal will be discussed with each employee and at the end of the quarter, the employee's performance will be judged based on that goal. Although MBO has been criticized for creating too much paperwork, it has been effective and is widely applied in business—both domestic-only and international—and is consistent with the empirical evidence on goal setting.

Employees report higher levels of motivation and usually perform better when they have set difficult but achievable goals. Challenging goals also fulfill a person's self-actualization and other intrinsic needs associated with self-efficacy and achievement satisfaction. When employees set their own goals, rather than having the company set goals for them, goals tend to be set somewhat higher. Self-set goals also have the effect of increasing employees' acceptance of the goal. Yet there are limits to difficult goals, if the goals become so difficult that employees no longer have the ability or tools to reach them. Consistent also with the predictions of expectancy theory, effort and measurable performance on the task falls significantly, as shown in Figure 7-7. The optimal range of goal difficulty is one in which the employee perceives a goal to be difficult, but achievable, and the believes that a strategy can be crafted to achieve that goal. Leaders in the organization have a key role to play in showing a path by which employees have some control over their work and can both achieve a goal and benefit from its achievement.

Goals must also be relevant to an individual's job and within his or her control. Telling an employee to work harder without a clear and achievable goal, relevant feedback, and a path to that goal will not motivate him or her and is likely to be confusing. Employees also should be involved in the goal-setting process. Participation in goal formation tends to increase commitment because employees take ownership of the goals, compared to those that are merely assigned by supervisors. In fact, today's employees increasingly expect to be involved in goal setting and other decisions that affect them. Participation may also improve goal quality, because employees have valuable information and knowledge that may not be known to those who initially formulated the goal. Thus, participation ensures that employees buy into the goals and have the competencies and resources necessary to accomplish them. Some managers believe that such participation is not expected

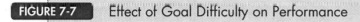

FIGURE 7-7 Effect of Goal Difficulty on Performance

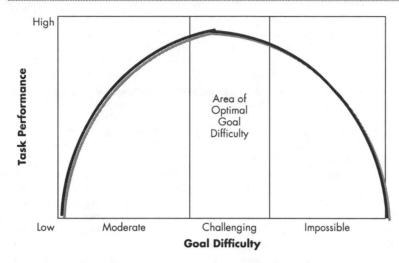

in their region of the world, and managers from China to Latin America report that generating such participation takes time to develop. However, employees ultimately want to participate in goal setting.

Feedback is another necessary condition for effective goal setting. In particular, experts emphasize that effective goal setting requires measurable feedback that matches the specific metrics of the goal. As discussed in Chapter 2, feedback is a powerful source of learning. In terms of goal setting, feedback lets us know whether we have achieved the goal or are properly directing our efforts toward it. Feedback is also a vital ingredient in motivation because employees need confirmation of their actions and goals and affirmation that they are doing a good job, as well as some censure if something needs to improve in their actions and performance.

Limitations Goal setting has a few limitations. One problem is that when goals are tied to monetary incentives, many employees may try to "game the system" by selecting easy goals, or negotiating performance goals that are already near completion. Employees with high self-efficacy, self-esteem, and need for achievement tend to set challenging goals whether or not they are financially rewarded for their results, while individuals who are lower on those scales are less likely to set high goals for themselves. Employers must balance these considerations in setting up a reward-and-evaluation system. Similarly, management needs to implement checks and balances on employee goals and behavior. For instance, if there are performance goals for production workers with no controls on the quality of what they produce, some employees may rush so they can produce more and be rewarded accordingly. But this will lead to higher levels of defects and product nonconformance, more material wastage, and an increased need for quality control checking and product reworking with all the incumbent costs. So quality control and teamwork goals need to be implemented along with production goals to minimize quality problems.

Another limitation is that goal setting cannot be applied to every performance dimension of every task. We can usually find some measurable goals, but many other dimensions of job performance are difficult to measure and have complex and long-term outcomes. The result is that goal setting potentially focuses employees on a narrow subset of short-term performance indicators. The saying "What gets measured, gets done" usually proves accurate. Thus, organizations must be

NORTH AMERICAN RETAILER: DISCOVERING THE POWER OF SHAME

Goal setting in North America can be a straightforward process and very successful. But as firms move internationally they may need to consider a richer set of motivations than commonly used in North America to be successful. One North American firm, one of the world's largest retailers, opened its first store in China in the late 1980s. Although it was a global firm, it was slow to enter the rapidly growing Chinese market for fear that it would have difficulty understanding the market. A year after entering the market, the firm found that the customers were not that hard to understand. The problem lay with understanding the local workforce and the rules they should impose on it. For example, the retailer was used to trusting employees and giving them a second chance if they were caught stealing. If an employee was caught a second time, only then would the retailer fire the employee and refer the matter to the local police. But the firm was warned by their local managers that this approach would not work in China, where retailers must be stricter and have zero tolerance for stealing. Local managers also suggested firing the employees and allowing shame to do the rest, but the retailer chose to stick to its global policy.

Not long after the retailer opened one of its first stores in China, the store's general manager discovered that a local employee had stolen several small electronics goods. The general manager decided to follow the firm's procedures and give the employee his warning, in spite of protests from the local manager, who argued that the employee should be fired at once. Afterward, the general manager asked that the employee be watched carefully. A few weeks later, the general manager learned that the same employee had once again stolen several more items. He decided to follow procedure, fired the employee, and referred the case to the local police. The police arrested the employee and held him without trial for several weeks. Later, the general manager learned that the employee had received a twelve-year jail sentence, which seemed harsh for petty theft. After that and several other theft incidents, the retailer tightened its security and procedures considerably, and changed to a policy of immediately discharging any employee caught stealing anything, even office supplies. It also changed its global policy by deciding not to notify police about a theft unless it was particularly serious. "Firing an employee and making the reason public is punishment enough; potentially wayward employees get the message quickly, and we have not had any major incidents in quite a while," the general manager said. "Anyway, the threat of several years' imprisonment is always there, though we'd rather not resort to that."

careful in setting goals and measuring employee output. Apart from such concerns, goal setting brings a wealth of well-tested evidence and tools to managers. It is widely supported by research and is generally successful in practice. Goal setting involves measurement of the task, an agreed outcome, and a goal for improving performance.

EMPLOYEE INTERESTS

Recall from the earlier discussion that performance is closely related to motivation, which itself is based on ability, values, and life interests. Life interests indicate whether an employee is likely to be interested in doing the job. Thus, motivation also concerns an employee and what they as individuals like to do. Timothy Butler and James Waldroop at Harvard University identify eight life interests (also called "job interests") that motivate when they fit with an employee's particular bent to do certain tasks.[xliii] For example, some people may like managing others (similar to McClelland's high nAff people). They would do better and be self-motivated (intrinsically motivated) to work on tasks associated with people management, but might not fare well in a job that required them to stare at a computer monitor for eight hours a day, even if they were good at it. Others may enjoy working with numbers or working with technology and would be intrinsically motivated to do that job. Butler and Waldroop give a list of job interests in Figure 7-8, and tasks and vocations that might fit people based on these interests are shown in Figure 7-9. Butler and Waldroop have developed a job-interest inventory that can be viewed at www.careerdiscovery.com, where people can discover their job

FIGURE 7-8   The Big 8 "Life Interests"

1. **Application of Technology** – People with these interests are curious about finding better ways to use technology to solve business problems.

2. **Quantitative Analysis** – Good at running the numbers; they see math as the best, and sometimes the only, way to figure out business solutions. Also see math as fun when others consider it very hard work.

3. **Theory Development and Conceptual Thinking** – People with this interest can be excited by building business models that explain competition within a given industry or by analyzing the competitive position of a business within a particular market.

4. **Creative Production** – Some people always enjoy the beginning of projects the most, when there are many unknowns and they can make something out of nothing. These individuals are frequently seen as imaginative, out-of-the-box thinkers. They seem most engaged when they are brainstorming or inventing unconventional solutions.

5. **Counseling and Mentoring** – Some people really enjoy teaching. In business, this is coaching or mentoring. These individuals are driven by the life interest of counseling and mentoring—guiding employees, peers, and clients to better performance.

6. **Managing People and Relationships** – Counseling and mentoring is a bit different from managing. Individuals with the managing life interest enjoy dealing with people on a day-to-day basis, but they focus much more on outcomes than do people in the counseling-and-mentoring category.

7. **Enterprise Control** – Such individuals seem happiest when running projects or teams; they enjoy "owning" a transaction such as a trade or a sale. These individuals also tend to ask for as much responsibility as possible in any work situation.

8. **Influence through Language and Ideas** – People in this category sometimes feel drawn to careers in public relations or advertising where they can write or communicate regularly. Sales, consulting and political/policy or even education careers are also common.

interests, what tasks may be most interesting to them, and why their current job may not be motivating them, irrespective of the money it pays. Bosses may find they can *add a task* to a job (such as creative production or influence through language and ideas—that is, a sales or corporate communications function) that fits with an employee's job interests. That new task will motivate the employee to work simply because of his or her interest in the task, even if there is no extra money for doing it. Of course the company must be careful not to overload hard-working employees and should try to take away tasks that those employees do not value.

For example, if you are an accountant, but have an interest in influencing through language and ideas, you may be interested in speaking publicly about the company and its work. That might mean helping in corporate communications, or sales and customer support. It may also mean traveling to university campuses to speak to classes, teaching a seminar, or participating in campus recruiting. Butler and Waldroop's work suggests that employee motivation largely depends on their being interested in their jobs. What employees want is something that firms, no matter in what nation they are operating, must determine.

SUMMARY

One of the main implications of content motivation theories is that different people have different needs at different times. That implies that to motivate employees (or anyone else, for that matter) we need to learn what their needs are. Some employees, particularly younger employees, are motivated by more money. Yet others may be reasonably satisfied with their current salaries and would like more interesting work or an opportunity to influence decisions in their organization.[xliv] Need theories remind us not to rely too heavily on financial rewards as a source of employee motivation. Although some scholars argue that content motivation theories are culture-bound, the evidence so far suggests otherwise. Process theories provide a unique perspective of employee motivation. Each looks at different variables in the workplace and the minds of employees. As a new generation of employees enters the workplace and as globalization creates a

FIGURE 7-9   Twelve Pairs of Life Interests & Possible Job Matches

1. **Enterprise Control and Managing People:**
   CEOs, presidents, division managers, and general managers who enjoy both strategy and the operational aspects of the position – the CEO who enjoys playing the COO role as well.

2. **Enterprise Control and Quantitative Analysis:**
   Investment bankers, other financial professionals who enjoy deal making, partners in Big Six firms, top-level executives in commercial and investment banks, investment managers.

3. **Application of Technology and Quantitative Analysis:**
   Individual contributors who have a strong interest in engineering analysis (systems analysts, tech consultants, process consultants); production and operations managers.

4. **Creative Production and Influence through Language and Ideas:**
   Advertising executives, brand managers, corporate trainers, salespeople, public relations specialists; people in the fashion, entertainment, and media industries.

5. **Counseling and Mentoring and Managing People:**
   Human-resources managers, managers who enjoy coaching and developing the people reporting to them, managers in nonprofit organizations with an altruistic mission.

6. **Enterprise Control and Influence through Language and Ideas:**
   Executives (CEOs, presidents, general managers) whose leadership style relies on persuasion and consensus building; marketing managers, salespeople.

7. **Application of Technology and Enterprise Control:**
   Managers and senior executives in high technology, telecommunications, biotech, information systems (internally or consulting), and other engineering-related fields.

8. **Theory Development and Quantitative Analysis:**
   Economic-model builders, quantitative analysts, "knowledge base" consultants, market forecasters, business professors.

9. **Creative Production and Enterprise Control:**
   Solo entrepreneurs, senior executives in industries where the product or service is of a creative nature (fashion, entertainment, advertising, media).

10. **Creative Production and Managing People:**
    Entrepreneurs who partner with a professional manager, short-term project managers, new-product developers, advertising "creatives"; individual contributors in fashion, entertainment, and media.

11. **Quantitative Analysis with Managing People and Relationships:**
    These individual like finance, yet they also enjoy managing people toward goals. Often enjoy corporate finance over investment banking and sometimes venture capital, although less than the Quantitative-Theory life interest combination.

12. **Application of Technology with Managing People and Relationships:**
    This is the engineer, computer scientist, or other technically oriented individual who enjoys leading a team, particularly long-running efforts as opposed to temporary project management.

Source: Adapted from Butler, T., & Waldroop, J. (1996). *Discovering Your Career In Business.* New York: Basic Books.

more diverse workforce, companies need to examine their motivational practices and check their systems for equity. Pulling these various theories together, an international firm can help to tailor its specific motivation system for a worldwide organization. Meeting employee needs, setting useful goals, and providing employees with work they find interesting and rewarding can all help to create a very motivated workforce, and many of these actions do not require any additional investment. Firms have the tools to motivate employees if care is taken to understand what workers want (see Take-Home Exercise #2).

MANAGERIAL GUIDELINES

1. Recognize employees' individual needs and job interests. Remember that most people, managers included, have an *extrinsic bias* when evaluating others' needs and values while failing to recognize their intrinsic motivators, such as job involvement and autonomy.

2. Give goals and clear feedback to employees
3. Allow employees to participate in decisions that affect them by letting them set their own goals and exercise ownership over their jobs by giving them tasks they want to do, and provide stock purchase options where possible.
4. Link rewards and performance (*expectancy*).
5. Check the system for equity. Some people are more sensitive to equity problems than others, so managers need to be sure these people feel they are treated equally. Some employees want to see a clear path to promotion; others are motivated by the opportunity to do new things. Each person can be highly motivated if management pays attention to different needs.
6. Improve communication. Most employees like ongoing communication with management and even higher-level employees must keep their bosses informed.
7. Set worthwhile goals. Employees respond well to goals, as well as to job feedback. Public goals and objectives (and small rewards for meeting them) motivate.
8. Facilitate interesting work. Much research on employee satisfaction and performance in recent years has emphasized that employees want interesting work they can understand.
9. Communicate the firm's mission. Excellent leaders motivate by communicating the mission clearly and telling employees the truth about challenges facing the organization.
10. Find out life interests of each employee. Try to put people in jobs or give them tasks that match their life interests.[xxxiv]
11. On an ongoing basis, look carefully at the extrinsic motivators you have at your disposal and use your knowledge of your team's values and interests.
12. Motivation can differ with culture and situation.
13. Poorly delivered criticism can be demotivating and significantly harm performance.
14. Link firm mission with motivation system.
15. The motivation or reward system needs to fit the job type.

Table 7-1 is useful to students and practitioners as they seek to analyze how motivation may vary in different areas of the world.

TABLE 7-1 Motivation around the World

Topic	Evidence
Motivation and money	Money is definitely a useful motivator. Most people want to make pretty good money, and some people are really motivated to make a lot of money. But if someone's monetary needs are fairly fulfilled, giving him or her the opportunity to earn more money may not work well, and may even hurt that person's motivation ("This company just likes to throw money at problems instead of addressing the real issues I have."). It is important to consider the employee's interests.
Regions where money may be more important than the average place in motivating	Money is important everywhere. But people in a high-masculine or production orientation culture may be more motivated by money than those who are not. For example, it is a good bet that people in Hong Kong will be motivated by the opportunity to earn more money. They'll work overtime or take on extra work. But people in a slower-moving place, such as Hawaii, may be more likely to figure out how much money they need and leave it at that. On average, they would be less likely to be motivated to accept extra work just to make a few more dollars.

TABLE 7-1 (Continued)

Topic	Evidence
Misunderstanding employee needs and demotivation	Correctly understanding employee needs is crucial to motivation. Managers will find that motivating people is difficult if they offer things that employees do not want. For example, not all people are motivated by fulfilling social needs, because they simply do not think it is necessary to meet social needs through work. When a company expends efforts on social activities for its employees, it should be sure that employees actually want and value this; if they do not, it will be a complete waste of money. Managers who value social activities themselves (possibly because they are from cultures with a high feminine or relational-value score) may be surprised that employees from other countries (that may have a higher masculine or production orientation score) don't share their enthusiasm for social activities. Managers shouldn't be surprised if employees do not want to participate in company activities.
Motivation across cultures	Sometimes managers find that employees will work hard without more money or any other extrinsic motivators, based on the theory of job interests (or life interests).[xl] A manager may discover that an employee will be willing to take on extra or new tasks simply because he or she enjoys them.
Going against culture	Companies must introduce motivation systems into a foreign location carefully. A slow introduction that allows employees to opt in at their own pace might be a good approach. If successful, the motivation system can then be made available to more employees. Offering employees a choice of gifts in a reward system is generally welcomed.

CULTURE AND DOING BUSINESS IN SOUTH AFRICA

South Africa is the richest nation in Africa. Its 44 million citizens have a per capita GDP of $11,000, and its stock market is one of the 10 largest in the world. South Africa is an ethnically diverse country. Widely diverse African tribes lived in the region when Dutch settlers began extensively settling it in 1652. The British seized the Cape of Good Hope area in 1806 and as a result, many of the Dutch settlers (called the Boers) went further north to establish their own republics. The Boers were finally defeated in the Boer War (1899–1902). The resulting Union of South Africa operated under a policy of apartheid, the separate development of the races. The 1990s brought an end to apartheid politically and ushered in black-majority rule.

Today South Africa has a wide diversity in its ethnic makeup. However, the country is best seen as a country with distinct ethnic groups rather than an integrated ethnic society, such as the U.S. or the United Kingdom. As a result, doing business in South Africa will vary depending on which ethnic group you are conducting business with. Individuals of British heritage tend to be quite reserved, while, those of a Boer background are quite blunt and forward. The native African business people typically have a background in the revolution movement that sought to overthrow the white-only rule. They often have far greater international experience than South African whites, because they were often forced into exile during the revolution. However, their international experience was often with the former communist nations of China and Russia that were supportive of the South Africans' effort to overturn white-only rule when most Western governments were not.

Networks of business people are particularly important in South Africa, although each of the three ethnic groups—the British, the Boers, and the native African business people—will have their own networks. Good educational backgrounds are valued by all the different parties.

ADDITIONAL RESOURCES

Butler, T. (2007). *Getting Unstuck: How Dead Ends Become New Paths*. Boston: Harvard Business School Press.
Wilson, T.B. (2002). *Innovative Reward Systems for the Changing Workplace* (2nd ed.). New York: McGraw-Hill.
Waldroop, J., & Butler, T. (1997). *Discovering Your Career in Business*. New York: Perseus Books Group.

EXERCISES

Opening Vignette Discussion Questions

1. What motivates you? When did you feel most motivated to do something voluntarily? Think about previous jobs or tasks, or a sport or hobby—what was the need that was pushing you to work as hard as you did?
2. Apart from rewards (or punishments), can you think of other things that have motivated you to work hard?

DISCUSSION QUESTIONS

1. Think about your motivation in this class. Which motivation theory best explains it?
2. Motivation is a function of your ability and tools to achieve a certain task, your goals, needs, and interest in the task. Think of a situation in which you were highly motivated. Assess that situation in terms of those four key items. Were all four working well for you?
3. Have you ever been in a situation in which your goals and needs were fulfilled by a job, and you had the right ability and tools but little interest in the work? Describe that situation and how you fixed it.
4. Many people believe that equity theory (inequitable situations) explains a lot of human action. That is, if people make less money than others, they get so upset that they will take tough union action, riot, or even revolt. Recent evidence suggests that equity may not be as important to everyone as was once thought. How upset would you be if you discovered that your friend and coworker, doing essentially the same work, was making more money than you? Suppose that your friend worked for another company. Would you have the same feeling?
5. Why do you think expectancy theory may be most useful in explaining the behavior of major league baseball players? How about highly paid surgeons?
6. In some Latin American countries, employees believe that pay levels should be partly determined by family needs. Their unions insist that those with more children should be paid more, particularly from multinational firms. Discuss this idea in the context of the equity theory model. Do you agree? What if you were an international manager of an MNC suddenly confronted with this demand by several workers—what would you do?

IN-CLASS EXERCISES

1. Equity sensitivity exercise

Measuring Your Equity Sensitivity

This self-assessment is designed to help you to estimate your level of equity sensitivity. Read each of the statements and circle the response that you believe best reflects your position. Then use the scoring key below to calculate your results. This exercise assesses your equity sensitivity. Complete the questionnaire without discussion or help from others.

	Strongly Agree	Agree	Neutral	Disagree	Strongly Disagree
1. I prefer to do as little as possible at work while getting as much as I can from my employer.	1	2	3	4	5
2. I am most satisfied at work when I have to do as little as possible.	1	2	3	4	5
3. When I am at my job, I think of ways to get out of work.	1	2	3	4	5
4. If I could get away with it, I would try to work just a little bit slower than the boss expects.	1	2	3	4	5
5. It is really satisfying to me when I can get something for nothing at work.	1	2	3	4	5
6. It is the smart employee who gets as much as he or she can while giving as little as possible in return.	1	2	3	4	5
7. Employees who are more concerned about what they can get from their employer rather than what they can give to their employer are the wise ones.	1	2	3	4	5
8. When I have completed my task for the day, I help out other employees who have yet to complete their tasks.	1	2	3	4	5
9. Even if I received low wages and poor benefits from my employer, I would still try to do my best at my job.	1	2	3	4	5
10. If I had to work hard all day at my job, I would probably quit.	1	2	3	4	5
11. I feel obligated to do more than I am paid to do at work.	1	2	3	4	5
12. At work, my greatest concern is whether or not I am doing the best job I can.	1	2	3	4	5
13. A job that requires me to be busy during the day is better than a job that allows me a lot time for loafing.	1	2	3	4	5
14. At work, I feel uneasy when there is little for me to do.	1	2	3	4	5
15. I would become very dissatisfied with my job if I had little or no work to do.	1	2	3	4	5
16. All other things being equal, it is better to have a job with a lot of duties and responsibilities than one with few duties and responsibilities.	1	2	3	4	5

Source: Sauley, K.S., & Bedeian, A.G. (2000). Equity sensitivity: Construction of a measure and examination of its psychometric properties. *Journal of Management* 26(5), 885–910.

Scoring Key for Equity Sensitivity

To score this equity scale, called the Equity Preference Questionnaire (EPQ), complete the three steps below.

Write your circled numbers for the items indicated below (statement numbers are in parentheses) and calculate Subtotal A.

____ + ____ + ____ + ____ + ____ + ____ + ____ + ____ = _____

 (1)   (2)   (3)   (4)   (5)   (6)   (7)   (10)   *Subtotal A*

The remaining items in the EPQ need to be reverse-scored. To calculate a reverse score, subtract the direct score from 6. For example, if you circled 4 in one of these items, the reverse score would be 2 (i.e., 6 − 4 = 2). If you circled 1, the reverse score would be 5 (i.e., 6 − 1 = 5). Calculate the reverse score for each of the items indicated below (statement numbers are in parentheses) and write them in the space provided. Then calculate Subtotal B by adding up these reverse scores.

____ + ____ + ____ + ____ + ____ + ____ + ____ + ____ = _____

 (8)   (9)   (11)   (12)   (13)   (14)   (15)   (16)   *Subtotal B*

Calculate your total score by summing Subtotal A and Subtotal B.

_____ + _____ = _____

(Subtotal A)   (Subtotal B)   *Total*

2. Professional athletes worldwide have seen significant salary increases since the 1970s. Such salary increases could have the dual effect of creating perceptions of inequity in those who have older contracts signed years before and who have thus fallen behind the increasing salary curve, and creating strong motivation in those individuals to improve performance so as to enhance their bargaining positions as they approach the end of their contracts. Indeed, one formal study of major league baseball in the United States showed that prospective free agents (players whose contracts have expired and are free to sign new contracts with any team in the off-season) typically earn less-than-average salaries. And after signing new contracts, they typically move well ahead of the average (Zimbalist, 1992).

Thus the rapid increase of salaries has often rendered a player's contract uncompetitive only a few years after it was signed. Differences of hundreds of thousands or even millions of dollars annually among coworkers and peers performing similar tasks in nearly identical organizations are highly unusual. Equity theory would predict that players might feel demotivated under those conditions.

In addition to the equity implications raised by salary differentials, high-guaranteed multiyear contracts signed by a large majority of free agents also raises motivational issues that are addressed by expectancy theory. Upon signing a new contract, will players feel the need to raise their performances to justify their large salaries, consistent with equity predictions? Or will players' motivation levels be reduced by contracts that are guaranteed regardless of how well they play, reflecting the predictions of expectancy theory?

TAKE-HOME EXERCISES

1. Assume that 20 Chinese managers are coming to your firm's new regional head-quarters. According to the market, they should be paid about $12,000 per year, which is not a lot by U.S. and European standards, but is a pretty good wage in terms of standard of living (purchasing-power parity) in China. But the Chinese

managers are asking to be paid the same as your European managers—about eight times more than the planned salary. This would increase your overhead considerably, and cause your now profitable China operation to lose money. What should you do about this? Should you just pay (after all, it is not your money, right?) and hope that the local managers will become more productive as a result? Should you convince them that they should not be given such a substantial raise? How would you do that? Or would you just fire everyone and try to recruit and train new local managers, which can be a slow and costly process? New hires might try to demand the same higher salaries as well. Describe your action and its pros and cons.

2. Many managers believe that most employees want higher salaries, followed by good working conditions. What do you think? Is this true for you? Take the "What Workers Want" survey below to find out. Remember to answer as if you are the manager in the first column (what you think your employees might want) then as an employee in the second column (what you want). Be ready to discuss your answers in class.

What Workers Want Questionnaire (rank from 1 to 10; 1 is highest)*

Needs	As a manager, what do you think your employees might want?	As an employee, what do you want?
Interesting work		
Full appreciation of work done		
Feeling of being involved		
Job security		
Very good wages		
Promotion and growth in the organization		
Very good working conditions		
Personal loyalty to employees		
Tactful discipline (when needed)		
Sympathetic help with personal problems		

*Adopted from Kovach, K.A. (1987, September–October). What motivates employees? Workers and supervisors give different answers. *Business Horizons*, pp. 58–65.

3. Think of a time when you were really motivated in performing a certain task (such as a sport or a hobby). You felt that you really wanted to wake up early to get at that task. Describe reasons why you felt so motivated. Do you feel this way about your current school work or job? Why or why not?

SHORT CASE QUESTIONS

Lincoln Electric in Mexico (p. 202)

1. How do you think Lincoln Electric would have to adjust its system if they opened a plant in China?
2. Would the result of Lincoln Electric's efforts have been different if it had tried to introduce its system in a desperately poor domain, such as the Sudan, rather than in a relatively wealthy nation, such as Mexico?
3. Why do you think more firms have not tried to copy a system like Lincoln Electric's?

8

LEADERSHIP

Overview

Leadership is the act of one person guiding others toward the attainment of common goals or objectives. How individuals lead and how people respond to that leadership can vary across cultures. For example, people from egalitarian Northern Europe tend to respond positively to leaders who empower them to take responsibility for their jobs. In a high power-distance country such as India, however, leaders are expected to make decisions with less consultation with lower levels; employees there believe decision making is part of a manager's role in the workplace.

Managers of multinational enterprises can face difficulty if they mindlessly transfer the leadership style that has worked for them in their home countries to a foreign setting. What works for a leader in one culture may not work at all in another culture. Instead, the culture and institutional environment of that country must be accounted for in the leadership style employed.

This chapter will establish the foundations for international managers to lead in different cultures. The topics that will be covered in this chapter include:

* Primary leadership theories and how culture affects them in different settings.

* How culture and the institutional setting of a multinational enterprise may necessitate changes in leadership style.

* An examination of different traits, competencies, and behaviors that leaders require when working with different cultures and strategic situations.

NORTH AMERICAN FOOD AND BEVERAGE MANUFACTURER'S LEARNING EXPERIENCE IN CHINA

It has long been a goal of breakfast cereal makers to introduce the Chinese consumer to breakfast cereal. Historically, such food has not been part of the Chinese diet, but with over 1.5 billion consumers the market potential is clear. With changing demographics of two working parents with more consumable income, higher availability of milk and milk-like beverages, and increasing urbanization of the Chinese market, cereal makers believe they may have a good opportunity to enter the Chinese market in a significant way. This pattern of changing social conditions is very similar to what occurred decades ago in North America that led to the increased popularity of easily prepared breakfast cereals.

U.S. and European cereal makers had long tested the market through exports and limited foreign direct investment, selling their products mostly to hotels and to stores where foreigners shopped. One leading U.S. firm invested in manufacturing facilities to prepare for what it hoped would be a big increase in demand as China continued its growth and urbanization. In the process, expatriate managers sought to learn all they could about leadership in China.

The desire to learn about Chinese leadership prompted the company to invest in training in which managers studied the works of Sun Tzu, reading books such as the *Art of War*. Managers also studied the *I Ching*, or "Book of changes"—a classic Chinese book that has been a source of wisdom and inspiration for thousand of years. This training taught managers about the inherent cooperative culture in greater China and about ways to be a successful manager or leader in China. The professors and consultants running the training argued that in China, striving for social needs without regard for immediate personal gain is symbiotic with the philosophy of the *I Ching*, which emphasizes that the greatest welfare is achieved though the joint efforts of individuals creating better social and physical environments. The implication for leadership was that the collective must be emphasized over the individual. Greater value is placed on the ability to lead groups to cooperative output than on giving individual attention and recognition.

However, the training was an idealized version of leadership in China and was not very useful to managers. One of the U.S. expatriate managers commented during the training:

> Given all the training on the idealized Chinese cultural and traditional values, I assumed I could craft a leadership and motivation strategy based on what I understood as Chinese culture. I sought to reward local employees, but only through group incentives. I was told that individual incentives would demoralize the group; it would disturb the group's *wa* or harmony. But for over a year, I had an unmotivated workforce, people were late for work, turnover was high, sick leave was up, and I was rated by the employees as an uninspiring leader—yes, charisma is valued in China unlike what the culture books said. Finally, I heard that other foreign firms in China were using a different system—basically the organization's leader was giving individual employees recognition in front of their peers. It was a remarkably simple system that gave recognition to the line employees and administrative workers. This was completely in contrast with what the consultants who trained us, and the professors whose work I read, stated. But I decided to try it—we changed the reward system to include some individual rewards, recognition from the firm's top management on a quarterly basis, and an award from the firm for high performers. We measured both individual performance and teamwork, and decided to risk some *wa* by recognizing employees— individually—at a quarterly company dinner, and at an annual awards banquet, modeled after the popular awards dinners done at the American firm Southwest Airlines. The consultants warned us not to make the changes, they said it flew in the face of China's harmony and collectivism and went against everything in the anthropology books about China. But we did it anyway. And the results have been quite good—top management's ratings from the employees have gone up, our turnover has gone down, and employee satisfaction with the compensation system is higher than my previous overseas assignments. Chinese employees do like individual rewards and public recognition, they told me that they had had enough of their hard work going unrecognized as under the old system with their boss or some lazy colleagues taking credit for their work. Now is their time to make money and be recognized for what they can do—individually.

Leadership requires the recognition that environments do change and even in cases where leaders think they are being culturally appropriate, they may not be. Thus, a leader is one who determines what needs to be accomplished in a given situation, aligns the goals of the organization with the needs and wants of the employees, and provides the necessary tools for the employees to meet those goals.

Ahlstrom, D. (2009). But Asians don't do that. *The Chinese University of Hong Kong Working Paper Series.*

Leadership is critical to the success of a business—both domestic and international. However, studying leadership in different cultures presents the challenge of first determining what is meant by the term "effective leadership." For example, the founder of the People's Republic of China, Mao Zedong, won a civil war against difficult odds, united a torn country, motivated a level of social change in one of the oldest cultures in the world, and eventually inspired such devotion that millions hung on his every word. However, he also pursued disastrous economic policies that led to the starvation of millions of his citizens, as well as starting and encouraging China's Cultural Revolution, which killed and maimed perhaps millions more. Mao was undeniably a charismatic leader, but was he an effective leader? It is possible to answer yes and no to that question. Charismatic leaders are skillful at inspiring action and change. But what change and at what cost? Thus, the concept of an "effective leader" clearly requires greater definition and qualification.[i]

Once we understand what effective leadership is, then we can examine how leadership changes in different countries and cultures. Well-known leadership scholar Gary Yukl has observed that much of the research on leadership during the decades following World War II was undertaken and published in Western Europe, the United States, and Canada.[ii] However, as argued throughout this text, many assumptions underlying U.S. management practice are somewhat different than in other countries and cultures.[iii] For example, market processes, the stress on the individual over the group, and an emphasis on management and leadership problems rather than on subordinates or followership challenges are aspects of U.S. management style. Another well-known leadership researcher, Robert House, adds that the major theories of leadership, along with most empirical evidence, are from North America and tend to emphasize individualism over collectivism, stress assumptions of rationality, highlight follower responsibilities, and take for granted the centrality of work and democratic values by leaders and followers.[iv]

We know from research in cross-cultural psychology and anthropology that many nations do not have the same cultural values as people in North America.[v] Thus, international business people must acquire a broader understanding of leadership than what is commonly found in the United States. An effective manager operating internationally needs to act in a manner appropriate for the setting in which he or she is located. A manager who fails to take into account the local setting may be seen as inadequate, unfair, or unjust by employees and ultimately be unsuccessful. This chapter will examine these complex issues of leadership around the world. Figure 8-1 summarizes the flow of material in this chapter.

FIGURE 8-1   Chapter 8 Conceptual Flow

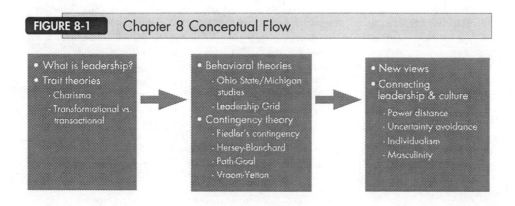

WHAT IS LEADERSHIP?

Leaders
Individuals who significantly affect the thoughts and behaviors of others, often through persuasion and influence.

Leaders are individuals who significantly affect the thoughts and behaviors of others, often through persuasion and influence. (These two related topics are examined more closely in Chapter 10.) Leadership in international and diverse settings therefore involves the ability to inspire the thinking, attitudes, and actions of a variety of individuals and cultures.[vi] Leadership is a relatively new concern for business. For example, while famed steel entrepreneur Andrew Carnegie is considered to have been an exemplary leader and philanthropist, no one in his day sought to offer courses or seminars based on his leadership style. (Contrast this with the books and seminars on Donald Trump or Richard Branson today.) This does not mean that the leadership concept is a new one. The symbols for "leader" existed in the ancient pictographic languages of Egypt and China.[vii] The Chinese philosopher Sun Tzu raised the issue of leadership as early as 400 BCE (see the Sun Tzu and Leadership Culture Box). While the study of leadership may be recent, the concept is one of humankind's oldest.

Leadership is different from management. Management consists of planning, organizing, leading, and controlling a group or organization; managing resources and scheduling is a major part of managing. Leadership, however, is about influencing, motivating, and assisting followers to desired levels of performance. It must also be recognized that simply inspiring individuals is not the sole characteristic of a leader. Leaders must also deliver positive outcomes. Individuals may disagree on whether an outcome is positive, but the results must be viewed as positive by at least some in the organization, or its broader stakeholders, in order for a person to be considered a leader.

In our prior example, it can be argued that Chairman Mao was a leader: he shepherded his followers through World War II and China's postwar revolution to create the People's Republic of China. China was poorly managed during the reign of its last emperor and after his fall in the early twentieth century, the country was ruled by warlords with little concern for the populace. Mao unified China and mobilized its citizens behind several ambitious goals to restore China's infrastructure, environment, and economy after decades of war. However, Mao's policies and his desire to hold onto power would subsequently lead to the disastrous Great Leap Forward of the late 1950s, which created the largest famine in world history,

---

SUN TZU AND LEADERSHIP

Sun Tzu is credited with writing a book titled *The Art of War* in China sometime between 400 and 320 BCE. There is no direct historical evidence that one man named Sun Tzu existed, and it is possible *The Art of War* may have been compiled by a group of philosophers. Nevertheless, the book is the oldest known work on military strategy and diplomacy. Today, *The Art of War* still shapes the strategy not only of the military but also of business around East Asia, which can be seen in negotiation strategies of parties in this region. For example, one of Sun Tzu's quotes is, "The best victory is when the opponent surrenders of its own accord before there are any actual hostilities . . . It is best to win without fighting."

The effect of this quotation can be seen in negotiating strategies in which Chinese parties will seek to delay decisions until just before the deadlines demanded by Western firms working with them. The Chinese hope the result of the delay will be that the Western firm concedes certain items. The Chinese parties will also seek to ensure that the opposing side has no options other than what they offer. Their goal is not to have a disruptive negotiation but instead, to ensure that the negotiation is successful from their perspective without any battles.

Sun Tzu also addressed leadership. He argued forcefully that a defeat of an army was not the responsibility of the soldiers, but instead of the general (the leader). He went on to argue that a general should lead by example and not by coersion. A successful leader is one who takes advantage of opportunities as they are presented. These characteristics match what a modern business student would think is essential to a leader, although students should remember that leadership styles need to change with the situation and the maturity of the followers.

and also the equally devastating Cultural Revolution just a few years later. There-fore, it is very difficult to argue that Mao was a successful leader given the catastrophic events that he set into motion.[viii]

LEADERSHIP THEORIES

Leadership theories can broadly be divided into four categories: trait theories, behavioral theories, contingency theories, and implicit theories of leadership. Each of these four categories will be examined in turn. As noted earlier, much of our understanding of leadership theories is based on research from North America. Therefore, the initial understanding of the theory will be presented and will be followed by the theory's implications for an international business as culture is considered. A richer discussion of how a student can integrate these various theories and the concepts of culture to help direct their managerial actions will follow.

Trait Theories of Leadership

Trait theory argues that there are underlying traits or characteristics of people that lead to either superior leader or follower performance, the right stuff as it were. These traits include a leader's knowledge, natural and learned abilities, values, and personality traits. From ancient times through World War II, most people automati-cally assumed that leaders were born, not made, and that leadership came naturally. As a result of this belief, schools sought ways in which leaders could be identified, particularly from a young age. Researchers looked for ways to differentiate leaders from non-leaders by their characteristics or traits, and initially focused on physical traits, such as height and physical appearance. However, it was quickly found that leaders come in all shapes and sizes, and all races and genders.

Researchers then turned to common personality traits, including charisma (discussed in greater length below), confidence, vision for the organization or team, decisiveness, and internal locus of control. **Internal locus of control** refers to whether people feel that they can control things themselves or whether outside forces control their future. Figure 8-2 lists some of the personality traits most commonly associated with leadership.

Today, research on personality traits has taken the path of studying competencies—mixtures of traits and learned skills. One trait that has received a great deal of attention and that deserves particular attention is charisma.

Charisma Charisma is the ability to inspire or influence others. This line of research developed primarily in the United States prior to World War II. However, the analysis of charisma fell out of favor after the war because of the strong

Trait theory
Argues that people have underlying traits or characteristics that lead to either superior leader or follower performance.

Internal locus of control
Whether people feel that they can control things themselves or whether forces outside them control their future.

FIGURE 8-2	Personality Traits Commonly Associated with Good Leadership

1. **Charisma** "Natural" gifted leader.

2. **Dominance** An individual's need to exert influence and control over others; helps a leader channel followers' efforts and abilities toward achieving group and organizational goals.

3. **Self-confidence** Helps a leader influence followers and persist in the face of obstacles or difficulties.

4. **Energy/activity levels** When high, help a leader deal with the many demands he or she faces on a day-to-day basis.

5. **Tolerance for stress** Helps a leader deal with the uncertainty inherent in any leadership role.

6. **Internal locus of control** Helps the leader take responsibility for an endeavor's success and not blame outside factors for failure.

7. **Integrity and honesty** Ensure that a leader behaves ethically and is worthy of followers' trust and confidence.

8. **Emotional intelligence** Ensures that a leader is not overly self-centered, has a steady disposition, and can accept criticism.

negatives associated with charismatic political leaders such as Adolf Hitler, Benito Mussolini, and Joseph Stalin. (The first two individuals were the charismatic leaders of the main Fascist movements in Europe, while the third was the powerful and ruthless leader of the Soviet Union.) It is interesting to note that in Germany today, individuals who are considered charismatic still do not do well as politicians. Instead, Germans favor soft-spoken politicians because of this negative association with charisma, and many German politicians have a style that many other countries would consider low key.

The benefits of charisma, along with its drawbacks, have been well documented.[ix] In recent years, however, charismatic leadership that combines learned skills with the ability to transform an organization, in addition to internal traits, has been the focus of research. This type of charisma is referred to as **transformational leadership** and has been shown to have positive effects on organizational climate and performance.[x]

Transformational leadership
A combination of learned skills and the ability to transform an organization in new, substantive ways.

Transformational leaders establish a vision and the key objectives that must be reached to move an organization forward. The charisma of a leader is necessary to generate awareness of a given problem, raise the interest of the followers to address that problem, and encourage their acceptance of the organization or team's purposes and mission. Charismatic leadership also can inspire followers to put the success of an organization and colleagues ahead of their own.[xi] Effective transformational leaders articulate a realistic vision of the future that can be shared, stimulate subordinates intellectually, and attend to the differences among subordinates.[xii] By defining the need for change, creating new visions, and mobilizing commitment to these visions, charismatic leaders can ultimately transform organizations. Follower transformation can be achieved by raising the awareness of the importance and value of desired outcomes and getting followers to transcend their own self-interests and focus on the needs of their colleagues and the organization, which is called employee engagement.[xiii]

Empirical Findings on Charisma The empirical results from decades of study on charismatic leadership show that leaders described as charismatic, visionary, or transformational often have a positive effect on their followers and organizations as a whole. This positive effect is both in terms of organizational performance and on follower satisfaction, organizational and team commitment, and organizational identification.[xiv] Charisma may also increase followers' perceptions of leaders' ability and effectiveness.[xv]

These positive results have been demonstrated in various organizational settings, including small groups, major units of complex organizations, corporations, and in studies on innovation, the military, and even the U.S. presidency.[xvi] Evidence supporting the value of transformational leadership has emerged from all around the world to which we now turn.[xvii]

International Perspective on Charisma The term *leader* evokes a positive image in the United States, but for people in many other parts of the world it evokes quite a negative image.[xviii] For some Europeans, for example, leadership is an unintended and undesirable consequence of democracy.[xix] British, Americans, and Canadians value charisma in their leaders and identify such business and political leaders as Lee Iacocca, former CEO of Chrysler Corporation, World War II British Prime Minister Winston Churchill, and former U.S. President Bill Clinton as effective, charismatic leaders.[xx] But as noted above, Germans do not value charisma in their contemporary business or government leaders. Many German people associate charisma with the blind obedience commanded by Hitler, and the resulting destruction of World War II.

Leadership scholar Bernard Bass notes that charismatic leaders are more likely to appear in societies with traditions of support for them and expectations about their emergence.[xxi] This implies that charismatic leadership might more easily surface in the Anglo-American societies where a preference for charisma exists. Yet there is also evidence that transformational leadership exists in various forms around the world, though perhaps less so in places such as Germany and Russia where people have experienced charisma's negative side in their leaders and are wary of it.[xxii]

Peter Dorfman compared leadership in Western and Asian countries.[xxiii] He and his colleagues showed that charismatic leaders' behaviors are widely accepted in both Asia and the West. The GLOBE study of leadership around the world also concurred. (This study was discussed in detail in Chapter 2.) The GLOBE study found that attributes of charismatic/transformational leadership, including foresight, encouraging, communicative, trustworthy, dynamic, positive, confidence builder, and motivational are universally endorsed as contributing to outstanding leadership. However, certain charismatic attributes were also identified as being culturally contingent. For example, attributes such as enthusiastic, risk taking, and ambitious were identified as characteristics of a leader in the West. In contrast, attributes such as self-effacing, self-sacrificial, sensitive, and compassionate were identified as leadership qualities in East Asian cultures. Charisma and many of its attributes are valued around the world, although different cultures have different ideas of what charisma is.

Transformational versus Transactional Leadership It was highlighted above that one type of leadership associated with charisma is transformational leadership. Transformational/charismatic leadership is traditionally contrasted with transactional leadership; the two concepts are seen as opposite approaches to leadership, though it is possible for a leader to manifest both charismatic and transactional qualities, depending on the situation.[xxiv] Political scientist James MacGregor Burns first introduced the concept of transactional leadership in his treatment of political leadership.[xxv] Researchers in social psychology have now adapted these concepts to the study of business leaders. For example, Bernard Bass defines a transactional leader as one who recognizes follower needs—recall how important identifying needs is to motivation—and tries to see that the organization satisfies those needs if employee performance warrants it.[xxvi] Thus, transactional leaders also use extrinsic motivators very effectively. For example, such a leader exchanges (promises) rewards for appropriate levels of effort, and responds to employees' self interests as long as they are getting the job done. Transactional leadership also seeks to acquire more followers through the exchange process.

Some have argued that transactional leadership is the best approach in dealing with followers in emerging economies where people are poorer and likely to be motivated by what Maslow would refer to as lower-order, material needs, such as money and housing. Research on the importance of social exchange and connections for conducting business in emerging economies, such as China and India, supports this view of the importance of transactional leadership.

In contrast to transactional leadership, transformational leadership occurs when a leader transforms his or her followers in ways that result in followers trusting the leader, performing behaviors that contribute to the achievement of organizational goals, and being motivated to perform at a high level. Transformational leaders increase followers' awareness of the importance of their tasks and of performing well. They not only make subordinates aware of their needs for personal growth, development, and accomplishment, but they also give subordinates a feeling of engagement with the organization by motivating them to work for the good of the organization in addition to their own personal gain. Figure 8-3 summarizes the characteristics of transformational leadership. While transactional leadership may work best in a more difficult environment where followers require

FIGURE 8-3   Attributes Associated with Transformational Leadership

1. Motive arouser

2. Foresight

3. Encouraging

4. Communicative

5. Trustworthy

6. Dynamic

7. Positive

8. Confidence builder

9. Motivational

Source: House, R.J., Hanges, P.J., Javidan, M., Dorfman, P.W., & Gupta, V. (Eds.) (2004). *Culture, Leadership, and Organizations: The GLOBE Study of 62 Societies.* Thousand Oaks, CA: Sage Publications.

the organization to "show us the money" (such as in lesser developed countries), in cultures that value empowerment and understanding the higher goals of the company, transformational, Steven Jobs-type leadership can work very well.

Behavioral Theories of Leadership

Behavioral theories

Leadership theories that argue that specific, learned behaviors can differentiate leaders from non-leaders (or successful leaders from unsuccessful leaders), and are behaviors that can be learned.

The next category of leadership theories is the behavioral theories. **Behavioral theories** of leadership argue that specific, learned behaviors can differentiate leaders from non-leaders (or successful leaders from unsuccessful leaders), and these behaviors can be learned. Unlike the trait theories of leadership, which imply that leaders need to be identified and perhaps nurtured, behavioral theories assume that effective leadership behaviors can be identified and taught to prospective leaders. The initial studies were done at Ohio State and the University of Michigan and established the domain of behavioral leadership. Building on these initial studies, researchers developed the Leadership Grid, which further extended the concepts of behavioral leadership.

Ohio State/Michigan Studies The behavioral perspective of leadership identifies two dimensions of leader behavior: task orientation and people orientation. Task-oriented behaviors include assigning employees to specific tasks, clarifying their work duties and procedures, ensuring that they follow company rules, and pushing them to reach their performance capacity. People-oriented behaviors include showing mutual trust and respect for subordinates, seeking to meet employee needs as a way to build relationships and loyalty to the company, and looking out for employee well-being to reduce turnover. This perspective has been used to argue that the most effective leaders exhibit high levels of both types of behaviors, irrespective of a given situation.

The foundational studies in this area are competing studies done at Ohio State University and the University of Michigan in the 1950s and 1960s. The Ohio State leadership studies argued that leadership behavior had two dimensions: initiating structure (task behavior) and consideration (people oriented behavior). The Michigan study used slightly different terms, production oriented and employee oriented, but the concepts used in both sets of studies are similar. Here we will use the terms task behavior and people-oriented behavior because they are widely used. Both studies argued that leadership behavior could be taught, and stressed the importance of a leader being high on both the task and people dimensions.

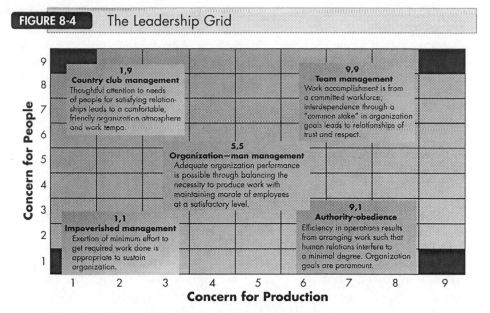

FIGURE 8-4 The Leadership Grid

Source: Blake, R. & Mouton, J.S. (1964). *The Managerial Grid*. Houston, TX: Gulf Publishing Company.

Leadership Grid A similar behavioral leadership theory that followed was the Leadership Grid, with categories based on a 9 by 9 matrix. This grid identifies various types of leadership behavior based on two independent dimensions of concern for production and concern for people. As in the Ohio State and Michigan studies, effective leaders must show high concern for both production and for people, and work to encourage employees to reach their highest levels of achievement. The ratings for leaders on both dimensions ranged from one to nine, with nine being the highest on both dimensions. Leaders were named according to their ratings on the Leadership Grid; for example the ideal leader was seen to be a "9,9" leader—someone who is highest on both concern for production and concern for people (see Figure 8-4).

In this view, the ideal 9,9 leader is seen as being flexible with the ability to get a great deal of effort from followers who maximize their effort for him or her; all of this while the leader works hard to meet the workers' needs. The 9,9 leaders are thought to be responsive to change and innovative. The opposite of a 9,9 leader is a 1,1 leader, who is considered to have impoverished leadership and management abilities. This type of leader exerts minimum effort and gets minimal output from workers, and has little concern for workers' needs. In this environment, managers will often find ways to minimize work, and will punish those who try to do extra for "creating more work for others."

The Leadership Grid identifies several other leadership styles. Familiar to most is the 9,1 or the Authority–Obedience leadership style. This leadership style stresses efficiency in operations and certain, specified results, and it offers no room for creativity. In this setting, working conditions are arranged so human actions are constrained and cannot interfere with the mechanistic output of the work system. A military boot camp is a classic example. A drill instructor is a 9,1 leader, with full attention given to drills and building unquestioning discipline in the troops. In these leaders' view, there is no room for individualism, creativity, or personal concern for the employees (soldiers), beyond what the system has built into it. Managers in more traditional organizations in developing countries are thought to fit this leadership profile, which is more likely to work best with difficult situations in which strict discipline is required and followers are not yet experienced enough to make decisions about their work. The 9,1 leadership approach is thought to be essential in training factory employees in emerging economies of Asia and Africa. But even these employees, many of whom are barely literate, are given room to innovate within their jobs after a year or two on the job. Once employees are able to demonstrate competence with their assigned tasks, supervisors have found that they are able to suggest improvements to individual tasks and maybe to the production process as a whole. This allows the leader to give more freedom to the employees and to "back off" from the strict 9,1 production orientation, giving more concern to the employees and their opinions and growth.

International Perspectives on Behavioral Theories There is evidence that different cultures will find different positions on the Leadership Grid to be most effective. For example, high power-distance cultures may be more open to the 9,1 form of leadership and less likely to question the orders and authority of a leader. In many Asian settings, such as China, this type of leadership is common. This style also characterizes Turkey and several other Middle Eastern countries.[xxvii] It is interesting to note that in many Korean firms, employees start their day with company songs and group exercises in a manner similar to the military, and, in Japan, leaders are often expected to be quite strict with employees, pushing them very hard for the good of the organization.[xxviii]

LEADERSHIP AT PHILIPS AND CHRYSLER

To illustrate different leadership styles, consider electronics manufacturing powerhouse Philips—one of the most well-known companies in Europe. Based in the Netherlands, its former CEO is Jan Timmer—an impressive figure both physically and mentally. Timmer is typically portrayed in the media as being charismatic and, while in office, he masterminded the turnaround of Philips, for which he was praised and admired. However, within months of stepping down, Timmer faced severe criticism, both in the company and the media.[xxix] As is common with many charismatic leaders, it was thought he had put his reputation ahead of the organization's well-being.

When a charismatic leader is primarily focused on his or her own reputation or advancement, the long-term impact on a firm can be negative. People thought that many of the strategic actions Timmer took were to benefit his own career and reputation, and not to help advance the growth and development of the firm, its shareholders, and employees. Timmer did engineer a fairly effective turnaround that helped Philips dig itself out of a big financial hole. Philips did well for a while, but as is the case with many charismatic leaders, Timmer seemed to lose interest and failed to train a top management team to take over

once he left the firm. Philips is still a leader in different segments of the electronics industry, but has not regained its leadership position in the industry.

This also seems to be the situation with Lee Iacocca, the charismatic former leader of Chrysler. Starting in 1979, Iacocca initiated the turnaround of the U.S. automaker, one of the greatest turnarounds in American business history. Chrysler's financial fortunes were greatly improved, its cars improved a great deal through the 1980s, and its strategic situation improved considerably. Throughout the 1980s, Iacocca appeared in a series of commercials for Chrysler's Dodge and Plymouth cars, using the ad campaign "The pride is back" to signal Chrysler's return as a contender in the field. But again, as with many charismatic leaders, Iacocca seemed to tire of the continuing effort needed to build a great firm. Starting in 1982, Iacocca headed the Statue of Liberty-Ellis Island Foundation, which was created to raise funds for the renovation and preservation of the Statue of Liberty. He took over the Italian sports car firm Maserati and U.S. automaker American Motors, and added Gulf Stream jets to Chrysler's increasingly diversified portfolio. Although Chrysler became a stronger car company during his tenure, by the

time Iacocca left in 1992, it was only marginally above where it had been in the late 1970s financially and in terms of rank in the U.S. auto market, and had no foreign presence.

It is common for organizations under charismatic leaders to do well while that leader mobilizes change, extracts hard work and commitment, and inspires financial markets and customers. But it is all too common for a leader to eventually do what's best for him or her personally and not the organization, leaving that organization in pretty much the same state as it was in when he or she took over.[xxx] Such a leader may fail to train and coach followers, fail to build a top management team, and rely too much on his or her own "genius" to get things done.[xxxi] Thus, the proper leadership role will vary not only in terms of local culture, but also by the nature of the situation that the firm faces and the needs for the business at that given time. Charismatic leaders can be particularly effective during a turnaround or other stressful situation, but if that leader cannot put the organization's needs first at all times, the organization and its stakeholders will eventually suffer. As *Good to Great* author Jim Collins puts it, "If you are president of Harvard [University] and it [your work] is all about you, then you shouldn't be president of Harvard."[xxxii]

Some cultures are particularly associated with a certain type of leadership. For example, the leadership style 5,5 is commonly referred to as "organization man management." Adequate organization performance is possible through balancing the necessity to produce while maintaining morale at a satisfactory level. Japanese leadership in average domestic firms is often associated with this style of leadership in which organization man loyalty is prized and promotion is still often based on seniority. Excepting the elite firms, productivity in most Japanese domestic firms is not especially high, and though employees work long hours, they do not have to work particularly hard; productivity in many Japanese service firms, for example, is rather low.[xxxiii]

Contingency Theory

The theories described in the preceding sections are limited to defining types of managers in absolute terms. According to the Leadership Grid, leaders fall into categories based on a 9 by 9 matrix. Behavioral theories imply that the 9,9 leader—the one high on both concern for production and concern for people—has the ideal leadership style. Recent evidence, however, suggests that leaders must adjust their management style to best handle different situations and to meet employee needs.[xxxiv] Sometimes leaders may generally be considered a 9,9, but at times must behave as a 9,1 (coercive, military style). For example, if a firm is in decline there may not be enough time to gather input from all employees to find ways to improve business; instead, decisions must be made and orders followed.[xxxv] In addition, not every culture values leaders who are overly concerned with employee interests. For the average person in more individualist societies, such as the U.S. and Australia, employees may see a manager with a rating of 9,9 as someone who is too personal and who prefers to "pass the buck" when making decisions. They also may not want their manager to be concerned with their personal lives. Indian workers, on the other hand, may find the Anglo-American participatory leadership style uncomfortable as employees tend to feel that a manager is paid to make decisions, and should not be concerned about the opinions of their staff. Students from East Asia and other more hierarchical cultures similarly report that they feel uncomfortable being asked too many questions or for input, because the professor (boss) should be telling them what to do.[1]

Many students may remember a time when a boss, teacher, or colleague asked questions that were too personal. You may have wanted to, or in fact did, tell that person to back off and give you more space and freedom with your work. Leaders need to be sensitive to individuals who may not want (or need) a 9,9 supervisor hovering over them; more individualistic cultures value that personal space. Recent stories about Chinese firms with branches or offices in North America have confirmed that more traditional Chinese bosses are seen as intrusive by North American workers. Those bosses ask specific and personal questions and micromanage employees, phoning them at night or on weekends about work, and even scold them for having turned off their mobile phones. Leaders must use different styles at different times in different settings. The adaptation models of leadership help individuals to understand how a leader may adjust behavior to better fit a particular situation and employees' maturity levels. The theories based on this model, recognizing the need for adaptation, are called **contingency theories.**

Contingency theory
Theory in which the type of leadership needed is based on the situation being faced.

---

[1]This is quite similar to students in the more traditional, hierarchical cultures in East Asia or Africa, who feel a teacher or trainer should have the answers. They tend to get frustrated with teachers or trainers who constantly ask them what they think. "Why doesn't the trainer simply give us the answers? We don't want to hear what these other students think, just what the teacher thinks," students commonly say.

Fiedler's Contingency Theory Leadership scholar Fred Fiedler developed the first contingency model in response to the realization about the impracticality of requiring leaders to behave the same way in all situations at all times. Fiedler argued that there are two fundamental types of leadership: task orientation and relationship orientation. (Notice the similarity to the Ohio State, Michigan, and Leadership Grid models.) Relationship-oriented leaders want to be liked by their subordinates and to get along with them. They are also referred to as high-LPC leaders because they tend to describe their LPC (Least Preferred Coworker) in relatively positive terms. Leaders who are task-oriented want their subordinates to perform at a high level and accomplish all of their assigned tasks. These leaders are also referred to as low-LPC leaders because they tend to describe their LPC in relatively negative terms.

The best leadership style is determined by three conditions or contingencies. The first contingency is the leader-member relationship, which includes the degree of confidence that followers have in their leader, the loyalty given to the leader, and the leader's appeal. The second contingency is task structure, which is the degree to which employees' tasks are routine, in contrast to varied tasks. The third contingency is the power inherent in the leadership position. This variable includes rewards and sanctions available to the position, the leader's formal authority (based on ranking in the managerial hierarchy), and the support that the leader receives from supervisors and the overall organization.

Looking at which leadership style works best in different situations, Fiedler argued that high-LPC leaders (relationship-oriented leaders) are most effective in situations that are moderately favorable for leading. That is, when a situation is not too ambiguous, people basically know what to do, but there is some degree of flexibility for leaders and followers. In contrast, low-LPC leaders (task-oriented leaders) are most effective in situations that are very favorable or very unfavorable for leading, such as unfavorable, mechanistic, or military (extreme leadership) environments.[xxxvi] Low-LPC does not imply that leaders should have no concern for employees, but that they cannot worry too much about being liked by employees; instead, the key is to command employee respect and be sure that workers carry out their duties.

The contingency theory argues that an effective leader's behavior is determined by both his or her personal characteristics and by the three types of situations in which leaders find themselves. This sheds light on why some leaders are effective and others, who may be equally qualified and respected, are ineffective in the same situation. It also helps to illustrate why a leader may be effective in one situation but not in another.

International Perspective on Contingency Theory Leaders from different cultures vary in the assumptions they make about how to lead. In the United States for example, many leaders assume that people's basic physiological needs for safety and security have been met and therefore only opportunities to satisfy higher-order needs will motivate them. They believe that denying these opportunities leads to alienation, lower productivity, and, ultimately, high levels of turnover. As a result, most U.S. leaders believe that the majority of the people who work for them want to develop interpersonal relationships characterized by trust and open communication and they assume that people produce more when a workplace is more democratic and open.

Fiedler's contingency theory of leadership reminds us that it is inappropriate to think there is a single best leadership style. At certain times leaders may need to be more autocratic and at other times less directive. An employee's behavior will affect the type of leadership style needed in a given situation. Fiedler's work encourages managers to consider not only the culture in which they are working but also the nature of the work environment in which the firm is located. Fiedler's work also brings out the important point that managers cannot focus solely on culture. The nature of the employees and the tasks to be accomplished also have a significant impact on the type of leadership that is required.

The nature of the task to be accomplished raises another significant issue that managers should consider as they determine an appropriate leadership style. As leaders move up within an organization, the nature of the needed leadership changes. The leadership behavior of a lower-level manager is commonly more directive and task oriented, and typically the manager's focus is simply on getting the job done. Senior and executive managers, however, are more focused on relationships.

Hersey–Blanchard Situational Leadership From Fiedler's foundation another contingency model was developed by Paul Hersey and Ken Blanchard (a co-author of the well-known book, *The One Minute Manager*). They argued that contingency was the appropriate approach because it allows flexibility in types of leadership as required in different settings.[xxxvii] Specifically, they argued that effective leaders must also vary their style of leadership based on the employees' level of maturity. Hersey and Blanchard identified a three-dimensional approach for assessing leadership effectiveness. An employee's maturity is determined by job maturity (job experience) and psychological maturity (employee self-confidence and ability to accept responsibility).

There are four levels of employee maturity. The least-mature employees must be given much more direction and discipline, while mature employees are more confident and can be given more independence. Training, personal motivation, maturity, and teamwork can substitute for leader discipline and direction. The effectiveness of a leader depends on how his or her style interrelates with employee maturity. Leadership should meet the needs of all employees, from telling employees what to do and how to do it at the lowest level of maturity; to selling ideas to employees at the next level of maturity; to participating with employees at the next level; and finally to delegating to employees at the highest level of maturity.

The willingness and ability (readiness) of an employee to do a particular task is an important situational factor. It's important to remember that employees become more mature with time and leaders must be able to adjust their leadership style appropriately. The degree to which a leader is able to vary his or her style to the level of an employee in a given situation can be crucial to the success of a team or organization (see Leadership under Changing Circumstances).

International Perspective on the Hersey–Blanchard Theory This approach to leadership has important implications for international business. Managers who move from a low power-distance country to a higher power-distance country will find that they must alter their style to fit that new environment. Many managers in the United States believe that people who work for them want to develop interpersonal relationships characterized by trust, communication, and empowerment. They may mistakenly assume that all employees want a democratic workplace and want to be involved in factory-floor decisions. That often is not the case. Employees in high power-distance countries may expect bosses to act in a more directive and formal way and keep their distance, although employees will often welcome a mentoring, teaching approach as they become more mature, consistent with the Hersey–Blanchard theory.

Path–Goal Theory The contingency model that developed next is the Path–Goal theory. The Path–Goal theory proposes that the most successful leaders are those who increase subordinate motivation by charting out and clarifying the paths to high performance.[xxxviii] This contingency model is based on the Expectancy Theory

LEADERSHIP UNDER CHANGING CIRCUMSTANCES

Many students will be familiar with the award-winning ten-part HBO film series *Band of Brothers*, produced by Steven Spielberg and Tom Hanks and based on historian Stephen Ambrose's book of the same title. *Band of Brothers* tells the story of a group of American soldiers' preparation and combat during World War II. The series followed one company of U.S. Army paratroopers from the famed 101st Airborne Division—Easy Company of the 506 Regiment—from their training in boot camp through the end of the war. In the first episode of the series, the recruits of Easy Company meet their new Commander, Lieutenant Herbert Sobel. Lieutenant Sobel trained his men mercilessly—a textbook 9,1 leader. His only concern was for the success of Easy Company (and thus his reputation and promotion) based on group performance measures set down by the Army. Sobel's superiors were confident that if the training measures were correct, everything else must also be going well. Easy Company's performance in physical drills and other competitions quickly earned Sobel a promotion to captain and the accolades of his regimental commander, Colonel Sink. But all was not well. As Easy Company graduated from basic training camp and began to prepare for combat in Europe—improving from raw recruits to more mature soldiers—Captain Sobel still continued to treat them like immature recruits.

That is, he treated them like the unwilling and unable followers at the starting point of the Hersey–Blanchard model, and continued using an ordering style that was abusive to his men. This abusive style had worked well during the initial training—Easy Company outdistanced the other eight companies in the 506th regiment—but as the soldiers prepared in England for the European invasion, Captain Sobel's overly strict treatment and his petty punishments and intimidations caused the men to rebel against his authority.

After several isolated incidents of near insubordination, followed by punishment, the non-commissioned officers (corporals and sergeants) in Easy Company all got together to write letters to Sobel's superior, Colonel Sink. Triggered by a trivial charge against the Easy Company executive officer (and highly respected leader), Lieutenant Richard Winters, and risking a firing squad for mutiny, the noncoms informed Colonel Sink that they did not want to serve under Captain Sobel in the upcoming invasion of Nazi-occupied Europe.[2] Colonel Sink angrily informed them that they could be shot for insubordination during wartime, but he finally took account of the sergeants' concerns about Sobel. Easy Company needed a leader who could adjust to the new, ambiguous (nontraining) combat situation with the now mature and well-trained soldiers. Sink removed Captain Sobel from command of Easy Company and gave him

command of an airborne training school. A more able combat commander took charge, who generally understood what Easy Company could do and led by example. Captain Sobel's tough discipline had given Easy Company the training to become a fine company, but his style was not appropriate in a leadership role when going into combat with more experienced soldiers. It took the inspired leadership of Lieutenant Richard Winters and others to help Easy Company finally realize its abilities and become one of the most celebrated units in U.S. military history.

Businesses face similar situations—there are times in which a firm needs authoritarian or even coercive leadership to obtain certain goals within a given time period. For example, the turnaround of the Australian firm Brambles after a poor merger took considerably quick decision-making. However, once the turnaround was complete, that same type of leadership wasn't required. In cases like this, firms form groups of CEOs and other leaders to conduct turnarounds. These individuals typically leave the firm after it returns to profit, because the skills they possess are not needed to run the business on a daily basis.

Ambrose, S.E. (1992). *Band of Brothers: E Company, 506th Regiment, 101st Airborne from Normandy to Hitler's Eagle's Nest*. New York: Simon & Schuster.

of Motivation (see Chapter 7, Motivation). The manager's job is viewed as coaching or guiding employees to choose the best paths (in terms of tasks and objectives) for reaching their goals. This is evaluated by the accompanying achievement of organizational goals and individual objectives. As can be seen by the theory's name, goal setting is central. As discussed in Chapter 7, goals are motivational and should be used by a leader to help direct and motivate followers. Further, the Path–Goal theory argues that leaders will have to engage in different types of leadership behavior depending on the nature and demands of a particular situation. It is the leader's job to assist employees in attaining goals and to provide direction and support.

[2]That is how it was portrayed in HBO's miniseries, though noncoms did not actually send the letters to Col. Sink. They planned to do so, but the company executive officer found out about their plan and talked them out of it. Sink got word of the mini-revolt anyway and decided to remove Cpt. Sobel from command of Easy Company, sending him to command a paratroop training school.

As a result, managers can have four different leadership styles. These styles include achievement-oriented (challenging goals are set and high performance encouraged), participative (decision making based on group consultation with information shared in the group), supportive (good relations with the group and sensitivity to subordinate needs), and directive (specific advice is given to the group and ground rules established). The effective leader uses each of these four styles as required in different settings.

International Perspective on the Path–Goal Theory Like the other contingency models of leadership, Path–Goal theory specifies different leadership styles for different situations. In **achievement-oriented** leadership, the leader sets challenging goals for employees, expects them to perform at their highest level, and shows confidence in their ability to meet this expectation. This style is appropriate when the employee is not challenged, tends to be mature, and knows his or her job inside and out. With a directive leadership style, the manager lets employees know what is expected of them and tells them how to perform their tasks. This style is appropriate when the follower has an ambiguous job or may not be ready to work independently. Though the leader must assess each setting and employee separately, this approach may generally work best in emerging economies where employees need to be told the exact steps to complete a job, and perhaps just as important, need a list of things not to do. Participative leadership involves managers consulting with employees and asking for their suggestions before making a decision, sometimes called the democratic style of leadership. This style is appropriate when an employee is using improper procedures or is making poor decisions, and should be helped to uncover these problems. In addition, and as will be discussed in the next section, this participative style is most appropriate when employee buy-in is needed for making a difficult decision. In supportive leadership, the manager is friendly, approachable, and shows concern for the employee's well-being. This style is appropriate when the followers lack self-confidence or have just gone through a difficult time at work.

Determining the appropriate leadership style to use involves knowing how employees see themselves in a given situation: are they in control of their success or is it controlled by external factors? For example, in India's newly industrializing regions, employees are characterized by not being in control of their success, perhaps for religious or cultural reasons. They are used to hierarchy and expect managers to take control of a situation. In contrast, employees who believe they have at least some personal control over their destiny will be happier with participative approaches. This will be elaborated on further in the section on Daniel Goleman's work on emotional intelligence and situational leadership below.

Vroom–Yetton Theory The last contingency leadership model was developed by Victor Vroom and Phillip Yetton. This model focuses on how leaders make business decisions. Specifically, this theory argues that the required type of leadership is contingent on these issues:

* whether decision quality is important and followers possess useful information
* whether a manager considers decision quality important while employees do not
* whether decision quality is important when a problem is unstructured and the manager lacks information and/or skill to make the decision alone
* whether decision acceptance is important and employees are unlikely to accept an autocratic decision
* whether decision acceptance is important but employees are likely to disagree with one another
* whether decision quality is not important but decision acceptance is critical

DANISH JOINT VENTURE IN THAILAND

The impact of different perceptions of control can be seen in a joint venture between a Danish manufacturer of building products and a partner firm in Thailand. The Danish expatriate managers had some difficulty managing the Thai workforce at the beginning of the joint venture. Thailand is high on Hofstede's power distance and uncertainty avoidance. Their relatively high power-distance score indicates a high level of inequality of power and wealth within the society, and a distance between bosses and subordinates. The high uncertainty-avoidance index indicates Thailand's low level of tolerance for uncertainty. To minimize uncertainty, Thai society generally has strict rules, laws, policies, and regulations. The ultimate goal of this population is to control everything in order to eliminate or avoid the unexpected.

Denmark and other Nordic countries are essentially the opposite of Thailand, very low on power distance and uncertainty avoidance. Scandinavian leaders typically believe that most people want to be empowered to make work-related decisions. Like

most people of this profile, they tend to project those beliefs onto their subordinates—even those in a foreign country. They develop a system characterized by trust and open communication, and assume that employees are most productive when the workplace is democratic and employees are empowered to make team-based decisions, much like employees in their native countries.

Early on the Thai employees were charged with recreating a team-oriented manufacturing system. This system had worked well in Scandinavia at Volvo and other major manufacturing firms in Denmark. The Danes believed that the Thai employees would understand the local environment better than the expatriates and should have input not just on the joint venture management but on the production system. Yet the first several months were unproductive, while the local employees waited for more instruction from the Danish managers. The result was not innovative changes that fit the local environment as the Danish expatriate managers had hoped, but stagnation.

After three months, the Danish managers changed their approach to a more structured, standard assembly line system. They created very specific jobs for each employee and did not look for employee input on innovative changes that could be made. After some time, the employees learned their jobs and became accustomed to the more democratic (though temporarily coercive) Scandinavian system. After 18 months had passed, the joint venture's production had risen to forecast levels and employees had started to suggest local improvements to production and product. The leadership, which had started out as too egalitarian and unstructured, had moved to a more structured system, and was now gradually loosening up and encouraging innovation. Thus, the leadership style of the managers had to change and evolve as employees evolved and learned more about what was expected and why. The patience of the Danish managers eventually paid off.

Hofstede, G. & Hofstede, G.J. (2005). *Cultures and Organizations: Software of the Mind.* New York: McGraw-Hill.

As a result of these seven contingencies the leader then makes decisions in one of five different ways:

* Autocratic 1—Problem is solved using information already available
* Autocratic 2—Additional information is obtained from group before leader makes decision
* Consultative 1—Leader discusses problem with subordinates individually before making a decision
* Consultative 2—Problem is discussed with the group before decision is made
* Group 2—Group makes decision about upon problem, with leader simply acting as chair

The Vroom–Yetton Model is typically applied using a decision tree. The seven contingencies highlighted above are asked as questions which then, depending on the answer, inform the manager about the required or appropriate style of management for that setting.

International Perspective on the Vroom–Yetton Theory Contingency models can be seen as growing more complex over time. As with many North American–developed theories, the Vroom–Yetton Model assumes participation is good, and this model has proven to be useful in more universalistic societies such as the Scandinavian countries that have a predilection to low hierarchy and power distance. It may be less useful in societies that are higher in power distance, and are more formal,

UNIVERSALISM VERSUS PARTICULARISM: WHEN IN ROME DO AS THE ROMANS?

Culture researcher Fons Trompenaars emphasizes his universalism versus particularism orientation as being a key differentiating dimension of cultures and countries (see In-class Exercise #1 in Chapter 2). In universalistic societies such as those of the United States, United Kingdom, and Germany, people believe in a universal definition of goodness or truth—one that is applicable to all situations. Judgments are likely to be made with little regard to a particular situation. In contrast, people in more particularistic societies, such as China, Russia, and some Latin American countries, take the notion of situational forces more seriously. Judgments take into account contingencies that affect most circumstances, in particular, one's position in a hierarchy and loyalty concerns, especially to family and friends.

When expatriates from universalistic societies work in particularistic societies, they can find themselves in conflict with other members of the local management team. That team may argue that giving special prices and kickbacks to key customers is necessary to facilitate business because of that customer's relation to the firm. Expatriate managers are likely to have problems with this sort of "business as usual" attitude, and may argue that loyalty to longtime customers or suppliers is not as important as offering a fair price and treating all firms in the same manner. A firm's code of conduct and the laws in its home country are important here because expatriate managers need to follow their firm's code and are subject to the laws of their firm's home country, as noted in Chapter 3. Yet a more particularistic society might argue that specific situations allow certain behavior that many in western countries would find unethical. This is becoming a bigger issue as firms from particularistic, developing countries do more and more business in countries such as Sudan, and argue that they have no right or responsibility to say anything about the turmoil and violence going on in those countries.[xxxix]

Trompenaars, F. (1993). *Riding the Waves of Culture.* London: Nicholas Brealey Publishing.

hierarchical, and particularistic. Culture affects values, and decisions are made based on how a decision-maker values an outcome. As we saw in Chapter 2, some cultures, often in the West, hold more universalistic values: universal definitions of goodness, truth, and fairness and the need to always abide by them. Other cultures, often in Asia and Latin America, are more likely to take into account contingencies and circumstances, in particular, one's position in a hierarchy and loyalty concerns (i.e., families and friends). Outsiders are not accorded the same courtesies.

New Views on International Leadership

The theories above were developed in North America. Each has implications for international management, but none directly provides insights as to what should occur internationally. As a result, practitioners have integrated these theories and developed practical means for managers to lead internationally. For example, recent research from the consulting firm the Hay Group studied over three thousand executives worldwide.[xl] The Hay Group has identified a number of different leadership styles, each springing from different components of emotional intelligence. Typically, a leader would call on each of these different styles of leadership in different settings. Daniel Goleman and colleagues built on the Hay Group's extensive empirical research classifications to examine their impact on organizations, and developed more fully the concepts behind each type of situational leadership behavior. The six different leadership styles they specified are coercive, authoritative, affiliative, democratic, pacesetting, and coaching. We will next discuss these concepts and what they mean in international terms. (See Figure 8-5.)

Coercive A coercive leader is typically quite strict, leading by intimidation, bullying tactics, and through direct orders to employees. Although these methods may be helpful in situations requiring a disciplinary style, as we saw in the Fiedler model, they may be disruptive in those settings where creativity and a variety of ideas are required. It is not difficult to understand why Goleman found this style of leadership to be the least effective in most situations. An extreme top-down decision

FIGURE 8-5	Goleman's Situational Leadership Styles

Leadership styles	Method	Phrase	Situation where useful and problematic
Coercive	Demands immediate compliance	"Do what I tell you"	Situation is highly structured and stressful; followers not mature or experienced, requiring strict, mechanistic leadership. Works poorly for an experienced or professional workforce that know their jobs well.
Authoritative / Charismatic	Mobilizes people toward a vision	"Come with me"	To motivate people during difficult circumstances, sell a vision, undertake a turnaround. More of a short-term solution, a telling, charismatic leadership can be hard on followers that might start to value more democratic leadership.
Affiliative	Creates harmony and builds emotional bonds	"People come first"	Build harmony in workforce, increase employee satisfaction and engagement, build loyalty, and reduce turnover. Works well with other leadership styles such as democratic and coaching.
Democratic	Forges consensus through participation	"What do you think?"	To build buy-in or consensus, or to get input from valuable employees—needed for long-term planning and major change. Decision making tends to be slow; does not work well in higher power-distance cultures that expect leaders to make decisions and tell people what to do.
Pacesetting	Sets high standards for performance	"Watch and do as I do, now"	To get quick results from a highly motivated and competent team, like project management, R&D, creative endeavors. Can be tough on a workforce that is being pushed too hard. Pacesetting leaders have a tendency to want to do things themselves rather than delegate. Employee development might suffer.
Coaching	Develops people for the future	"Try this" and "I'll help you"	To help an employee improve performance or develop long-term strengths. Often improves organizational climate significantly. Coaching style takes a lot of time but can be very valuable for employee development and engagement.

Adopted from Goleman, D. (2000). Leadership that gets results. *Harvard Business Review*, March-April, 78–90.

making style stunts innovation: people are afraid to give suggestions or make mistakes. This does not mean, though, that it is always ineffective. In settings in which employees do not want to be accountable for their performance and refuse to respect authority, it can be effective. Firms that operate successfully using this type of leadership are characterized as having rapid decision making and the ability to change course quickly. The coercive style of management does not work well in industries that require innovation and leading-edge development.[xli]

Given the often negative impact of a coercive style on an organization's climate, it should be used with caution and only in special circumstances, but there are times it can be useful. Using a coercive style can break failed businesses of bad habits and shock people into new ways of working. The coercive style is appropriate during an emergency, such as when a company is on the verge of failing; in the face of a disaster such as a fire, a bomb threat, or hurricane; or with problem employees when all else has failed. However, if a leader fails to change his or her style as the situation changes, the long-term impact on the organizational climate can be quite negative. Employee morale is likely to decline if the coercive style remains in place for longer than absolutely necessary. Higher power-distance cultures are more accepting of a coercive leadership style as they are more likely to believe that leaders should act in this way (which does not mean that they necessarily like it).

Authoritative Authoritative leadership is similar to the coercive style, in that it is used to change people's minds in unfavorable situations. Any similarities stop there, however. One of the main differences between the two is that the authoritative leadership style is characterized by enthusiasm and vision rather than criticism and negative tactics—hence it has also been called the charismatic style of leadership.[xlii] This style is called authoritative because leaders tend to impose their vision on the company or team in an assertive manner.

Research has shown that the authoritative style can be one of the most effective approaches to leadership. Authoritative (or charismatic) leaders are visionary and motivating, which gives employees a strong sense of task identity and significance—they know what they are doing and why there are doing it.[xliii] Unlike the coercive leader, the authoritative leader's standards for success are clear and employees are given room to innovate and are not punished for making honest mistakes. Because of its positive impact, authoritative leadership works well in organizational settings such as when a business is adrift. An authoritative leader charts a new course and sells employees on a fresh, long-term vision.

Authoritative leadership also typically works well in high power-distance situations with strong group relationships. For example, Carlos Ghosn, a Brazilian-Lebanese employee of Renault, was sent to turn around the Japanese company Nissan—a company in which Renault has major investments. In three years, Ghosn improved Nissan's performance from $22.9 billion in losses to $7 billion in profits. He was able to do this by ignoring the firm's historic suppliers. Those that came from the *keiretsu* or business group of which Nissan had long been a part. Ghosn instead awarded contracts based on cost and quality considerations rather than on longstanding relationships and traditions. He focused Nissan on building fewer, better products on a narrower range of platforms to increase efficiency, and promoted employees based on talent and performance, not age or seniority (the typical Japanese method). Ghosn also looked for talented people outside of Japan. He consulted his employees for solutions to various issues, but was also able to make decisions on his own when appropriate. Today Ghosn is recognized as one of the top ten business leaders in the world after leading Nissan through an expected and almost unprecedented turnaround.

The authoritative style may be problematic in lower power-distance countries when a leader is trying to lead a team of experts or peers with more experience who may see the leader as overbearing or just out of touch.[xliv] This may also be true in many knowledge industries where employees know their jobs well and do not need enthusiastic cheerleading to get their jobs done. However, authoritarian leadership can be very effective in situations in which quick, dramatic action is required to lead a declining company back to success.

AUTHORITATIVE LEADERSHIP AND RESTRUCTURING

In authoritative leadership, managers and other leaders must be able to make decisions quickly and encourage workers to follow them based on their vision. When a firm restructures, it must make hard choices on what businesses to keep and what businesses to shut down. However, such decisions are not easy and involve sensitive ethical choices for the manager, particularly when a firm is making high profits and chooses to lay workers off in a restructuring effort. But, at the same time, such restructuring can be essential to the long-term health of the firm.

Unilever is the world's third-biggest food and consumer-goods company. The Anglo-Dutch firm's 400-plus brands include Dove soap, Knorr soups, and Sunsilk shampoo. In 2007 it announced a reduction in workforce by 20,000 in Europe—about 10 percent of its worldwide workforce. The goal was to save over $2 billion a year in reduced personnel costs. However, the announcement came as the firm also announced high profits and its surpassing the original profit estimates made to stock analysts.

Patrick Cescau is CEO of Unilever. He is well known for his strong commitment to the betterment of society. In particular, Cescau argues for social innovation in which new products and services are developed to not only meet consumers' need and desire for tasty food or clean clothes, but also for their wider aspirations as citizens. It was clear to Cescau that embarking on the firm's single highest number of layoffs at a time of high profits would be controversial. To successfully complete the layoffs, he relied on authoritative methods. Cescau knew that many people, both inside and outside the firm, would not understand the need for layoffs, but he was confident that it was necessary for Unilever's long-term success. Continued success does not mean, however, that the ethical issues surrounding layoffs like this no longer need to be considered or discussed—they do.

Unilever to cut 20K jobs in Europe. (2007, August 3). *New York Post*. http://www.nypost.com/seven/08032007/business/unilever_set_to_cut_20k_jobs_in_europe_business_.htm.

ETHICS

Affiliative While a coercive leader demands that people do what he or she says and an authoritative leader urges, an affiliative leader believes that people come first. This leadership style revolves around people—its proponents value individuals and their emotions more than tasks and goals. An affiliative leader strives to keep employees happy and to create harmony among them. He or she manages by building strong emotional bonds among employees. This style places a premium on communication and flexibility within an organization.

The affiliative leader is quick to offer positive feedback. Such feedback has special potency in the workplace because it is all too rare—outside of an annual review, most people usually get no feedback on day-to-day efforts or receive only negative feedback. This lack of feedback typically makes the affiliative leader's positive words all the more motivating. Finally, affiliative leaders are masters at building a sense of belonging. They are natural relationship builders.

Affiliative leadership is more likely to be successful where there are lower levels of power distance and more focus on individuality. One of prime example is SAS, the world's largest privately held software company that makes software for analyzing and managing large databases.[xlv] Jim Goodnight was a professor at North Carolina State University when he and several colleagues founded the firm in 1976. SAS today is still largely run a little like a university with the business's culture focused on positive encouragement. SAS believes happy employees will make happy customers. The firm also offers its employees on-site health clubs, day care and medical facilities, hefty cash bonuses, and profit sharing, which helps to build high levels of employee satisfaction and engagement and reduces turnover and absenteeism. As a result, SAS employees are known for being highly committed to the firm. As successful as affirmative leadership has been for SAS, companies that are in decline or in other less-than-optimal situations are less able to benefit from it.

Democratic Style This style is very consultative and is most often associated with the Japanese style of leadership and decision making. It permits a management team and employees to discuss plans and goals and reach decisions collectively, allowing for people to buy into the decision. The democratic style is slow, but when implemented it usually moves along rapidly with few objections. This contrasts with the coercive style, where decisions are handed down by a coercive or authoritarian leader with expectations that the orders will be implemented without question. By letting employees have a say in decisions that affect their goals and how they do their work, a democratic leader increases flexibility and responsibility and keeps employee morale high by listening to employees' concerns. Finally, because they have a say in setting their own goals and the standards for evaluating success, people operating in a democratic system tend to be very realistic about what can and cannot be accomplished.

However, the democratic style has its drawbacks. One of its more frustrating consequences can be endless meetings in which ideas are mulled over, consensus is sought over other goals, and employees are asked about every detail, including how to word trivial memos, announcements, and even meeting minutes. And in the end, the meeting's result can just be an agreement to meet again the following week. Some democratic leaders can use the style to put off making crucial decisions, hoping that meetings will eventually yield a blinding insight, or somehow help them to avoid responsibility. If the democratic style is taken to the extreme, an organization can seem leaderless. Nissan, prior to the appointment of Carlos Ghosn, experienced the risks of this style firsthand. Nissan had been on a downward spiral and appeared unable to address its problems. The business continued much as it had always done, employing a democratic leadership style, while it got into deeper trouble. No one wanted to make any big decisions until Ghosn came along and changed the firm's leadership and decision-making style.

Firms in which democratic leadership works best normally would be associated with very low power distance and a strong emphasis on individuality. Such leadership is typified by Scandinavian firms. For example, the company headquarters of Enator, a Swedish computer consulting company, has an architectural style that typifies management's leadership approach. Management's goal was to optimize their office space to suit the "idea workers" that the firm employs. For example, the building allows people to change their workspace inside the building easily. Also, nameplates and numbers are not on the office doors, so finding someone requires human contact. Enator's goal was to have maximum interaction among diverse people in order to help encourage the generation of new ideas. Democratic leadership also works best in situations that require most people in a department (or firm) to buy into a decision and support it as if it were their own. This may occur when a firm has to make a difficult decision about layoffs or shutting down a product line. Getting people's input about what to do and being transparent about the decision will generally have a positive impact on the organization's climate and the decision outcome.[xlvi]

Pacesetting A pacesetting leader is obsessive about doing things better and faster, and asks much the same of his or her employees. If employees do not deliver, they are out. In this sort of firm, performance can be high for a time, but employee turnover is also high. The difficulty for pacesetting leaders is that often employees feel overwhelmed by managerial demands for excellence, and morale drops. Guidelines for working may be clear in the leader's head, but often he or she does not state them clearly. The pacesetter sees their role as selecting the right people, and training has a much lower priority. In the minds of some pacesetting leaders training should not even be needed if the right people were hired in the first place. Steve Jobs in his first run at Apple was the archetypical pacesetter: a remarkably creative and hard worker, but domineering and terrorizing if employees did not meet his high standards. Apple finally rebelled against Jobs' impossible demands, but not before it was almost torn apart by dissension. Jobs lost the board's support and he resigned in 1985.[xlvii] However, Jobs learned a great deal from his experiences at Apple and came back to the firm about a decade later with a toned-down pacesetting style to lead the company in a very successful turnaround and entry into consumer electronics and retailing.

Cultures that are very high in masculinity often produce more pacesetting leaders, and these do not work well with higher quality-of-life cultures (feminine culture in Hofstede's terms). A pacesetting approach works best when all employees are self-motivated, highly competent, and need little direction or coordination. For example, it can work for R&D groups or legal teams. Japanese culture scores extremely high on the masculinity dimension and are typically thought of as having self-motivated employees who will work long hours with only general directions from management. Thus, pacesetting works well for them.

Coaching This style is more like a counselor than a traditional boss. Coaching leaders help employees identify their unique strengths and weaknesses and tie them to their personal and career aspirations. They encourage employees to establish long-term development goals and help conceptualize a plan for attaining them. They make agreements with employees about their roles and responsibilities in enacting development plans, and they give plentiful instruction and feedback. Coaching leaders excel at delegating. They give employees challenging assignments, even if that means the employees may not be able to accomplish the assignments without help, in order to help the employees grow into their jobs.

Research suggests that of the six styles, the coaching style is used least often but should be used much more. It fits with most cultures and produces a positive

Although coaching focuses primarily on personal development, not on increasing productivity at work-related tasks, it can improve business performance.

organizational climate.[xlviii] Admittedly, there is a paradox in coaching's positive effect on business performance because coaching focuses primarily on personal development, not on increasing productivity at work-related tasks. Even so, coaching can improve business performance. When an employee knows the boss is using a coaching style and cares about the employee's improvement, that employee feels free to experiment and is not afraid of making mistakes. After all, the employee is sure to get quick and constructive feedback and will be able to learn and become more satisfied and productive.

The coaching style works well in many business situations, but it is perhaps most effective when people on the receiving end of the coaching are supportive of its use. For instance, coaching works particularly well when employees are already aware of their weaknesses and wish to improve their performance. Coaching also works well when employees realize how cultivating new abilities can help them advance. In short, it works best with employees who want to be coached.

Implicit leadership
Recognizes the process by which persons are perceived as leaders and follows the same basic social-cognitive processes that occur in other contexts of perceptions of persons.

Implicit Leadership Another relatively recent development in leadership theory is **implicit leadership**. This theory recognizes that the process by which persons are perceived as leaders follows the same basic social-cognitive processes occurring in other contexts. From this background it is known that people generally find it difficult to cope with large amounts of information they receive from their environment and, as a result, develop cognitive structures—shortcuts to analyze information. These shortcuts include creating categories, schemas, scripts, and implicit theories. A type of script familiar to students is a "date." When a friend tells you that he or she is going out on a date, you immediately understand what that means. No one within the same culture needs the term "date" explained to them—that script is quite familiar. Such cognitive shortcuts are convenient and help people organize and process information more efficiently.

An implicit theory of leadership is similar in that people have certain ideas about the characteristics of leaders and the nature of leadership, and they develop idiosyncratic theories of leadership. As such, an individual's implicit theory of leadership refers to beliefs held about leaders' characteristics and behavior.[xlix] Leadership can also be based on the idea of a leader's characteristics and what a leader should be.[l] Jeffrey Garten in his book *The Mind of the CEO* described a meeting with the former CEO of AT&T, Michael Armstrong, in complimentary terms, stating that Armstrong showed confidence, enthusiasm, and energy. Garten, showing a common United States and Western Europe implicit view of leadership, based his analysis of Armstrong on traits he thought were appropriate for leaders, stating that if Hollywood were looking to cast someone as a CEO, it would choose Armstrong.[li]

Employees decide about leadership through their ideas about what leader characteristics should be. This suggests that different cultures will vary in their conceptions of effective leadership's most important characteristics. Thus, different leadership prototypes emerge from different cultures.[lii] In some cultures, an individual might need to take strong decisive action in order to be seen as a leader, whereas in other cultures, consultation and a democratic approach may be more generally accepted. In a culture that endorses a more coercive style of leadership, concern expressed by a leader might be interpreted as weak, whereas in cultures endorsing a more affiliative style, such concern proves essential for effective leadership. Recent studies in Europe, for example, have found, as in the United States, those persons perceived as excellent managers and leaders are expected to be high on inspirational leadership. In Eastern Europe, which was long influenced by the technocratic, totalitarian requirements of the Soviet Union, inspirational leadership is not perceived as a characteristic of successful leaders. Instead, excellent leaders in Eastern Europe are those who are thought to be administratively competent. As is expected from the longtime Soviet influence, supervisors in Eastern European firms are often chosen based on their technical skills, while middle managers are often chosen on the basis of political skills and perceived ability to work with senior managers.[liii] Thus implicit leadership theories affect not only how people view leaders, but also how managers are selected. It is easy to see how conflicts arise over differing implicit theories, even for Western European firms based in Eastern Europe.

CONNECTING LEADERSHIP AND CULTURE

The preceding sections presented the major theories and the current trends in leadership. The discussion made clear the possible impacts of different national settings for each of the theories discussed. Despite each theory's differences, you should by now see some commonalities in the suggested leadership style for different cultural settings. This section will integrate and discuss more precisely the appropriate leadership style in specific cultural settings. Hofstede's dimensions of cultures will be used to organize this discussion.[liv] Recall that Hofstede's dimensions of culture are uncertainty avoidance, power distance, masculinity femininity, and individualism collectivism. Each dimension of culture will be discussed in order show how students can develop guidelines to deal with leadership in different environments.

Power Distance and Leadership

Hofstede argued that participatory leadership, which has long been encouraged by North American theorists and managers, is not suitable for all cultures.[lv] As noted, employees in high power-distance cultures, such as India for example, expect a manager to act as a strong leader, and become uncomfortable with leaders delegating decisions. In a culture that endorses a more authoritarian style, leader sensitivity might be interpreted as being weak, whereas in cultures endorsing a more nurturing style, the same sensitivity is likely to prove essential for effective leadership. A less negative attitude toward authoritarian leadership will be found in high power-distance societies. In such societies, dominance and ostentatious displays of authority and order-giving might be seen as desirable actions for a leader, such as in South Asia or the Middle East. This contrasts with lower power-distance cultures that prefer their leaders to empower and encourage employee participation in decision making. In more egalitarian societies, such as in Scandinavia or Australia, leaders should emphasize egalitarian leadership when the situation permits (see the Culture box titled Culture and Doing Business in Australia).

Uncertainty Avoidance and Leadership

High uncertainty-avoidance cultures that have an emphasis on rules, procedures, and traditions, may place demands on leaders not expected in low uncertainty-avoidance cultures. In such environments, it can be assumed that leaders are more directive and rely on rules to help guide their decision making. It is important, however, that a leader ensures that members of the organization are clear on the nature of the rules and regulations that are motivating their actions. Environments with high uncertainty avoidance, ensuring that information is well communicated so that there are no surprises, help the members of an organization accept management's actions. One side effect of this approach is that more innovative behaviors may be expected in low uncertainty-avoidance cultures. This can reduce the ability of the leader to respond quickly to decline or strategically threatening situations.

Individualism and Leadership

A high degree of individualism implies that leaders must allow employees to make decisions about their work. This encourages risk-taking, out-of-the-box thinking, and innovation. In a more collective society, a leader may ask for a group consensus before adjudicating the final decision. For example, in Japan, leadership is oriented toward forming and reaching group goals, and leadership also is geared toward preserving group harmony and not publicly questioning leaders. As noted before in discussing Nissan, such consensus-building can be useful to build buy-in, but it can also delay responses when there are critical issues facing the firm.

Masculinity and Leadership

Countries high in masculinity will more commonly place emphasis on male leadership and production along the lines of the 9,1 leader. These countries include Japan and many of the South American countries. In contrast, Sweden is much lower on the masculinity scale, along with the Netherlands and Thailand, and it could be expected to have more female leaders than most countries and place more value on relations and quality of life in the company. Sweden is also a pioneer in creating excellent quality of life within a firm and building workspaces that promote creativity. In spite of cultural proclivities in some countries against women leaders, research suggests that women expatriates coming in from the outside are more readily accepted as leaders than local women are.[lvi] Thailand has a number of women in leadership positions. It should be noted that women are increasingly able to take up leadership positions in even masculine societies. The Philippines, with a strong influence from the Spanish and East Asian masculine societies, has had two strong female presidents in the past twenty years—Corazon Aquino and Gloria Macapagal-Arroyo. Even the high-masculine scoring country

FUJIO MITARAI, CEO OF CANON

Fujio Mitarai of Canon is one of the most respected business leaders in the world. Mitarai has led Canon to becoming the leading producer of cameras and camera equipment in the world. He has been successful by combining traditional Japanese management with Western focus on profit. Mitarai's focus on profit was developed during his leadership of Canon's U.S. subsidiary. He took over the subsidiary in 1961 when it had only seven employees and quickly adapted to the U.S. business environment. Soon after arriving in the U.S. Mitarai put together his first annual report, which showed a profit of $6,000 on sales of $3 million. The low profit rate raised the concerns of the Internal Revenue Service (IRS) who suspected tax fraud. After an audit, it was found that Mitarai had been honest in his profit claims. However, the IRS agents suggested that he close the business and

place the money he would have spent on operating the business in a savings account instead, where he'd earn more money. It was at that stage that Mitarai realized that profits, not sales, on which many Japanese firms focus, are what must be made. Over the next 38 years in the U.S., he built Canon into a major force in the production of camera and copy equipment.

In 1995 Mitarai became president of the Canon Corporation, and in 1997 its CEO. Mitarai is far more decisive than many traditional Japanese managers, who look for consensus. For example, he quickly acted in eliminating divisions that sold unsuccessful products, such as personal computers, electric typewriters, and liquid crystal displays. He merged the remaining divisions into four: copiers, printers, cameras, and optical equipment. To increase coordination among the divisions, Mitarai

adopted consolidated balance sheets for the units. Mitarai has also kept a strong focus on profit. To encourage employees, he started having daily lunch meetings with senior managers and monthly meetings with middle managers, in which he personally explained his vision and outlined what needed to be done. This communication level is unique in Japan.

However, Mitarai retains many Japanese leadership characteristics, such as maintaining lifetime employment of workers, a traditional Japanese approach to employment that many firms have now dropped. He argues that such commitment to employees will build similar employee commitment to the firm. Thus, Mitarai has combined aspects of traditional Japanese management with aspects from other cultures to produce a unique and highly competitive form of leadership at Canon.

of Germany has elected its first female prime minister, much to the surprise of many German citizens, suggesting that culture is not necessarily destiny.

OVERVIEW OF CULTURE AND LEADERSHIP

In countries with different cultures there may be several appropriate approaches to leadership. No one type of leadership is best, but rather the goal is to match the needs of the local culture with the right style of leadership. It has been noted that making quick or innovative actions can be difficult in countries whose cultures do not support such action. This does not mean that such actions cannot be pursued. Instead, it means that a business person needs to be aware of potential conflict that can arise when actions are not consistent with the culture. In those situations the business person needs a strategy on how to address the potential conflict. The greatest danger is not the potential conflict, but in being caught unaware of that conflict. If that occurs, the individual will spend significant time working to overcome a problem that could have been avoided.

It is also important to remember that in all cultures, a leader needs to build trust with followers. A leader is also, by definition, responsible. Thus, while leaders may approach that responsibility in different ways in different settings, they cannot be afraid to be out in front when necessary. Leaders must also remember that they must have a high degree of integrity, and must be perceived as treating everyone fairly. Finally, a leader in an unfamiliar environment should be willing to admit when he or she does not know something and seek assistance to get the needed answers. There are individuals in all organizations that are willing to help, and employees do not expect a manager to know everything.

SUMMARY

In North America, charisma is often thought of as central to leadership. However, this chapter reminds us that there is much more to leadership than just charisma. Some leadership situations demand strong, charismatic leaders, while there are other situations in which such a person will be quite ineffective. Additionally, although charismatic leaders are effective in many countries and in a variety of situations, there are other leadership styles that can get useful results. Thus, it is critical that business people recognize that culture dictates the leadership approach.

In addition to the trait theories of which charisma is a part are the behavioral theories of leadership. Originally, there were two main behavioral leadership dimensions: task orientation and people orientation. Leaders could be high, moderate, or low on both of those dimensions. It was originally assumed that a leader who was high on task and people orientation would be the most effective leader. Subsequent research on other key conditions, such as employee experience and the favorability or unfavorability of a situation, has given more depth and detail to the behavior model of leadership. Contingency models of leadership, including the Path–Goal and Vroom–Yetton theories have been developed to help differentiate the situations under which a leader should be more directive or democratic in decision making.

Recent empirically grounded work by Daniel Goleman and colleagues has agreed that task orientation and people orientation are inadequate, and has identified six distinct leadership styles ranging from coercive to democratic, depending on organizational goals, the situation, and employee needs. Implicit leadership theories serve to remind us that different cultures are more likely to favor different types of leaders, and this will influence leadership selection. Even cultures that are relatively close to us, such as those in Western and Eastern Europe, place different value on more charismatic, inspirational leadership. Whichever leadership style you choose, be sure that it fits the follower maturity and the demands of the situation. Simply stated, good leadership brings to a situation what the followers lack, be it discipline, vision or just coordination.

MANAGERIAL GUIDELINES

When trying to inspire employees to reach goals and objectives, managers should remember:

1. leadership in different cultures will mean different things.
2. even a concept such as charisma, which has been shown to have a positive impact in a wide variety of settings, can take different forms in different settings.
3. coercive and authoritarian leaders—the more task-oriented leaders—work best under unfavorable situations. Affiliative leaders work well in moderately favorable leadership situations in which they can give employees more freedom.
4. democratic leaders who seek consensus, discussion, and are slow to make decisions are most effective in getting employee buy-in to facilitate employee input and implementation. This is most helpful with long-term planning and major change initiatives across an organization.
5. affiliative leaders who are good at listening to employees and handling employee relations are usually also good at leading employees during stressful circumstances.
6. pacesetting leaders obtain the fastest results from a highly motivated and competent team—project management, R&D, or creative input. Often, a pacesetting leader is a high performer in the field in which he or she is leading.
7. coaching leaders can be effective. Coaching helps an employee improve performance or develop long-term strengths. Novice employees often argue that they prefer this style to help them develop in their jobs.

8. if a firm cannot change leaders to match a situation, then that leader should try to modify his or her behavior to conform to the situation. This is difficult for some people, which is why Professor Morgan McCall recommends carefully taking into account a prospective manager's background or "professional upbringing" when selecting a leader and not his or her "right stuff" traits. For example, if you are trying to get a new overseas office going in your company that requires the general manager to build the business from the ground up, it would be best to look for someone with experience in fast-growing entrepreneurial firms. That person would understand how to get a new business going, particularly in the face of the many constraints faced by new organizations. In contrast, if you needed someone to run an established factory overseas, McCall argues that an "entrepreneurial upbringing" would not be of much help; the manager in that position needs to have experience in budgeting, scheduling, dealing with government officials, unions, and many other challenges that entrepreneurs seldom face. International experience is also important for anyone being given a key international assignment.[lii] That is not to say people cannot learn a much different job—they can, but there will be a learning curve, and many costs to the company as the firm "pays for the education" of the new manager as he or she grows into the job. This may not be an option for a firm that needs a manager to hit the ground running, particularly in a difficult international assignment.

Table 8-1 will be helpful to students and managers as they examine different aspects of leadership.

TABLE 8-1 Leadership Styles and Culture

Leadership Style	Leadership Style and Culture
Coercive	Coercive leadership is necessary in many unfavorable situations where the work has to get done quickly, with little discussion. The challenge for a coercive leader is when to adjust his or her style with the improvement of the situation and the maturity of the followers. Higher power-distance cultures are more accepting of a coercive leadership style, because they are more likely to believe that leaders should act in this way. Still, leaders can have a mini-revolt on their hands if they keep treating followers in a coercive, tyrannical manner if the situation does not call for it and the followers are mature and know their jobs.
Authoritarian (Charismatic)	There is evidence that charisma is positively associated with effective leadership. However, charismatic leaders who cannot put an organization's goals ahead of their own, even at the expense of their own goals and reputation, can be a liability to the organization. Charismatic leaders may be more effective during turnaround situations and other situations requiring radical change. Certain countries with bad experiences with charisma, such as Germany or Italy, may be more hesitant to accept a charismatic leader.
Affiliative	Unlike the coercive and authoritarian styles, an affiliative leader believes that people and relationships are very important to maintain. Proponents of affiliative leadership value individuals and their emotions more than tasks and goals. This style places a premium on communication and flexibility within an organization. Affirmative leadership is more likely to be successful in cultures with lower levels of power distance and more focus on individuality.
Democratic	Will only countries with a democratic tradition accept democratic-style leaders? That is far from certain; democratic, inclusive leadership seems to depend more on the situation and the maturity of the leader and followers. If the followers know a lot about the job, they will expect to be consulted. One problem is that a leader brought up in a high power-distance country where bosses make decisions and followers carry out decisions may find it hard to act in a consultative manner, and followers may find it hard to accept responsibility. But that leader must learn how to encourage discussion and accept decisions from subordinates, particularly in situations where no one is the expert and the leader needs "buy in" from followers.

TABLE 8-1 (Continued)

Leadership Style	Leadership Style and Culture
Pacesetting	A pacesetting leader is obsessive about doing things better and faster, and asks much the same of his or her employees. Pacesetters lead by example and see their role as selecting the right people. Cultures that are very high in masculinity often produce more pacesetting leaders, and these do not work well with the more feminine cultures, in Hofstede's terms. But the pacesetting approach can work well irrespective of culture if all employees are self-motivated, highly competent, and need little direction or coordination, such as with R&D groups, consultants, or legal teams.
Coaching	Coaching is thought to be effective in all cultures, though higher power-distance cultures are less likely to expect coaching. Coaching can help an employee improve performance or develop long term strengths. Coaching takes a lot of time but can be very valuable for employee development and engagement, and often improves an organizational climate significantly. Similarly, the style works well when employees realize how cultivating new abilities can help them advance.

CULTURE AND DOING BUSINESS IN AUSTRALIA

Australia has an egalitarian culture, which is reflected by the low power-distance score in Hofstede's model of cultural values. The familiarity of the culture is reflected in the Mick Dundee character made popular by Australian actor Paul Hogan in the *Crocodile Dundee* films. The concept of "mateship," the leader being "one of the boys," was one of the typically Australian leadership dimensions that reflects the high value placed on egalitarianism and a leader's ability to earn respect through his or her skills, not by the office held. This egalitarianism means that Australian employees will commonly call their boss by his or her first name, or sometimes a nickname. Students in Australia also often address professors by their first name, or the short version of their name (like "GB" for Garry Bruton, or "Dave" for David), and would think it pretentious of professors to want to be addressed by their titles. This is the opposite of how it is in Germany, where professors are often called "professor doctor"—"professor" representing the job title and "doctor" representing the academic degree held. Australian leaders are expected to inspire high levels of performance,

as in most countries, but they are expected to do so without giving the impression of using charisma or of not being anything more than "one of the mates."

Mateship also results in Australians being suspicious of those who offer excessive praise. Instead, their focus is on the facts. The focus on mateship also emphasizes an egalitarian approach to decision making or group decision making on many matters. As a result, decision making in Australia can take longer than in other western countries. Australia has about 21 million citizens and a per capita GDP of roughly $30,000 per year. Australia's economy has been one of the strongest in recent years of all the developed economies. It is difficult to say if this is because of the egalitarian culture, but Australian culture and leadership styles are likely influencing business practices in the Asia Pacific region.

Ashkanasy, N. M. (2007). The Australian Enigma. In Chhokar, J., Brodbeck, F.C., & House, R.J. (Eds.), *Culture and Leadership across the World: The GLOBE Book of In-Depth Studies of 25 Societies*, (299–333). Mahwah, NJ: Lawrence Erlbaum Associates.

ADDITIONAL RESOURCES

Ambrose, S.E. 1992. *Band of Brothers: E Company, 506th Regiment, 101st Airborne from Normandy to Hitler's Eagle's Nest.* New York: Simon & Schuster.

Goleman, D., Boyatzis, R., & McKee, A. 2002. *Primal Leadership: Realizing the Power of Emotional Intelligence.* Cambridge, MA: Harvard Business School Press.

Goodwin, D.K. 2005. *Teams of Rivals: The Political Genius of Abraham Lincoln.* New York: Simon & Schuster.

Maxwell, J.C. 2005. *The 360 Degree Leader: Developing Your Influence from Anywhere in the Organization.* Nashville, TN: Nelson Business.

Useem, M. 1999. *The Leadership Moment: Nine True Stories of Triumph and Disaster and Their Lessons for Us All.* New York: Three Rivers Press.

EXERCISES

Opening Vignette Discussion Questions

1. Why do you think there are differences in the theoretical advice offered to the managers going to China and what actually worked?
2. As you think about the potential for developing a major new market for cereal in China, what might be some other domains that may offer similar major-market opportunities that would be related?

DISCUSSION QUESTIONS

1. Discuss what you think an effective leader would be like if you were in Australia. Contrast that with what an effective leader would be like in India.
2. What would be the potential leadership problems a Chinese manager at Lenovo might encounter as he or she moves into a senior management position at the firm's new New York offices, where he or she will work with former IBM employees?
3. If a South American manager is sent to manage a joint venture in Sweden, what would be the potential problems that he or she could encounter in seeking to lead the organization?

IN-CLASS EXERCISES

1. Give examples of effective leaders, particularly in business. Consider leaders at all levels from CEOs to supervisors to sports coaches.
2. What do effective leaders do?
3. What are the main goals of an effective leader in most organizations?
4. Think of two ways a leader can build trust in his or her ability to lead.
5. Recently in Japan, a train driver for one of the big railroad firms stated that he was compelled to undergo 71 days of re-education, which included cleaning trains and writing essays reflecting on his "mistake." What was this serious error the operator was forced to write about? It was overshooting a train platform by two meters. What type of leadership style is this company employing? Do you think it will be effective in Japan? How about in western countries, such as the U.K. or the United States? See the article below to help you on this exercise.

Faiola, A. (2005, November 30). U.S. baseball manager's softer style throws Japan's social order a curve. *The Wall Street Journal (Asia)*, p. 32.

TAKE-HOME EXERCISES

1. Several management scholars have argued that charisma is not enough for someone to be a leader. Explain why they argue this.
2. How could charisma actually hinder a leader from being effective and under what circumstances?
3. Many people from the West would argue that democratic leadership in which the leader gives followers a say in decisions is the preferred leadership style. When would a democratic leadership style be effective? When would it be ineffective?

4. In Japan, China, and many other Asian countries, a tough, autocratic leader is thought to be necessary to motivate the workforce. Many leaders (including managers, coaches, teachers, and even parents) believe that praise to followers should rarely if ever be given. Why do you think this is the case? Do you agree with this approach to leadership and motivation?

SHORT CASE QUESTIONS

Leadership under Changing Circumstances (p. 246)

1. Studying military history is recommended to learn more about issues such as training, strategy, logistics, management, and leadership. What do you think can be learned from a military setting about these three key concepts? Keep in mind that although the military regularly trains to fight, most armed forces actually spend only a small amount of time actually fighting, and in fact face many of the same strategic and managerial problems that all large organizations face.
2. Why did the invasion of Europe in WWII ("D-Day") require a change in the way Easy Company, as described in *Band of Brothers*, was to be led?
3. Why do you think the "telling and yelling" style of Captain Sobel, the commanding officer of Easy Company, would not have worked well under conditions of combat? Don't most military officers just yell out orders anyway?
4. What type of leadership style would be necessary under combat conditions?
5. Why do you think the regimental commander (Captain Sobel's boss, Colonel Sink) was unaware of Sobel's failings as a leader? What measures was he relying upon to judge Easy's performance? What does this say about how managers should assess the performance of their units and the fitness of the leaders they appoint?

9

DECISION MAKING

Overview

This chapter examines decision making in the international management arena. As has been demonstrated throughout the text, managing a business becomes more complex as the firm internationalizes, not only due to greater physical distance between various parts of the firm, but also because of the cultural distance. Decisions that are relatively easy in firms that are located in a single country may become very difficult in an international setting. This chapter will examine the following topics:

* Models of decision making, including the rational decision-making model and the positive decision-making model

* Current decision-making concerns, including decision heuristics and biases including loss framing and escalating commitment

* Effective decision making in international business

* Group decision making and the problem of groupthink

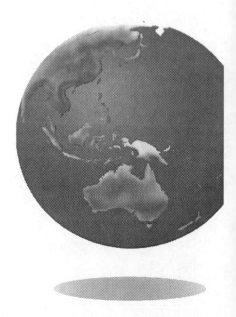

OCEAN PARK IN HONG KONG

Ocean Park is an amusement park in Hong Kong. With the opening of Disneyland in the Hong Kong market, it was widely assumed that Ocean Park would be driven out of business. Disney is a well known, global theme park operator with deep pockets and an excellent reputation. Ocean Park was an older park with crumbling facilities and it was losing money. Its future was not bright.

The Hong Kong government did something unusual at that point. It asked Allan Zeman, a Canadian-born businessman well known in Hong Kong as the developer of the Lan Kwai Fung entertainment section of Hong Kong, to take over Ocean Park's management even though he had never been there. The Lan Kwai Fung district includes bars and restaurants that are situated in what previously was a red light district. Zeman was able to come in and help to develop the area, which is now the major area of entertainment for young professionals in Hong Kong.

Hong Kong, a city of 7 million people, has proven able to support the two major amusement parks. Disney has largely taken the model for managing their parks in the United States and applied it to its park in Hong Kong. Decision making about how to run the Hong Kong park was often centered in the U.S. and only limited adaptations were made. For example, the entry to the Hong Kong park is the same U.S. main street that appears in all Disney parks. Some of the adaptations that Disney did implement have not turned out well. A case in point is interpreting the safety consciousness of the people in Hong Kong as a reason to slow down the rides. This only made the rides less thrilling for teenagers and young adults visiting from both mainland China and Hong Kong.

Zeman, despite being born in Canada, has been making decisions for the park in a manner more like a native of Hong Kong. He incorporated more Hong Kong people into decisions to revamp Ocean Park., and the decisions at Ocean Park have fit better with the local people's desires. For example, typical in Chinese culture, Hong Kong is very family oriented. Ocean Park offers grandparents free entry on certain days, based on numbers in their citizen identity cards. The grandparents then bring their grandchildren to the park and spend a lot of money on them. This promotion also fits with the Chinese interest in lucky numbers. Notice the next time you eat a fortune cookie at a Chinese restaurant in the United States—there will likely be lucky numbers on it.

Zeman has also been able to incorporate unique things into Ocean Park that may seem unusual in the U.S. but that fit well in Hong Kong. He has been able to do this not only from his own knowledge of the Hong Kong environment but also by allowing people from Hong Kong to contribute to decision making. For example, Halloween has become a popular holiday in Hong Kong. The city, from its British roots, has celebrated Halloween to some extent for a number of years. But Zeman has incorporated into this Western celebration other things that are unique to Chinese culture, such as images of paper dolls that are believed to travel with the deceased to the next world. Having individuals dressed up as these dolls and walking around in the park is a unique aspect that only comes from decision making that is sensitive to local culture and traditions. As a result of Zeman's effective strategizing and marketing, attendance at Ocean Park over the last four years has increased by over one and a half million, and the park is in a solid financial position once again, in spite of the new competition from Hong Kong Disneyland.

Smooth operator. (2007, October 20). *The Economist*, p. 88.

Individuals make hundreds of decisions every day: when to get up in the morning, what to eat for breakfast, what to wear for the day, and, if it's a workday, how to get to work. Some of these decisions are interdependent; for example, on a workday you will pick clothes appropriate for the workplace, not for the beach. When a person gets to work, the choices increase and become more complex. Decisions regarding who to use for suppliers or how to market a product are complex and often must balance a myriad of consequences and constraints. Many of the decisions managers make will be routine, but others will not. This chapter will focus both on the nature of the decisions themselves and on the process by which they are made. The chapter will also focus on how to avoid decision-making problems. Decision-making problems often can be traced back to a lack of adequate preparation, reflected in the information that is sought (or ignored), how that information is evaluated, and how possible alternatives are assessed. These mistakes tend to be systematic (i.e., they are

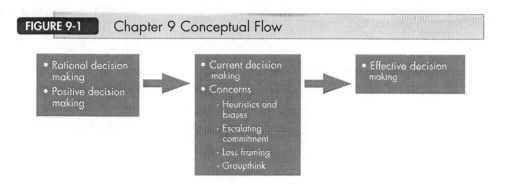

FIGURE 9-1   Chapter 9 Conceptual Flow

consistent and to a certain degree predictable), and because of this they can also be reduced. This is important because decision errors such as wasteful investments or missed opportunities can be very costly.

The higher an individual rises in management, the greater the number of difficult decisions that demand attention, so there is a need to understand the impact of contingencies such as level of responsibility in the organization and its impact on decision making. In international firms particularly, there is also a need to understand any additional complexities and how these complexities impact decision making. This chapter will explore these international dimensions to decision making.

The chapter begins by describing a model broadly known as the rational model of decision making. This model is then examined more critically, by identifying the cognitive limitations that impede such "textbook" approaches to decision making. The latter part of the chapter explores the forms and levels of employee involvement in decision making, including a detailed discussion of self-directed work teams and socio-technical systems. Finally, we discuss the potential benefits and limitations of employee involvement and identify some cultural forces at work. Figure 9-1 summarizes the chapter flow.

RATIONAL MODEL OF DECISION MAKING

The historical foundation for the examination of decision making is what is generally called the rational model of decision making. This model dominated thinking on decision making from the 1800s to the mid-1950s, and is still commonly employed by many individuals. In this model, decision makers determine the appropriate decision criteria, such as price and quality, and then assign weights or levels of importance to them. Different people may place different weights on a criterion because they may value that attribute differently. A manager will then try to rank each decision as to importance and determine the optimal choice, based on these weighted criteria. Decisions under this model are seen as being logically sound, uninfluenced by emotion or other non-rational factors.

The rational decision model has had a major impact on many aspects of business management; most large organizations try to employ numerous decision and operations management tools in their decision making. For example, a central tenet of the rational decision-making model is that there is logical consistency across decisions, regardless of the manner in which available choices are presented. This assumption still lies at the heart of a number of widely used models in finance and economics, such as game theory,[i] which is used to evaluate how

---

FIGURE 9-2   Rational Decision-Making Model

* Define the problem.
* Identify the key decision criteria (based on values).
* Allocate relative weights to the criteria.
* Determine the decision style.
* List solutions and develop any alternatives.
* Evaluate the alternatives.
* Select the choice that maximizes utility based on the weighted criteria of all the feasible alternatives.
* Mobilize resources.

---

different competitors may act and which firms will survive or thrive. In many financial-related businesses, firms employ game theory as the foundation for planning, partly because of the availability of valid and reliable data about the risk and return of assets such as firm stocks or the price of commodities. Thus, the rational decision model provides a useful basis of decision making, not only because it is still used in practice when data are available, but also because it allows us to contrast other decision models with it. We will next discuss each of the component parts of rational decision making in depth. The rational model of decision making is shown in Figure 9-2.

Problem Identification

Problem
Arises when there is a discrepancy between the present situation and the optimal outcome.

Problem identification is the first step in decision making and is arguably the most important. A **problem** arises when there is a discrepancy between the present situation and the optimal outcome. This deviation can be a symptom of more fundamental difficulties within the organization. Therefore, we need to ensure we identify a problem correctly in order to choose the best solution. The decision process is directed toward changing the root causes of difficulties so that the symptoms are reduced or eliminated. This should also lead to the development of decision criteria by which the decision can be weighted.

Appropriate Decision Style

Programmed decision
A decision that follows standard operating procedures. There is no need to explore alternative solutions because the optimal solution has already been identified and documented.

The second step is to determine the most appropriate decision style. A decision maker must choose between a programmed decision or a non-programmed decision. A **programmed decision** follows standard operating procedures, and there is no need to explore alternative solutions because the optimal solution has already been identified and documented. For example, when customers call a General Electric customer service center, operators key the problem into a computer database of 1.5 million issues, and the database provides the best solution. In contrast, new, complex, or abstract problems require non-programmed decisions. In these cases, decision makers must search for alternatives and possibly craft a unique solution. As problems reappear, however, programmed decision routines are formed and knowledge becomes more codified and explicit. In this respect, programmed decisions drive out non-programmed ones. Programmed decisions are faster, more predictable, and routine, and usually do not need an expert to handle them, which lowers costs and enables a firm to serve more customers.[ii]

List of Solutions

The third step in the rational decision model is to develop a list of possible solutions. This usually begins by searching for ready-made, already proven solutions to existing problems. If decision makers cannot find an acceptable ready-made solution, then they would normally try to design a custom-made solution or modify an existing one. All these solutions must first be added to the final list.

Choose Best Alternative

The fourth step in the rational decision-making model involves choosing the best alternative. In a purely rational process, this would involve identifying all the main selection criteria that can help to rate all alternatives. The selection criteria must be ranked by importance and given a weighted rating such as from 1 to 10 or some other scale; then each alternative's total value is calculated from the ratings and criteria weights.

Mobilize Resources

In the fifth step, decision makers must rally employees and prepare sufficient resources to make and implement the decision; a decision that cannot be implemented is just a speculative exercise. Firms must consider the motivation, ability, and role perceptions of employees implementing the solution, as well as situational contingencies to facilitate its implementation. Part of this last step entails evaluating whether the gap has narrowed between "what is" and "what ought to be." Ideally, this information should be based on systematic benchmarks and feedback, so that relevant results and reactions are objective and easily observed.

Problems with Rational Decision Model

Extensive research from cognition, social psychology and behavioral finance has shown that people's decisions are strongly affected by the nature of the data informing a decision and the setting in which that decision is made.[iii] For example, research has shown that it is much easier for a decision maker to cancel a failing project if that person is not the one who approved the project in the first place.[iv] As a result, the rational decision model itself is now recognized as insufficient in describing people's behavior under many conditions. In fact, although organizations want to employ rational, systematic approaches to decision making, particularly with major investments, research suggests that the rational model may be more of an exception than the rule.[v] And when you introduce additional variables such as cross-cultural interaction within an international setting, additional contingencies arise that the rational model cannot address. Thus, while the rational model of decision making is still taught in economics and statistics textbooks as a **normative model** (how things ought to be), it is now recognized that it is not the **positive model** (how people actually behave) of decision making we now commonly recognize in management.

Normative model of decision making
Decision making using a rational model (i.e., how things ought to be).

Positive model of decision making
Actual, day-to-day decision-making model, not idealized.

POSITIVE MODEL OF DECISION MAKING

While we now know that decision making often does not follow the prescribed methods laid out in the rational model, the steps in that model still provide a useful means for understanding how actual practice deviates from the rational model, shedding light on what actually occurs in decision making. In the next

GREATER INTERNATIONALIZATION OF FIRMS AND DECISION MAKING

Chinese firms typically allocate a given percentage of their budget each year to entertainment. This is a throwback to the time when Chinese firms were all state-owned entities and the government ensured that services were provided to employees. Today these funds are typically used both for employees and visiting business people.

One firm that did quite a lot of entertaining was a traditional and well-established Chinese organization. The firm had brought in many foreigners from the West and also had many foreign clients visiting. A high percentage of its entertainment funds were typically spent on these visitors, but some was also spent to offer periodic employee dinners. During a review of how to spend money on employee and visitor activities, the senior managers argued that money should be spent as in the past, that is, on regular lunches, teas, and Chinese-style banquets for both employees and visitors. "That is what the people expect," intoned one senior manager.

But the firm now had young managers from China who had gone to school outside of China as well as a few Western managers. These individuals argued that the younger employees and foreign visitors did not value the regular lunches and banquets; indeed they were complaining that the company had little meeting space, no outside areas to sit in, no coffee room with comfortable seating, and so forth. A local coffee shop had offered to set up a small stand on the company's large premises but this would have required additional outside seating. When the managers reported this to the senior managers they were very surprised, almost shocked. The question they kept asking was, "Why would anyone want to sit outside at lunchtime? How can they have a proper hot meal outside?" One Western manager answered, "They just want to have a sandwich and a coffee and take a break at lunch." The senior manager responded, "Who wants to eat sandwiches everyday? Sandwiches are not a proper lunch. And anyway," he added, "they should be drinking tea and not coffee!"

The company still has not established any break facilities or coffee room, let alone an outside seating area. At this Chinese company, lunch is thought of only in terms of Chinese noodles and dim sum under bright fluorescent lights; anything else, like having a sandwich outside or just a coffee and muffin is not a "proper lunch." The values of the senior executives and their projection made it difficult for them to understand those of the younger employees and foreigners in the organization. Decision making in this setting was difficult because it was hard for the leaders to relate to (much less understand) what the younger and more Westernized employees wanted.

section, we will go back through the steps to look at when and how we now commonly alter the rational model based on our understanding of how decision making actually works.

Problem Identification

Problems, as with opportunities, do not publicly announce themselves. They are recognized and ultimately defined by the decision maker. However, people are neither perfectly efficient nor objective, so problems are often misdiagnosed and opportunities overlooked. One of the key issues in identifying problems is the decision maker's bounded rationality.

Herbert Simon,[vi] in his administrative theory of individual decision making, describes the process that managers (and likely the majority of us) use to make decisions as **bounded rationality**. According to Simon, managers make choices based on simplified and subjective sets of choices. People do not have the ability to process all of the information and analyze all of the possible solutions to a problem. Thus, they employ a means of dealing with this information overload that allows them to narrow problems and possible choices down to something they can process in a reasonable manner. This is why giving a customer or other decision maker too many choices can cause them to freeze up and become unable to make any decision at all. The outcome, however, is that in most cases a manager will make a decision based on limited information and a reduced choice set. A boundedly rational approach to decision making is convenient under some circumstances—how many people have time to evaluate every toothpaste on the

Bounded rationality
According to Herbert Simon, people do not have the ability to process all of the information and solutions that face them. This inability leads them to limit their problems and solutions.

market when they go to the store to buy toothpaste? They make a choice based on very limited information search and evaluation. But for major decisions, particularly ones involving risk and strategizing about the future, boundedly rational decision making can lead to suboptimal decisions because a certain amount of useful information and choices are necessarily ignored. Bounded rationality affects not only the identification of a problem but, ultimately, also the identification of solutions to that problem. Later in the chapter we will see several examples of this.

Appropriate Decision Style

The rational model argues that there are programmed and non-programmed decisions. Programmed decisions are those that largely follow a formula—for example, last month a firm's sales were X, so this month it knows to order X + 1. The impact of bounded rationality is greatest when trying to make non-programmed decisions, and can be viewed along a continuum of rationality. At one end are the programmed types of decisions, and here the rational model is strong and the impact of bounded rationality is limited.

But at the other end of the continuum are non-programmed decisions, where managers must tailor each decision to a particular situation. It is at this end of the continuum that the potential impact of bounded rationality is greatest, because the decision-making procedure here is based on the values, beliefs, attitudes, and behavioral patterns of the decision makers rather than on a strictly rational model. It is important to note, too, that the impact of values, beliefs, and attitudes on decision making is particularly problematic for firms with diverse international settings.

In reality, most firms will have a mixture of both programmed and non-programmed decisions. Some are truly unique and every manager must make a decision based on the reality they perceive. But other decisions may be of a nature where a rational model will work well.

List of Solutions

Upon recognizing that a problem exists, a manager must generate solutions. The key to generating such solutions is gathering relevant information. The psychologist Carl Jung suggested that people have two primary modes of gathering information (i.e., of perceiving): sensing and intuition.[vii] Individuals whose primary mode is sensing use their five senses to gather empirical evidence about a situation. In contrast, individuals who use intuition to assemble (in their minds) the relevant details will depend heavily on their own judgment and less on specific empirical evidence or experience. "Sensors" rely on facts and empirical evidence and are often more inductive, whereas intuitive people rely more heavily on images, emotion and logic and are often more deductive, drawing heavily on certain basic principles from which they prefer not to deviate.

In providing potential solutions, bounded rational decision makers tend to focus on alternatives that are "good enough" rather than on finding the best possible solution. In other words, they engage in **satisficing** (rather than maximizing) by choosing the first "good enough" choice that comes along early in the process. Satisficing occurs because it is difficult to identify all the possible alternatives, and because information about available alternatives is imperfect or ambiguous. It also occurs because decision makers tend to evaluate alternatives sequentially. What constitutes a "good enough" solution depends on the availability of acceptable alternatives. Standards rise when acceptable alternatives are found easily, and they fall when few are available. As in the case of the toothpaste example above, when making smaller purchases (and even some big ones), people will often choose the first pretty good alternative that comes along. They will not make an exhaustive search of all the alternatives. Thus, the satisficing approach may result in people accepting a suboptimal decision in order to save time.

Satisficing
Alternatives that are acceptable or "good enough," rather than the best possible solutions.

PHARMACEUTICAL FIRMS AND IDENTIFYING THE PROBLEM

As stated in Chapter 4, some of the most profitable firms in the world are pharmaceutical firms. These firms must consider current scientific fact while remaining open to new discoveries in approaches to treatment medical conditions.

Physicians treating common peptic ulcers long believed that stress-produced stomach acid was the main cause. Ulcers were thus treated by bland diets, medicines to reduce stomach acid, and if necessary, a difficult and complicated abdominal surgery. Few challenged the status quo, and powerful medical specialists—gastroenterologists and surgeons—controlled the treatment regimen for ulcers.

This paradigm went unchallenged for decades until Dr. Barry Marshall, a family physician in Australia, and a colleague, Dr. Robin Warren, discovered that a bacterial infection was often the cause of peptic ulcers. For years Dr. Marshall argued with the medical establishment and requested funding to study this bacteria, to no avail. He produced data showing the relation between this bacteria and ulcers, but

few physicians took note. Finally, in desperation, Dr. Marshall drank a beaker full of a solution of H. pylori bacteria in front of some colleagues at a medical conference. For a week after he drank the H. pylori, nothing happened. Then, suddenly, Dr. Marshall became sick to his stomach and within a week, he was ill. A colleague performed an endoscopy by inserting a tiny videocamera down Marshall's throat to inspect his stomach. He found the telltale signs of an ulcer: the redness and inflammation of gastritis. Armed with this "discovery," and his finding of H. pylori in nearly all the ulcer patients he had biopsied, Marshall began traveling to conventions of gastroenterologists. After his exuberant speeches announcing that ulcers were caused by bacteria, he was practically laughed off the stage by the specialists. How could bacteria cause ulcers? It took years and years of research in the face of very strong opposition from physicians who would later report that they ignored the data (selective perception), but later found it to be accurate. Their problem was they

simply could not believe that something as common as the H. pylori bacillus caused ulcers, so it had to be something else. The pharmaceutical firms were simply indifferent—more money was to be made in selling antacids and other medicines than a two-week course of antibiotics to kill H. pylori.

Finally, the data did win out, although it was first widely reported in the U.S. tabloid *The National Enquirer*, of all places. In 2005, Drs. Marshall and Warren were awarded the Nobel Prize in medicine for their work on peptic ulcers. Most peptic ulcers would neither have been cured nor the number of surgeries significantly reduced had it not been for these doctors' ability to look beyond standard practice and belief and identify the correct problem. If the medical profession had continued to search for solutions to ulcers only in the area of acid reduction and hormone treatments, the H. pylori bacillus—the real cause of most peptic ulcers—would likely never have been identified.

O'Reilly, B. (1997, June 9). Why doctors aren't curing ulcers. *Fortune*, pp.100–112.

In terms of culture, it is important to remember that different societies vary in how they process information. Recall the discussion of high-context and low-context societies in Chapter 2. Individuals in high-context cultures, such as Arab countries in the Middle East and North Africa, rely much on who is providing the information, their position, and how they present it. Those from low-context societies, such as the United States or Canada, tend to rely more on facts and empirical evidence, though almost anyone can be moved by expert opinion to some extent.[viii] It is relatively easy, then, to imagine how difficult it may be for a firm with operations in both North America and the Middle East to generate potential solutions that both groups agree are useful and to present them in a way that both groups can analyze.

Choose Best Alternative

Evidence-based information search
A process of information search and decision making that does not start with a presumed decision and seeks to evaluate a range of evidence and challenge the emerging solution as it is gradually shaped.

Verdict-based information search
A process of information search and decision making that starts with the presumed answer to the decision and proceeds to only seek out information that confirms the initial verdict or decision.

In choosing the best alternative, an important factor is whether the manager relies on an **evidence-based information search** or a **verdict-based information search** for decision making. Although a manager may be characterized as a "sensing" decision maker, preferring empirical evidence over intuition, these styles of information search are very important in determining what kind of evidence is actually sought out and applied to a decision about the problem. The key difference in the two types of search is the extent to which the decision maker relies on preconceived notions to search for information and frame alternatives. To illustrate the difference between evidence-based and verdict-based approaches, think about the joke where two economists are walking down the street and spot a $20 bill on the sidewalk. The first economist says, "Look, a $20 note. Let's pick it up." The second replies, "It can't possibly be a $20 note, because if it were really a $20 note it would not be lying on the sidewalk. Someone would have picked it up by now." One economist sees the money and wants it. But the other has a preconceived idea that a $20 bill could never be left on the street and so rejects the idea and does not investigate further—using verdict-based information search and decision making, he already knows the bill cannot be real and does not investigate further (losing out on the money in the process).

As another example, consider a decision-making exercise familiar to most of us: a jury used in a court case. Most of the jury may enter the deliberation room "believing" the defendant is guilty and as a result, employ a verdict-based information search where they primarily seek out information (courtroom evidence) that confirms their initial guilty verdict. Such a jury will emphasize evidence that confirms the defendant's guilt; any other evidence that might throw doubt on that guilt is ignored or its source criticized.[2] In contrast, juries that keep an open mind evaluate the evidence as it is made available, and are not afraid to consider evidence that they disagree with or find disconcerting are using an evidence-based approach for their information search and eventual decision making. Juries that use a verdict-based approach able to move more quickly and do not get hung up on technicalities. But they also can overlook important information and are more prone to errors in judgment. People define problems or opportunities based on their perceptions, values, and assumptions. These selective attention mechanisms screen out relevant information, and the quality of the problem definition is lost.

The verdict-based approach to information gathering and decision making creates a *confirming-evidence bias*. This bias leads people to seek out information that supports their existing instincts or points of view while avoiding information that fails to support their beliefs. The confirming-evidence bias not only affects where we go to collect evidence but also how we interpret the evidence we do receive, leading us to give too much weight to supporting information and too little to conflicting information, and even preventing us from searching out information that might challenge our beliefs. It is important to the decision process to seek out a range of information and to avoid premature judgments that will cut short the information search process when useful information for the decision process is still available. That is why it is a good idea to ask people to write down some ideas before coming to a meeting where a key issue is to be discussed and thus avoid being prematurely influenced by those at the meeting.

Moreover, employees, clients, and others with vested interests can influence a decision maker's perceptions and bias them toward a premature decision. Research on strategy has shown how managers with the same type of training and background will often search in one area for a solution and ignore other areas (a problem we will revisit when we discuss the problem of groupthink later in the chapter). For example, the top managers of former Fortune 500 minicomputer maker Digital Equipment Corporation (DEC) all had similar training, had worked as minicomputer engineers for years, and were recognized as leaders in their particular domain. When desktop personal computers started to enter the market, DEC leadership continued to look for minicomputer-related solutions to some of the problems that PCs were starting to be used to solve. DEC's chairman

---

[2]Some students may have seen the classic 1957 film *12 Angry Men*. In that movie, 11 out of 12 jurors are convinced the defendant is guilty of murder and state that verdict out loud to each other, right at the beginning of their deliberations, before even giving their views of the evidence. In fact most of the jurors do not even want to hear about evidence that the defendant is innocent and ridicule the single juror (played by Henry Fonda) who insists on considering all of the available evidence, regardless of its source.

and founder, Ken Olsen, famously stated in 1977, "There is no reason for any individual to have a computer in his home."[ix] As a result, DEC rapidly fell behind microcomputer pioneers such as Apple and IBM, and was unable to participate in the desktop revolution, although it had the engineering talent, resources, and customer relations to be a major player in that business. It was stymied in part by the "verdict" that microcomputers were not that useful, minicomputers were much more powerful, and computing was best done at a central location with computer power piped out to users over wires. In a final irony, DEC was bought out in 1998 by one of the PC companies, Compaq Computer, and much of DEC's technology and product lines were discontinued.

Once a verdict-based decision maker has made up his or her mind, he or she will not examine any evidence that could challenge a conclusion or improve the decision. When confronted with that evidence, they will immediately discount it as unreliable or inapplicable because it came from some particular source with which they seldom agree (though they may never have taken the time to really read or listen to that source), and not because of some concrete concern about its validity.

Too often, verdict-based decision making shows up in organizational settings. Decision makers typically screen out a number of items from consideration to save time. Such screening of evidence is a particular problem internationally, where there is often greater diversity of information. This diversity of information can lead to potentially confounding evidence that the manager will likely ignore or downplay because the bearer of that information is not an insider in the corporation but from one of its distant units.[x] Yet it might be useful inside information about a local market that the headquarters should consider.

Research shows that while evidence-based decision making, which employs a broader information search, is much more likely to lead to better decisions, verdict-based decision making is still very common.[xi] If everyone in a team follows verdict-based decision making and becomes biased in the same direction in this manner, a group-level phenomena called *groupthink* is likely to arise.[xii] Such uncritical consensus thinking is the source of many serious decision errors and suboptimal decision making.[xiii] Groupthink will be considered later in the chapter. The vignette about the Columbia space shuttle accident illustrates the problem of verdict-based information search and decision making.

When diverse opinions are squelched and useful data are ignored when they are presented, important alternatives will go unexamined, and the probability of good decisions is reduced.[xiv] There are several things that firms and individuals can do to help overcome these problems:

* Always check to ensure people are examining a range of evidence with equal rigor.
* Do not lock out otherwise reliable information simply because you do not like its source. Check the information itself for its validity.
* Avoid the tendency to accept confirming evidence without question, particularly when it is from a source that you like.
* Seek evidence that *challenges* your ideas, particularly initial points of view and key assumptions.
* Try to build counterarguments yourself and ask for challenges and comments.
* Give someone in the group charged with making a decision or evaluating a proposal the role of **devil's advocate**,[3] to argue against the decision you are contemplating and challenge its assumptions.

---

[3] The term "devil's advocate" (*advocatus diaboli* in Latin) comes from the Roman Catholic Church. It was a temporary position assigned to someone during the church's process of selecting candidates for sainthood. During the canonization process, the devil's advocate was charged to argue against the sainthood of the candidate. This was to ensure that all the evidence was considered regarding the life of the prospective saint, and that any negatives would be brought to light.

COLUMBIA SPACE SHUTTLE AND DECISION MAKING

Like the earlier Challenger space shuttle, the last Columbia space shuttle mission ended in disaster. During its launch in January 2003, foam insulation debris hit the shuttle, creating a hole in the left wing. Although a couple of NASA engineers suspected the damage to be potentially serious, no one was sure, and thus nothing was done about it, not even figuring out the extent of the wing's damage. When the shuttle's orbiter re-entered Earth's atmosphere, it broke up because of the extreme heat and fire on the wing. Columbia's failure is an interesting and tragic example of verdict-based information search. Post-flight investigations confirmed what the engineers had suspected: the left wing had been damaged by foam insulation that had broken off from the shuttle during takeoff and smashed a hole in the wing.

During the two-week period from Columbia's takeoff to its expected re-entry, top managers of the Mission Management Team (MMT) ignored requests from lower-level engineering staff that the Department of Defense be asked to use its spy satellites to photograph potentially damaged areas of the shuttle. The managers could not believe that the foam could have caused any damage, and they refused to consider investigating the problem.

In trying to understand how these disasters came about, consider the following exchange between a Columbia disaster investigator and the MMT chairwoman:

Investigator: "As a manager, how do you seek out dissenting opinions?"
MMT Chairwoman: "Well, when I hear about them..."
Investigator: "By their very nature you may not have heard about them... What techniques do you use to get them? That is, how do you encourage some dissent or questioning of assumptions and plans?"

The chairwoman didn't have an answer.[xv]

When the evidence collected by the Columbia Accident Investigation Board had been sifted through, it became clear that the team had had an opportunity to make a different decision that would have improved the crew's chances of surviving. The team leaders had been asked on different occasions to permit certain members to collect the information they needed to make a reasonable estimate of the shuttle's safety. Team leaders had been advised that the foam might have inflicted enough damage to cause "burn-through"—heat burning through the protective tiles and into the shuttle's fuselage—when the shuttle re-entered the Earth's atmosphere. The possibility was raised that the debris damage might have been severe. And yet the MMT as a whole never came close to making the right decision, or to even seeking out the potentially available evidence. Though many mistakes were made in the decision process, the one that stands out is the verdict-based decision that the breakaway foam probably wouldn't cause any damage, and even if it did, nothing could be done about it, so no further information about the foam strike would be pursued. Unofficially, some of the team's engineers did develop plans to determine how to save the astronauts if there was severe damage to the shuttle's orbiter. Yet the verdict-based information search made by the head of the mission management team stood, and the opportunity to attempt to save Columbia's crew was lost.

BETTER DECISION MAKING

A number of strategies to help managers overcome these problems have been developed within the context of the positive model of decision making. These include creating an early warning system, implementing systems for systematic evaluation, establishing decision support systems, and instituting scenario planning.

Early Warning Systems

A manager can help to avoid the issues discussed above by taking the time to identify in advance any critical issues that could potentially confront the firm. These investigations can be made through discussions with a wide variety of managers within the organization. The firm can then institute an early warning system to identify a problem if it starts to occur. Thus, the manager would not have to be on constant alert to pick out the problem from the constant stream of information. Instead, a system would be in place to help bring the situation to the manager's attention.

To illustrate, it may be difficult given the quantity of data coming into modern organizations to quickly spot a problem in a firm's major product line or to adequately forecast the year-end profit figures. But the firm can use specific warning mechanisms to alert management to potential problems. For example, customer satisfaction ratings falling below a certain threshold or a drop off in repeat business could signal a quality control or service problem, while costs increasing above a predetermined threshold could indicate declining profit margins. Some of these figures are not readily available from typical financial data, or may be difficult to pinpoint, particularly in the case of cost accounting data on allocated costs. Such warning thresholds can be derived from past experience or from pre-set goals for major stakeholders (customers, shareholders, employees, and so forth). The effectiveness of these early warning systems is only as good as their development. However, if carefully planned, alerts can spur an organization to action and prevent conditions from deteriorating further.

Some firms engage in wide data search and data mining to help identify potential issues, using computer programs to search through large databases and organize this information into meaningful trends. Data mining minimizes the perceptual problems that occur when manually looking for trends and patterns in mountains of data.

Systems for Systematic Evaluation

Firms can create processes to ensure systematic evaluation of certain critical information and key forecasts. For example, it is possible for a firm to identify in advance and systematically analyze alternatives for some given problems on a weekly, monthly, or quarterly basis. Typically, such systems are driven by human input (computer-driven systems will be discussed below). To illustrate, when a firm needs to select a job applicant, a systematic evaluation is required that would include (1) identifying the relevant factors against which applicants are judged, (2) measuring applicants on each factor, (3) weighting the importance of each factor, and (4) computing an overall score for each applicant based on the weights and ratings for each factor. (The process for the selection of job candidates will be discussed in detail in Chapter 12, Human Resources Management.)

To illustrate further, Dow Chemical relies on systematic evaluation when deciding which information technology projects to pursue. The company has a cross-functional committee that evaluates each proposal using a point system that factors in the quality of the vendors, the logic of the proposal, and Dow's technical and organizational readiness for change. This process tends to minimize satisficing limitations in the decision process. It also aids information processing because the calculations are systematic rather than based on intuition.

Decision Support Structures

A complementary strategy to systematic evaluation is to create decision support systems to guide the decision-making process. Decision support systems are computer-based programs that guide people through the decision-making process; systems for systematic evaluation are typically human driven instead of computer driven. For example, one firm with which the authors are quite familiar—software developer Cerner Corporation—uses a case-based reasoning process at its help desk. Callers' problems or questions are entered into the system in simple English, and the system replies with questions and eventually solutions to the problems presented. These solutions are organized by topic and made available to all employees online. This decision support system cut in half Cerner's backlog of unresolved client issues and increased customer satisfaction ratings to high levels. Notice that this decision support software turns a seemingly non-programmed decision into a programmed decision. It helps employees identify the problem systematically and search out past solutions that then point to a ready-made solution without the need to evaluate alternatives.

Scenario Planning

Another method that firms use to ensure that they have fully analyzed all potential problems is to employ scenario planning. This method requires a firm to think about what would happen if a significant environmental condition changed, and what the organization should do to anticipate and react to such an outcome. A good question to ask is, "Where are our future revenue and profits coming from, particularly if something important to our firm changes significantly?" Scenario planning explores potential problems and opportunities and asks firms to think about difficult circumstances and competitive challenges. Firms such as the Dutch/British firm Shell Oil and Huawei in China are well known for employing this method to enable them to better think through their assumptions and develop two or three alternative "what if" scenarios associated with major decisions or strategic plans. The advantage of scenario thinking is that the importance of one or two key criteria such as the cost of a raw material or the price of a substitute product can be clearly identified and properly dealt with. See the Ethics Box for ways in which global warming can be thought of in terms of different scenarios with broadly framed costs and benefits of major decisions.

DECISION MAKING ON GLOBAL WARMING

The best science available today on possible global warming scenarios shows that though some causes are natural, various human and industrial activities contribute to global warming. Decision makers who contribute to government policy on this issue must determine the most relevant factors needed to frame the decision making to slow global warming or mitigate its effects. One method being considered is a tax to reduce carbon emissions—thus reducing possible global warming. With this tax, society will sacrifice wealth today, and probably some in the future (called a "welfare loss" by economists) in return for the future benefits of less global warming and fewer associated problems and costs. But to properly make this decision, first it is essential to have a reasonable idea of what the costs would be of global warming if it is left unmanaged, and what the costs would be of stopping it or slowing it down significantly.

The challenge in making assessments about the costs of global warming is that changes in climate set off a complicated set of feedback effects on weather and the environment. Some of these will tend to magnify global warming, yet some will also reduce it. For example, more carbon dioxide should lead to faster plant growth; this pulls CO_2 out of the atmosphere and therefore reduces global warming. But as the atmosphere heats up, polar ice caps melt, causing rising waters and further warming the planet. The list of potential feedback effects is very long, and many effects are interrelated. Because global warming's outcomes are essentially unknown, it is very difficult to assign accurate probabilities, leaving scientists to guess at feedbacks and other long-term outcomes.

These uncertainties are what makes forecasting the climate and determining likely costs of global warming difficult. Estimates of the impact of doubling CO_2 in the atmosphere with no feedback effects is about a 1 degree Celsius increase in temperature—a very manageable increase. But a more likely scenario (with some hypothesized feedbacks included) from the United Nations Intergovernmental Panel on Climate Change (IPCC) argues that a doubling of CO_2 will more likely result in about a 3 degree Celsius increase in temperature over the next century. The current IPCC consensus forecast is that, under a fairly reasonable decades-long modeling project by the Yale School of Forestry & Environmental Studies and Department of Economics, this amount of warming should result in minor net average global economic costs through the year 2100. Larger negative impacts are predicted in poorer tropical areas, while large northern landmass regions such as Russia, North America, and Northern Europe are projected to benefit. The continental United States and China are projected to experience roughly break-even net impacts. Only if temperatures continued to grow well beyond this level would high costs be incurred. This would lead to potentially costly climate changes that would be felt in the twenty-second and twenty-third centuries, although by a much wealthier and more technologically advanced society. According to the most recent IPCC Summary for Policymakers, a higher end 4 degree Celsius increase in temperatures would cause greater economic losses of 1 to 5 percent of global GDP.

Many advocates of strict global measures to reduce carbon emissions present the issue in terms of the avoidance of costs associated with global warming of about 3 percent of global GDP. This benefit (cost savings) would be realized maybe one hundred or more years later—by future and much wealthier generations. But these rather modest cost savings would justify only very mild abatement of carbon emissions, and there is current thought arguing that this goal can be more productively achieved by innovative firms and entrepreneurs, sometimes in partnership with governments, rather than by large tax increases. That is, the costs of a new tax regime seem higher than the long term benefits, particularly if innovation and incentives to innovate through venture capital and entrepreneurship are downplayed by policymakers and discouraged by much higher taxes. Proponents of more modest efforts to slow global warming also point out that by slowing down economic growth by one percentage point, as the more aggressive carbon taxes would, world economic growth would be greatly reduced in the long run. For example, this reduction would mean the difference between a society that

ETHICS

(Continued)

ETHICS

is four times wealthier than today compared to a society that would otherwise grow sixteen times richer in a 100 years' time. They argue that the much richer society will have many more financial and technological resources to deal with global warming problems.

But costs of global warming are not isolated to small (or even big) future costs associated with managing higher temperatures and sea levels. There is a possibility of more specific climate catastrophes, such as the shutdown of the Gulf Stream or large sea level rises, although accurate probabilities of such events are nearly impossible to assign. Advocates of strict global warming control, who advocate rapid carbon abatement, contend that the downside risks are so catastrophic that we should pay any price to avoid any chance of their occurrence, a concept known as the

Precautionary Principle. It is difficult (some would argue impossible) to determine the probability of events that have never occurred and that have very complex causal mechanisms. If it were possible to determine the probability of such catastrophic events, rational decision analysis could be used to justify the expenditure of large sums to avoid those events.[xvi] For now, policymakers have to weigh the costs of slowing global warming against the significantly reduced economic growth that would ensue given the more aggressive carbon tax and related proposals to determine if the world can live with a slowly warming climate, at least for the time being while technologies are developed to address the problem more fully. Thus, there are rich issues on both sides of this important issue that need to be considered.

CURRENT CONCERNS IN DECISION MAKING

In addition to information search and processing problems, there have arisen a number of more current concerns regarding decision making in organizations. These include heuristics and biases, escalation of commitment, loss framing, and groupthink. Each of these will be examined in turn. See Figure 9-3 for a summary of heuristics and biases.

Heuristics and Biases

In recent years, research has increasingly focused on identifying the cognitive shortcuts individuals use to cope with the complexity inherent in many decisions and their application in the world of business and finance.[xvii] These shortcuts are formally known as **heuristics**. Heuristics simplify the decision making process by providing certain types of mental shortcuts that decision makers can use to make decisions more quickly. As noted earlier, shortcuts serve us well in most situations. Imagine how long it would take to buy toothpaste (or most other products) without relying on expert judgment from a dental association or the recommendations of others for the purchase. As the world has become more complicated, heuristics or decision shortcuts are increasingly helpful in simplifying our lives.

Cognitive psychologist Daniel Kahneman has done a great deal of research on heuristics in decision making, work for which he won the Nobel Prize in 2002. Prior to Kahneman, decision errors were identified with emotion—if a decision maker did not use a textbook rational approach for decision making, then that decision maker was simply being "emotional." In this view, any decision that went awry must have been an "emotional" decision. But later research in psychology,

FIGURE 9-3   Heuristics and Biases

- **Anchoring.** Anchoring occurs when a person is anchored by an initial impression or relies on one piece of information as the key to decision making.
- **Availability.** The availability heuristic leads to a bias whereby people base their decisions on how easily an example can be brought to mind.
- **Representativeness.** The representativeness heuristic occurs when objects of similar appearance or patterns are assumed to represent something that the data do not warrant.

management, and political science showed that people regularly make decision errors that have nothing to do with any discernible emotional state. Rather, they made consistent mistakes and persistent miscalculations in seeking out information and making decisions. This finding lies at the core of Professor Kahneman and colleagues' research on decision making, which is broadly referred to as **prospect theory**. Prospect theory examines a number of decision-making errors people regularly make stemming from risk assessment, loss aversion, and dependence on a reference (comparison) point. The rational model of decision making assumes that people make decisions based on the optimization of individual self-interest. But people have been shown often to rely instead on heuristics and logical inconsistencies. As a result it seems that mistakes in human decision making are the rule, rather than the exception.

Kahneman and others have shown that although decision heuristics or shortcuts can be helpful to us, they are not always benign. Researchers from psychology, finance, economics, and management have identified a whole range of heuristics people commonly use in making decisions that lead to systematic biases that lead to (highly predictable) decision errors. Even with very simple, one-step decisions, heuristics can push decision makers away from more optimal alternatives. For example, consider a very simple problem: Alternative A offers you a 50-50 chance (like a coin flip) of receiving $1000 or nothing. Alternative B offers you a certain $400. Which option will you take? A quick look at the math tells you that the expected value of alternative A is $500 ($1000 × .50 + $0 × .50), while alternative B is worth $400. Thus, the rational, optimal choice would be alternative A. But if you are like most people, you will not make the optimal choice, but will select the certain $400. Most people hate the feeling of losing something—and if they take the risk and choose the coin flip, they have a 50 percent chance of receiving nothing—so they opt for the certain $400 instead of ending up with no money. This common decision-making bias is known as loss aversion in that people will forgo a superior choice (a potential benefit) to avoid a loss. Even with a simple, one-step, easy-to-calculate decision, the average decision maker can make very big decision errors influenced by heuristics and other common cognitive limitations.

Most people use these shortcuts or heuristics automatically and do not realize they are happening. Heuristics create unperceived biases—traps that increase the possibility of suboptimal decision making. But if an individual can recognize these heuristics and the traps that follow, then that individual can create a process to avoid them rather than accepting information and judgments that are biased and likely incorrect. The heuristics that will be examined include anchoring, availability, and representativeness.

Anchoring Anchoring occurs when a person is unduly influenced by an initial impression or relies on one piece of information as the key to decision making. For example, in one study Kahneman asked individuals to guess the percentage of African nations that are members of the United Nations. People who were asked if the figure was more or less than 45 percent consistently made a lower guess than others who were asked if it was more or less than 65 percent. The only difference was the initial point on which the decision maker (the person answering the question) was "anchored" by the questioner—the higher percentage influenced respondents to make a higher guess. This pattern has held true in many other experiments for a wide variety of guesses on different topics.

Usually once an anchor is set, it biases people toward that value and anchors discussion on that attribute of the product or service. When considering a decision, the mind gives disproportionate weight to the first information it receives. Similar to the verdict-based approach to information search, such initial impressions, estimates, or data anchor subsequent discussion, information search, and

Prospect Theory
Examines risk assessment, loss aversion, and dependence on a reference or starting point. Explains why individuals consistently behave in ways different from what traditional economic and decision theory would predict.

Anchoring
When a manager relies on one piece of information as the key to his or her decision making.

judgments. Recall our discussion of international mergers and acquisitions in Chapter 4, in which we noted that a majority of international mergers and acquisitions fail because managers too often focus solely on rates of return and do not consider key issues like integrating the firms and managing the impact of different cultures on the newly merged firm.

Others have suggested that anchoring affects other kinds of estimates, like perceptions of fair prices and good deals. Anchors take many guises. They can be as simple and seemingly innocuous as a colleague's comment or a statistic from the morning newspaper. Or they can be as insidious as stereotypes about a person's accent, culture, or clothes. In business, one of the most common types of anchors is a past event. As business students you should know that past financial performance is not a guarantee of future performance. Other factors need to be weighed as well. In situations characterized by rapid changes in the marketplace, historical anchors can lead to poor forecasts and, in turn, misguided choices. In addition, because anchors can establish the terms on which a decision will be made, such as the starting price of a negotiation to buy a car or house, the anchors are often exploited as a bargaining tactic by savvy negotiators. Be careful of where you anchor or start out a negotiation, even in a simple bargaining situation at an auto dealer or with your employer; do not anchor yourself in an unfavorable starting place.

Availability

The availability heuristic leads to a bias whereby people base their decisions heavily on an example that can be easily be brought to mind.

Availability A second well-studied and common cognitive shortcut is availability. The availability heuristic leads to a bias whereby people base their decisions heavily on an example that can be easily brought to mind. In these instances, the ease of imagining an example or the vividness and emotional impact of that example becomes more credible than actual statistical probability.

Essentially, the availability heuristic operates on the notion that if you can think of something, it must be important and will become part of your decision. This bias occurs when people place excessive importance on relatively rare, though vivid, events or circumstances. For example, many people believe that "Chinese firms make everything" and have taken over the world's manufacturing and trade. This is because Chinese products are more "available" in cognitive terms: many consumer goods such as clothes and light electronics are made in China, so naturally the "made in China" label seems to be everywhere. The truth is somewhat more complex. China has a much smaller share of world trade than the United States and several other countries.[xviii] And, quite often, Chinese-owned firms are not the ones doing the manufacturing and exporting; it is just that the factory happens to be located in China. Everything is not made in China, but the availability or vividness of consumer goods made in China makes people exaggerate China's importance (or threat) with respect to world trade.[xix]

Media coverage can also help fuel people's availability bias with widespread and extensive coverage of unusual events, such as airline accidents, and less coverage of more routine, less sensational—but perhaps more important—events such as automobile accidents. For example, when asked to rate the probability of a variety of causes of death, people tend to rate more newsworthy events as more likely because they can more readily recall an example from memory. For example, most people believe that having a gun in the house is quite dangerous for children. But few know that children living in homes with a swimming pool are more than 100 times more likely to die in an accident involving the pool compared to children that live in a house with a gun being fatally shot.[xx] Similarly, people often rate the chance of death by plane crash as higher than the chance by car crash. In actuality, death from car accidents is much more common than airline accidents, particularly in many emerging economies with poor roads and little traffic control. People may be afraid to travel to India because of the news of terrorist attacks and sectarian violence, but the probability of encountering such problems in a country the size of India are remote (unless one is seeking out the trouble spots). Yet the likelihood of being in a car accident on one of India's roads is much greater. Additional rare forms of death and injury also seem much more common than they really are because of their inherent drama, such as shark attacks, lightning, and terrorism. The problem lies when people make decisions based on faulty or incomplete information. People are more likely to believe that plane crashes kill more people than car accidents and thus pay relatively little for auto safety, although it would be a relatively simple thing to improve road maintenance and safety to significantly reduce accidents. This can push organizations and governments to invest a great deal of money to prevent very remote events while neglecting safety measures such as improved road safety because safer roads are not vivid or newsworthy.[xxi]

One final cautionary example. When the anthrax scare occurred in 2001 in the United States, the U.S. Postal Service spent $5 billion to acquire equipment to prevent future poisoning of the mail. This was done in spite of a lack of evidence of terrorist involvement (probably a rogue scientist) or evidence that it would continue to be a threat. Five people died from the anthrax attacks, which is most certainly a tragedy, but thoughtful arguments have been made that that amount of public money could have been spent on other safety measures to address much more likely and serious problems. But anthrax was very vivid and dramatic, thus biasing decision making about where to spend money on safety and public health.

In international business, the impact of the availability heuristics can be seen in how Americans view potential markets. For example, today's media representations of Russia are almost universally negative in the United States. Russia is seen as a corrupt, criminal, and dangerous place, almost always hostile to the United States. The result is that most Americans do not recognize that the Russian economy is rapidly growing, its capital markets have done very well in recent years, the rule of law is improving, and tremendous opportunities for American and other foreign firms are emerging.

Representativeness The representativeness heuristic occurs when seeming patterns are assumed to represent something that the data do not warrant. While sometimes useful in everyday life, representativeness can also result from misunderstanding probabilities, seeing patterns where none exist, and neglecting relevant base rates—that is, the underlying relevant population from which that small (pattern) sample is being drawn. For example, people tend to judge an event's probability by finding a "comparable" known event or situation and then assuming that the probabilities will be similar. The vignette about the "hot hand" illustrates this issue.

Humans, as part of making sense of their observations, need to classify things. If something does not fit exactly into a known category or pattern, or have a visible cause, most people will approximate with the nearest similar category available or make a guess as to the cause. This can lead to some significant biases, such as assuming people with certain characteristics will have (or lack) certain skills and knowledge. The representativeness heuristic leads people to believe in spurious causes, such as the mythical "hot hand" in basketball. As noted above, people often incorrectly believe a "hot" player is more likely to perform well at that moment. This all happens because people tend to ignore *base rates* (the relative frequency or likely probability that an event, like making a basket, typically occurs). People also misunderstand that there are always runs (hot streaks) and that over time these tend to even out as performances return back to their averages (i.e., regress toward the mean). This

Representativeness
The representativeness heuristic is when seeming patterns of data are assumed (incorrectly) to represent something that the data do not warrant.

INTERNATIONAL BUSINESS AND THE HOT HAND

Suppose you are the coach of a men's basketball team. Your team is behind by 1 point with only a few seconds left, so a single basket will win the game. Your best player, who has made about 56 percent of his shots in his career, is having a bad night and has made only three of twelve shots. Another player on your team has made his previous six shots, including a couple of long three pointers and has scored 30 points, but his career average over many years is only 46 percent and he's more known for his defense. The defenders guarding those two players are approximately equal in skill, and the other three players are not reliable scorers. Since the game is on the line and you only have time for one more play, which player would you pass the ball to for the game's last shot—your best shooter or the player having the big day? Most people when asked that question would recommend passing the ball to the player who is having the big scoring game, as he has the "hot hand." Yet research on sports and performance confirm what decision-making scholars would argue, that this would be an incorrect decision, and it would be best to ignore the representativeness heuristic and give the ball to the player with the best career average.

Many people, especially sports fans and announcers, would incorrectly recommend giving the ball to the player who has scored 30 points as he is "hot." (Try this question with friends who are basketball fans.) They believe the player with the hot hand is the obvious choice as he has a better chance of making the next shot and the other guy is "cold" anyway. This idea of the hot hand is very common in sports and yet it does not hold up to empirical scrutiny. Basketball players are not more likely to make a shot simply because they have just made several in a row. Players (and anyone else, for that matter) are most likely to perform to their average, or in this case, return to their average—a phenomenon known as regression to the mean. Research has shown that no matter how many shots a player has made or missed in a game, the odds that he will make or miss his next shot do not change and will generally be consistent with his career averages. The idea that someone on a hot streak is more likely to perform better is an example of the representativeness heuristic—people seeing patterns that are not there, or at least that cannot be explained by anything other than natural streaks or base-rate probabilities.[xxii]

The idea of a hot hand can also be applied to international business, particularly in the area of finance. We will discuss this in more detail in Chapter 11.

misunderstanding of what (apparent) patterns truly represent (or do not represent) leads gamblers and investors to believe in runs of good and bad luck or streaks of hot and cold. Many streaks and other clusters of similar events are usually little more than the naturally occurring variation that exists with any probabilistic series of events. For example, some people claim to see clusters of cancer incidence near power lines running through certain communities; this was the basis for a large number of lawsuits in North America in the 1990s. When carefully studied, these clusters turned out to be naturally occurring random patterns. No statistical link between power lines and cancer incidence was found, and no study ever showed that brain tumors were caused by low levels of exposure to electric power lines. But tens of millions of dollars had already been spent in lawsuits and bogus awards.[xxiii]

Assumptions about how groups of individuals may act or what they will buy are often based on representativeness assumptions. For example, in the United States, people often assume all Latin Americans will want the same things or act in the same way as Mexicans, only because Mexicans are the Hispanic group that Americans know best. The reality is that many Latin Americans have tastes and behaviors that are very distinct from those of Mexicans, and to simply assume that just because someone speaks Spanish he or she will behave like individuals from Mexico is a mistake. A simple illustration is food: Mexican food is often spicy, but food in Argentina and some other parts of Latin America tends to be relatively bland.

Overcoming Heuristics/Biases No one can avoid the influence of heuristics because they are part of our cognitive makeup, and some mental shortcuts are useful. But managers can reduce the impact of anchors, availability, and representativeness by using the following techniques:

- Always view a problem from different perspectives. Try using alternative starting points and approaches rather than sticking with the first line of thought that occurs to you or that comes up in a meeting.
- Think about the problem on your own before consulting others in order to avoid becoming anchored by their ideas.
- Be open minded. Seek information and opinions from a variety of people to widen your frame of reference and to push your mind in fresh directions. Do not reject ideas out of hand based only on their source. People with a different background or political point of view may have something useful to add to the decision process. Diversity can improve group decision making.
- Be careful when using advisers, consultants, and others. Tell them as little as possible about your own ideas, estimates, and tentative decisions. If you reveal too much, your own preconceptions may simply anchor the discussion prematurely.

Escalation of Commitment

Another more current area of concern is known as **escalation of commitment**, which is the tendency to allocate more resources to a failing course of action. (In poker, this is called "throwing good money after bad.") There are plenty of examples of escalation of commitment in organizational settings. One of the most prominent occurred years ago when the British and French governments continued funding the Concorde supersonic jet long after its lack of commercial viability was apparent. To this day, many refer to escalation of commitment as the "Concorde fallacy." A variety of the escalation of commitment occurs in organizations where significant investment has been made in a project, but the decision makers do not want to go back on that decision and cancel the funding. This specific aspect of escalation of commitment is called the **sunk-cost trap** (see Figure 9-4).

Sunk-Cost Trap What helps to energize the escalation of commitment problem is the sunk-cost trap, which is the deep-seated bias to make present decisions in order to justify past choices. Even when the past choices no longer seem valid, individuals are too often unwilling to give them up. For example, many individuals will refuse to sell a stock or a mutual fund at a loss even though it may be clear that the investment will not turn around. When you do this you are foregoing other, more attractive investments, but doing otherwise would require you to admit that you made a mistake and realize the loss. Firms often put enormous effort into improving the performance of an employee who most individuals recognize should not have been

Escalation of commitment
The tendency to repeat an apparently bad decision or allocate more resources to a failing course of action. (In poker, this is called "throwing good money after bad.")

Sunk-cost trap
Making decisions in order to justify past choices.

FIGURE 9-4   Escalation and Sunk-Cost Fallacy (Sometimes Cognitive, Sometimes Social Psychological)

- **Escalation of Commitment**. An increased commitment to a previous decision in spite of negative information (chasing sunk costs).
- Are you swayed by arguments that a certain infrastructure project must be finished because "so much has been completed already"?
- If the answer is yes, then you too have been a victim of what psychologists call the "sunk-cost fallacy"—the human tendency to judge options according to the size of previous investments rather than the size of the expected return.
- Truly rational choices would be made only after weighing future costs and benefits. Past costs and benefits are quite irrelevant.

hired in the first place. But firing the person would require acknowledging that past decisions and the associated investments of time or money are now irrecoverable. We know, rationally, that sunk costs should be rendered irrelevant to the present decision, but nevertheless sunk costs still affect people's decisions.

Sometimes a corporate culture reinforces the sunk-cost trap. If the penalties for making a decision that leads to an unfavorable outcome are overly severe, managers will be motivated to let failed projects drag on endlessly in the vain hope that they will somehow be able to transform the projects into successes. Such a culture can also limit risk taking because managers will fear proposing anything remotely risky for fear of failing and being punished. Executives should recognize that in an uncertain world where unforeseeable events are common, good decisions can sometimes lead to bad outcomes. By acknowledging that some good ideas will end in failure, executives will encourage people to cut their losses rather than let them mount.

Causes of Escalating Commitment Researchers have identified several factors that lead to the sunk-cost trap and, in turn, an escalating commitment. These include self-justification, the gambler's fallacy, perceptual blinders, and closing costs.

Escalation of commitment sometimes occurs because people want to present themselves in a positive light, that is, they want to create self-justification for their actions. Individuals who are personally identified with a decision tend to persist because this demonstrates confidence in their own decision-making ability. This persistence is also the decision maker's way of saving face to avoid the embarrassment of admitting past errors. Some cultures (even corporate cultures) have a stronger emphasis on saving face than do others, so escalation of commitment may be more common in those societies where leaders rarely admit mistakes. Thus, in more hierarchical societies, such as in East Asia and Latin America, escalating commitment problems can be particularly widespread.

Many projects result in escalation of commitment because decision makers commit the gambler's fallacy, that is, they underestimate the risk and overestimate their probability of success. They become victims of the gambler's fallacy by having inflated expectations of their ability to control any problems that may arise. In other words, decision makers falsely believe that luck is on their side, so they invest more in a losing course of action.

Escalation of commitment can occur if decision makers do not see the problems soon enough. Through these perceptual blinders, as discussed earlier in this chapter, the decision makers unconsciously screen out or explain away negative information. Serious problems initially look like minor errors. The information necessary to pinpoint and define major problems is downplayed, so the problems are ignored and remain unsolved.

Even when a project's success is in doubt, decision makers will persist because the closing costs of ending the project are high or unknown. Terminating a major project may involve large financial penalties, a bad public image, or personal political costs. This explains in part why BHP's hot briquetted iron (HBI) plant in Western Australia long continued to receive financial support in spite of very high cost overruns. The plant cost about $2 billion to build and was not competitive. Terminating the project proved difficult because of the estimated costs of around $1 billion for doing so and the embarrassment of a number of BHP principals and politicians. The plant was finally closed in 2007 after several years of losses and other problems.[xxiv]

Overcoming Escalating Commitment Problems Managers in particular should be on the lookout for the influence of sunk-cost biases in decisions and recommendations made by their subordinates. Managers can do several things to overcome escalating commitment problems:

* One effective way to minimize escalation of commitment decision problems is to separate decision choosers from decision evaluators. This tends to avoid the problem of escalating investments because a decision maker had to "prove" that he/she was right. For example, banks have been found to be more likely to take action against bad loans after the executive responsible has left. In other words, problem loans were effectively managed when someone else took over the portfolio.
* Publicly establish a preset threshold. If the resulting test falls in the alert region, the decision is to be abandoned or re-evaluated. This is similar to a stop-loss order in the stock market, when stock will be sold if it falls below a certain price.
* Seek to avoid creating a failure-fearing culture that leads employees to perpetuate their mistakes. In East Asian firms, for example, this is thought to be a particular challenge. Such firms are often organized around principles of filial piety, which means loyalty to the father or father figure, such as a boss in the organization. To go against the boss or the decisions they have made would be considered improper and would show poor upbringing and disloyalty.[xxv] Thus, it can be difficult to organize for innovation because employees fear that they will be criticized as disloyal or punished for pointing out errors such as failing projects. A decision or judgment gets evaluated for its loyalty to top management, not its accuracy.
* Recognize that the source of escalation of commitment has deep psychological roots in our desire to protect our egos or prove to others that we were correct. Breaking from the status quo also means taking action, and when we take action, we take responsibility, thus opening ourselves to criticism and to regret. Most individuals will stick with the status quo because it is the safer course, putting us at less psychological risk.
* In rewarding people, look at the quality of their decision making and their decision process, taking into account what was known at the time their decisions were made, not just the quality of the outcomes.

Loss Framing

A third current concern was also identified by Kahneman, who found that most people feel worse about a loss of a given amount than they would feel good about a gain of a similar amount. This loss framing, or loss aversion, means that people tend to focus more on losses (or loss avoidance) than they do on benefits in making decisions. To illustrate, homeowners are more likely to purchase energy-saving insulation when the cost savings are presented in terms of losing money through energy wastage, instead of on any payback or gains provided through lower utility bills.[xxvi] This higher valuing of losses (and thus being more influenced by them) holds for money, opportunities, and other items. People consistently are more influenced by avoiding potential losses than by gains. (See Figure 9-5 for summary of loss framing.)

FIGURE 9-5   Loss Framing

* The loss framing bias means that most people feel worse about a loss of a given amount than they would feel good about a gain of a similar amount. That means people tend to focus on losses (or loss avoidance) in making decisions.
* There is evidence that managers place more importance on information about potential losses than benefits of approximately equal value.
* Items and opportunities are seen to be more valuable as they become less available. This latter propensity is also called the scarcity principle.

That decision makers value losses more than gains of the same amount is reflected in how people value products that are hard to get. Study after study shows that people dislike losses greatly, or missing out on a perceived benefit. Thus, items and opportunities are seen to be more valuable as they become scarcer. (This latter propensity is called the scarcity principle and will be covered in more detail Chapter 10, Influence and Negotiation.) It's important to understand how people value losses. One well-known study showed that potential losses played a far bigger part in managers' decision making than potential gains.[xxvii] Policymakers rate and codify the potential losses associated with every decision. An extreme example is the methodology of "worst-case analysis," which was once popular in the design of numerous organizational systems and is still used in certain engineering and regulatory settings. The idea was to avoid the "worst" worst case scenario, but this may bring higher costs than is necessary.

What can managers do about loss framing? In Chapter 10, we will learn about how loss framing can be used to influence people to buy our products or ideas. A poorly framed problem can undermine even the best-considered decision. But the adverse effects of framing can be limited by taking the following precautions:

* First, do no automatically accept the initial frame, whether it was formulated by you or by someone else. Always try to reframe the problem in various ways. Look for distortions caused by the frames.
* Second, be aware of being overly sensitive to losses, which can also lead to risk aversion. Firms that are afraid to risk anything also miss out on major opportunities.

Groupthink

Groupthink
A mode of thought whereby individuals intentionally and prematurely conform to what they perceive to be the consensus of the group and preference of the leader.

The last major current concern in decision making that will be examined here is groupthink. After the severe blunders at Pearl Harbor and other attacks on the allied forces during World War II, researchers started to examine catastrophic decision failures, especially those originating from groups. In the 1970s, psychologist Irving Janis theorized a group interaction phenomenon he called groupthink, and credited it with being a potentially important influence on group decision making. Although groups generally make better decisions than individuals, **groupthink** is the downside of group decision making, and it must be carefully avoided. Janis defined groupthink as a mode of thinking that people engage in when they are deeply involved in a cohesive in-group, and when the members' striving for agreement override their motivation to realistically appraise alternative courses of action.[xxviii] More generally, groupthink is a problematic manner of decision making that can arise during the group decision process, whereby individuals intentionally conform to what they perceive to be the consensus of the group and preference of the leader. (See Figure 9-6 for details on groupthink.) This emphasis on group harmony and agreement

---

FIGURE 9-6   Groupthink

* Groupthink is formally defined as "a mode of thinking that people engage in when they are deeply involved in a cohesive in-group, when the members' striving for agreement overrides their motivation to realistically appraise alternative courses of action (or even examine assumptions)."
* Individuals intentionally conform to what they perceive to be the group consensus and the preference of the leader.
* Groupthink may cause the group—typically a committee or organization—to make poorly supported, too-fast decisions which are likely to prove suboptimal or even catastrophic.

FIGURE 9-7   The 8 Symptoms of Groupthink, Divided into 3 Categories

Category I: Overconfidence in the Group's Abilities

* Symptom #1 Illusion of Invulnerability—People are more risk-seeking in a group (risky shift—some exceptions)
* Symptom #2 Belief in Inherent Morality of the Group—Related to fundamental attribution error (the other guys are "in it for the money/power, etc.")

Category II: Closed-mindedness of the Group

* Symptom #3 Rationalization—Ignoring contrary evidence and basing decisions only on past (limited) experience (related to verdict-based decision making)
* Symptom #4 (External) Stereotyping of Out-groups

Category III: Group Pressure to Conform

* Symptom #5 (Internal) Self-Censorship—"We don't do that around here," Not Invented Here (NIH) syndrome
* Symptom #6 Direct Pressure—Subtle threats to dissenters
* Symptom #7 Mindguards—Keep dissenting opinions away from leaders; excessive centralization
* Symptom #8 Illusion of Unanimity—Overlook quiet dissent and the leader makes his/her opinion clearly known

overrides the ability to consider relevant evidence and the merits of a decision. More specifically, groupthink can cause the decision-making group—typically a committee or large organization—to make poorly supported, hasty, and suboptimal decisions that each member might individually consider to be unwise and would disagree with in private. Team-based decision making provides many benefits—speed, flexibility, and positive team member development. But such teams are also subject to the effects of groupthink, and this can be a major problem because many important decisions about organizational strategy, key threats, or forecasts about the future should be made by decision-making teams or groups.

In his research, Dr. Janis identified eight symptoms that could indicate that groupthink may be occurring. If this is the case, there will be a higher probability of that group making a decision that will be unsuccessful, and possibly even catastrophic. The first two characteristics of groupthink stem from overconfidence in the group's prowess. The next pair reflect the tunnel vision members use to view a problem. The final four are signs of strong conformity pressure within the group. (See Figure 9-7 for a summary of these eight symptoms of groupthink.) These symptoms have shown up in numerous flawed decision processes, for example, the 1986 *Challenger* space shuttle accident, the decisive defeat of French and Allied forces at the start of World War II in 1940, and the failure of the Russian navy to save its ill-fated *Kursk* submarine in 2000.[xxix] These examples will be discussed in greater detail below, along with the eight groupthink symptoms.

1. *Illusion of Invulnerability.* The attack on Pearl Harbor is often cited as a classic example of an illusion of invulnerability. The American naval and army commands never thought that the Japanese naval and armed forces could travel thousands of miles undetected to attack U.S. military bases at Pearl Harbor in Hawaii, and as a result they did not test that very important assumption. This illusion of invulnerability led military authorities to fail to prepare for possible attack, in spite of numerous warnings that war with Japan was imminent, which resulted in perhaps the worst defeat ever inflicted on U.S. military forces.

2. *Belief in Inherent Morality of the Group.* Group members automatically assume the rightness of their cause, and dissenters are judged as unethical or even immoral. At the hearing about the *Challenger* accident in 1986, one engineer noted that NASA managers had shifted the decision rules under which they operated, remarking that the engineers felt they were in the position of having

to prove that the space shuttle was unsafe instead of proving that it might not be safe and that dangers could not be ruled out.

3. *Collective Rationalization*. Despite the launch pad fire that killed three astronauts in 1967 and the close call of Apollo 13, the American space program had never experienced an in-flight fatality. When engineers raised the possibility of catastrophic O-ring blow-by, it was argued that the shuttle had flown successfully about 20 times and there was little reason to think that this would not continue.

4. *Out-group Stereotypes*. Getting critical outside testimony and evidence is important for groups seeking effective decisions. In 1940, French and Allied (British, Dutch, Belgian) forces were defeated in a shocking six weeks by the German *Wehrmacht* with just a little help from their Italian allies.[xxx] The French high command at the start of World War II in Europe failed to learn lessons from the German *blitzkrieg* attacks on Poland. The French generals argued that the Poles were not up to the standard of the French armed forces and Poland was not like France. Thus information about German tank battalions and their coordination with armed troop carriers and *Stuka* dive bombers was mostly ignored.[xxxi]

5. *Self-Censorship*. Returning to the *Challenger* accident, main contractor Morton-Thiokol wanted to postpone the flight. But instead of the engineers clearly stating that they certainly should not launch below 53 degree Fahrenheit (about 11 degree Celsius), they offered equivocating opinions. One engineer suggested that lower temperatures were not in "the direction of goodness" for the O-rings. Managers instructed engineers to make a management decision rather than an engineering one, presumably asking them to ignore some of their data and take a risk—something engineers are loath to do when human life is involved. Engineers were reprimanded by their superiors, so they did not press the issue directly with NASA even when they could have spoken up at the final preflight launch meeting

6. *Illusion of Unanimity*. NASA managers perpetuated the fiction that everyone was fully in accord on the launch recommendation. The managers admitted to the presidential commission that they did not report Thiokol's hesitancy to their superiors. As often happens in such cases, the flight readiness team interpreted silence as agreement.[xxxii]

7. *Direct Pressure on Dissenters*. During the momentous decade of the 1930s in the run-up to World War II, Charles de Gaulle, then a major in the French army, wrote a well-read article and later a book that described the importance of armored vehicles, separate tank battalions, and close ground-air cooperation. He was ignored by the French high command, which temporarily removed him from the promotion list for disagreeing with commanders. The French high command pointed out that they would not tolerate dissent (often termed "disloyalty") such as de Gaulle's. One well-known French staff officer added: "Everyone got the message, and a profound silence reigned until the awakening of 1940 [the German invasion of France in World War II]."[xxxiii]

8. *Self-Appointed Mindguards*. "Mindguards" protect a leader from assault by troublesome ideas. During China's long war with the Japanese during World War II and subsequent fight against Mao Zedong's Communist forces, China's Generalissimo Chiang Kai Shek was well known for not wanting to hear bad news. When asked who his best generals were, he would usually reply that it was those that were the most loyal and did not question his orders. Even when the general was losing all battles he was fighting, Chiang would still be heard to remark "yes, but he is loyal."[xxxiv] In spite of having more resources and troops at his disposal, and assistance at various times from both the Soviet Union and the United States, Chiang

managed to lose most of the battles he fought and was eventually driven out of the Chinese mainland by the victorious Communist armies. A weak grasp of the concepts of total war and grand strategy exacerbated by weak group decision processes that would not give Chiang bad news or suggest the need to change strategy and tactics almost certainly hastened the defeat of Chiang's government forces.[xxxv] Attempting to prove loyalty or to avoid disrupting the harmony of the group by keeping bad news from the group leader or higher management is more likely to lead to groupthink and ill-informed decisions and is most assuredly inadvisable.

As can be seen, groupthink can occur in a variety of settings, including commercial, noncommercial, and professional environments. And groupthink can spoil a decision process to the extent that key assumptions are not tested and alternative strategies (visions) and scenarios are not examined. This is because groups engaged in groupthink tend to lock out outside points of view, employ verdict-based information search (not searching out anything that might disagree with their narrow points of view), suppress internal discussion, fail to challenge key assumptions (and make unwarranted assumptions), fail to consider alternatives, take excessive risk, and do not use the information they have. This creates a poor decision process that can lead to suboptimal and even catastrophic results.

Avoiding Groupthink There are ways that firms can overcome groupthink:

* Take the time to recognize and understand the vastly different ways that people's minds work. Howard Gardner's classic book *Frames of Mind*[xxxvi] explores various different intelligences (linguistic, musical, logical-mathematical, spatial, bodily-kinesthetic, inter- and intra-personal) that, if acknowledged and allowed to interact, can bring a surprising and exciting array of new data into any decision-making process. Ensure that a mixture of different mindsets are present in the group. This diversity can bring different perspectives to problems. But notice that it is diversity of thought and background.
* People also interact and process data in a variety of ways. Each person contains a mix of orientations, from task centered, to learning centered, to people centered. Each of us learn in different "directions," some moving from "the big picture" to the specifics of the particular task or project, and others beginning with details and moving outward to the bigger picture. We also organize data differently, some through step-by-step chronological planning, which is more common in Northern European cultures, and others by starting up something, stopping, and then coming back to it again. Creating space for a variety of cognitive approaches may take time initially, but in the long term, it ensures decision processes that are more creative and effective at problem solving and responding to the unexpected.
* Avoid overly valuing consensus and harmony, especially as a team leader. Remember that harmony is not the ultimate goal: the best decision is. Not everyone has to fully agree; they just have to agree enough to get the job done. Important decisions need to be evaluated on their merits, not because they make boss feel good or contribute to group harmony and agreement. Make sure that differences of opinion are encouraged and appreciated (not just tolerated). Take time to allow every member of the team to express themselves, and work hard to avoid putting pressure on dissenters to conform.
* Create partnerships of people from diverse disciplines, departments, or backgrounds when facing new projects or creative challenges. For example, under the leadership of Jerry Hirshberg, the Nissan Design Center in San Diego, California, hired designers in complementary pairs—people who were as unlike each other as possible—in order to ensure that they would avoid routine thinking and would lead one another into new avenues of creativity.

- Ensure effective processes for aggregating the group's input. Diversity is important, but groups ultimately need to land somewhere; decisions need to be made. It is crucial, therefore, to have effective processes for bringing all the divergent data into a cohesive whole and setting a time limit. It is important to resist the temptation to move into this phase too soon, but when the time is right, the group must be brought together in some way, or chaos, rather than creativity, will result.
- Voting is a method to be used only sparingly, perhaps at the end if no agreement has yet been reached. In some situations more than one alternative can be tried, and the results tested before a final course is chosen.
- In many groups that have taken the time to explore collective wisdom in depth, ongoing debate and dialogue can result in surprising new thinking, shared by the entire group, which opens the doors to the best decision. In this scenario, while consensus is not a goal of the group, it is frequently the result of effective processes. A well-known Native American Indian chief, in explaining how his tribal councils made major decisions, expressed it well in saying that they kept talking until there was nothing left but the obvious truth.[xxxvii]
- Finally, if a group is to be involved in the decision-making process, let it actually make decisions. If the group is treated simply as an advisory structure, or if its findings are dismissed or minimized, group members will simply check out of the process, and the group will experience "death by committee."

In an increasingly globalized and complex world, the collective intelligence of a group or organization is more important than ever. There are now a number of ways for a group's collective wisdom to be developed and utilized, though traditional meetings or via newer technologies. Whether through releasing the potential in relational tools like team building, or drawing on the technological dialogues made available through blogging or other information gathering and discussion, organizations need to work to take advantage of this diversity of thought and experience while avoiding the symptoms of groupthink.

GROUP DECISION MAKING

It is important to note when we discuss groupthink that this is a dysfunctional approach to group decision making. Groupthink and the effective group decision-making process are two very different things. But if a group is functiong well, then group decisions can be very effective.[xxxviii] A group, if it is more organized, is also called a team; a larger, less organized group might be called a "crowd" or a market. It is commonly believed that with a group, you get an average intelligence (and thus an average decision), and that an expert should always be called on to make important, difficult decisions—even unstructured ones where the solution may have a complex series of pathways to the answer.

In fact, group decisions in less structured decision areas like strategizing, making estimates about future price movements, and guessing about capital markets will typically be much better than any one individual's decisions. There are many famous examples of contests where people can win a prize if they guess an object's weight or the number of units in a container. One individual typically gets close, out of the thousands of guesses submitted. But if you average all the guesses together they are almost always exactly on point. To illustrate further, consider the space shuttle crash discussed earlier. Just ten minutes after the *Challenger* exploded over the southern Atlantic Ocean, the stock market pushed down the price of the shares of the four major contractors who were seen as potentially responsible for the crash. By the end of that day, three stocks had recovered to their original price with minor losses. Only the stock of contractor Morton-Thiokol of Utah in the United States, stayed low, indicating that the market was betting that Morton-Thiokol was most responsible for the accident. There is no way the market could have known this: insiders had not dumped the stock, and it would be months before government inquiries uncovered the cause of the accident. But the market came to a "group" decision that ultimately proved correct: it was later determined that the failure of one of Morton-Thiokol's poorly designed O-rings caused the accident.[xxxix]

People often believe that any group is not as smart as the smartest person in the group. Most people also think that one or two experts will be smarter than a group. It is also commonly believed that when using a group (or the market) to make a decision, a simple agreement or consensus will be reached. None of the above is correct or true. The intelligence (wisdom) of a group is not the "average" of the intelligence of each individual in the group. Moreover, the wisdom of groups and markets is not about consensus. Wisdom really emerges from disagreement and even conflict. It is what one might call the "collective opinion" of the group (like the price of a stock, or of any product), but it is not an opinion that everyone in the group can agree on specifically. That means you are not likely to find collective wisdom by simple compromise or harmony-maintaining approaches. Some dissent and the giving of opinions are needed. Experts, no matter how smart, only have limited amounts of information. They have cognitive biases like everyone else. It is very rare that one person can know more than the sum of a large group of people, and almost never does that same person know more about a whole series of questions, some of which fall outside of his or her expertise. Thus, the current evidence is that group decisions are more effective than individually directed decisions under certain specific, though commonly occurring circumstances:

1. The decision involves a long-range forecast or prediction, or
2. The situation is strategic (development of a strategic plan).
3. The situation is complex, requiring multiple skills.
4. The situation is such that no one person is an expert on that topic. This could be in a movement out of the organization's traditional area of expertise.

EVALUATING DECISION MAKING IN INTERNATIONAL BUSINESS

Too often, decision makers in international business are not effective or efficient. One concern is that after making a choice, decision makers tend to inflate the quality of the selected alternative and deflate the quality of the discarded alternatives. This perceptual distortion, known as post-hoc justification, results from the need to maintain a positive self-identity. We encountered post-hoc justification with the problem of escalation of commitment also. Post-hoc justification generally gives decision-makers an excessively optimistic evaluation of their decisions, but only until they receive very clear and undeniable information to the contrary. Unfortunately, post-decisional justification also inflates the decision maker's initial evaluation of the decision, so reality often comes as a painful shock when objective feedback is finally received.

ALCATEL-LUCENT

Alcatel is a leading French technology company that acquired Lucent in 2006 for $11 billion. Lucent was formerly known as Western Electric, the manufacturing division of American telecommunications giant AT&T, and home to the legendary Bell Labs where many famous technologies, such as the transistor, were developed. Lucent represented high technology and innovation in the United States, even after being spun off from AT&T in the telecommunication deregulations of the 1980s. With the addition of Lucent, Alcatel hoped to build a world-class global business that could dominate the wireless and hardwired telecommunications industry. Alcatel had strong relationships with European operators, while Lucent had strong ties to North American carriers who had been its customers for many decades. The companies believed that combining their businesses would allow them to address customers across both continents and improve their operational efficiencies to compete in Asia. Alcatel also believed it could generate about $1.7 billion in cost savings over three years based on synergistic economies of scale and scope from the merger.

Prior to the acquisition, Alcatel had shown a strong ability to make good decisions quickly. For example, Alcatel had recently sold many of its unprofitable businesses, such as microelectronics, batteries, cables, and mobile handsets, choosing to focus on fiber optics and mobile telephony. It also bought into the IP service-router business by snapping up California start-up TiMetra Networks, which now ranks second only to Cisco in this high-growth sector.

However, the acquisition of the much larger Lucent did not generate the expected benefits for Alcatel-Lucent. Part of the difficulties that the firm faced in its decision making related to the organization of the combined firms. To address these issues the firm developed an executive committee of seven senior executives from both companies in 2007 to make crucial decisions about the combined firm's strategy and integration. However, just two of the committee members were former Lucent employees: Cindy Christy, who added Central and Latin America to her existing responsibility for North American sales, and John Meyer, head of services. The merging of North America with Central and Latin America sought to simplify decision making, resulting in just two regions—the Americas and the rest of the world (Sayer, 2007). Alcatel-Lucent at this time also sought to make some changes in the firm's personnel, with the appointment of a new CFO. The outcome of these changes still did not reverse the decline of the firm.

Another key part of the difficulties that faced the combined firms' decision making was their cultural differences. For example, it has been noted before that the French are very hierarchical with a high power distance. In contrast, Americans tend to prefer very participative decision making and have fairly low power distance. The CEO of the firm came from Lucent while the chairman of the board came from Alcatel. One issue that was difficult to resolve was having headquarters in France while the CEO was in the United States. This physical distance between the CEO and headquarters made decision making slow and collaboration difficult.

The numbers for Alcatel-Lucent do not look good. Since the 2006 merger, the $27.5 billion company has posted six quarterly losses, taken billions of dollars in equipment and asset write downs, and seen its stock price plummet by 50% to less than $10 per share. Not all of this is the sluggish economy after the merger. Telecom investment worldwide is set to rise 2.5% to 5.5% in 2008, while Alcatel-Lucent estimates its sales may decline by low-to-mid single digits.

The outcome was that by 2008 the firm's losses were mounting and dramatic changes were called for. The CEO was fired (from the original Lucent) and the chairman of the board (from the original Alcatel) had to resign. The firm was faced with having to integrate the businesses much

(Continued)

more thoroughly and reduce decision time while increasing decision quality. The firm has had problems in integrating its much different styles. Lucent's decision-style is slow and deliberate, owing to its long association with AT&T in a regulated environment and having many very long-term customers. Alcatel, in contrast, was a much looser confederation of divisions and product lines with a freewheeling style. As the merger progressed it was estimated that Alcatel was utilizing around 20 different accounting and reporting systems in various parts of the firm. Given the differences in decision style and data reporting, it has proved more difficult than either side anticipated to integrate the two firms and realize the planned cost savings, let alone any synergistic benefits from combining the product line and development efforts. Only time will tell if the new chairperson and CEO can get the Alcatel-Lucent ship back in shape, but a great deal of work in integrating the two firms and aligning the decision systems and data reporting seems to remain.

Sayer, P. (2007). Alcatel-Lucent CFO leaves in management change. Computerworld. http://www.computerworld.com.au/index.php/id;164868684.

Matlack, C. & Schenker, J.L. (2008, June 18). Alcatel-Lucent's troubled marriage. *Business Week.* http://www. businessweek.com/magazine/content/08_26/b4090056678890.htm (accessed July 29, 2008)

Michelson, M. & Wendlandt, A. (2008). Loss-making Alcatel-Lucent dumps CEO and chairman. *Reuters.* http://www.reuters.com/article/newsOne/idUSWEA355220080729.

* The communications, group dynamics, and decision-making processes involved are quite complex in international business. In small groups, diversity of opinion is the single best guarantee that the group will reap benefits from face-to-face discussion. What this means is that diversity—that much-discussed feature of today's work environment—is a very important factor in collective intelligence. While gender, race, age, and cultural diversity all have a role to play, the primary element in effective teams is **cognitive diversity**, the ability of members of the group to *think* differently (not just *be* different in terms of race or gender) and to express their opinions and findings opening in an organizational setting. International companies need to tap the power of cognitive diversity naturally present in their offices and partners around the world.

Cognitive diversity
The ability of members of the group to think differently, and to express their opinions and findings.

DEALING WITH CULTURE AND DECISION MAKING

It has been highlighted throughout this text that culture is an important consideration for those doing business internationally. It is worth discussing specifically some of the cultural factors that can affect decision making. For example, based on differences in a society's orientation to activity—to "getting things done" (see Chapter 1)—some cultures emphasize solving problems, while others focus on accepting situations as they are. In certain cultures, such as the United States, managers perceive most situations as problems to be solved and as opportunities for improvement through change. Other cultures, such as the Indonesian, Malay, and Thai cultures, tend to see no need to change most situations, but rather individuals attempt to accept life as it is and be patient with the situation.

If a "problem-solving" manager receives a notice that a prime supplier will be three months late in delivering needed construction materials, he or she will immediately attempt to speed up delivery or find an alternate supplier. If, by contrast, a "situation-accepting" manager receives a similar notice of delay, he or she might simply accept that the project will be delayed. Situation-accepting managers believe that they neither can nor should alter every situation that confronts them. Problem-solving managers believe that they both can and should change situations to their own benefit. Situation-accepting managers generally believe that fate or God will intervene in the production process (external attribution), whereas problem-solving managers are more likely to believe that they themselves are the prime or only influence on the same process (internal attribution). Consequently, when viewing exactly the same situation, American managers might identify a problem long before their counterparts from the county of Georgia might. Comparative research has demonstrated that managers' perceptions of situations and their definitions of problems vary across cultures.

A key aspect of culture that affects a firm is who makes the firm's decisions. Based on a culture's view of the relationships among people (see Chapters 1 and 2), either individuals or groups will hold primary decision-making responsibility. In North American business, individuals usually make decisions. The popular expression "The buck stops here" reflects the belief that ultimately a single person holds responsibility for a particular decision. In Japan, groups make decisions; most Japanese would find it inconceivable for an individual to make a decision prior to consulting his or her immediate colleagues and gaining their agreement.[xl]

At what level are decisions made? In more hierarchical cultures (see the discussion of Hofstede's power-distance dimension in Chapter 2), only very senior managers make decisions. Lower-level personnel are given responsibility for implementing decisions. Most lower-level Indian employees, for example, would wonder about the competence of a superior who consulted them on routine decisions. The majority of Indian managers prefer a more directive style, and up to 85 percent of their surveyed

---

DECISION MAKING AND VALUES IN THE UNITED STATES AND CHINA

In the classic 1945 film *Valley of Decision*, Gregory Peck stars as Paul Scott, the son of a wealthy industrialist in one of the great U.S. steel centers who has many ideas about newer production practices and better labor relations, which are alien to those of his parents and their business associates. Greer Garson stars as the family's maid, Mary Rafferty, and her father is an employee in one of the plants owned by Scott's father. Scott becomes attracted to the maid's personality and sympathy for the plant workers. In the meantime, labor trouble erupts in the plant—the workers go on strike for higher wages and better working conditions. A group of strike breakers are called in; Scott attempts to persuade his father and his advisers to call off the strike breakers and discuss terms with the labor leaders. But while his father, under pressure from his son, exchanges views with the labor leader, a riot breaks out between the workers and the strike breakers. Scott's father is killed, many men are injured, and the family's home is destroyed. Mary Rafferty's father is killed also. After order is restored, Scott takes over the management of the business and liberalizes its labor policies. As a result, Scott's unsympathetic wife demands a divorce, and Scott and Rafferty are then married.

Chinese-American anthropologist Francis Hsu observed both Chinese and American responses to this film when it was released at the end of World War II. Americans considered the movie to be good drama, because every conflict was resolved in a desirable way. Conflicts with production methods in the workplace were resolved by introducing new views on manufacturing; liberal attitudes toward labor won out; Scott, the progressive son, replaced his conservative father; and true love triumphed in the end.

According to Hsu, Chinese people who saw the film did not agree. Hsu reports that one of his Chinese friends understood the considerable size and extent of American industry and wealth, and he had some understanding of the acrimony in American industrial disputes. He was also aware that Americans are usually ready to experiment with new ideas or to introduce novel methods of production. But they considered both the Peck and Garson characters to be villains. Peck's character, Paul Scott, had no filial piety because he was opposed to his father, and his decision to encourage his father to work more closely with the union undid all that his parents had done. The maid was practically the sole cause of the breakdown of Scott's marriage, his family's ruin, the destruction of Scott's home, and both of their fathers' deaths. When the maid first entered the picture, the family was prosperous, dignified, and intact. If she had not encouraged her young boss in his views, he would not have asked his father to negotiate with the laborers and the father would not have been exposed to their fatal attack. Her own father would not have died in the ensuing battle.

To the Chinese audience, a son in conflict with his father was a bad son, and a maid who would help such a son in his endeavors was bad woman. Through the same Chinese lens, Scott's wife was regarded as an extremely virtuous woman who suffered at malicious hands. The question of the son's unhappiness with his wife as opposed to his possible happiness with the maid should never have been raised. Hsu noted, however, that while the Chinese audience's thoughts about the son's decisions were dominated by concerns about the family and its business, it took almost no account of the workers' difficult situation. The Chinese audience argued that the workers should accept their lot; the hierarchy should remain intact and everyone should know their places—workers, maids, and sons alike.

Hsu, F.L.K. (1981). *Americans and Chinese: Passages to Differences* (3rd ed.). Honolulu, HI: University of Hawaii Press.

subordinates believe they work better under supervision.[xli] By contrast, most lower level Swedish employees expect to make most of their own decisions about day-to-day operations. Thus, it would not be surprising that Swedes, not Indians, were among the first to experiment with autonomous work groups and platform manufacturing. At Volvo's Kalmar plant, Swedish management gave groups of employees total responsibility for producing cars.[xlii] The group, not senior management, took responsibility for allocating and scheduling tasks as well as for allocating rewards among employees. Senior management could more easliy delegate this amount of discretion to the shop floor in a low power-distance country such as Sweden.

Are decisions made slowly or quickly? American business people pride themselves on being quick decision makers. In the United States, being called "decisive" is a compliment. By contrast, many other cultures downplay time urgency. Some cultures even rate a decision's value proportionally to the length of time spent in making it. In addition, more traditional collective cultures might be concerned that the wishes of the more senior people are respected, whereas in a more Anglo-American context, individual choices are more recognized and expected.

When managers from quick-paced cultures, such as the United States, attempt to conduct business with people from more slow-paced cultures, such as Egypt and Pakistan, the mismatched timing causes problems. Americans, for example, typically become frustrated at Egyptians' slow, deliberate pace and begin to believe that their Middle Eastern counterparts lack the commitment to getting the job done. Egyptians, on the other hand, in observing the Americans' haste to make decisions, typically conclude that Americans' unwillingness to take more time reflects the lack of importance they place on the business relationship and the particular work at hand. The cultural perception of time and other values is a crucial dimension in understanding decision-making behavior cross-culturally.

SUMMARY

Decision making is a challenging task for organizations. Organizations face many important decisions on a regular basis, and decision errors can have serious consequences. First, it is important to remember there are strong psychological forces at work in decision making that affect everyone. These psychological forces or heuristics can be useful because they help us to screen out excess information for trivial and day-to-day decisions, but they can also can create information search and decision biases that push us toward deficient and even irrational decision making. These irrational decisions are not limited to emotional decisions leaped to with little thought, but even seemingly calm and cool decisions can prove to be very suboptimal if cognitive biases are not accounted for. First, decision makers must be sure to conduct earnest information searches for important decisions. It is important to understand that people routinely overestimate their own abilities and knowledge, and tend to assume that their view (or the view of their group or department) is the right one. This causes people to employ verdict-based information search and to search out information that only confirms their initial decision or some other preconceived bias. Research suggests that this is a substandard approach to gathering the information you need to make an informed decision. It is better to practice evidence-based information search, withholding your decision about something until you have sought out adequate evidence, and not just evidence that conforms to a preconceived notion about something. It is the contrary evidence that helps an organization work the kinks out of a difficult decision. Avoid being too dogmatic and didactic ("I'm telling you the way it is," or the more colloquial, "It's my way or the highway").

Money that is already spent is money that no longer should figure in future decisions. The sunk cost fallacy is one of the more common decision-making fallacies, and it results in financial decisions that are incorrectly based on previous investments or expenditures. Such a tendency is problematic for the simple reason that past investments should not affect your future decisions. What matters is how much you need to spend to accomplish what you were trying to do versus the best alternative. Past investment should not count, only what is likely to happen from the present.

In terms of information search and investment, it is hard for people to admit mistakes. That is why it is hard for managers to terminate a failing investment or for people to search for and accept information that goes against their basic beliefs, even if the evidence is sound. People like to try to confirm what they already believe or have decided. This confirmation bias of evidence makes it hard to change patterns of thought and behavior, as well as policies. This is as true for highly rational scientists as it is for business people.

Remember that people tend to weigh certain facts, figures, and events too heavily, putting too much stock in them, which can be explained by a number of decision-making heuristic problems. Anchoring, for example, explains how people fixate on a specific amount or topic and negotiate around that. Similarly, people also tend to place too much emphasis on especially available or vivid information. They also misunderstand probabilities and try to find cause and effect in data that is in fact random.

Another basic principle of decision theory states that it matters how you frame decisions. Since most people tend to be loss averse, if a decision is framed as a loss (or a missed benefit), people are more likely to try to avoid that loss than if the same decision were framed as a benefit. It is important to understand this propensity to loss aversion and how it may cause people to almost irrationally seek to avoid a loss and weight information about losses more heavily than about potential benefits. Also be aware of the groupthink problem, which can harm the otherwise effective group decision process. Allow the group decision process to operate; value diversity of opinion, particularly dissenting views. Encourage innovative thinking, even if it goes against the grain of what your company has practiced for years. Firms grow through the development of new products, new markets, and new businesses, often outside of traditional domains.[xliii]

MANAGERIAL GUIDELINES

What can be done to improve decisions?

- Analyze the situation carefully, and do not rush into major decisions. The "just do it" attitude that the popular culture tends to promote can lead to poorly thought-out decisions, prematurely arrived at.
- Avoid strict dogma. Be open to contrary evidence and publications from a different point of view than your own. Assess the *evidence presented* rather than dismissing it by criticizing the messenger's background, politics, or training, which are not relevant to the *accuracy* and applicability of the evidence itself.
- Be aware of the common heuristics that lead to biases, both for individuals and groups, and try to avoid them. For example, do not be overly influenced by available or vivid information. Just because there were three terrorist bombings in India last year, for example, does not mean that such bombings are "always happening," nor does it mean that traveling to India is particularly unsafe. Try to gather as much data as is feasible to make your decision, and do not let any one piece of data dominate the decision.
- Combine rational analysis with intuition, but understand that "common sense" or intuition is often flawed and affected by the common cognitive biases described in this chapter.
- When possible, treat decisions as part of a series of decisions. That is, do not be too risk averse to avoid a single mistake. Successful decisions cannot occur if you do not make any.
- Use group decision making for unstructured, predictive, ambiguous, or otherwise difficult decisions, particularly where no one is the expert. But beware of groupthink or premature conclusions, which can lead to catastrophic decision errors.

DOING BUSINESS IN THE COUNTRY OF GEORGIA

CULTURE

When many Americans hear Georgia they think of the state in the southern United States. But Georgia is also a country of over 4 million in the Caucasus Mountains around the Black Sea. Georgia was a republic in the USSR until its breakup. From the time of its independence in 1992 until 2004, Georgia was ruled by former Communist Party officials. But in what is now called the Rose Revolution, the population demanded a true democracy. As a result, Georgia has quickly instituted a reformed, market-oriented economy and active democratic institutions. Georgia has even begun conversations to both enter NATO and the European Union.

As part of the political changes in Georgia there has been a strong effort at market liberalization. Georgia is now ranked by the World Bank as number 18 out of approximately 180 countries for ease of doing business. Now investor confidence is strong and the economic growth is approximately 10 percent per year. There are large numbers of Russians and Armenians living in the country. Georgian, the official language, is ancient and very unique, and its written form is unlike any other. Almost all documents must be translated into Georgian if someone wishes to do business there.

Georgia's efforts to enter NATO has angered Russia, which still sees that country as part of its sphere of influence. The result has been that Russia has instituted strong controls on Georgian exports. While this has caused many difficulties for some businesses, it has also forced Georgians to build more connections to Europe and market their products there. Today Germany is one of Georgia's major trade partners. Culturally, Georgians are more conservative than many Europeans. But as Georgia integrates with Europe, it is quickly taking on more typical European attitudes. Family remains a central concern in Georgia and the culture is much more hierarchical than in most European countries.

In 2008 almost all the progress in the Georgian economy was brought to a halt as the country fought a border war with Russia. Although much larger, Russia invaded Georgia and helped two regions whose ethnic origins are Russian declare their independence. These regions are now planning to join Russia as provinces of that nation.

ADDITIONAL RESOURCES

Belsky, G., & Gilovich, T. (2000). *Why Smart People Make Big Money Mistakes and How to Correct Them: Lessons from the New Science of Behavioral Economics* (115–116). New York: Simon & Schuster.

Langewiesche, W. (2003). Columbia's last flight. *The Atlantic Monthly*, 292(4), November, 58–82.

Lomborg, B. (2007). *Cool It: The Skeptical Environmentalist's Guide to Global Warming*. New York: Knopf.

Lomborg, B. (Ed.) (2004). *Global Crises, Global Solutions*. Cambridge: Cambridge University Press.

EXERCISES

Opening Vignette Discussion Questions

1. Recall Chapter 5 in which global and multi-domestic strategies were discussed. Which strategy would Disney represent? How can a firm like Disney still adapt to a local market but also maintain the strong brand image that is so critical to its success around the world?

2. Do you think it's important for executives like Allan Zeman to be familiar with a firm or its products before becoming that firm's leader? Give the pros and cons.

3. Tourists from mainland China are critical of both Ocean Park and Disney in Hong Kong. Do you think the people of Hong Kong would automatically understand customers from China? How should both firms ensure they are able to meet those customers' needs?

DISCUSSION QUESTIONS

1. Think about the eight symptoms of groupthink as discussed in the text. Have you experienced these symptoms in groups that you are a part of or are aware of? How was the decision affected?
2. In this and other classes you have had to conduct projects in teams or groups. Discuss the difficulties in making decisions you have experienced in these groups.
3. Suppose you are a government official of a small but fast growing emerging economy. You have been asked to allow a commonplace recreational product—swimming pools—to be installed in your country for the first time by an American multinational corporation. You have been told that swimming pools directly lead to the death of 600 Americans every year—many of them children—and also cause brain damage in several thousand more children. Should you allow that product into your country? Discuss the pros and cons.
4. Once again, suppose you are a government official of a small but fast growing emerging economy. A company wants to come to your country to start selling a clean fuel that has previously been unavailable there, and it wants to pump the fuel directly into your country's homes. Although it can be burned for heat or energy, the fuel has been known to explode occasionally if improperly handled. It is odorless, colorless, and poisonous; you can not see it escaping from a malfunctioning valve and filling your house. Not surprisingly, this fuel kills about 400 Americans per year. Will you allow companies to sell this potentially dangerous gas in your country? What fuel do you think this is? What decision-making heuristic is implied here that might bias your decision?
5. Think of a time when you conducted an informational search to help you make a major decision, such as to which universities to apply. How did you gather information and finally come to a decision? Did you practice evidence-based or verdict-based decision making?
6. Is there a time you used verdict-based information search that helped to limit your information search but produced a sub-optimal decision? What decision was it and how could that decision have been better made?

IN-CLASS EXERCISES

1. A software developer in Hong Kong is experiencing an increasing number of customer complaints and a general trend toward lower sales. Describe three reasons why senior executives in this organization might be slow to realize that a problem exists or to identify the main cause(s) of these symptoms.
2. A manufacturing company hires a management consultancy to determine the best site for its next production facility. The consultancy has had several meetings with the company's senior executives regarding the factors to consider when making its recommendation. Discuss three decision-making problems that might prevent the consultancy from choosing the best site location.
3. A developer received financial backing for a new business financial center along a derelict section of the waterfront in a large European city, a few miles from the current business district. The idea was to build several high-rise buildings, attract a lot of new tenants to those sites, and have the city extend transportation systems into the newly developed location. The developer believed that over the next decade others would build in the area, thereby attracting regional or national offices of many financial institutions. Interest from potential tenants was much lower than initially predicted and the city did not build transportation systems as quickly as expected. Still, the builder proceeded with the original plans. Only after financial support was curtailed did the developer reconsider the project. Using your knowledge of escalation

of commitment, discuss three possible reasons why the developer was motivated to continue with the project despite its escalating losses.

4. The Ancient Book Company has a problem with new book projects. Even when it is apparent to others that a book is far behind schedule and may not have much public interest, sponsoring editors are reluctant to terminate contracts with authors. The result is that editors invest and therefore waste more time with these projects rather than on more promising projects. As a form of escalation of commitment, describe two methods that The Ancient Book Company can use to minimize this problem.

5. When a large law firm needed to create a task force to make some significant strategic decisions, it put together what it considered a diverse group. The group consisted of three men and three women, all in their late thirties, representing different racial and ethnic backgrounds. The individuals had been active together in a recent political campaign for a certain candidate in that state and would all describe themselves as "progressive." Each person in the group was a lawyer. Though they came from different parts of the United States, they all went to either Harvard or Yale Law School and graduated around the same time. Is this a diverse group? Comment on the pros and cons of this group and the possibility for groupthink.

TAKE-HOME EXERCISES

1. Research both the Cuban Missile Crisis and the Challenger space shuttle crash on the Internet. Develop your own list of advice on how to avoid groupthink.
2. Using your knowledge of culture, research the cultural dimensions of the Arab countries of the Middle East. What aspects of this culture and society do you think would affect your decision making if you were sent there as a manager for a multinational firm?
3. In relation to Take-Home Exercise 2, do you think the decision making in Israel will be different from that in other Middle Eastern countries? Explain why and how. If necessary, select one particular country from the Middle East to discuss this question.

SHORT CASE QUESTIONS

Alcatel-Lucent (p. 290)

1. How could Alcatel-Lucent improve their decision making in the future?
2. Do you think such difficulty is one of the key issues that faces most mergers and acquisitions?
3. Do you think that these decision-making problems would have been present in a Swedish-U.S. merger?

10

INFLUENCE AND NEGOTIATION

Overview

International business people must seek to influence others and negotiate with them in a wide variety of situations. For example, someone in a sales or marketing position must regularly influence customers to buy the firm's products and then must negotiate a price. Managers, especially international managers, will find it difficult simply to order people to do things; instead, it is a process of influence and negotiation that leads to getting things done. This chapter draws on extensive work in psychology, marketing, and negotiation to examine questions of influence and negotiation in international business.

As the text has emphasized, in international settings managers must consciously seek to address the impact of culture on activities such as influence and negotiations. As has been seen throughout the text, culture can affect a wide variety of human interactions in international business, including influence and negotiation. It is important in reading this chapter to remember the problem of projection; that is, do not assume that everyone else will share your values and will play by those rules. What influences you to buy may not influence others, since they may have completely different buying criteria than you. Although principles of influence and negotiation have proven to be fairly uniform across cultures, there are often different conditions present in different cultures, and this creates a variety of ways to implement influence and negotiation principles.

The issues addressed in this chapter include:

* Understanding what persuasion is and its role in the influence process.
* Six primary approaches to influence.
* Negotiations.
* International applications and concerns.

Chapter 10 Conceptual Flow

- Persuasion
- Influence
  - Six means to influence individuals
    - Social proof
    - Authority
    - Liking
    - Consistency
    - Reciprocation
    - Scarcity

- Negotiations
  - Cognitive shortcuts
  - Types of negotiations
- Negotiation process
  - Heuristics & biases
  - BATNA
  - Reservation price
  - Target price
- Impasses

Global managers spend a great deal of time in trying to **influence** people informally and seeking to negotiate with them formally. Think about your day. How often do you ask people to do things? How often can you simply order people to do things? If you are making significant requests, chances are that you almost always have to influence others to do things. Simply ordering them to act in the manner you want is typically not successful. Students may like to think that most managers can simply issue orders, as in the armed services, and then sit back and supervise performance. That is not the case because managers, as opposed to military officers, must regularly influence and negotiate with others to get them to

Influence
Seeking to change people's behaviors.

NEGOTIATIONS FOR UNILEVER IN AFRICA: DOING GOOD WHILE DOING WELL

Unilever, an Anglo-Dutch firm, is one of the world's largest consumer goods companies with sales of over €5 billion. Africa is one of the poorest regions in the world, and more than 40 percent of sub-Saharan Africa lives on less than a $1 a day. Two nations, South Africa and Nigeria, comprise 54 percent of the region's economic output.

Simple sanitary items such as soap are often not used in these impoverished nations and about 140 out of every 1000 children under the age of five die every year. Of these deaths, 17 percent are due to diarrhea and 21 percent to pneumonia—diseases that can be controlled or even prevented by simple handwashing. This has prompted a unique public–private relationship between Unilever and non-profits, such as Unicef, USAid, London School of Hygiene and Tropical Medicine, and the Gates Foundation, all of whom want to promote more handwashing. Specifically, Unilever hopes to promote its product

Lifebuoy (note that the spelling in the United States of this product is Lifeboy), an antibacterial soap that is ideally suited for these consumers. Unilever is now third in the Ugandan soap market.

The relationship here between the for-profit firm and the non-profits is not typical. There is often much suspicion between these two types of groups, and this agreement took much negotiation between the various parties. In particular the different sides report differences in how they viewed the timing of the program. Unilever was ready once it committed to move forward in an aggressive manner. But the non-profits had extensive bureaucracies and wished to reach a consensus on each issue with all items specified to a great detail. The result was that each side had to come to an understanding of the other. The non-profits needed to begin to trust Unilever, but Unilever knew that the timing of the campaign was vital. In many rural poor nations, individuals may not

have radios. As a result firms and non-profits develop road shows where a truck with a stage takes an entertainment show to remote areas. In this case, the show was to be centered on good health, with speeches on the need for everyone to wash their hands. Unilever with its marketing expertise knew that at certain times of the year like the rainy season or harvesting when people are very busy, the impact of road shows or advertisements is lessened. But this was a new concept to the non-profits.

Unilever and the non-profits together were able to help each other and to help the citizens of Uganda. But it was critical in the negotiation process to reach a better understanding of each other and not allow their biases to interfere with reaching a mutually beneficial agreement.

Russell, A. (2007, November 15). Growth data fuel hopes of new business era in Africa. *Financial Times*, p. 12.

Unilever looks to clean up in Africa (2007, November 15). *Financial Times*, p.18.

Persuasion
Seeking to change people's beliefs or attitudes.

do things. Even military officers cannot always issue orders and expect them to be followed. The U.S. president Abraham Lincoln, who was known for his **persuasion** and influence skills, had to spend a great deal of time trying to convince his subordinates to execute his orders.[i] Even as Commander-in-Chief of the U.S. armed forces, Lincoln had to "sell" his often slow-moving generals on the idea of carrying out needed campaigns to defeat the Confederate rebellion in the U.S. Civil War. President Lincoln even stated that he would hold one general's horse if that general would just go out and win some battles against the Confederacy.[ii] As a testament to the importance and ubiquity of influence skills, Lincoln's generals sometimes came around to his way of thinking, while others regularly refused to heed his orders until finally Lincoln had to replace them.[iii] In this chapter, the focus is on understanding influence and negotiation in cross-cultural settings. The chapter will initially examine these issues as short-term concerns, then examine them as longer-term issues. We will begin by defining and discussing what is meant by persuasion, since persuasion is the foundation for understanding the influence and negotiation process. We will examine six of the main principles of influence identified by well-known social-psychologist Robert Cialdini and other experts in the field that are used in organizations today to influence others in an ethical manner.[iv] We will apply these principles to illustrative situations, including more formal influence and decision-making situations found in negotiations.

PERSUASION

The opening vignette illustrates features of the persuasion that individuals are exposed to literally hundreds of times daily in advertising, promotions, or emails from colleagues and friends.[v] First, it is important to distinguish between persuasion and influence. Persuasion is the effort to change people's beliefs or attitudes, whereas influence is convincing people to actually do something, like purchase a product. Both are important. Many studies on persuasion have focused on attitude adjustment; that is, changing an individual's attitude toward something or some idea.

One very consistent finding in research around the world is that strong attitudes resist change. In fact, when faced with challenges to those strong attitudes, most people will not only seek out sources (people, media, or data) that support their initial beliefs, but they will also ignore any competing views and even lock them out of meetings and discussions. (Recall Chapter 9's discussion about verdict-based information search, the struggle to have the cure for peptic ulcers widely accepted in the medical community, and the problem of groupthink). Even if the data for those alternative views are strong, most individuals will ignore that data, even going so far as criticizing or attacking the messenger rather than arguing against the content of the message. We learned in Chapter 9 that this type of verdict-based information search is more likely to lead to decision errors and can also create the pernicious groupthink problem that is common in all types of organizations today. In this chapter, we look at the problem from the other angle—that is, how one persuades and influences people, especially people with strongly held attitudes that they have always made very public.

Persuasion and Influence

Though the words are often used interchangeably, persuasion and influence are not identical. Persuasion is a change in a private attitude or belief resulting from the receipt of a message. Influence is an action that leads to a change in behavior. The two approaches, persuasion and influence, can work together. For example, you might persuade someone about the importance of a healthy lifestyle and work habits, and then influence them to implement that lifestyle.[vi]

Persuasion is a deeper form of change than influence. To illustrate, if your friend is constantly troubling you about supporting his or her favorite cause, then you might say yes just to stop the incessant banter, while not really being persuaded. If you are really serious about persuading someone to accept a new idea, it is good to recall the words of the Greek philosopher Aristotle who reminded us: "The fool persuades me with his reasons; the wise man persuades me with my own." It is good to remember that just repeating the same things over and over is not likely to be effective if you fail to listen to the other person's comments, problems, objections, or objectives. There are tactics that help you to persuade someone—understanding what they value or what problems they may need to solve is the first place to start, because people will rarely go against their own values.

Early efforts to understand persuasion emphasized the importance of the message itself. Thus, the focus was on issues like the message's clarity, logic, or ease of recall because it was believed that the target person's comprehension and learning of the message's content were crucial to persuasion.[vii] Today, more emphasis is placed on understanding what encourages people to change their attitudes and beliefs. This draws on the **cognitive response model** and focuses on communication and the understanding of individuals' wants, beliefs, and the problems they need to have solved. Individuals' key wants and beliefs are known as the **self-talk of the target audience**.[viii] Persuasion occurs not only in what the communicator says to the target but also in what the target says in response. Thus, it is important for the persuader to listen carefully to the concerns of the target audience. It bears repeating that listening to and understanding the individual you are trying to persuade is quite important, so you must learn to ask questions (or do research) and then listen and summarize.

In particular, it is important to comprehend the most basic reasons why people may respond to a persuasive message. First, many people would like to build a more accurate view of the world and how it works. If a person has a sensing personality and prefers data and evidence, then providing data that is meaningful to that person can be a big first step toward persuading him or her about a new idea or product. Second, people would like to be consistent with their own values. This principle, known as the consistency principle, is important to both persuasion and influence, and will be discussed in the influence section later in this chapter. For now, it is sufficient to say that people would like to be consistent with their values in order to avoid **cognitive dissonance**, which is a negative feeling caused by holding two contradictory ideas simultaneously. Often this means having attitudes, values, or beliefs that do not match one's own behavior.[ix] When this occurs, people will try to remove that dissonance or discrepancy. If you can show how the message helps the listener do that, there is an increased chance that the message will succeed in persuading (or influencing) that person. Third, in addition to caring about what they believe, people also care about what others think. Therefore, a message may work if it helps the target person build social approval and demonstrate the logic and consistency of their new views and behavior (see Figure 10-2).

It is important to remember these three factors because they will make persuasion easier. For potential customers, try to find out what *needs* they have and what *problems* they are trying to solve and then show how your product solves their problem (more on this later in the chapter). Simply repeating your position or

Cognitive response model of persuasion
A model of persuasion that views the most direct cause of persuasion as the self-talk of the target audience, not the persuasion method itself or its deliverer.

Cognitive dissonance
The negative feeling caused by holding two contradictory ideas simultaneously.

| FIGURE 10-2 | Why Do People Yield to a Persuasive Message? |

People may change their minds based on a persuasive message in order to:

* Build a more accurate view of the world and how it works.
* Be consistent with their own values and previous commitments.
* Build social approval and demonstrate the logic and consistency of their new views.

views on a topic (or a standard sales pitch about your product's features) is usually not very persuasive. You also need to *listen to the problems* of the other person in an empathetic manner and then show that person (or target market) how your product or idea solves that problem or fits with that person's values or publicly stated position.[x] This approach to persuasion is similar to the marketing process whereby a firm seeks to find out the *problems and needs of the consumer* and then shows how the product or service can solve those particular problems.[xi]

This process sounds obvious, but think about how most products are designed and sold. How helpful are the frequently asked questions (FAQs) on a manufacturer's website? Do they just state the obvious about the product or tout its features without explaining common uses, tricky features, or potential problems? If your experience is like that of most customers, it is likely that most firms you encounter tend to emphasize their product's features and functions—how many features they have, how fast the product is, how well it works, and so forth—and not how their products can *solve your problems*. For example, at trade shows where firms pitch new consumer electronics technology products such as advanced mobile phones, you will typically hear all about a phone's functions and technological features—its capacity, upload and download speeds, ability to function as a video phone, and so forth. This is all impressive, to be sure, but you will hear very little about the *problems* of the customer and how the phone's features actually can solve those problems. This is also true for advertisements. For example, much has been made about the video function of the 3G and other new phones, but rarely is a problem directly identified that the video phone solves. Do you have a problem that requires you to see who you are speaking to on the phone? Probably not, unless you are a physician or someone else that needs to follow someone's actions or diagnose. Though the video phone has been around since the New York World's Fair of 1964, there has been little demand for it. The technology's sponsors have long failed to show what customer problems are addressed by the video phone, and instead continue to talk about service enhancements and the phone's newest specifications. Customer response has been predictably indifferent, and the proponents of 3G have added another common refrain typical of an improperly positioned and packaged product—upping the features and functions, then complaining that the product is ahead of its time and suggesting that customers just need to be educated about the product. This complaint about uneducated customers is commonly made by firms that have failed to address customer needs or to communicate how their product can help to solve specific customer problems—or even find out customers' problems, for that matter.

This is also quite consistent with what venture capitalists remind entrepreneurs: Do not ask customers to make lifestyle changes in order to adopt a product; that is, do not spend a lot of time educating the customer. It is very hard to make people change their lifestyles; it is far easier to persuade them to change their attitudes toward your product or industry by showing them how your product solves their problems or is very consistent with their current lifestyle and points of view. The failure of Toshiba's HD-DVD format in its battle with Sony's Blu-ray has been attributed to Toshiba's attempts to educate the consumer about HD-DVD's superior technology rather than describing how the format helps users watch and store movies, which is the main problem to be solved for DVD consumers.[xii] See Figure 10-3 for some questions to ask related to this application of the persuasion process in the marketplace.

Given the importance of self-talk and understanding people's problems and situations, it suggests that a manager's criticism of an employee's or position is not likely to help the persuasion attempt; beyond that, the manager needs to seek to connect to the employee's needs.[xiii] Let's consider a company memo intended to

---

FIGURE 10-3 How to Make Your Selling Message More Persuasive

* Does the message about your product help prospective customers understand their situations better?
* Does it solve a particular problem that the customers have? How will it solve that problem? Is that problem solving being communicated clearly to the customers, or are your promotions only mentioning the great features and functions of your product or company?
* Will the innovation help customers do what they are already trying to do more easily and effectively?
* Do you understand their needs and values such that you can identify what they are trying to do? Or are you selling something that does not address any problem or need and is not consistent with their values? If the latter is the case, then you will need to rethink the selling message or the product itself.

---

persuade employees to support a new pay-for-performance plan in a Latin American plant. The plan will be a tough sell in this setting because the Latin American employees typically experience a guaranteed wage with pay standards typically set at the same level throughout the country by negotiations between a union and the employers' association. The union does not prohibit pay-for-performance schemes, so the manager of a foreign-owned plant in that country might think it will be easy to implement such a plan. This would allow the plant to take on a pay structure consistent with those of the company's other factories around the world. But the manager may face far more opposition if he attempts to implement the system without using a more democratic form of leadership and consulting the employees. The manager must think about what the employees would say in response to the letter introducing the plan. The manager will want to find ways to stimulate positive responses in the letter to the employees introducing the plan. In addition to considering features of the intended message (e.g., the strength and logic of the arguments), the manager should take into account an entirely different set of factors that are likely to enhance positive cognitive responses to the message. For instance, the manager may want to lay the groundwork for introducing the pay-for-performance system by sending plant leaders a memo outlining various pay systems and including news stories from the business press about them, including the one that the manger is seeking to implement. The manager will also want to meet with opinion leaders among the employees to ask them to give the plan a try in order to see if more money can be made with the pay-for-performance plan—rather than unilaterally implementing it and "hoping for the best."[xiv] By understanding the employees' situation, the manager can pursue actions that help to prepare workers and their leaders for the changes ahead.

PERSUASION THROUGH PARODY AND ONE INDUSTRY'S RESPONSE

One powerful form of persuasion is parody. Consider the cigarette industry, an industry that has undergone dramatic changes over the last 40 years. These changes ultimately resulted in a ban of all tobacco advertising in 1969. You might think that the tobacco industry argued vigorously against such a ban, but surprisingly, they supported it.[xv] Their support was actually central in creating this ban on TV and radio that has been in place since 1971 in the United States.

What could explain the tobacco industry's support? In the 1960s, the newly passed Fairness Doctrine and public service announcements were granted equal time to explain the health consequences of smoking. This ruling by the U.S. Federal Communication Commission allowed anti-tobacco groups, such as the American Cancer Society, to run ads that parodied the tobacco ads' images of attractiveness and rugged independence (such as the famous Marlboro Man) showing that cigarette smoking led to illness, damaged attractiveness, and addiction. The advertisements were so effective in mocking the tobacco industry's image that cigarette consumption started to decline in the U.S. after the ads started

running in the 1960s. But with the tobacco ads prohibited after 1971, anti-tobacco forces were no longer able to receive free air time for their ads. In the first year after the ban on tobacco ads went into effect, cigarette consumption in the U.S. actually rose by three percent, and to top it off, tobacco firms were able to reduce their advertising expenditures by 30 percent.[xvi] The tobacco firms were then able to focus their advertising money on print and outdoor ads and on sponsorship of sporting events, which proved very profitable for them and may have led to an increase in tobacco consumption worldwide.[xvii]

INFLUENCE

Next, we will discuss something that companies in particular are interested in: ethically influencing employees to work effectively for their teams, colleagues, and customers. This is the process of influence, or stated more formally, **social influence**, which is defined as encouraging a change in behavior that was caused by real or imagined external pressure.[xviii] Defining influence in terms of a change in behavior distinguishes it from *persuasion*, which, as discussed earlier, refers to an attempt to change attitudes or beliefs but which may not necessarily lead to immediate behavior change. There are three behavior outcomes deriving from a successful influence attempt: conformity, compliance, and obedience, which will be addressed first.[xix]

Conformity
Changing one's behavior to match the responses or actions of others, to fit in with those in proximity.

    Conformity involves changing one's behavior to match the perceived requirements of others—that is, to fit in with those around us. Think of how out of place you would feel if you were not dressed as formally as everyone else at a dinner party. Or maybe everyone was exchanging business cards at a meeting, but you forgot to bring yours along—you probably would not forget them the next time. The key here is that the group or an opinion leader increases your desire to conform by just showing that everyone else is doing things a particular way.

    The second and third types of behavioral change are in response to more overt forms of influence. **Compliance** refers to the act of changing one's behavior in response to a direct request. The request may be coming from someone who is not in authority over you, but he or she may be in a position to command some kind of power, such as that possessed by an expert like a physician. Finally, **obedience** is a special type of compliance that involves changing one's behavior in response to an authority's command. For example, a police officer may order a driver to pull over and show his or her license and registration, or a supervisor may require you to work on a new task. Firms around the world normally think it is helpful to seek less overt forms of influence—that is, firms believe it is good to influence employees, customers, and colleagues if the targets of the influence believe the ideas are their own and they do not feel coerced, as with conformity.

Compliance
The act of changing one's behavior in response to a direct request.

Obedience
A special type of compliance that involves changing one's behavior in response to a directive from an authority figure.

Six Universal Principles of Influence

Social psychologist Robert Cialdini has distilled six universal principles of influence from the manifold research on this topic. The principles are universal in that they show up in a range of situations and across cultures.[xx] Figure 10-4 summarizes these principles, and each will now be examined in turn.

FIGURE 10-4   Six Universal Principles of Influence

Research in social psychology has identified six universal principles of influence:

1. **Social proof.** People get their "proof" about a product or idea based on validation from the group.
2. **Authority.** People are influenced by credible authorities. This authority can be the influencer or the testimony of an outside authority.
3. **Liking.** People are more influenced by people they like and have some positive relationship with.
4. **Consistency.** People like to be consistent with their values, and with statements they have made in the past. These values and statements will act to influence them toward making decisions that they feel are consistent with those past actions and statements.
5. **Reciprocation.** People are more likely to say yes to a request from those who have helped them or given them something before.
6. **Scarcity.** The scarcity and uniqueness of a product, service, or activity causes people to more highly value it and want it more.

1. **Social Proof** (also known as the consensus or social validation principle). Research shows that people are more likely to be influenced if they see evidence that many others, especially others they perceive as similar to themselves, are also doing a particular activity or buying a product. It is called "social proof" because the proof comes, not from the product, but from the group of people that is using or recommending the product. Marketers employ this principle in claiming that their products are the fastest growing or largest selling in the market, and by using phrases like, "Do not miss the action and excitement your friends are experiencing."

2. **Authority** (also called the expert principle). As with social proof, people often look for some kind of external validation before they make a decision, and are willing to follow the directions or recommendations of a trusted authority. For example, advertisers often succeed merely by employing believable actors dressed to look like experts (health care professionals, police officers, etc.), who may already be playing those characters on television or in the movies.[xxi]

3. **Liking**. People prefer to listen to individuals who they like or see some connection or similarity with, because they feel that people they like or have some connection with are likely to understand them and have their best interests at heart.[xxii] Research shows that people are more willing to buy insurance from agents who are similar to them in age and political and social preferences, including liking similar brands of beverages and cigarettes.[xxiii]

4. **Consistency**. People are more likely to say yes to a request or agree with something if they see it as consistent with an existing or recently made commitment of their own. The key word here is "precedent." If someone has made a public statement about a subject in the past, that person will be more likely to follow through on that statement, particularly if reminded of it. That is why publicly stated goals are much more motivational than private goals, and good managers will ask their staff to write down their goals for the year. Salespeople understand this influence principle and will ask a prospective buyer (the person they want to influence) questions about their preferences and values and then remind them of how their preferences fit the product. This works because people will rarely go against their own stated values.[xxiv]

5. **Reciprocation**. People are more willing to comply with requests from those who have given them something first. People around the world feel an obligation to reciprocate, so companies provide free samples, home owners put out free drinks to prospective buyers during an open house, and salespeople do favors for customers in hopes that they will purchase something in return.[xxv] Research shows that people are more likely to say yes to something if they perceive that request reciprocation for something that was done for them first.[xxvi] This is true even if the initial gift or favor is much smaller than the subsequent request.[xxvii]

6. **Scarcity**. People want to buy things or do things that they perceive are scarce, unusual, or limited in number. Thus, store promotions warn customers that the most you can buy of an object is six (implying a limited availability), or declare that there is only one day left to make a purchase (implying limited time), or tout a product's differentiated attributes and unique value-add. Scarcity is an effective influencer because people want to avoid any feeling of regret over missing out on something.[xxviii]

Each of these six influence principles will next be examined in greater detail.

Social Proof

There is strong evidence that people like to follow the crowd. That is, people are influenced to act when they think many others are behaving in a certain way or buying a certain product. Because of this, it is helpful to appeal to what the larger

---

Social proof
A principle of influence that states people are more likely to want to do something if they believe that many others are doing the same thing or buying the same product.

Authority
A principle of influence that states people are more likely to say yes to a request or purchase a product if an authority says it is good to do so.

Liking
A principle of influence that holds that people are more likely to be influenced by those whom they like or with whom they have similarities.

Consistency
A principle of influence that indicates how people are influenced by showing how their previous statements or stated values fit with a recommendation or request.

Reciprocation
A principle of influence that states people are more likely to say yes to a request when the requester has done something for that person in the past.

Scarcity
A principle of influence that argues that people are more likely to buy a product or want to do something that they perceive as scarce, unique, or dwindling in availability.

group is doing. Recall from Chapter 7 on motivation that this appeal to the group is how Lincoln Electric influenced workers at their new plant in Mexico to accept Lincoln's strict pay-for-performance system. Rather than implementing their motivation system by fiat, Lincoln Electric started with social proof. The workers in Mexico were not used to a piece-rate system and were more accustomed to very egalitarian pay rates. Lincoln Electric wisely decided not to force the radically different system on the workers all at once; rather, they selected a couple of volunteer employees to try it out first. When other employees started to see how well the volunteers were doing in terms of pay and bonuses, they started to opt into the system. The whole plant gradually moved to the pay-for-performance system within two years. Productivity went up and worker pay rose. Perhaps most importantly, it was the workers' idea to change, not the company's, so the change was more likely to stick.[xxix]

This use of the influence principle of social proof is but one of several examples of how these principles can be used ethically to influence subordinates, colleagues, customers, and even bosses to accept your ideas or to buy your products, and for them to do so willingly. Using an opinion leader is quite important (and having two is better), particularly in developing countries where competitive market systems are new. Firms should try to find one or two opinion leaders who can be early adopters of the firm's system, of performance-based pay, for example. When opinion leaders accept your system, and say so publicly, others are more likely to follow, as in the Lincoln Electric example, particularly if the opinion leaders can be seen to be doing well under the new system.

People faced with strong group consensus sometimes go along even though they think the others may be incorrect. This occurs even if there is strong evidence that the group is wrong. This phenomenon was investigated in a series of experiments conducted by psychologist Solomon Asch in the 1950s as he sought to understand why so many Germans and Japanese conformed to the destructive and often brutal orders of their leaders in World War II.[xxx] Asch was interested not only in the submission of individuals to group pressure, but also in people's ability to go against those conformity pressures. In one well-known experiment, Asch asked university students in groups of eight to match the lengths of two lines with a comparison line. It was easy to see which of the two lines was the best match. In the control condition, in which there was no group pressure about the choice, 95 percent of the participants got all 12 line matches correct.

But for the subjects in the experimental condition, the results were much different. Five confederates in the room had been instructed by Asch to give wrong answers. Asch's intent was to learn if students could be influenced to go along with the group and select an answer that was obviously wrong. Even though the students saw the right answer, 75 percent went against their own judgment and conformed to the group in giving the wrong answers.

Recently, Dr. Gregory Berns of Emory University conducted a similar experiment and used MRI brain-monitoring devices to learn which parts of the brain were used to process answers to questions. Berns' research confirmed Asch's conclusions that social pressure to conform creates major errors in judgment. As with Asch's study, Berns placed confederates in the group who were instructed to give the wrong answer before asking the lone study participant to answer. The lone participants almost always gave the wrong answers to a shape-matching test, although they had answered correctly when working alone on the same task earlier. People who had been getting near 100 percent of the answers correct when working alone started to get most questions wrong when people before them had answered incorrectly (out loud) first. One participant in the study later said he actually came to believe that the group was correct, and thought he must have been seeing things incorrectly. An MRI of the respondents' brains when they answered revealed that the respondents' visual cortexes were lighting up. The MRI indicated that the people in the experiment were struggling to see if they could believe what their eyes were telling them, particularly when the confederates in the group were telling them to believe something else by giving wrong answers.[xxxi]

It is easy to imagine that in cultures with high group cohesiveness, such as those in East Asia, social validation is extra important. And companies can utilize social proof in a number of other ways. For example, individuals are influenced by knowing that many people are adopting a certain mobile phone and plan, and by the belief that these people are similar to them. If you are a student or business person who travels overseas regularly, you might be looking for a good mobile phone plan that works in foreign countries. You could compare multiple plans, but there is a good chance you would be more influenced by friends who have similar requirements as you do. This is particularly helpful when you are uncertain about what you want. Firms can use this approach on a business-to-business level by pointing out to a prospect that other companies have purchased this product and are doing well with it. They would then put the prospect in touch with some of those similar clients who could explain how they use the company's product. This is particularly helpful in international business because such showcase clients in a foreign location can serve as reference points for other prospective customers there. It also explains why a firm may be willing to sell a new system at a break-even price to a new overseas client just to "get in the door" of that foreign country and showcase the new account to other potential clients there.

Another important point to remember is that if you want to discourage a behavior, it is best *not* to say, "Many people are doing this, but don't you do it." For example, one study looking at "no-shows" in a physician's office (no-shows are people who make an appointment but don't show up for it) noted that after putting up signs saying "No-shows are costly" and "We had 220 no-shows last month," the number of no-shows climbed to about 300 the next month.[xxxii] The fact that so many others were not showing up for their appointments influenced even more patients to miss them. This is also true with public service announcements. Ads that try to discourage behavior such as littering by showing how dirty a place is are essentially telling viewers, "Everyone is doing this, but you should not do it even though everyone else is." This type of message has been shown to *increase* the very behavior that the public service commercial is trying to discourage, so be careful how you use social proof. The lesson is clear: if you want to encourage something, show that many others are doing that same thing, particularly people who are similar to those you are trying to influence. But if you want to discourage behavior, do not say that many others are doing the action you want to discourage. Finally, it should also be noted that when you say, "We have a consensus, so that should convince this particular individual," this is not a correct application of the social proof principle. Social proof means that *many others*, especially others like the person you are trying to influence, are doing something, or buying this product. It is the consensus of the people "out there" that does the influencing.

Authority

People are also influenced by authority and expertise because as with social proof, it gives them a shortcut to an assessment or decision—if the authority says so, it must be ok. The authority principle is helpful to some extent because we do not have time to evaluate every decision we make. The authority principle is a powerful influencer. For instance, would you obey orders from a researcher directing a study (wearing an authoritative-looking white coat) to deliver painful electric shocks to another study participant in response to that study participant's incorrect answer to a quiz question that you just posed? And if so, what would the victim have to say to get you to stop obeying such orders? Or would you stop?

Social psychologist Stanley Milgram sought to answer this very question in a series of famous studies in the 1960s that showed how powerful an authority figure could be in influencing someone to continue with a seemingly harmful experiment.[xxxiii] This hearkened back to the argument given by those accused of war crimes after World War II at the Nuremberg Trials in Germany. The accused individuals repeatedly defended themselves by arguing that they had only been following orders in carrying out mass arrests and executions. In Milgram's experiments, three people took part: the "experimentor," the "learner," and the "teacher." Only the teacher was an actual participant; the experimentor was running the experiment while the learner was a confederate of the experimenter who had specific instructions on how to behave. The teacher was instructed to ask quiz questions of the learner, who was on the other side of a wall. Every time the learner would get a question wrong, the teacher was to give the learner an electric shock as a penalty. The voltage would be increased as they worked through the quiz, to a lethal 450 volts. It should quickly be pointed out that the learners were not really receiving electric shocks, but the person asking the quiz questions did not know this and thought the shocks he or she was administering were real.[1]

Before conducting his experiment, Milgram polled Yale students and professors as to what they thought would be the results, that is, would the teachers in the study continue to ask questions and administer increasingly powerful electric shocks to the learners behind the wall. Generally, the poll respondents believed that very few teachers would inflict a very strong shock, guessing around one percent.[xxxiv] They were in for a shock of their own. Even in the benign setting of a Yale University lab, some two-thirds of the teachers persisted in asking quiz questions all the way to the end of the list and administered supposedly lethal-level shocks of 450 volts, even when the learner answering the questions had fallen silent and was apparently injured or worse. Even when faced with the victims' repeated yelps and subsequent silence, those giving the shocks continued to do so because the authority figure of the lab researcher told them they had to do it—they had agreed and must continue, and that the experimenter would take all responsibility.[xxxv] Although not everyone went all the way up to 450 volts, very few teachers stopped before a possibly lethal 300-volt level.[xxxvi] Subsequent studies had similar results, in a variety of settings.[xxxvii] This study is a strong testimony to the power of authority to influence people to do things and also highlights the need to use authority judiciously and ethically.

As introduced in Chapter 9, the authority or expertise principle provides a helpful decision shortcut because we do not have time to evaluate each and every decision we make. Even in an organizational setting when we make purchases, it is helpful to have some expert opinion on what might be the best product. This could include an objective study or the recommendation of a technical expert who has no financial relationship to the product. Reliance on expert authority, however, can lead us to respond to the trappings (symbols) of authority, such as the style (a manner of speaking or the type of clothing worn), rather than the substance of genuine authority or expertise.[xxxviii] Why else would something as simple as a necktie be called a "power tie"? An expensive tie seems to be worn by people in authority or with high expertise in a certain area.

Indeed, much research suggests that people are more influenced by those who display their credentials and awards as a signal of their authority. Physical thera-pists who posted their credentials found that they significantly increased the compliance of their patients to the physical therapy regimens.[xxxix] Similarly, firms harness the power of authority by touting their experience, expertise, or scientific recognition (recall the well-known "Four out of five dentists surveyed..." adver-tisements for Trident sugarless gum). Though it may seem boastful to some people and some cultures, research shows that posting credentials, certificates, and other symbols of expertise is highly influential for employees, clients, colleagues, even patients.[xl] Even in countries such as Japan and China that emphasize the value of

---

[1] No study fooling people into believing they were significantly harming others would be permitted today.

In China, firms welcome and document visits from high-ranking government officials. Associating with a local authority figure lends legitimacy to their operation.

personal humility, credentialed people are seen as highly credible and are thus influential, and their authority is particularly potent.[xli]

The authority principle is widely seen in international business. For example, in China it is common when a high-ranking government official visits a plant or factory for photos and video to be taken with the official. Those photos will then be widely distributed and hung near the company entrance. This presentation of authority demonstrates that the firm has the right to exist in an environment that can sometimes be hostile to private business as it indicates some level of official support for the firm.[xlii] More recently, firms in China have been basing some of their operations near or on military bases for the same reason—to associate with a local authority figure that lends legitimacy to their operation and can influence local government officials to leave the firm alone and not interfere with its operation. It is important also to note that in influencing someone, you can be an authority and thus wield influence yourself, or you can refer to another authority to do the influencing.

Liking

It can be seen from the preceding discussion that people seek affirmation for their choices from both society ("Everyone is buying this") and from experts ("Expert research shows this is high quality"). They also seek opinions from and are thus influenced by those who they like, are similar to, or feel connected with in some way. Controlled research has identified several factors that reliably increase liking, but two factors stand out as especially compelling: similarity and praise. Similarity increases liking. People who have learned they share social values and political beliefs stand closer together and listen more closely to one another.[xliii] The converse is also true: differences decrease liking and thus influence. If someone disagrees with your political beliefs, you will reduce your influence with that person by rambling on and on about your political views every time you talk to that person. This is especially true if you never bother to listen to other people's views or even try to understand their position. With customers, bosses, colleagues, family, and friends, try to listen more than you talk, particularly if you want to build liking and influence.

Managers can also use similarities to build relations with customers external to the firm and internally. With both groups, informal conversations create ideal opportunities to discover common areas of enjoyment, be it a hobby, a certain sports team, or a type of cuisine. The important thing is to establish connections early, because they create a presumption of similarity and trustworthiness in subsequent interactions. It is much easier to influence people to buy a product, or to build support for a new project internal to the firm, when the people you are trying to influence are already leaning in your direction on other issues.

Praise can also establish liking and increase the probability that someone will say yes to a request. Research has shown that people feel great regard for others who have praised them regularly.[xliv] Although we don't recommend that you give disingenuous flattery, it should be pointed out that even false praise increases liking by those hearing the praise.[xlv] The importance of praise was further confirmed by experimental data showing that positive remarks about another person's traits, attitudes, and performance reliably generates liking for those offering the praise, as well as increasing the subsequent willingness to comply with requests made by the person offering the praise.[xlvi]

As might be expected, while praise can increase someone's liking of you, criticism can have the opposite effect. When a manager criticizes a person's actions and beliefs they are reducing their influence with that person. Certainly, a manager or supervisor must give employees frank assessments (which will be discussed in greater detail in Chapter 12, Human Resource Management). But managers should do so carefully—perhaps starting out with some praise, and an understanding of the employee's situation (note the importance of listening and asking questions again). If the employee did a bad job, take some time to find out what went wrong. Maybe the employee worked late hours but did not focus on the right things. Try to acknowledge the good first, before giving any critique. A person will usually be more open to criticism if they think you care about and are empathic to their situation. Use criticism very carefully, and only when necessary. For example, if you come into someone's office to ask them to do something, it is not a good idea to start with negative comments (like "You know the air conditioning is really too low in here" or "You are having lunch at your desk today? You know that is not good for you"). These criticisms will *reduce* your influence and make it *less* likely that the person will do what you ask. Criticize carefully, prefacing with praise and empathy when possible. Criticism, negative comments, and inflammatory statements reduce your influence. Because words can wound, choose them very carefully, and avoid unnecessary negatives and complaints.[xlvii]

What does a manager do if they have already damaged a relationship by making negative or careless remarks? Able managers can use praise to repair a relationship. Imagine you are the manager and your work necessarily brings you into contact with an employee whom you have come to dislike. No matter how much you help out this employee, it is never enough. Even worse, this employee never seems to believe that you are doing the best you can for him. The department's performance is suffering because of this conflict, and the situation is consistently uncomfortable. Research suggests ways of improving the relationship and your department's performance. Some praise for this employee's work will help to improve the relationship. That praise can be as simple as acknowledging the hard work they are doing or that they are handling a tough job that no one else wanted to do. If you do that, the employee will be more open to subsequent suggestions of how they can improve.

Internationally, there are cultures where negative comments may be even more damaging than in others. For example, in Thailand it is very rare to raise your voice or to offer negative feedback, particularly in the presence of others. The Thai society prizes very positive interactions and careful, face-saving criticism. If a manager from the West imposes a style of feedback characterized by a loud, stern voice in which negative feedback is provided, sometimes with other people present (a style that may be acceptable in the United States and other Western countries), a Thai individual is most likely to completely shut everything out because their response to the negative feedback is so strong. Therefore, in cultures where negative feedback is so damaging, try to give some praise first, do not criticize the employee in front of others, and focus on the person's performance, emphasizing what you would do instead.

Another strategy to build liking (in addition to praise) is to make sure you focus on others' needs instead of frequently talking about what you want.[xlviii] If you find that you are always telling others what you need to get done and what your goals are while failing to ask what the other person may need to get done, then you are focusing only on your situation. Taking the time to listen to someone's specific concerns (as opposed to just asking the superficial, "How are you doing?") will help to build liking (and influence) with that person. Understanding someone else's problems and what they value also helps with the next influence principle—consistency.

Consistency

The fourth universal principle of influence is consistency. Once individuals take a stand or go on record in favor of an idea or product, they typically prefer to stick to that position. A personal commitment ties an individual's identity to a position or course of action, making it more likely that he or she will follow through. This is because most individuals prefer to be consistent with statements and beliefs that they have made public so as to reduce cognitive dissonance, the discrepancy between what someone believes and how they act. Thus, seemingly insignificant commitments can lead to large behavior changes. For example, someone doing fundraising for a charity may be able to improve compliance with a request for money by first getting people to comply with a smaller, related request. In one classic study, researchers in a large city in Israel went to a large local apartment complex, knocked on half of the doors, and asked residents to sign a petition about establishing a recreation center for the handicapped. Because the cause was a good one, almost everyone signed the petition. Residents in the other apartments did not receive a visit and thus served as a control group for the study. Two weeks later, all the residents in the apartment complex were approached and asked to give some money for the recreation center. Among those who had not been asked to sign the petition, the control group, about half agreed to contribute. But nearly all of the people who had signed the petition two weeks earlier, thus making a public commitment in support of the center, donated money.[xlix]

Recall how powerful commitments can be in decision making (Chapter 9). Decision makers in organizations have a tendency to escalate their commitments to investments or decisions that are not working out and should be terminated. Although it is easy to say that a failing investment should be canceled, research shows it can be very difficult for decision makers to do so. Once someone has publicly stated or written something that makes their views explicit, that person's behavior is likely to adhere to that statement. Managers who can obtain a public statement from an employee committing to a goal or action are more likely to see the employee following through on that action. It is particularly effective if you can get it in writing; for example, ask people to send you an email detailing what they will do and when. One senior manager for a major firm in Hong Kong told us that he will send an email asking an employee for a confirmation of some task they will do, but in the email, that manager will deliberately make a small mistake, like writing down the wrong completion date. The employee invariably will come back with an email saying, "No, I agreed to do it by this date." As a result the manager has the employee's commitment in writing—not coerced, but fully voluntary. Indeed, numerous studies have shown how even a small, seemingly trivial commitment can have a powerful effect on future actions. As influence expert Robert Cialdini reminds us, people live up to what they write down.[l] It is important to notice that it is not *your* commitment that will influence people. It is *their* commitment, and your reminding them of that commitment can help to influence them.

Reciprocation

People are more willing to comply with requests from those who have provided something to them first. All societies subscribe to a norm that obligates individuals to repay in kind what they have received (in Portuguese, the word *obrigado* is used for "thank you," but it literally means "I am obligated"). Gifts can increase the numbers of donors and donations.[li] Free samples in supermarkets, free home inspections by pest control companies, and free gifts through the mail from marketers or fundraisers are all highly effective ways to increase compliance with a follow-up request.[lii] The evidence from the United States is that mailing out a simple appeal for donations produces an 18 percent success rate, but adding a small gift such as personalized address labels nearly doubles the donation rate to 35 percent.[liii] And this is with a gift that costs much less than the requested donation, which is consistent with much research into the reciprocation principle: an initial gift can be much lower in value than the subsequent request. Recently, charities in Hong Kong have also started to enclose self-stick personalized address labels with requests for donations.

In the United States, it has been found that purchasing managers who receive a gift are willing to purchase products and services they would have otherwise declined. This raises some discomfort and is why in some firms like Wal-Mart an employee can be fired if he or she has accepted any type of gift from a potential vendor, including a free meal. But in China and many developing countries, gift giving is a legal and established part of the business culture and builds relationships with clients.[liv] In China, it is assumed gift giving will lead to some form of reciprocity, and Chinese managers are known to tell people what they will give in return at the same time they ask for something.[lv] The key for a manager is interpreting the give and take in balancing the reciprocity.[lvi] By contrast, Westerners may deem such a "quid pro quo" scheme (i.e., **balanced reciprocity**, or the asking of something in return right away for a favor done) as inappropriate and too materialistic.[lvii] International managers need to understand reciprocity in the society in which they are working and to ensure that at the same time they are building relationships, they are also responding properly to those who may feel that they have provided something that results in a debt to be repaid.

Balanced reciprocity
Securing a promise of a near-immediate return for a favor done or a gift given; thought to be particularly important in China and in ethnic Chinese communities around the world.

Scarcity

People find objects and opportunities more attractive to the degree that they are scarce, rare, or dwindling in availability. At Florida State University in the 1970s, psychologist Stephen West surveyed students about the campus cafeteria food. He found that food's ratings rose significantly from one particular week to the next, even though there had been no change in the menu, food quality, or preparation. Instead, the improvement in perception of the food seemed to have come from the fact that the cafeteria had partially burned down and cafeteria meals would not be available again for several weeks. FSU students and staff were influenced by the sudden scarcity of the cafeteria and its food, which caused them to rate the desirability of the food much higher than before.[lviii] This illustrates a basic psychological principle called reactance.[lix] Reactance basically states that when we are told that we cannot have or do something, then we want it more. This psychological reaction common to all people helps to explain why scarcity operates as an influence principle. Promotions like "Only two more days to buy" or "You are limited to a maximum of three" encourages people to hurry up by touting scarcity.

Proprietors of nightclubs and restaurant use the scarcity principle by artificially limiting the availability of space. Nightclub owners, for example, commonly restrict the number of people allowed inside even though there is plenty of space, not because of maximum occupancy laws, but because their apparent inaccessibility makes these establishments seem more desirable. Similarly, some restaurant managers use scarcity to limit the number of seats available in order to build up their restaurant's desirability and ratings, particularly among opinion leaders in the community.

Internationally, firms often use the principle of scarcity. For example, the two main supermarket chains in Hong Kong emphasized that unless customers acted quickly, they would miss out on an opportunity to try several new healthy cereal products from the United States. Rather than emphasizing the health benefits of the cereal products the way they were commonly promoted in North America, the Hong Kong supermarkets shrewdly suggested in their ads and promotions that this particular brand was very difficult to get and that customers should take the opportunity to try it during its limited trial run. By emphasizing both the uniqueness of the product and its scarcity (limited availability and limited time), the supermarkets were able to create a buzz for their whole line of cereal products and health foods. Several years later these brands are hard to find in Hong Kong and South China, and when available, they carry a significant price premium.

Scarcity does not just influence consumers but also can be influential inside firms as well. A 1994 study detailed in the journal *Organizational Behavior and Human Decision Processes* showed that potential losses figure more heavily in managers' decision making than potential gains.[lx] This can drive managers to focus on information about threats while ignoring possible opportunities, and can encourage them to be overly risk-averse by trying too hard to minimize losses and avoid making mistakes, as discussed in Ch. 9. It is important to remember that being overly risk-averse and avoiding making mistakes will lead to not trying to do anything. Hockey great Wayne Gretsky once said that he certainly had missed every shot that he did not take. Avoiding mistakes will also increase errors of omission (deciding not to do something that was likely to have worked) and thus potential opportunities will be missed. Managers should be reminded to avoid creating an organizational culture that encourages risk aversion and discourages trial and error in new business opportunities. Scarcity is a powerful influencer, so use it ethically to bring out information about how your product or idea is unique and can bring useful benefits to clients that they do not want to miss out on. Similarly, do not let scarcity and fear of a mistake create too much risk aversion such that you or your organization fail to try anything new or different.

INFLUENCE PRINCIPLES IN FOUR DIFFERENT CULTURES

CULTURE

Do the six universal principles of influence operate the same in different countries and cultures? Are they truly universal? Research suggests positive answers to those questions. Consider the principle of reciprocation. Although some people talk about reciprocation like it only exists in some societies (China in the form of guanxi or connections, for example), research in sociology and social psychology has found that it exists in all societies.[lxi] For example, when Christopher Columbus traveled to the Western hemisphere and discovered the Caribbean Islands, he had no way of communicating with the natives there. How did Columbus signal that his intentions were peaceful? By giving the natives gifts. What

did the natives do in return? They gave gifts. Imagine, two cultures (European and Caribbean Islanders) that had been separated by at least ten thousand years with no common language, being able to communicate. Somehow they knew about reciprocation and knew to give gifts of approximately the same value.[lxii]

People are susceptible to the basic decision shortcuts and cognitive tendencies that characterize all societies. But cultural differences, institutions, and recent history in a country can modify the importance of different influence principles and how they are implemented. Three Stanford University researchers studied worldwide employees of a global bank, examining

(Continued)

four particular societies: the United States, China, Spain, and Germany. They surveyed the bank's branches within each country, asking employees if they would assist a colleague if requested to do so. Specifically, the researchers wanted to know which of the six main principles of influence might be most useful in influencing these employees to offer assistance. As you might guess, it was different for each culture.

The Germans were most compelled by authority; they were more likely to comply with the request in order to follow the organization's rules and regulations. They decided whether to comply by asking if official regulations allowed them to assist others. If the answer was yes, they granted the request.

U.S. employees favored a reciprocation-based approach to the decision to comply. They asked the question, "What has this person done for me recently?" and felt obligated to volunteer if they owed the requester a favor.

Employees in Spain based the decision mostly on friendship and loyalty, regardless of position or status. They asked, "Is this person connected to my friends?" If the answer was yes, they were especially likely to want to comply.

Chinese employees responded primarily to authority, in the form of loyalties to those with high status within their group or organization. When given a request, they asked, "Is this requester connected to someone in my unit, especially my boss or someone high up in the organization?" If the answer was yes, they were more likely to comply.

Although all human societies seem to respond to the same set of influence principles, the weights assigned to the various principles can differ across cultures. Persuasive appeals to audiences in distinct cultures need to take such differences into account.[lxiii]

NEGOTIATIONS

Negotiating
A process in which at least two partners with different needs and viewpoints try to reach agreement on matters of mutual interest.

Building on our understanding of persuasion and influence, we next look at another practical application of those topics: negotiations. Just as people regularly try to influence and persuade others, individuals and organizations regularly carry on negotiations. We negotiate with co-workers over a project's schedule and goals, with other organizations over deliverables and dates, with vendors over price, and with family, neighbors, landlords and even the city government. **Negotiating** is the process in which at least two parties with different needs and viewpoints try to reach agreement on matters of mutual interest. There are a number of issues that concern a negotiator, including the familiar cognitive shortcuts that we have seen in this chapter and in Chapter 9—balance of power, rational approaches to negotiations, and types of negotiations. We will examine each in turn.

Cognitive Shortcuts and Negotiation

We have already discussed cognitive shortcuts and is important to be aware that these same decision heuristics can push people toward suboptimal decisions in negotiations. Even in the careful, studied process of a long negotiation, people's decisions can be affected, perhaps overly so, by availability (vivid examples and stories, particularly emotional ones), loss aversion (not wanting to walk away from a deal that took months to arrange), consistency, and other heuristics that bias decisions. Negotiators need to be aware of these biases because they can and do occur in negotiations.

You will recall from Chapter 9 that it is not necessary to conduct an extensive analysis for most decisions. Similarly, it is not necessary to conduct negotiations in order to influence people: most everyday decisions do not require extensive analysis and negotiation. For a firm, bargaining over an item that is already fairly priced wastes time and money. Many firms today do not competitively bid all products, choosing instead to pay a little more and rely on certain suppliers that they can trust.

You will also recall that a set of decisions may be integrated together in order to make one big decision. For example, durable goods are typically expensive and issues such as delivery and installation must also be negotiated. In China, a negotiator for a state-owned enterprise (SOE) often needs to be able to show his

NEGOTIATION AND COMMUNICATION

"What we've got here is a failure to communicate."

—The prison warden to a rebellious prisoner (played by Paul Newman) who he had just knocked to the ground in the 1967 film *Cool Hand Luke*.

Cognitive shortcuts shape people's behavior in many ways. One critical shortcut involves our perceptions of the world. The role of perception is so great that it has given rise to a new philosophy, referred to as *solipsism*, which argues that the whole world is essentially created by an individual and his or her perceptions. It turns out that solipsism has a very practical side known as *plural solipsism*, which basically means to have a common world view. If you hold a plural solipsism of the world, you believe in a planet populated by friendly people who believe in a world like the one portrayed in the old Coca-Cola commercial with everyone singing about wanting to "teach the world to sing in perfect harmony." In this view, after all the cultural rituals are performed and languages translated, people still need to eat, sleep and take care of their families and friends, and so people are all the same. This philosophy underlies the premise suggested above in the famous film *Cool Hand Luke* and can be detected in a great deal of media and popular culture around the world: We are all the same deep down. Pacific Islanders, Middle Easterners, and business students.

If the whole world is like you and me, then most conflicts must simply be, like the warden said, a result of a failure to communicate. But as we saw in Chapter 2, Culture and International Management, and in this chapter, projecting our own feelings, beliefs, and world views onto others, and assuming others will share our way of thinking and behave as we do can be risky. Studies of cultural values and other differences around the world suggest that people hold some profoundly different world views, and these differences are not simply ones of style, fashion, or language. A contrary view is that culture and context matter a great deal, and in practice, people will have positions that are difficult to reconcile. This confirms the importance of understanding the process of negotiation. Different cultures emphasize different tactics in negotiations and can hold significantly different values.

Nordic and northern European cultures, as well as the U.S., emphasize fairness in negotiations and are more likely to present a reasonable position. Many other cultures, particularly in the lesser developed economies of the Middle East and parts of East and South Asia, are more likely to start out with a more extreme position to test how far their opponent can be pushed. A Chinese negotiator may start out with a requirement that a partner firm turn over its intellectual property so they can properly produce the product. However, if you are negotiating for your firm, you know this would be impossible. How can the negotiator seriously believe you would do this? Is it just an intimidation tactic? Is it an effort to anchor the discussion around your intellectual property? Is the negotiator really serious? It may be one or all three, and therefore you must be aware of the different processes of negotiation within different cultures along with the differing values and goals they hold.

Hofstede, G., & Hofstede, G. J. (2004). *Cultures and Organizations: Software of the Mind.* New York: McGraw-Hill.

Nisbett, R. (2004). *The Geography of Thought: How Asians and Westerners Think Differently . . . and Why.* New York: Free Press.

or her superiors a concession that was obtained from a foreign multinational enterprise, in order to prove the negotiation was handled in an aggressive manner. The MNE can make a number of small concessions that will help the Chinese negotiator look good in front of superiors and show that he or she is not falling prey to the type of unequal treaties that were foisted upon China by the European powers and Japan and in the 19th and early 20th centuries.[lxiv] Smaller concessions might come out of areas such as delivery, installation, and maintenance. It may not seem much to you or your firm, but to the SOE negotiator (or anyone with whom you are negotiating) it might be enough to satisfy the person's supervisors and seal the deal. It is not unlike a gardener agreeing to give greater care to one section of your lawn in exchange for less care over a section you seldom use.

A Rational Approach to Negotiation

In practice, no strategy can solve every negotiation problem. Starting out by asking for a high price in negotiations works in some cultures, such as in China or the Middle East, and in fact may be expected, but in other cultures, such as those in northern Europe, a negotiator who does this might be seen as tricky and dishonest. This increases the likelihood of the deal falling through and bad feelings all around.

Think of a time you had to negotiate something simple, like the price of a watch from a street vendor. Anyone who has traveled to East Asia, Africa, or the Middle East, or even to a number of ethnic neighborhoods in large North American cities, has probably had this experience. How did you feel when the vendor asked $75 for a watch that you knew would probably only sell for about $15 at a retail store, and with no purchase guarantee? Did you take it as just part of the negotiations—part of the fun of bargaining? Or did you think that the vendor was a crook with whom you would certainly never do business? If you thought the former, you are probably from a culture that typically bargains very hard and has a long history of trade, travel, and barter. Such cultures start high and ask for $75 because they expect you to start very low, say at $5, and negotiations proceed from those two extreme positions. By starting high, the seller is trying to anchor the negotiations near that number. Cultures in the Middle East and East Asia, particularly China, will often start negotiations at extremes to test the other party and gauge their commitment to the deal.

But individuals from northern Europe or Anglo-American backgrounds will likely respond negatively to a high initial price. In these cultures, negotiators generally expect each side to bargain fairly and not seek significant advantage. This may be related to the more egalitarian nature of these cultures—the relatively low power distance in the Northern European and Anglo countries—or by the sense of fairness Anglo and northern European cultures try to portray toward strangers.[lxv] If you are the type of person who does not like to start at an extreme price, resist the temptation to call the other side crooks and walk away if they start out the negotiations too high, whether you are buying a watch or negotiating for a long-term lease on a factory in southern China. In international business, it is essential to avoid projecting your own value system onto others, as well as understanding that a person's initial negotiation stance might be part of their culture, or may even reflect what is expected of them by their superiors or the government.[lxvi] Problems in negotiations are often not due only to a failure to communicate.

In this section, we survey some basic principles of negotiation and return to some irrational tendencies discussed earlier that commonly arise in negotiations. When you understand the underlying dynamics of negotiation, you will be able to isolate common biases and mistakes that lead to suboptimal agreements and instead base your decisions on sound business principles. We then discuss specific strategies that strengthen negotiation skills during each of the three stages of a negotiation: preparation, bargaining, and settlement.

Balance of Power

In any negotiation, one side may have more leverage than the other side. Recall from our discussion of Porter's Five Forces model in Chapter 5 that large customers can reduce the profitability of an industry. This is because in negotiations between big and small companies, the large company typically has greater leverage over price. A negotiation's outcome may be of much greater overall importance to the small company, or perhaps even essential to survival, while the large company's threats of walking away may leave the smaller company with no choice but to accept the larger firm's demands.

But it is not always clear which firm has the power in a relationship. An MNE may find that it must tread very carefully in a developing country because its negotiation partner may have the backing of the government. The government may want an MNE to open a factory in their country, but it may also have the choice of several MNEs in that industry and may be able to play each MNE off one another in the negotiation. Negotiating skill is especially critical in such a case because it can help maximize what you receive from the negotiations.

FIGURE 10-5 Two General Types of Negotiations

- **Distributive negotiations.** This type of negotiation assumes a fixed set of resources to bargain over, although this assumption may not be accurate and should be challenged by the other side. It is also known as fixed-pie negotiations.
- **Integrative negotiations.** This type looks aggressively for win-win solutions that also enlarge the resources that both sides might capture in negotiations. It is also known as expanding-pie negotiations.

Types of Negotiations

Negotiations and negotiation issues can be classified into two broad types: distributive (sometimes colloquially known as "fixed-pie") and integrative (also called "expanding-pie") negotiations.

Distributive Negotiations

In all negotiations, the parties seek to divide up available resources. Distributive negotiations are those in which opposing negotiators are concerned only with how the (apparent) fixed pie will be divided. In dividing the pie unevenly, one party's gain would represent the other party's loss; the more one party receives, the less the other party receives. Sometimes negotiations may involve only one issue, such as the cash sale of a watch from a street vendor in Chinatown. In such cases, any gain for one party is at the expense of the other party. The resource they are negotiating for is fixed (the selling price of a good), and the negotiation is purely distributive.

Integrative Negotiations

An integrative negotiation differs from a distributive one in that integrative negotiations have the potential to expand the size of the resources available for the negotiators to divide. Integrative negotiations do this in two ways. First, they expand the range of items of interest in a negotiation and thus make the deal bigger. Second, they try to identify and incorporate issues that the two sides value differently to create additional room for trade-offs and needed concessions. When parties value items differently, they can give some concessions on certain items they value less in exchange for gaining concessions on those they value more, which adds value for both parties.

Negotiation must involve more than one item to be integrative. Even though negotiating multiple topics simultaneously can complicate the negotiations, including multiple issues can add value for both parties. In practice, an integrative negotiation produces greater winnings for everyone involved. The negotiator with less power in the deal often has more to gain from an integrative negotiation because a purely distributive negotiation awards more of the pie to the stronger side. A negotiator who is in a weaker position should seek an integrative negotiation in which other items are brought into the negotiation. For example, in negotiating a joint venture in a developing country where the government might be involved, an MNE that has less leverage than the local firm may bring other items to the table to help promote the establishment of the joint venture. The Chinese government is typically interested in acquiring technology, both in terms of products and manufacturing processes.[lxvii] Thus, the MNE can use the issue of creating jobs as well as bringing new technology to the region.

CLINICAL TRIALS IN EMERGING ECONOMIES: SOME ETHICAL ISSUES

Many organizations have outsourced a variety of tasks to emerging economies around the world. We have all experienced the overseas call centers for banks, software manufacturers, and hotel reservation lines. In recent years pharmaceutical firms have also started doing some of their clinical trials for drugs in emerging economies.[2] Pharmaceutical firms must extensively research and test their products before public consumption is permitted and governments in emerging economies are very supportive to firms bringing in knowledge industries such as drug and medical device research and development. Basic research is carried out in labs, usually in the firm's home country. Initial tests are done on animals, and later on healthy human volunteers. When a drug is determined to be safe with no apparent side effects the drug is given to humans in clinical trials. In 1997 over 80 percent of these clinical trials occurred in the United States and less than five percent were in countries outside of Western Europe or the U.S. But by 2007 less than 60 percent of clinical drug trials were conducted in the U.S. with approximately 30 percent conducted outside the U.S. and Western Europe. Evidence shows that the number of trials done in China and Southeast Asia will increase rapidly in the coming years.

One reason that many more clinical trials are being done in emerging economies is the diffusion of safety and test standards spurred by globalization. Whereas in the past, the regulations for drug efficacy and safety in the developing world were comparatively lax, today they are becoming much stricter. China, Taiwan, and South Korea, for example, all now require drug trials to be carried out locally before they will approve drugs for their citizens. Other countries such as Singapore and Thailand would like to see more local tests but are likely to approve drugs that are already approved in North America or Europe.

A second reason for the increasing number of clinical trials outside of North America and Europe is medicine's better understanding of regional diseases, both communicable and inherited. For example, there may be as many as 350 million sufferers of Hepatitis B in Asia, compared with around five million in North America. Drug firms have noticed opportunities for developing treatments for populations that suffer from diseases that may be more specific to a particular region. To do so, research protocol suggests that they conduct at least

some of this research in the countries that suffer more from the disease. In the case of Hepatitis B, it would be China, where about 15 percent of the population is thought to suffer from that disease. Yet drug firms have been hesitant to conduct the necessary research for a major new drug largely for Asia partly because of the unknowns involved in the research process and working with regulatory agencies. But they will have to set aside these concerns in doing basic research in Asia and following up with clinical trials in several Asian countries to be able to meet this and other difficult diseases such as stomach cancer (also much more common in East Asia) head on.

Clinical trials cost only about half as much in emerging economies. A physician in Thailand will have training comparable to most physicians in the developed world but that costs a lot less. This will facilitate additional research in Asia and help drug companies overcome their resistance to committing basic research there. Nevertheless, drug firms still have concerns about the testing standards in some countries such as China, where some serious patient problems and breaches of testing protocol have occurred with clinical trials; some subjects in clinical trials have died during poorly managed tests. A decrease in the cost and time required in offshore drug testing may lead to drugs being available faster, resulting in the saving of many lives, but many ethical concerns must be taken into consideration as testing and regulatory standards continue to be problematic, even though they are improving. Would you recommend that pharmaceutical firms be more aggressive in researching and testing new drugs in emerging economies? How can they better control the drug testing process in emerging economies where regulations and scientific testing protocol are not well developed? What challenges would you foresee for Western pharmaceutical firms seeking to do more clinical trials in China, particularly with the help of Chinese drug firms and hospitals?

Eaton, M.A. (2004). *Ethics and the Business of Bioscience*. Stanford, CA: Stanford Business Books.

Jack, A. (2008, January 29). New lease on life? The ethics of offshoring clinical trials. *Financial Times*, p. 9.

Troy, D. B. (2006). *Remington: The Science and Practice of Pharmacy* (21st ed.). Philadelphia: Lippincott Williams & Wilkins.

ETHICS

THE NEGOTIATION PROCESS

Sometimes negotiations end with one party dissatisfied. Human error is one reason this occurs. We process information incorrectly or allow our judgments to be swayed by emotions or irrelevant events. In this section we examine those

[2]Understand that by doing clinical trials overseas, North American and European pharmaceutical firms are *not* replacing their local clinical trials with those done overseas. To get a drug approved in the United States, for example, a pharmaceutical firm must go through double-blind tests of their drug versus a placebo as well as some other tests (in most cases). The regulations in Europe are slightly less strict, but clinical trials must also be conducted there. Trials done in emerging economies cannot be substituted for locally conducted trials in the U.S. or Europe for the purpose of securing drug approval (Eaton, 2004; Troy, 2006).

things that can affect an international manager's negotiations. We will first return to issues of heuristics, biases, and culture, and introduce some common negotiating terms—Best Alternative to a Negotiated Agreement (BATNA) reservation price, target price, and positioning—as well as the importance of information, trust, impasses, and positive emotion.

Heuristics and Biases Revisited

In Chapter 9, we discussed a number of shortcuts or heuristics that people use in making decisions. Some of decision-making heuristics are quite useful because they reduce the amount of time and effort needed to make a decision, such as leaning on the expert opinion of a pharmacist when buying over-the-counter medicine. But sometimes heuristics can lead to an overemphasis on some information and the complete overlooking of other relevant information. In negotiations the same biases can occur. Some of the most common biases appear at the start of a negotiation, such as unrealistic expectations, improper frames, and anchors. Subsequent problems can occur during the negotiation if previous commitments are over-valued, leading to the escalation of commitment. The heuristics and biases we will examine include the role of unrealistic expectations, anchors, escalation of commitment, over-competitiveness, and framing.

Unrealistic Expectations

Negotiators need to recognize that unrealistic expectations can include those that are too high or too low. An underconfident negotiator who starts out by undervaluing his or her position and bargaining power will make unnecessary concessions or choose a low starting point (anchor). This lack of confidence affects the other members of his bargaining team, and everyone starts to undervalue the team itself. As a result, the team's assets are not well represented. In other cases, negotiators can be overconfident and believe that they know in advance how a negotiation should end, not taking the time to find out what the other side values. This lack of empathy can lead to a confirming-evidence bias that shuts out new sources of information and possible alternatives that may provide value to both sides.

Anchors

Recall that **anchoring** is a cognitive bias that describes the common human tendency to rely too heavily, or anchor, on one piece of information when making decisions. During the decision-making or negotiation process, individuals may anchor on a specific topic or value such as a starting price, and then discussion may proceed around that value or topic. For instance, novice car salespeople often make the mistake of bringing up an item that is not that important to the sales negotiation, such as the price of an option that the customer has not mentioned, and discussion can get sidetracked around that option.

An anchor may be set by a previous transaction price, an industry standard, or a rumored price, as well as an initial offer. In one study on anchoring, a group was asked to write down the last two numbers of their government identity numbers. Right after that, they were asked to submit mock bids on some luxury items. It was found that the half of the audience with higher two-digit ID numbers submitted bids that were consistently higher. Writing down the unrelated first number determined the second number, even though there was no logical connection between them.[lxviii] Because we want signposts and guides to help us with our judgments, the natural tendency is to focus on an anchor, even when that anchor has very little applicability to the current situation or is pushing in an unwanted direction.[lxix] Those bidding first can use anchors to their favor by setting the numbers and topics around which the negotiations will focus. The other side must then try to re-anchor the negotiations in a different area, sometimes by suggesting small concessions or by other means of changing the topic.

Escalation of Commitment

Managers like to succeed and follow through with what they stated they will accomplish. Pressure caused by the threat of failure or not reaching an agreement in a negotiation can be significant. This leads managers to sometimes escalate their commitment during a negotiation until they end up accepting a deal that they should have walked away from. Chinese negotiators are famous for recognizing this characteristic and delaying negotiations until the last minute before their counterparts need to catch a plane, hoping to clinch favorable deals from executives who do not want to leave China empty-handed. Business people should recognize this tactic and be prepared for it. It is also important to avoid escalation of commitment; once a negotiator has committed time and energy to a negotiation, that negotiator must fight against the natural instinct to agree to a deal simply to reach an agreement. Never be afraid to walk away from a deal if it is not what you want, that is, you must know your alternatives, particularly your BATNA and reservation price, which are discussed below.

The Best Alternative to a Negotiated Agreement (BATNA)

BATNA
Best alternative to a negotiated agreement.

Decisions should not be evaluated in isolation, but must be assessed in the context of what other *reasonable alternatives* may be at hand. In particular, negotiators must be fully aware of their **BATNA** or best alternative to a negotiated agreement. This brings one brief historical example to mind. After one particularly large battle between a U.S. (Union) army and a Rebel (Confederate) army during the American Civil War of the mid-nineteenth century, U.S. President Abraham Lincoln was being pushed by his advisors to replace the talented but overly cautious General George McClellan, who was properly blamed for the battle's so-so outcome as well as his failure to follow up and pursue the Rebel army. They urged President Lincoln to replace McClellan with anyone. In the true spirit of a negotiator Lincoln replied, "Anyone may be fine for you, but I must have someone."[lxx] Lincoln understood that McClellan was his best alternative until he could find some suitable (and willing) replacement commanders, which required a lot of trial and error until good leaders such as General Ulysses S. Grant finally emerged.[lxxi]

This example highlights the point that having and identifying alternatives to various key decisions in a negotiation are very important. Decisions should not be evaluated in isolation, but must be assessed in the context of what other reasonable alternatives may be at hand. For example, it is not very helpful to say that a certain decision is bad and that you disagreed with it without proposing *what you would have recommended instead*. In this way, you can make comparisons between your decision and the chosen one and the strengths and weaknesses of both choices. As President Lincoln pointed out, he still had to select *some* general; "anyone" was not a real choice. Practically speaking, this means that negotiators must be fully aware of their alternatives, particularly their BATNA. It is better to quit a lengthy negotiation than to accept a deal at a loss. Do not be afraid to walk away from any negotiation that provides terms that are worse than your best alternative to the negotiated agreement. Remember what the avoidance of escalation of commitment implies here: it is better to quit a lengthy negotiation than to accept a bad deal just to show something for the effort.

The Importance of Information

All of the discussion above about best alternatives, concessions, and positions reminds us once again that having well-organized and relevant information is crucial to effective negotiations. The ancient Chinese philosopher Sun Tzu wrote about the value of information in negotiation and conflict, particularly understanding the other side's strengths, weaknesses, and goals.[lxxii] Many negotiations are multidimensional and offer opportunities for integrative, resource-enlarging solutions. If the negotiating parties do not stay open to mutually beneficial proposals, a negotiation may falter and valuable opportunities may remain unexplored, leaving potential value undiscovered. This is particularly important to enterprises seeking cooperation on development projects and joint ventures. Significant value can be left in the negotiation room if the two sides do not have the tools and information by which agreement can be reached. The more information open to the negotiators, the more likely the "goods on the table" can be identified and made useful to both sides, creating an integrative, win-win negotiation.

It is important to collect as much information as possible because most negotiators will not offer the information up front. Once you and your opponent's underlying interests are known, you can begin to assess relative values. You can trade off concessions on issues that are less important to you in exchange for concessions on issues that are less important to your opponent. Understanding your counterpart's BATNA and reservation price is very valuable, but this is difficult to determine. For example, your negotiation partner might ask, "What's the maximum you will pay?" In effect, he is essentially asking for your **reservation price**, which is something you should never reveal. Sometimes you can answer a different question, or move the discussion toward other topics such as guarantees or delivery dates.

Reservation Price
A reservation price is the absolute bottom price that is acceptable.

ALEX RODRIGUEZ'S NEGOTIATION

The contract negotiations of baseball's Alex Rodriguez in 2000 and again in 2007 are an example of the negotiation process. In 2007, Rodriguez shocked the New York Yankees and Major League Baseball by activating an opt-out clause with three years and $81 million remaining in his contract, and notifying the Yankees in the middle of the 2007 World Series that he wanted a new contract. It was rumored that Rodriguez wanted a new 10-year contract for about $350 million, though he finally did re-sign with the Yankees for less than that. The contract that Rodriguez had opted out of was a 10-year, $252 million, guaranteed contract signed in 2000 with the Texas Rangers—by far the highest contract in sports history, eclipsing the previous record by over 100 percent. (Rodriguez was traded to the New York Yankees in 2004.)

How did Rodriguez's agent, Scott Boras, originally negotiate such a rich contract? In part, Boras reframed the negotiations by distributing a 70-page booklet to interested teams that summarized Rodriguez's statistics and his individual, incremental contribution to team revenues, so teams could see how much he was really worth. The booklet was full of data about how much ticket sales, parking fees, and food concessions went up when Rodriguez was playing. In this way, Boras was able to anchor the negotiations around the total package that Rodriguez brought to his team in terms of extra revenue and profit, and frame discussions away from comparisons with other players in professional baseball and their (much lower) salaries. It certainly made a difference—Rodriguez wanted to sign with his original team in 2000, but ended up with a much more lucrative deal by moving to the Rangers. Finding a more favorable anchor (incremental revenue brought in when Rodriguez is in the game), and reframing away from strict comparison with other players' salaries was key to the quarter of a billion dollar contract. Boras wanted to negotiate a new contract with the Yankees or other teams in 2007 and he convinced his client to exercise the opt-out clause in the original 10 year deal signed in 2000. Rodriguez eventually signed another 10 year contract that basically amounted to an extension of his current one. The Yankees had managed to persuade Rodriguez to drop his $35 million annual salary demand by reframing the negotiations in terms of Rodriguez becoming the greatest third baseman in baseball history and breaking the career homerun record in storied Yankee Stadium.

In order to assess your own strength and set your own BATNA and reservation price, you need to know both your own main or proximate alternatives and those of your counterpart. Your negotiating team's strategic positioning relies on the underlying goals and interests of your opponent and your opponent's stated position. To negotiate most effectively, negotiators need to base their decisions on reliable information. But here, too, individuals are subject to several common biases that influence how information is acquired and processed.

First among these biases is that most people make decisions based on vivid experiences and events. Unfortunately, memory is often selective and subject to the availability heuristic. People make decisions and draw conclusions based on the information and events that they can remember, instead of the necessary facts. We remember vivid, spectacular, or catastrophic events more readily than mundane ones. For example, the Great Depression of the 1930s permanently imprinted the memories of many Americans and Europeans from that era. Experience taught them that neither investments nor jobs could be counted on, and that no amount of savings was enough. Many of those people refused to process information about the safety and profitability of a diversified portfolio of securities and other long-term investments. Instead, they put their money in low-interest, insured accounts and lived more frugally than necessary. Many older Americans still use the expression "play the stock market" like it is a game and not an investment. This problem was not confined to the United States. For decades, some Japanese people kept their savings in accounts with the Japanese Post Office at interest rates hovering around 1 percent. Only in recent years have they learned the value of compound interest and started to demand higher returns on their money.

Second, individuals are often as impressed by the theatricality of a presentation as its substance. Because we more easily recall facts or events that are described to us in vivid terms, negotiators who use picturesque language and concrete examples are more effective in influencing others than negotiators who supply the same information in less vivid terms. Do not be overly influenced by salesmanship and emotion. Cast a skeptical eye on the other side's enthusiasm for their product or capabilities. Beware of statements such as "Our market is huge" or that "Nine times out of ten" something will happen. Instead, seek out hard figures and evaluate them carefully. Negotiators should be sure to provide that data or tell customers where it can be found. It should be noted that it is sometimes said that Chinese negotiators do not like to provide data with their presentations. That preference may be limited to the old state-owned enterprises that were not charged with making a profit but with maximizing production or employment. Newer Chinese organizations today are concerned with profits and data, and that information should be sought out. Negotiators should not settle for broad, unsubstantiated generalizations such as "The market is very big"; rather, they must determine with the help of consulting firms or other knowledgeable people how big the given product market is in specific areas, such as the coastal provinces or major city markets.[lxxiii]

This emphasis on information is also a reminder that a decision *must* be assessed in comparison with other possible decisions. No decision should ever be assessed in isolation. There are always alternatives and opportunity costs; even if the only alternative is doing nothing, it is still an alternative.

Reservation Price

A reservation price is the firm's absolute bottom price that is acceptable. For a firm selling something, the reservation price would be just *above* the BATNA. Reservation prices are most easily defined in single-issue, distributive negotiations and are more difficult to establish in more complex, integrative negotiations. Nonetheless, it is always useful to establish a set of conditions that describes the reservation price. This set of conditions can serve as a benchmark for other offers and help

Visual aids can be very effective when making a presentation because the audience is more likely to understand and recall facts or events that have been described in vivid, picturesque terms.

suggest your position to your opponents without giving away too much information about what you can pay and what you wish to pay.[lxxiv]

Target Price

Negotiators should also set targets for what the price they wish to pay or receive. This is the value that you would like to have—your preferred, or "blue sky," agreement. While reservation price establishes the lowest price you will accept, target price shifts your focus from getting just enough to negotiating what you and the other side want. Focusing on your target during the negotiation gives you a clear vision of what you hope to achieve. The negotiator needs to create doubt in the opponent's mind about the point at which they would prefer to walk away rather than reach an undesirable deal. The negotiating team can create such doubt by emphasizing the target price (not the reservation price) and negotiating terms on other items. If the other side demands concessions, follow the reciprocation principle and ask for concessions in return right away—the other side will be more likely to reciprocate with concessions if you ask right after they asked you for concessions.

Framing

Recall our earlier discussion of loss framing's effect on people's decision making. Research shows that negotiators can react very differently to identical proposals when the perspective, or framing, changes. As anchoring on a specific number can strongly influence negotiations, the way a situation is framed or presented also greatly influences the action taken. If a frame is poorly constructed, a negotiator may unwittingly make a money-losing choice. For example, managers can err by framing an investment solely in terms of gross margins rather than in terms of the strategic value of the decision.

One example from high-end consumer sales shows a very interesting approach to framing. A company offered a range of spas, from the basic outdoor variety for a few thousand dollars to a fancier indoor spa complete with its own room for $15,000, and it was having trouble selling the more expensive spa. Prospects were comparing the expensive interior spa with the cheaper outdoor models and concluding that they were just too expensive. Finally, the firm hit on an idea. Rather than emphasizing the more expensive spa's fancier features and functions (remember the problem of simply pushing features and functions while not listening to and addressing customer needs), they asked prospective customers about something they are all concerned with: the value of their homes. The spa salesperson then asked the customers how much they thought their homes would go up by in value if they added an extra room. Depending on which area of North America they lived in, that answer could be $30,000 or more. The spa salesperson then asked how much it would cost to add a room such as an enclosed porch or a small den to their home, something that could easily top $25,000. The salesperson then pointed out to prospects that buyers of the top-of-the-line spa were able to add value to their homes because the enclosed spa was considered to be an additional room for the house. By adding the spa, customers would meet two of their stated needs: getting the spa they wanted and adding another room to their home. Given the increase in their homes' values, the spa would be an excellent value, in fact it would practically pay for itself. When framed as a comparison with adding a room to the house, instead of in comparison to the cheaper spas, the high-end $15,000 spa became quite desirable and even economical.[lxxv]

Framing is essential to negotiation. For example, instead of focusing on risks in a negotiation, you might want to focus on opportunities. In negotiating your salary, rather than focusing only on the asking salary, you might want to focus on the benefits you can bring in. The type of information brought into a negotiation "sets the table" for the interpretation and understanding of all negotiating that follows.

Finally, remember loss framing and the scarcity principle. People are more influenced by avoiding a loss (or not missing out on some benefit) than by equivalent gains. If you can cast your negotiations in terms of helping the other side not miss out on some benefit, that is usually a more effective frame. In any case, negotiators will want to understand both their own frames and their negotiating partner's, and it may be necessary to test different types of analyses and perspectives to achieve a win-win agreement.[lxxvi]

Fairness and Trust

Most people are very sensitive to fairness issues. Some people will walk away from a good deal just to punish someone on the other side of the negotiation who they perceived as behaving unfairly or being deceptive—even if they would have been better off with that deal. This is illustrated in a well-known experiment often run by economists called the ultimatum game.[lxxvii] There are several versions of the experiment, most of which give two or more participants the chance to split up a sum of money, say $20. If the players can't agree on how to split the money, neither side gets any of it. The players have a limited amount of time to negotiate the distribution of funds. If on the last round, Player 1 seeks to keep, say, $15 for himself and leave just $5 for Player 2, studies show that Player 2 will reject that split, even if by rejecting it he or she is left with nothing as the game ends. Thus, Player 2 will typically punish Player 1 for not being fair, even if it is clear he would be better off by accepting the final $5 offer. After all, his BATNA is zero dollars, and the reservation price would just likely be just a few cents above that. Although people are usually loss-averse, that loss aversion may be overridden by a sense of equity and the desire to punish unfairness. Why else would we make multiple phone calls and write letters about a small sum of cash that we think a company cheated us out of? Most people will say, "It is not the money that is important but the principle of the thing," when explaining an irrational decision to punish unfairness and "get even" at a significant cost to themselves. Interestingly enough, people from poorer countries such as Indonesia will also reject unfair splits in the money—even rejecting final offers equivalent to three days' wages and walking away with nothing—just to get even with those they feel are bargaining unfairly and make sure they also walk away with little or nothing.[lxxviii]

In negotiations, the dynamics can be quite similar. Negotiators often will walk away from an economically rational agreement if they believe they have been unfairly treated or deceived in some way. They will do this even if this agreement is above the reservation price and should be accepted. This problem can be compounded by culture. What is fair for all sides is often difficult to define. A fair outcome for a negotiator from an egalitarian society such as Sweden might be one in which parties share benefits more or less equally. For another society, such as Latin America, a fair distribution would be based on the relative resources and work each person contributed. Someone from yet another culture, as in China or India, might argue that it is fairest to allocate benefits according to need, even if the split in money is very uneven.[lxxix]

Therefore, it is essential that a negotiator be cognizant that fairness is an issue. People who feel they are being treated unfairly become angry and walk away from what still are good deals. Emotions are a part of any negotiation, but negotiators who focus on getting back at the other side because of their unfair tactics may end up hurting themselves as well. Negotiators are much more likely to achieve compromises with opposing parties they like and trust. When we trust someone, we are less likely to suspect ulterior motives, traps, or deception and minimize any perceived unfairness. Most negotiations are not one-shot deals, and we usually expect to maintain an ongoing relationship after an agreement is reached. If you expect to do more deals in the future, trust is essential. Thus, it is valuable to a firm to build trust over time.

Impasses in Negotiations

An **impasse** simply means that you and your partner cannot reach an agreement. The situation may arise that no agreement is improving either side's BATNA. In such cases, a manager needs do some creative, integrative problem solving to create more value, or be willing to walk away from the negotiations. In contrast, a "sweet deal" may exist for both sides but a handshake cannot be reached because the solution is distributive and both sides are holding out for a bigger piece of the negotiation pie and do not want to feel unfairly treated.

Several strategies can help restart stalled negotiations. First, try to focus on underlying interests or values rather than only on positions. Positions may become more matters of pride or fairness rather than substance; in this case, return to what people value and need. Also try to meet your opponent's needs in appearance while fulfilling your team's interests in substance. By focusing on the substance of your interests, you are more likely to uncover new integrative proposals that enlarge the pie for both sides. Second, as the reciprocation principle recommends, make an initial small concession, then suggest one in return. Sometimes people need to be shaken from entrenched positions before they can make significant moves. One arbitrator who works on cases in North America told us that he starts out a negotiation between two parties by offering both of them a concession: he

Impasse
When a manager and his or her negotiating partner cannot reach an agreement.

gives them the first hour of the arbitration at no charge (a substantial gift). He then asks in return that both sides promise to bargain fairly during the negotiation. Research in social psychology over the past 60 years suggests that most people will reciprocate.[lxxx] Third, the arbitrator also suggested that it may be helpful to bring in a third party. A fresh perspective sometimes gets a negotiation back on track.

In some cases, you will not be able to reach agreement. Always terminate a negotiation cordially. Inform the other party that you are sorry no agreement was possible at this time, but that you hope new opportunities will arise in the future. Being genial encourages future agreements and makes it easier to restart negotiations later if circumstances change.

Ultimatum
Requiring someone or a group to do specific thing in a specific way in order for negotiations to continue.

An **ultimatum** is an attempt to break an impasse and force a deal, whereby one party says that the other party must agree to X or the negotiations are terminated. Such an approach is a double-edged sword. It can sometimes get the other side to give in, but it can also prematurely end a negotiation. Managers should always avoid using ultimatums in negotiations unless he or she is willing to carry through with them. If a negotiator makes an ultimatum and then fails to act on it, the negotiator's credibility will suffer. However, it may be possible to keep the door open for resuming negotiations later. If the manager is given an ultimatum by the other party, he or she should realize that sometimes an ultimatum is serious but at other times it may be a bluff. If a manager is faced with an ultimatum from the other party, ignoring it is often the best possible response. It may be possible to pick up the negotiation again and set aside the ultimatum.

Positive Emotion

Anger, pride, overconfidence, and over-competitiveness can all work against you in a negotiation. But emotional reactions can also have positive effects. Negotiators who are in positive moods are more likely to achieve integrative agreements. Amicable, trusting relationships can lead to mutually beneficial exchanges of information and the discovery of opportunities to add value for both parties.[lxxxi]

It is ironic that many aggressive negotiators, who often consider themselves to be the most savvy of business people, fail to understand how much business they may be losing when others perceive them to be unfair or arrogant. People prefer to do business and negotiate with people whom they like and feel to be fair and can develop some relationship with. If a negotiator constantly seeks to squeeze advantages from others, then he or she may only get the one-time business, particularly with Northern European or North American cultures that have expectations of equitable behavior in negotiations.

Moods are also important in negotiations. Studies show that people that are in a sad emotional state are likely to pay about 30 percent more for an item than those in a neutral state. Similarly, they also are likely to sell an item for about 33 percent less than they would otherwise.[lxxxii] Emotions can be very important in negotiation and decision making, and it is important to account for them and not to ignore them. Do not hesitate to replace a negotiator who is not in top form.

Culture in Negotiations

There is a growing literature documenting international negotiating styles.[lxxxiii] Research and descriptions can be found about the negotiating style of Latin Americans such as Brazilians and Mexicans,[lxxxiv] East Asians (including Chinese, Japanese, and Koreans),[lxxxv] people from the Middle East,[lxxxvi] Russians, and others.[lxxxvii] For example, research suggests that Russians are more likely to base their arguments on asserted principles or ideals, somewhat similar to the verdict-based information search discussed earlier. People from China and the Middle East are more likely to start a negotiation at a number that's very favorable to them,

NEGOTIATIONS TRAP

Misunderstanding the culture and negotiation standards of another country can lead to a breakdown in the negotiation process. While politeness and respect may be the way one country negotiates a business proposition, another might use extreme bidding, coercion, and even deception as acceptable ways to negotiate. Countries with similar cultures might be expected to negotiate in similar ways, but this is not always the case, because culture is only one of the many things that determines a country's negotiation style. For example, although China and Taiwan are both Chinese and follow similar tenets of Chinese culture, their negotiations tactics are significantly different.[lxxxviii] Recent history and legal institutions can play a big role in negotiation. A Chinese business person negotiating a deal related to employment head count with a British MNE may refer to aspects of China's socialist system, while a Taiwanese business person would be more likely to appeal to the joint commercial values held by the British and Taiwanese government and industrials systems. This also becomes clear when comparing Austria's negotiation tactics with Germany, a country with which it shares cultural similarities.

Austria

At first glance, Austria would seem to be like Germany. Austria is a central European country that borders Germany, German is the national language, and Austria is culturally very similar to Germany. Yet Austria also has its own identity, rich history, and traditions. Located just south of Germany, Austria is much smaller than her powerful northern neighbor, with a relatively small population of 8.3 million people. Yet Austria has one of the highest economic output per capita with a total GDP of $409 billion, or approximately $49,000 per person. Austria's economy is one of the strongest and best performing in the Euro Zone (the European countries whose currency is the Euro).

History plays a critical role in Austria's identity, and differentiates that country from Germany. For example, the only country the Soviet Union (predecessor to Russia) occupied and then left following World War II was Austria. All other countries the Soviets occupied either were incorporated into the Soviet Union or became puppet states that the Soviet Union controlled through proxy governments. It was for this reason Austria is strongly neutral—they refused to take sides in the Cold War between the forces of the North Atlantic Treaty Organization (NATO) and the Soviet Bloc. Austria still refuses to join NATO. Like Switzerland, Austria has used its neutrality to establish relations with former Soviet Bloc countries and their firms.

These connections to Eastern Europe do not rest on Austria's current position in Europe alone. Further back in history, Austria was the center of the Hapsburg Empire, which existed for several hundred years in central Europe and included Austria, Hungary, Spain, Bulgaria, Romania, and other countries at various times. As a result of these various relationships with surrounding countries, Austrian firms have been able to easily do business with and invest in them as they have liberalized, and have established strong trading and investment relationships.

The two countries' cultures are similar in many ways if one looks just at Hofstede's four cultural dimensions. However, there are other subtle but strong differences between the two countries. For example, Germany has a large and vibrant immigrant community, particularly Turks (immigration into Germany is comparable to immigration into the United States). This immigrant community has integrated in many ways much better than anywhere else in Europe. In contrast, Austria has very few immigrant communities and is also historically xenophobic, which may have limited Austria's access to emerging economies outside of Europe. This can also change the criteria that firms use to negotiate with Austrian counterparts. For example, while Germany might welcome foreign direct investment from Turkey and other countries from West Asia or the Middle East, Austria has been less welcoming in that regard, preferring to focus on developing its Eastern European and Balkan ties. Austria feels that it is a small country and its identity could become overwhelmed by large numbers of immigrants, though they would probably benefit the economy. Germany's population is nearly ten times that of Austria and the country feels more able to encourage foreign direct investment and immigration.

perhaps overly favorable, which can stir resentment in North European negotiating partners. See Figure 10-6 for a summary of regional negotiating styles.

As a negotiation progresses, Russian and Chinese negotiators are known to make fewer concessions than their counterparts and protest about the disrespectful treatment accorded to them. The other side should be ready to have a lot of small points to concede so the Chinese or Russian negotiators can show they are tough bargainers and are making a lot of progress against the foreign firm. Middle Eastern and South Asian negotiators are thought to use more emotional appeals based on subjective feeling. North Americans are more likely to use a factual approach to negotiating, rather than an emotional one, appealing to more objective and provable facts.[lxxxix] South Americans and Arabs may feel unconstrained by

---

FIGURE 10-6   Regional Negotiating Styles

* Russian negotiators are more likely to use an axiomatic approach to negotiating, appealing to basic principles of fairness and the negotiation process.
* Russian and Chinese negotiators are known to make fewer concessions than their counterparts.
* Middle Easterners, Africans, and South Asian negotiators (e.g., India, Pakistan, Sri Lanka) are thought to use more emotional appeals, whereas European and North American negotiators emphasize data and evidence. Emotional stories and appeals can also be influential to those groups.
* Arab negotiators do not feel limited by time or authority; they frequently approach deadlines casually. This is true with many countries in Latin America as well, although there are exceptions, such as Guatemala and Argentina.
* Chinese negotiators will often use time against Western firms, which feel rushed to complete their "China deals." Savvy Western firms will try to rise above their cultural proclivity to want to "get it done" and take the necessary time to complete the deal favorably.

---

time limits, and approach deadlines very casually.[xc] In contrast, North Americans generally take deadlines very seriously—even artificial ones—and usually have broad authority to reach an agreement in the time allocated.[xci]

A negotiation becomes cross-cultural when the parties involved belong to different cultures and therefore do not share the same values and behaviors. Many negotiations are cross-cultural as are some domestic negotiations that include multiple ethnic groups. A Singaporean business person negotiating a new e-commerce agreement with a Brazilian, two Malaysian citizens—one an ethnic Chinese and one a Malay—negotiating a large land sale, a U.N. official negotiating with ambassadors from several countries concerning a trade summit's agenda, Mexican executives considering a potential strategic alliance with Norwegians, and Flemish- and French- speaking Belgians determining national language legislation—these are all cross-cultural negotiations. Effective cross-cultural negotiations contain all of the complexity of domestic negotiations with the added dimension of cultural diversity.

It was noted earlier that Chinese negotiators are well known for driving a hard bargain, particularly those connected to the government or state firms.[xcii] But this is not the only tactic that Chinese negotiators use to persuade the other party to reach an agreement favorable to themselves. For example, in formal negotiation sessions Chinese negotiators are also well known for using flattery, identifying the opponent's problems, deception, shaming, and pitting competing foreign companies against one another.[xciii]

International managers facing tough negotiators in China can still be successful, however, if they are firm on what they can offer and what they cannot. They also should seek to build credibility with their Chinese partners by dealing with them fairly. Such credibility can be built not only in formal negotiating sessions but also between sessions. One manager gave the following example:

> Once one of the Chinese negotiators for a client of ours in China insisted that our new machines had some problems and that our technology did not work well. I did not say anything, but when I returned to my hotel, I called the head office and asked an engineer from our home office to check on the problem in the Chinese factory. It turned out that there was no problem, and perhaps something had been set up incorrectly. A couple of days later over the dinner I privately told the Chinese manager that there may have been an error in the set-up as the machine had started working and ran for two days without any problem. I had not said anything at that day's staff meeting so as not to embarrass him in front of his staff and gave him my direct number (at the Hong Kong office) and told him to call me directly with any other problems. After that he became very friendly and even helped us to get that and other orders.

Implied in this story is the recommendation that you do not confront people, particularly more senior people, in meetings about a mistake or a misjudgment he

---

NEGOTIATION TACTICS ACROSS CULTURES

The use of silence and feigned outrage are two extreme tactics used in negotiation. Japanese often use silence in negotiations, while Americans use it much less and Chinese are somewhere in between.[xciv] Chinese negotiators can alternate between long periods of silence and inaction and blaming and shaming their negotiation partners.[xcv] How do Americans often respond to silence? Past research has shown that American negotiators tend to assume that an offer is not going to be accepted if a Japanese group is silent for an extended period of time. An American negotiator may tend to argue in response to the apparently uncomfortable silence. While the Japanese silently consider the Americans' offer, the Americans interpret the silence as rejection and respond by making concessions (e.g., by lowering the price). Similar dynamics occur when nonnative English speakers negotiate in English. If nonnative English speakers hesitate during a negotiation, usually to make sure they are comprehending what is being said, Americans may also wrongly assume that their offer is being rejected. Silence should never be interpreted as a rejection of a position, and neither should a request for a closer examination of the proposal. A negotiation depends on the information gathered, and the relationships established.

Chinese negotiators may use a different approach. They have learned that repeatedly telling people they made a mistake, it will make them more likely to admit the mistake and perhaps make additional concessions.[xcvi] Chinese negotiators have also been known to regularly remind parties with whom they are negotiating how China was forced into unfair treaties in the nineteenth century and that they will not allow that to happen again. Sometimes the negotiator's country is blamed for concessions given to the European powers or for the Sino-Japanese conflicts of the past 120 years. Research suggests that it is helpful to admit to the problems of the past rather than argue about them. Although the United States never had significant concessions in China, and even donated reparation money granted from a treaty at the end of the Boxer Rebellion to support the founding of Ching Hwa University in Beijing, it may help nevertheless to acknowledge the problems that occurred in those days before moving forward.[xcvii] Research on influence also indicates that it is best to openly acknowledge a past mistake or weakness to get it out of the way and build credibility with the other party. Even making a small concession up front that you may feel is unimportant but that would show good faith to the other side may prove very helpful.

---

or she might have made when dealing with traditional and high power-distance societies such as in China, Japan, or the Middle East. If a negotiator from the West points out a mistake loudly and publicly, the senior negotiator on the Chinese side will lose face. It is better to take that negotiator aside to mention this, or even speak to his or her subordinate separately, so the problem can be communicated without a loss of face. If possible, the negotiator can try to show concern for the senior negotiator on the other side and acknowledge that they have helped to solve a problem in the negotiation.

SUMMARY

Persuasion and influence are important skills that international managers can learn that will help them in negotiating, selling, and managing on a day-to-day basis. Persuasion is getting someone to change their mind about something, while influence is defined as eliciting a change in behavior or a decision in response to your request. Six universal principles of influence help firms and individuals generate a positive response to a request. These are social proof, authority, liking, consistency, reciprocation, and scarcity. Knowledge of these principles can help managers and organizations empower employees, customers, or clients to make better-informed decisions about, for example, whether to purchase a product or support a particular plan or policy. The six principles are universal in that they apply to different industries and settings around the world, but cultural norms and traditions can affect how a principle may be implemented and which one may be most important.

Some common judgment errors often undermine our abilities to negotiate optimal agreements:

1. Under- or overconfidence. Because of underconfidence, we fail to value our assets adequately. Or because of overconfidence in our own strengths, we fail to consider all relevant information and end up with no deal or one that is below standards. Asking questions, exchanging information, listening carefully to the other party, consulting with others, and taking time to evaluate alternatives thoroughly can all help in assessing issues realistically and rationally.
2. Escalation of commitment. Out of desire to accomplish something or to win, we can escalate our commitments to irrational levels. We control escalation of commitment by evaluating our best alternative to a negotiated agreement (BATNA), establishing a firm reservation price, and walking away from a deal when pressured or not given that reservation price.
3. Over-competitiveness. We can become too competitive and succumb to the myth of the fixed pie. We take "your loss is my gain" positions and fail to explore the full potential of a negotiation. Focusing on underlying interests rather than stated positions is essential for overcoming excessive competitiveness. Remember that both sides can win!
4. Irrelevant anchors. We anchor our bids and offers around historical figures, industry standards, or even first offers that often have little or no relevance to the current negotiation. Information is the key to avoiding getting stuck on irrelevant anchors. Research, ask questions, and listen. Base figures on the most relevant data and reject irrelevant figures.
5. Biased framing. We frame problems too narrowly, take biased perspectives, and fail to consider the most critical issues. Consulting others, calling in third parties, and testing alternative assessment models can help your team gain new perspectives on negotiation issues, as can learning what the other side values and how to frame opportunities in those terms.
6. Unrealistic risk assessment. People often either overestimate or underestimate risks. To improve our risk assessment, list the risks and the rewards and assess the probabilities.

Managers should understand their own goals, evaluate their BATNA, and set their reservation price. They should take their time, ask questions, research information, and exchange information. Search for trade-offs and opportunities to expand and improve your agreement. Then evaluate proposals thoroughly, remaining open to integrative solutions. Never waste time on battling your opponent just for the sake of "winning" the negotiation. Drive home the best possible deal for your team.

MANAGERIAL GUIDELINES

Persuasion and influence are very important skills for managers and business people to have today, particularly those doing business globally. In today's business environment it is difficult to simply order people to do things. They often must be carefully influenced to do things. International business people must work with other departments, alliance and joint-venture partners abroad, government officials, military officers, and a range of customers and stakeholders from around the world, and these people cannot be ordered to do anything. The good news is that persuasion and influence skills can be learned. Effective persuasion to convince others to change an attitude or belief starts with empathy or trying to understand that person's position or underlying values. It is important to remember the old adage, "If you're talking, you ain't learning." And persuasion is all about listening and learning about the other person's problems, concerns, or tasks they need to get done. Only with an understanding of these issues can you identify how your product or service will benefit them *by solving their problems and addressing their concerns*. If you frame things in terms of their problems or stated beliefs, your arguments will be much more persuasive. Be patient and observant. Be a good listener and learn how to ask questions instead of making speeches about your company, your product or your ideas.

The influence principles not only help us to ethically influence people, they also suggest things not to do, such as being quick to criticize someone's work or point of view, constantly bringing up controversial issues unnecessarily, or being negative in your conversation. Doing those things will drive people away from you and *reduce your influence* with them. Unfortunately, these negative behaviors are all too common in day-to-day interactions, but you now know to steer clear of these unhelpful behaviors.

In negotiations, there are some additional precepts apart from the persuasion and influence principles discussed above. In some cases, a deal that is too biased toward your own team may back your opponent into a corner. For example, it may be impossible for them to deliver the goods as promised or to make the payments required. Or if he or she has felt unfairly treated, your opponent's team may not deliver the goods as agreed in the terms of the deal. Expedited service, special treatment in emergencies, and customized production may be essential to a successful partnership, and maintaining a cooperative relationship can be critical. Managers are well served to remember the following in negotiations:

1. Do not insist on too good a deal; remember that some cultures such as North European and North American may see extreme starting positions as a signal of dishonesty. Try to make sure your opponent's position will be viable; that is, look for win-win solutions. Most deals are not one-time-only deals. You also want to build long-term partnerships.

2. Be gracious when you receive concessions. Reassure your opponent that the concession is fair and in the interests of both parties, and helps to meet the other party's needs. After the negotiation is finished, your opponent will be looking for confirmation that they made a good decision. Be sure to give that to them.

3. Be sure that the other party understands the cost of the concessions to your own team, but avoid pouting or bitterness after you have made them. Once you have reached an agreement, you and the other party are now partners and should act accordingly.

4. Avoid misrepresentation. Certain forms of game playing are expected in negotiations, but dishonesty should be minimized under most conditions. You might want to disguise your eagerness to reach an agreement or to frame financial terms in language that is most favorable to you, but direct misrepresentations should be avoided.

5. Distrust will undermine your long-term agreements and block future agreements. Even in one-time business deals, every business person has a responsibility to act ethically. All businesses benefit from a trusting, efficient business environment. Plus, in today's globalized world, word gets around fast if you are always out to squeeze the last dollar out of every deal. Some industries are very clubby and tight, and you and your firm's reputations can precede you. Remember also that reciprocation pays dividends, but to engender reciprocation, you must act first. Be generous when you can and build good will.

DOING BUSINESS IN GUATEMALA

Guatemala is a Central American country of approximately 13 million people and with an annual GDP of approximately $33 billion per year. Guatemala has the second largest economy in Central America and its wealth is heavily concentrated in Guatemala City, the capital, with a population of 2.5 million. Poverty in Guatemala is extensive in rural areas where 60 percent of the population lives. The rural population is over 80 percent indigenous, descendents of the ancient Mayan empire. Approximately 40 percent of Guatemala's population lives on less than $2 a day.

Guatemala shares many of the same cultural characteristics of other Latin American states. There is a strong emphasis on family and a strong desire to have a relationship with an individual before starting business. Thus, business people are well served in seeking to meet and build relationships over time with other business people. This process includes getting to know the family of the person you would like to do business with. There is also a strong emphasis on titles and showing respect to other individuals.

Guatemala has unique differences as well. Guatemalans are typically more prompt than most other Latin Americans. If a time is set for a meeting, they expect that you will be on time. The significant indigenous population raises special concerns. Several Latin American countries, such as Peru and Bolivia, also have large indigenous populations, while others, such as Argentina, have much smaller ones. Indigenous populations have their own languages and cultures. In Guatemala, 23 official indigenous languages are recognized. The business people that you may deal with are likely to be bilingual in Spanish and English due to the strong business connections between the United States and South America. However, if you operate a manufacturing facility or some other factory or plant employing large numbers of people it is likely that many different languages will be spoken in the workplace. The cultural differences in a group like this will vary as well and will present another challenge for management staff.

CULTURE

EXERCISES

1. Do you think that partnerships between non-profit and for-profit entities have the opportunity to be beneficial to all parties as it was in this case?
2. What other societal problems do you think could be solved by for-profit and non-profit entities working together?
3. What are the difficulties that could arise in the negotiations between the parties in those settings?

DISCUSSION QUESTIONS

Opening Vignette Discussion Questions

1. American political consultants now often work for politicians in other countries. Why do you think their persuasion and promotion techniques seem to be transferable to other countries and cultures worldwide?
2. Why might advertising campaigns have to be changed to be effective while campaign methods would not?
3. How must your negotiation style change when dealing with a unionized plant as an active multinational enterprise in a Latin American country versus that in the United States?
4. What differences in cultural biases in making decisions do you think would exist between North American and European managers?
5. Suppose someone says: "I cannot understand why that guy [a mutual friend] did not help me out last week. I mean, we are friends, aren't we?" What influence principle is your friend invoking? What is the downside of depending too much on that principle and what might you recommend to him in dealing with that other guy in the future?

IN-CLASS EXERCISES

* Break into an equal number of teams and then pair up into teams of two. One team will be the seller of a product while the other will be the buyer. Your instructor will give each team some business specifics that the other team is not to know about. Conduct a negotiation to buy a given number of products.
* Influencing someone to do something and motivating someone to do something seem to be about the same. Discuss with your neighbor how these two general actions are different and give one action for each.
* Why is it good to acknowledge a weakness in your argument or position first before proceeding with trying to persuade someone? What does research show about how you will most likely be perceived?
* Break into teams of two. Discuss buying a lathe (a machining tool) and what types of information you might need to have before entering into the negotiation process.

TAKE-HOME EXERCISES

* Research a failed negotiation using an online search engine like Google. Identify what you think was the principal cause of the failed negotiation.
* Research a recent labor or sports figure negotiation. Detail the nature of these negotiations and how they illustrate the concepts discussed in this chapter.
* Based on earlier discussions of mergers and acquisitions, identify an international merger or acquisition using an online search engine. What were the nature of the negotiations that occurred for that M&A? How long did the negotiations take?
* Research negotiations that have attempted to end a standoff in a country or region facing severe political impasses. How do these negotiations differ from those in business?

SHORT CASE QUESTIONS

Negotiations Trap (p. 327)

1. What do you think the differences would be in negotiations in Ireland and Britain? Scotland and Britain?
2. Do you think regional differences in a large country like China also have an impact with different regions having different styles of negotiations?
3. What might be the differences in the negotiations in the same industry, such as venture capital, around the world?

12

HUMAN RESOURCES MANAGEMENT

Overview

In operating internationally, one of the most vital assets a firm has is its human resources. The firm needs people both from its home country and the foreign countries in which it operates. If it gets staffing wrong, the added cost to the firm can be inordinately high. Effective management of human resources can be a source of advantage for firms, particularly as they move internationally. Significant problems can also occur if a firm does not manage its human resources effectively. In particular, the ability to place an expatriate employee quickly into an international environment to seize new opportunities or correct problems is important. But if the expatriate is a poor fit and quits the post early, the cost to the firm is very high as the position must be filled again with all the incumbent costs of posting a manager abroad.

Therefore, this chapter will examine how an international firm's decisions regarding hiring, training, employee appraisal and compensation often differ from the firm's home country environment. This chapter will specifically provide insights on the following:

* The role of human resources management in international business

* The major functions of human resources: selection techniques and implementation of selection; training of employees; appraisal, compensation, and rewards; and socialization

* Problems and solutions in international postings—the expatriate dilemma

ASIMCO: EXPATRIATE PITFALLS

An assignment in China can prove to be very challenging for many expatriates—even those who are familiar with the language and culture. After working for a few years in accounting in the United Kingdom, British businessman Tim Clissold went to China to learn Chinese, hoping to work for his firm or another bank there. In the early 1990s, Clissold was hired by Asimco, one of the largest foreign investors in China at the time, to help it secure and oversee its China investments. Started by Jack Perkowski, a successful American banker, and run in China by Clissold, Asimco was able to raise a total of $434 million from private equity firms and private investors. The money was invested in a variety of state and private enterprises in China, such as car-component factories and breweries, with the ambitious goal of creating a large conglomerate of low-cost divisions, chosen from the best of China's state enterprises and other overlooked firms, often in China's interior.

Clissold spoke Chinese well and spent much time and effort courting key government officials to gather support for each venture. But he and his assistants were not able to watch over the farflung ventures that were often located in hard-to-access regions of

China's interior. Asimco's best manager, who ran a rubber-parts factory in the mountainous in isolated Anhui Province in eastern China, secretly set up a rival plant nearby that he financed by siphoning money and equipment from the Asimco joint venture. When that manager was eventually found out and fired, he told his workers to package defective products from his own production line in Asimco boxes and send them to customers so they would cancel orders from Asimco. There were battles on the street and around the factory with knives and broken bottles between workers loyal to Asimco and those loyal to the former factory boss. Police and later the army had to be called out to quell the situation.

While that was going on, in southern Zhuhai, near the border with Macau, the director of Asimco's brake-pads factory absconded to the United States with $10 million worth of company letters of credit, assisted by a local bank manager, leaving behind his entire family. Asimco sued the bank for validating the certificates, but ended up liable for the money. An anti-corruption official based in adjacent Guangdong Province promised Clissold he would investigate, but only if he was given

a car and money to fund the investigation. Eventually, nearly all of Asimco's $434 million disappeared in such investments around China with investors getting little but some scattered assets in return.

This cautionary tale carries several lessons for doing business in China, but in terms of human resources, it shows how important it is to place the right people in foreign subsidiaries, and to take enough time to find the right middle managers. One or two young, energetic expatriates flying around a country is seldom enough, particularly in a developing economy such as China or India. A factory manager, the head of finance or accounting, and at least one middle manager whose loyalty is to the parent firm are the bare minimum needed to run and monitor a significant operation in China, Russia, or most other developing economies. The expatriates must know the local environment and rely on loyal middle managers and finance managers who can monitor their investments and safeguard company accounts and "chops" (stamps used as proxies for signatures on financial transactions in China), otherwise millions of dollars can be lost.[i]

The human resources management (HRM) function is one the most important for firms in operating internationally. For example, a critical issue facing international firms is staffing of international locations. HRM has an impact on a number of functions in an international firm. These include selection, training, appraisal, and compensation. The flow of the chapter in discussing these issues is summarized in Figure 12-1.

THE IMPORTANCE OF INTERNATIONAL HRM

Finding the right people to fill positions in a division or department of the company that is doing business internationally is difficult, and the wrong person can be very costly. This is especially true if the individual is sent to a foreign location from the firm's home market. These individuals are referred to as **expatriates**. The cost of hiring and placing an expatriate in a foreign location can range from 50 to 200 percent of the expatriate's salary. When hiring an expatriate, costs to the firm include not only finding the right person but also relocation costs

Expatriate
A person from one country who is working and residing in another country.

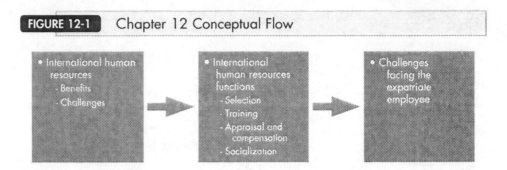

FIGURE 12-1   Chapter 12 Conceptual Flow

- International human resources
  - Benefits
  - Challenges

- International human resources functions
  - Selection
  - Training
  - Appraisal and compensation
  - Socialization

- Challenges facing the expatriate employee

to the foreign locale for the expatriate and his or her family as well as training about the local culture and other preparation costs.

Maintaining an expatriate employee in a foreign location is also expensive, with the expatriate often receiving return flights to the home country for holidays, the firm paying for private school costs for children, and trying to make the expatriate's compensation **tax neutral**. The United States is one of the few countries in the world that charges taxes on the income earned overseas by U.S. citizens.[1] Thus, firms should try to ensure that the employee is tax neutral—that is, the expat should not be paying so much in new taxes that he or she effectively earns less money than back in the home country. In addition, if the expatriate assignment fails, and the person leaves the job and returns home early, there will be lost productivity at the foreign location, new recruiting, training, and travel costs for the next employee, and other expenses commonly associated with employee turnover. With many knowledge-based jobs such as quality assurance, running a research center, or managing engineers, the loss of an expatriate manager may even cause the facility to shut down until a replacement is found. This is very expensive in terms of lost productivity and missed sales opportunities; the firm will also have to search for another person to fill that overseas position, and may have to pay relocation costs and other direct, hard dollar expenses. Thus, the cost estimate of expatriate failure ranges from half a year's salary to two years of salary from the person who left. Since human resources are so important to an international firm, and expatriate failure is very expensive, it is vital that the firm has effective HRM to ensure that the right people with the right skills are available when needed and that turnover is minimized.[ii] Figure 12-2 highlights the extensive nature of this problem for many U.S. firms. Though they have come down somewhat in recent years, expat failures are still a source of concern to management.[iii]

HUMAN RESOURCES MANAGEMENT (HRM) FUNCTIONS

In developing human resources to meet the demands illustrated above, there are several major functions to direct. Apart from record keeping and basic administration, often brought to mind by the older term for the HR department, "personnel," HR is sometimes summarized by its basic functions: selection, training and development, appraisal and compensation, and socialization. These functions in an international firm are addressed below, along with examples from firms thought of as exemplary in those areas.

Tax neutral

Firms will try to ensure that an expatriate does not pay more tax by being posted abroad.

[1]U.S. citizens must pay U.S. taxes on foreign income earned over approximately $80,000 (the first $80,000 earned is exempt), though many of the taxes paid to the foreign locality can be subtracted from the U.S. tax liability.

FIGURE 12-2 Expatriate Recall Rates from Abroad

Recall Rate Percent	Percent of Companies
U.S. multinationals	
20–40%	7%
10–20	69
<10	24
European multinationals	
11–15%	3%
6–10	38
<5	59
Japanese multinationals	
11–19%	14%
6–10	10
<5	76

Source: Tung, R.L. (1982). Selection and Training Procedures of U.S., European, and Japanese multinationals. *California Management Review.* 25(1) 51–71.

LINCOLN ELECTRIC IN EUROPE

Lincoln Electric's experiences in Mexico were discussed in Chapter 7. Its experience in Europe also offers valuable insights on the functions of international HR. In the late 1980s and early 1990s, Lincoln spent almost $325 million expanding beyond its U.S. base to Europe, Japan, and Latin America. None of Lincoln Electric's board of directors had any significant international experience, and no one challenged the significant international expansion plans to multiple foreign countries. The European operations ran into trouble early, losing millions of dollars and causing Lincoln Electric to run a consolidated loss—something they almost never did. The individual European businesses would submit extremely overly optimistic sales-and-profits targets in their budgets, but they invariably missed the targets, often by quite a bit. Even more worrisome, nobody seemed to have a handle on why the targets were being missed or what to do

about the gaps apart from just cutting budgets. The European managers had not been brought up under the Lincoln Electric system and seemed content to let the European recession run its course rather than working more aggressively to increase revenue and establish the Lincoln Electric brand in new markets. In the newly acquired German plant, some people were not even working. On one visit that had been announced in advance, three employees were found sleeping on the job. Lincoln Electric decided they had to get out of that plant.

The root cause of the crisis was that Lincoln Electric's leaders had grown overconfident in the company's abilities and systems. They believed that their unique culture and incentive system—along with the dedicated, skilled workforce that the company had built over the decades—were the main source of its competitive advantage, and assumed that the incentive system

and culture could be directly transferred abroad. Lincoln Electric employed a polycentric hiring approach, trying to localize its management, but it failed to realize that these managers had not been through the Lincoln Electric system and were not nearly as aggressive in sales and production incentives. Although Lincoln Electric went through a couple of very difficult years, it did finally learn from its mistakes. As former CEO Donald Hastings recalled, "Competing globally requires a lot more time, money, and management resources than we realized. At least five years before we launched our expansion in 1987, we should have started building a management team and a hoard of directors from whom we could have learned how to proceed."[iv]After its initial false start, Lincoln is doing well in its international markets and has successfully implemented its pay for performance system in a number of plants worldwide.[v]

Selection

Effective employee selection can prove to be a major task. A number of challenges surround selection, including the method used and the firm's general approach. In addition to standard selection problems, there are numerous problems with the criteria used to choose expatriates. There are three common methods for selecting new employees: interviews, observation, and various types of written tests. Each will be reviewed in turn with emphasis later in this section given to selecting employees for foreign postings.

Interviews Many firms use interviews to screen people for overseas assignments, agreeing that extensive interviewing of candidates (and their spouses) by senior executives still provide an effective method of selection. The spouse should be interviewed as well because the family plays such a critical role in whether the employee will be able to remain in the international job or will be compelled to return home to keep the family happy. If the family is not happy, it is likely that the expatriate employee will leave, no matter how well the job is going and how successful the employee is.

Professor Rosalie Tung's research on international human resources and expatriates supports the belief on the importance of the family and their involvement in the interview process. For example, in one major study, 52 percent of the U.S. multinational corporations she surveyed reported that they conducted interviews with both the prospective manager and his or her spouse for an international position, and 47 percent conducted interviews with the candidate alone. For technically oriented positions, 40 percent of the firms interviewed both the candidate and the spouse, and 59 percent conducted interviews with the candidate alone.[vi]

Although single individual interviews are a common selection method, research suggests that a single interview by itself is not a very valid predictor of performance.[vii] Instead, multiple individual interviews are more useful. Often, a prospective employee will be sent to speak to multiple people in the group. For example, when Apple was interviewing for new members of the original Macintosh development team, it had someone interview with each member of the team. Only if the whole team liked that prospective employee would the person be hired.[viii] Multiple interviews are also commonly used for higher-level and professional jobs including expatriate positions. Multiple interviews can provide diversity of opinion about the job candidate along with some consensus on whether he or she should be hired.

In China, many multinationals have found that individual interviews are useful in interviewing Chinese job applicants, but there is a need to employ both expatriate and local interviewers. The expatriate ensures that attention is focused on the key selection criteria so that individuals who are offered jobs will indeed have the abilities, skills, and training to do the work. The local person ensures that the prospective hire knows the local culture and customs, and can provide insights regarding the applicant's responses and other behaviors that can be problematic in the international location. Together, the two are able to help identify those candidates most likely to do the best job.

Group interviews
Selection tool in which typically there are multiple candidates and multiple interviewers present at the same time.

Group Interviews Also fairly effective for certain types of jobs—customer service jobs, or factory or facility management—is the group interview. In group interviews typically there are both multiple candidates and multiple interviewers present at the same time. In this case, the expatriate interacts with potential clients (real and role-playing) and potential colleagues. Emphasis is given to how the candidate responds to real situations and how they cooperate with others. Southwest Airlines in the United States has used group interviews very effectively to hire new flight attendants. Prospective flight attendants are evaluated by current flight attendants, the Human Resources (HR) department (called the "People Department" at Southwest), and customers (airline passengers). Similarly, Southwest Airlines will have mechanics interview mechanics, and pilots interview pilots. Southwest's belief is that the employees in the field doing the job will know best the kinds of people needed.

Cathay Pacific Airlines in Hong Kong also uses group interviews to evaluate prospective flight attendants' personalities and how they interact with various groups and each other. The goal of this Asia-based airline is similar to Southwest's in that they hire service personnel with engaging personalities who can work well with others and have an even temperament. Group interviews are often employed for filling midlevel and lower-level positions. Group interviews also facilitate another type of selection method, the observation method, because the way interviewees interact with customers and potential colleagues is one good indication of how they might fit in and perform.

Observation Method The hiring decision can also be accomplished through observation of the prospective employee interacting with colleagues, giving a presentation, or actually performing a job. This method is more common for certain jobs—research, engineering, professional organizations, governments, and universities. To illustrate, it is typical for a job candidate applying for a faculty position in a university to present his or her research to a group of professors and to a class of students to see how he or she interacts with individuals in each situation. Firms do similar things. As mentioned above, Southwest Airlines includes observation in some of its selection processes. The firm wishes to see how the individual will act in the actual setting. Southwest's former chairmen Herb Kelleher told the story of how he liked to place an individual who was actually already a Southwest Airlines pilot among a group of pilot applicants. The Southwest pilot would observe the applicants when they thought no one from the firm was present. Southwest also watches applicants in other settings, such as when they go to the cafeteria for lunch. The firm wants to see how they relate to people while there, particularly when the applicants do not know they are being observed.[ix]

The observation method is particularly helpful in selecting individuals for overseas assignments. For example, a prospective employee may be asked to give a presentation to a group that does not speak the same first language as the potential expatriate, such as a group of Chinese retail managers currently visiting the home office in the United States for training. The firm wants to see if the applicant is able to modify his or her speaking style in response to the demands of the setting. For example, does the prospective expatriate use a lot of slang and uncommon terms in his or her daily speech that will present problems when dealing with local employees and clients in non-English-speaking countries? Many North American idioms such as calling an idea "cutting edge" (or even worse, "bleeding edge"), often are confusing to others outside North America. A "punt" in North American football means to kick away the ball and is used to mean to dispose of an unwanted situation or responsibility. Yet in Britain and other parts of the current and former British Commonwealth (Australia, New Zealand, Jamaica, Hong Kong, Singapore, and so forth), a punt is a wager, and a "punter" is not a kicker but a gambler. Baseball metaphors such as "out in left field" or "that was a home run" should be avoided, as they will not be understood by most non-native English speakers. It is important for the expatriate to make efforts to rid his or her speech of slang, impenetrable idioms, and references to very local issues so as to improve his or her understandability.

Similarly, does the prospective expatriate speak at the same speed with individuals who are non-native speakers? Ideally you should speak a little more slowly and pronounce words more carefully in speaking to non-native speakers who do not have a lot of experience with your language. Additionally, the firm will want to observe if the applicant expresses a condescending or impatient attitude toward foreign listeners who fail to understand what the expatriate said the first time. The firm needs to know whether the applicant can adapt and change as the setting requires, and the observation method of selection is well suited to identify likely troubles before the firm expends extensive resources placing someone into an international setting.

To illustrate, one HR professional with whom the authors are acquainted told a story about observational interviewing for an important job in Taiwan. He recalled:

> I had been interviewing for a Taiwan posting and had settled on two roughly equal job candidates. At a lunch in a Chinese restaurant, I saw that one of the candidates was uncomfortable with the food—he was scooping through the food with his spoon, apparently looking for something. I asked him what was wrong. He said that he was looking for "weird seafood" in his bowl. After that lunch I decided that he might have trouble acculturating to Taiwan, particularly given that food is such a center of business and social activity for most Chinese people, especially business people. If the person is only comfortable eating at McDonalds or Burger King, why go abroad?

Written tests Another method used in hiring is written tests. One such test is the Structured Questionnaire Method. Arco, a large oil and energy company, has used this method effectively to test for management and marketing savvy, as well as temperament (happiness, anger, or patience). Other written tests used, typically together, include intelligence (IQ) tests and integrity tests. Another written test that may be used when hiring individuals to place in international assignments is one that measures the candidate's **cultural toughness**. This test assesses whether the candidate appears able to work in a specific country.[x] A similar test is the **cultural intelligence test (CQ)**. The higher an individual's score on the CQ test, the more likely that person can succeed in a cross-cultural setting such as an expatriate assignment.[xi]

It should be recognized, however, that written tests also have their limitations. To illustrate, in China selection tests have been found to have limited value. For example, one large U.S. consumer goods firm has reported that the analytical problem-solving tests that it uses in screening applicants will eliminate half of the applicants from North America and Europe, but only 12 percent of Chinese applicants. This is a result of the outstanding analytical training that these individuals receive at prestigious Chinese universities.[xii] So the company needed to find other tests for identifying the very best applicants, as analytical ability is only one of several skills needed in managerial positions. Similarly, the use of psychological testing or Western-style assessment center exercises does not have a good reputation in China. For one thing, the Chinese education system generally does not train students to analyze open-ended hypothetical situations whereby they

Cultural toughness
Selection test that assesses whether a candidate appears able to work in a specific country.

Cultural intelligence test (CQ)
Selection test that evaluates a person's ability in a cross-cultural setting.

CHINESE FIRMS EXPAND TO EUROPE AND NORTH AMERICA

CULTURE

As the Chinese economy continues to grow, Chinese firms are increasingly going global themselves, many for the first time. Chinese companies have had both successful and unsuccessful experiences on their road to globalization. They have taken over parts of venerable western firms with long histories such as IBM, Thomson, and RCA. Chinese managers have found it is more difficult than they thought to communicate with European employees. They have also reported difficulty in keeping employees happy. The employees assume that Chinese management knows very little about modern management system and process. For example, Mr. Li, a manager at China's TCL subsidiary in France (taken over from French appliance firm Thomson) complained that his French colleagues turn off their mobile phones on the weekend and this hurts their work. Other local employees have complained about the late hours the Chinese parent insists on. Chinese firms in the United States have also experienced problems with the workforce. American employees in one major Chinese firm reported that they like to know what management is planning, but in the Chinese firm they feel they are on a purely need-to-know basis. Thus they are told about their immediate job and little else. Employees in both firms reported that the Chinese management did not take their suggestions seriously. This has led to difficulties in recruiting talent and a lot of turnover at these firms with the resulting costs. It takes much longer for a company to build the capabilities to operate and manage global businesses, as evidenced by the fact that Japanese, Korean, and Taiwanese companies typically spend over 10 years to build their global capabilities and suffer a lot of turnover and problems with local staff. These capabilities can by no means be developed in a short time.

Zhang, J. (2005, June). Global misadventures. *China International Business*, pp. 20–22.

must build an argument and supply evidence for a certain position. Nor does it teach lateral thinking (thinking beyond the literal answer to the actual problem at hand) particularly well. As a result, expatriate evaluators find it hard to draw conclusions about the suitability of the Chinese candidates based on their performance in problem-solving exercises alone.

Overview of Selection Methods

It should be recognized that whether a firm uses interviews, observation, or written tests, the most useful test for a given firm will also take local culture into account. For example, in Anglo-Saxon cultures, what is generally tested is how much the individual can contribute to the tasks of the organization. In these cultures, assessment center exercises, intelligence tests, and measurements of competencies are the norm. In Germanic cultures, the emphasis is more on the quality of education geared toward a particular (job) function. The recruitment process in Far Eastern cultures is very often characterized by ascertaining how well a person fits in with the larger group. This is judged in part by the elitism of higher educational institutes attended, such as the University of Tokyo in Japan. Latin cultures will tend to emphasize personality, communication, and social skills more than intelligence or job function.[xiii] The acceptance of selection devices vary around the world. For example, Hong Kong and Taiwan are averse to questionnaires.[xiv] Written references are less common in France than other European and Anglo countries as French people are reluctant to give written references. Situational and scenario tests are used more in the United Kingdom, Holland, and Germany than in France and Belgium. In contrast, multiple choice tests are more common in France and Belgium than in the Northern European and Anglo countries.[xv] Whichever selection tests are employed, they should be used judiciously, employing local versions of the tests when possible.

Implementing Expatriate Selection In making their selection firms may employ some or all the methods above. However, in implementing these selection methods a firm should focus on learning specific things about the potential job candidate. Particularly, for those positions which require that the individual be stationed abroad there are some key factors to focus on, including adaptability to different cultural settings, self-reliance, health, a balance of age and experience, motivation for international job, and family.

Adaptability to Cultural Change While it was noted above that people with international postings must have a certain level of cultural intelligence, they must also be able to adapt to different and changing circumstances. No matter how well they think they know a culture, they will have some degree of culture shock at the start, and will continue to encounter frustrations in their new environment, even after becoming accustomed to that environment. In fact, it is expected that many of the most effective international managers suffer this cultural shock, because it shows that the expatriate manager is becoming involved in the new culture and not just isolating him or herself from the environment. To illustrate the culture shock that can occur, one North American assigned to Japan described this experience to the authors in the following way:

> On my first week in Japan, living in an isolated area in the foothills of Mount Fuji, I was getting tired of the monotony of the salty Japanese cafeteria food of fish and pickled vegetables, so I walked down to the local Mom and Pop store to buy something more familiar to eat. As yet unable to read Japanese, I decided to pick up what looked like a jar of peanut butter. I was not sure that's what it was, but it looked like peanut butter, and there was a picture of what looked like a peanut on the package. I bought the jar and some bread and eagerly went back to the

company dorm to have a peanut butter sandwich. To my dismay, when I opened the jar and started to spread the paste on the bread it didn't smell like peanut butter. Turns out, it was some kind of raw soybean paste. It had almost the same color and texture of peanut butter but certainly did not taste like peanut butter. And it had the same salty taste that almost all of the cafeteria food had. I later found I had to walk about seven miles downhill to a larger store to buy peanut butter and other more familiar foods, and then seven miles uphill back to my living quarters. This was all a surprise to me to live like that in "modern Japan." .

While many expatriates are typically very happy at the start of their overseas assignments, after a few months there is often a downturn in contentment with the job and the foreign location, which can lead to a significant drop in mood. But if the expatriate understands that this downturn in mood after a few months is very common and is to be expected, he or she will be better able to weather this period and adjust. In fact, after the first two years, most people become more satisfied with their overseas assignment than when they first arrived. So if you feel very discontented after working in a new country for a few months, do not worry, this downtown in mood is very common and should pass in time.

Organizations examine a number of characteristics in determining whether an individual is adaptable. Examples include experiences with cultures other than one's own, previous overseas travel, a knowledge of foreign languages (fluency generally is not necessary, however), and recent immigration background or heritage. Others include (1) the ability to integrate with different people, cultures, and types of business organizations; (2) the ability to sense developments in the host country and accurately assess them; (3) the ability to solve problems within different frameworks and from different perspectives; (4) sensitivity to differences and nuances in culture, politics, religion, and ethics; and (5) flexibility in managing operations on a continuous basis despite a lack of assistance and gaps in information.

When are expatriates better able to adjust? In research conducted among expatriates in China, Professor Jan Selmer found that those who were best able to deal with their new situation had developed coping strategies characterized by sociocultural and psychological adjustments, including (1) having experience in adjusting to new situations, (2) learning how to interact well with host-country nationals outside of work, and (3) feeling reasonably happy and being able to enjoy day-to-day activities. In addition, if the expatriate possesses the personality trait of openness to new experience, this also helps with cross-cultural adjustment. Sociability was also correlated with effective adjustment, as the expat can get to know people in the foreign office better.[xvi]

Independence and Self-Reliance In many overseas assignments, expatriates have more responsibility than they had at the home office. They also have fewer people to call on for assistance and guidance. At company headquarters, a large staff of advisors may have been available to provide assistance and guidance, but in foreign assignments, expats must be more self-reliant. Some of the indicators of independence and self-reliance that employers are looking for include prior experience working with customers in the field, special project or task force experience, a hobby that requires a high degree of self-reliance, and a record of extracurricular activities or athletics in school. Most organizations also require that their expatriate managers be in good physical and emotional health, because developing countries often do not have the all of the medical resources available in more developed countries.

A firm is not only interested in an employee's physical health but also their psychological health. For example, it is important that an individual have the ability to withstand culture shock. Key parts of this evaluation would include the person's marital status and family setting. If a person is in a troubled marriage, the person's psychological stress will grow worse when he or she moves overseas. A prospective expat who has a child with a special need will often find moving

CULTURAL SENSITIVITY: HOW MUCH IS TOO MUCH?

Firms often seek to adapt to the culture of different key customers, such as the Chinese high-rollers in Las Vegas casinos. The casinos refer to Chinese people who are willing to spend $50,000 on a single hand of cards or a million dollars in a weekend as whales. It is estimated that 80 percent of whales are from Asia, because gambling is a key part of Chinese culture.

Las Vegas casinos have also sought to adjust their product mix and presentation to attract these customers. For example, many casinos offer Asian-themed baccarat salons and noodle bars. Asians on the whole prefer card games rather than roulette or craps because they feel they have some control over baccarat and their skill can allow them to be successful. Other casinos have built their facilities to make the Chinese feel comfortable. For example, Harrah's opened a gambling and dining area inspired by architectural elements of the Ming and Song Dynasties at their Showboat Casino in Atlantic City. Hong Kong and Taiwan singers regularly perform to majority Chinese audiences in Las Vegas showrooms.

But firms can go too far in seeking to be multicultural. Coca-Cola is often thought of as the prototypical culturally sensitive global firm. Robert Goizetta, Coke's longtime chairman who oversaw Coke's rapid growth in the 1980s and 1990s, was originally from Cuba. Doug Daft was one of Goizetta's successors and hailed from Australia, though Daft worked all around the world. But some have argued that Daft carried cultural sensitivity too far. When he was appointed CEO in 1999, Daft wanted to internationalize Coke's traditional U.S. headquarters in Atlanta, Georgia. As part of this effort he brought in a Feng Shui master, a person who specializes in the Eastern philosophy of arranging interior facilities to keep them in harmony with nature.

Feng Shui is drawn from Taoism and sees energy throughout the world. Its goal is to ensure that all things are in harmony with their surroundings by balancing the energies of any given space to assure the health and good fortune for people. There is an effort to place objects in a manner so as to improve *chi* or energy. Gentle wind and smooth water have positive connotations, while harsh winds and stagnant water are linked with negative elements. Feng Shui consultants try to promote the flow of positive energy, prevent the leakage of nourishing energy, and curb the development of negative energy.

The Feng Shui master hired by Coke reorganized the firm's Atlanta lobby and some executive offices according to Feng Shui principles. Desks were turned in various ways so they were "properly" facing doors to allow good energy to flow in. Many mirrors and objects with points on them were removed because of the bad luck they could project. These changes happened in spite of the desk owners who protested that the move was inconvenient for them. The Feng Shui master also had several statues, including a large green dragon, placed in Coca-Cola's lobby, presumably to scare away evil spirits. For a number of employees, that was the last straw. They complained to management about the inconvenient desk arrangements, uncomfortable furniture, loss of space, and ugly gargoyle-like statues placed where fine art had been. Being a culturally sensitive company is one thing, but ignoring local tastes, in this case those of Americans, is not a good thing for any company to do. And besides, the American employees argued that Coca-Cola was not being sensitive to their culture.[xvii]

Firms have to be careful how they choose to internationalize their settings. It can work well in some situations, but the Coke example shows how firms can push their employees to the point that they do not feel comfortable.

Hays, C. (2004). *Pop: Truth and Power at the Coca-Cola Company.* London: Hutchinson.

Rivlin, G. (2007, June 13). Las Vegas caters to Asia's high rollers. *The New York Times*, p. B1.

abroad more difficult because the special services on which they may depend are not as readily available. As a result, many firms have very specific characteristics that they look for in an employee. For example, one U.S. oil company operating in the Middle East considers middle-aged men with grown children to be the best able to cope with cultural shock, and for some locations in the desert, people from Texas or southern California can adjust better than those from New England.

Education, Age, and Experience. Education is important in selecting individuals for international assignments, and almost all firms will build on formal education through their own training and development efforts. For example, Germany's Siemens corporation gives its international management team specific training designed to help them deal more effectively with the types of problems they will face on the job. Most firms placing an employee in an expatriate position will also strive for a balance between age and experience. There is evidence that younger managers are more eager for international assignments and have more openness to new experiences and new cultures—important traits for succeeding as an expat.

CULTURE

HIERARCHY AND PROTOCOL: AN AMERICAN EXECUTIVE IN LONDON

An American executive moved to London to manage his company's British headquarters. Although the initial few weeks passed relatively uneventfully, it bothered the executive that visitors were never sent directly to his office. A visitor first had to speak with the receptionist, then the secretary, and then the office manager. Finally, the office manager would escort the visitor to see him. The American became annoyed with this practice, which he considered a total waste of time. When the manager finally spoke with his British employees and urged them to be less formal and to send visitors directly to him, they seemed upset.

After a number of delicate conversations, the American executive began to understand the greater emphasis on formality and hierarchy in many British firms, particularly in well-established, traditional organizations like banks and trading firms. He slowly learned to be more patient when his colleagues greeted guests using their more formal, multi-step approach. Visitors to the British headquarters continued to see the receptionist, secretary, and office manager before meeting the American executive. The executive was better able to get things done after understanding British protocol and not fighting it, frustrating as it seemed to him at the beginning.[xviii]

But by the same token, young people often are the least developed in terms of management experience and technical skills.

To gain the desired balance, many firms send both young and seasoned personnel to the same overseas post. A team should be selected for both its youth and its experience, taking into consideration reporting relationships, specific responsibilities, authority, necessary connections, and professional judgment as to how much experience is best suited to a specific job. Many companies consider an academic degree, preferably a graduate degree, to be important to an international executive, as well as some international exposure, which helps to reduce the expatriate's learning curve in the new country.[xix]

Language Training In implementing the selection process, language ability is very important. English is the primary language of international business, and most expatriates from all countries can converse in English. However, those who can speak only English are at a disadvantage when doing business in non-English-speaking countries. Language is an effective method of learning about a country and the customs of its people. Traditionally, U.S. managers have done rather poorly in learning foreign languages and tend to downplay their importance. Executives in Japan, Western Europe, and South America, however, placed a high priority on speaking more than one language, which is often compulsory in their countries from an early age. Prospective expats should show some commitment to foreign language learning if they are to be posted to a non-English speaking country for an extended period of time. Previous study is particularly helpful.

Motivation for a Foreign Posting When evaluating candidates for overseas assignments, a firm also should consider the employee's reasons for wanting to work abroad. Just wanting to work overseas is not sufficient motivation. Individuals must be engaged at work and believe in the significance of the job. Applicants who are unhappy with their current situation and want to get away are less likely to become effective expatriates. Successful expats often will also exhibit openness and a pioneering spirit. Other motivators include the desire to increase one's chances for promotion and the desire to establish the firm in a foreign location. Several large European and U.S. multinationals treat international experience and an understanding of the overseas environment as being critical for promotion to the upper ranks. Even firms with limited international activity have realized that having middle and top managers with international experience on staff is important in case the firm wants to expand its international activities.[xx]

Many expats are also encouraged by extrinsic motivators such as a supplemental wage and benefit package. For example, Lockheed Martin provides expats with housing while in the foreign country, compensation for their children's schooling, trips home each year for the family, as well as a food and expense allowance. As a result, many expatriates are able to save a great deal of money while working for the firm abroad.

Utilizing Expatriates for Foreign Assignments

A key question in the selection process is when to use an expatriate and when to rely on a local employee. The discussion above suggests that expatriates can be relatively expensive in comparison with local employees, especially in emerging economies. But there can be reasons to use a local employee beyond just cost savings (we discuss the pros and cons of hiring local employees later in the chapter). First, however, we examine the benefits and drawbacks of using expatriates.[xxi]

Advantages to Using Expatriates

There are distinct advantages to using an expatriate as opposed to a host-country local for a foreign assignment. These include their knowledge of the firm, their loyalty to the firm, and the symbolism for the business.

First, because they have worked for the company in the home country, expatriates are familiar with the company's resources, processes, and values.[xxii] They also have knowledge of the firm's management processes and culture. Expatriates also have a detailed knowledge of company policies, procedures, and corporate culture and how to transfer them to new local hires. Second, using expatriates enables companies to maintain a "foreign image" in the host country which may enhance its legitimacy.[xxiii] This can improve marketing and open doors for the firm. In China, for example, an expatriate may be thought of as having extra expertise, and certainly having a different background and experience than locals. This can come in handy to international firms in knowledge industries such as consulting.[xxiv] The placement of the expatriates also demonstrates the firm's commitment to the international aspects of the business.

Third, allegiance to the firm is another advantage in filling a foreign posting with an expat. The expatriate often is highly loyal to the firm and has many connections within it, in contrast to someone from the local country who may

An expatriate can help establish a firm's commitment to the international aspects of the business, while simultaneously bringing knowledge and experience to the firm's host-country location.

Michael Newman/PhotoEdit

not have worked for the company very long at a high-level position. (This issue is addressed further below.) Thus, using an expatriate enables international firms to select people with proven loyalty to the company (recall the Asimco in China story above). This helps provide credibility at headquarters when the expatriate conveys information, especially information concerning the adaptations the company must make to succeed in the foreign market.[xxv]

Disadvantages of Using Expatriates There are, however, some disadvantages to using expatriates in an international setting. These include the expenses involved, the person's unfamiliarity with local needs, and the inability to adapt.

First, expatriates are expensive. A full expatriate compensation package in an important position that includes salary, benefits and relocation expenses and vacation passage home for the whole family can cost from $300,000 to $1 million annually.[xxvi] This may be one of the biggest HR expenditures a firm has to make, apart from CEO compensation. Adding to the expenses is the fact that the expatriate posting is often unsuccessful, creating additional expenses for the firm in finding a replacement. Research has shown that 10 percent to 20 percent of all U.S. managers sent abroad returned early because of difficulties in adjusting to the foreign country or related job satisfaction. Moreover, many of those who stayed for the duration of the posting did not perform up to their firms' expectations, and many also quit to join a competitor.[xxvii]

These expenses and potential problems mean that training is also important in preparing expatriates before they start their foreign assignment. This is not as much of a problem for large international business enterprises as it is for small and medium-size enterprises (SMEs) that compete in the global arena, because smaller firms often do not have the financial means to establish such programs. Smaller firms can send their expatriate candidates for private training, particularly language training, but this is also costly. Yet without such training, expatriates are more likely to make costly mistakes in conducting business abroad.[xxviii]

Second, the expatriate and/or his or her family may not be particularly motivated to learn about the new culture and may not adapt to it well. This could result in expatriate failure—bringing the expatriate back to the home country early, which as we have seen can end up costing the firm about the equivalent of two years' salary.[xxix] Even when an expatriate is able to adapt, there is still a significant learning curve. Initially, even after going through the training program, the expatriate is still not completely familiar with the subtleties of the local culture, language, laws, and legal processes. People can be taught the formal systems, but informal, tacit knowledge has to be gained through field experience. Lack of such knowledge can hurt performance. Where to buy certain things, whom to call, which government agency needs to be consulted, where the best deals are for products and spare parts, and many other day-to-day details of business can be difficult for expatriates.

Communication problems may amplify some of these problems, and miscommunication is very common. For people in societies that ranked high on performance orientation, such as those in North America, presenting objective information in a direct and explicit way is an important and expected manner of communication, whereas in China, Russia, or other lower-context countries, this type of direct, factual communication may be misunderstood, at least initially. Russia, for example, ranked low on performance orientation, and hard facts and figures are not readily available or taken seriously there. In those cases, a more indirect approach may be better. For instance, if someone in China has made a mistake, an expat from North America may want to use a direct approach and point that mistake out, even in front of other staff. A less direct, more diplomatic approach would be to take that person aside and ask what he or she thought about the problem and how it could have been avoided. While some would find this approach frustratingly slow and sometimes confusing, people from countries ranking lower on Hofstede's production orientation scale prefer such discourse and place a premium on relationships.

Given the 20 percent failure rate in expatriate assignments, firms need to work harder to ensure that those individuals are successful. For example, HRM should establish the selection criteria for the expatriate. Management's involvement ensures that the selection will be based not only on technical know-how but also on acculturation skills. Others outside human resources typically focus on technical skills because the failure of the home-country national on the job is most often directly linked to technical shortcomings.[xxx] But the human resources manager knows that issues such as family can also affect the success of a foreign posting.[xxxi] Thus, it is important to have the human resources manager ensure that a rich set of concerns are incorporated into the selection process.

The firm can help to ease the family's transition into the new environment. The evidence is that most international firms do not take the family into consideration when making assignments. It has been found that prospective expats who were interviewed with their spouses for a job are more likely to succeed than those who were interviewed alone. Previous studies have shown that 70 percent of international firms did not have comprehensive pre-assimilation or preparation training programs.[xxxii] Only short briefings were done, and this has not improved much in recent years.[xxxiii] But such assimilation programs have been shown to be important to the success of the expatriate.

Utilizing Host-Country Employees for Foreign Assigments

Just as with expatriates, there are both benefits and drawbacks to hiring local host-country employees as managers, particularly senior managers. A firm must balance these advantages and disadvantages against those of the expatriate when choosing which to employ in a given country.

Advantages of Using Host-Country Employees Hiring a number of locals, particularly in management positions, can enhance a company's image in the host country and even give it additional bargaining power with the local government. Such locals also know the language and customs and have extensive tacit knowledge about how things are done in that country and region.

First, host-country locals are already familiar with the local language, culture, and customs, so they do not require expensive training in language proficiency or acculturation. The locals also know their way around. They know the government, the financial people, where to buy things, whom to call, and how to get things done. In addition, locals may be productive right away. Unlike expatriates, local employees do not need time to adapt to the local environment and can be productive from the beginning of the assignment if they know their job and the company system. Yet a firm may also need to train them directly. For example, Wal-Mart in China felt that local managers needed time to work with managers from the United States who knew the Wal-Mart system. This is consistent with what professor Morgan McCall has called "selection stressing experience and professional upbringing."[xxxiv] The professional upbringing of the manager suggests where the manager should be placed in the organization and what type of job he or she can best cover.

Another advantage to filling management positions locally in a foreign country is the locals' tacit knowledge. Host-country nationals have important tacit knowledge about idiosyncratic local commercial practices. Host-country nationals understand the subtleties of the local business situation, information that can help establish and maintain a good relationship with customers, clients, government agencies, employees, and the general public. Also, employing host-country nationals is often less expensive than employing home-country or third-country nationals (such as a Malaysian posted to China from an American firm), especially in lower-wage countries. In China, for example, managers are paid salaries and other benefit packages that are only 10 percent to 15 percent of expatriates' or third-country nationals, and no expensive repatriation programs are needed.

Third, having host-country nationals in management positions, especially at higher levels, may enhance the company's reputation in a foreign country that has strong nationalistic or populist movements. It may also enhance host-country employees' morale because these employees may appreciate working for a boss of the same nationality rather than for a foreigner, and they may also appreciate the opportunity for advancement within an organization that employs many local managers and supervisors. Frequently, international firms recruit students from universities located in the region of their foreign plant. For example, Gillette uses the AIESEC student exchange program, and Emerson Electric recruits host country locals right out of local universities in the foreign location. General Electric and Wal-Mart also recruit new management trainees from foreign universities in the country in which they intend to hire. The selector needs to be thoroughly educated about the specific educational institution, its language, and the culture-based courses that it offers to the students who are being selected. The intent is to hire people directly into the firm's system. When it moved into China, Wal-Mart found that local retailers and their employees had a much different view of what retail sales and service meant. Wal-Mart felt that the local retail workforce had learned a number of bad work habits, possibly from years of working in Chinese state-owned enterprises. It decided early on to hire new employees right out of China's universities and inculcate them with Wal-Mart's low-cost and service culture and work ethic. Wal-Mart had some unexpected difficulty early with employee behavior that they did not expect: there was significant employee pilferage and employees regularly took naps during office hours. The latter behavior is not uncommon in state enterprises in mainland China. Wal-Mart dealt quickly to eliminate undesirable behaviors, particularly insisting on no employee naps, even on break times. Wal-Mart has become a preferred place for China's graduates who are interested in retail or service business in general as a result of its training and development programs and excellent reputation in China. In the process of such training, the firm has also developed very good connections with local governments in China.[xxxv] Many Wal-Mart employees have returned to their home towns, bringing back their excellent training in retail to start specialty retail chains. China's retail industry has been transformed in just two decades from a Soviet Union style system of products being locked inside glass cases to a system that looks just like a modern, advanced retail system in Hong Kong, Japan, or the West.

Disadvantages of Using Host-Country Locals There are also some disadvantages to host-country locals, including difficulty finding qualified people, possible mixed loyalties, and lack of understanding of the company's culture and processes.

First, it may be difficult to find qualified people at the local level with the right skills for the assignment, especially in less-developed countries. Currently in China there is much talk of the war for talent among larger firms. There are significant shortages of middle managers in particular.[xxxvi] And it also may be difficult to assess local people's ability. Sometimes a degree or training program in the local country may not be equivalent to what is earned at an internationally recognized institution.

To illustrate, in China some 33 percent of the university students study engineering, compared with 20 percent in Germany and just 4 percent in India. But an engineering program in China can often mean little more than a technical-school training program. Moreover, relative to engineering graduates in Europe and North America, Chinese students get little practical experience in projects or teamwork. The result is that China's pool of young engineers considered suitable for work in multinationals is thought to be just 160,000—much fewer than in America and no larger than that of the United Kingdom.[xxxvii] Shortages of trained personal are now being reported in China, hindering its entrance into information technology and outsourcing service businesses. This is a concern for foreign firms making a new investment in China or any foreign market—the labor market has to be investigated with a local consultant before settling on a suitable location.

Second, the host-country employee's loyalty to his or her country or community may interfere with company policies.[xxxviii] Thus, in settings such as Bolivia or Venezuela, where political leaders are charismatic, nationalistic, and seek to limit the profits of international firms operating in their countries, local managers can prove difficult to manage. Their friends and family are often pressuring them to cooperate with the political leaders, but if they do their actions will hurt their international employers.

To illustrate the issue of loyalty, consider that in China, as in many developing countries, laws and institutions are somewhat underdeveloped, making personal connections especially important for getting things done, particularly in transactions with other organizations and the government. Connections, or *guanxi*, are very important, and foreign firms going to China are tempted to hire those with good *guanxi*. That is generally a good practice, but it must be considered carefully. Sometimes loyalty to an individual goes far beyond company loyalty. One major multinational snack food company hired a senior local sales manager to run its sales efforts in China. That manager had excellent training with another multinational firm, knew many local and regional distributors, and could speak English quite well, which made it easy for him to work with the firm's top management back at the home office. The manager then proceeded to build up the sales staff directly with his own network of contacts, many from his previous firm. In a short time, he had built up this sales force with people who were directly loyal to him, not to the company. The snack foods firm was initially pleased with the swiftness with which the manager built up the sales force and energized sales. Later, however, it came to the firm's attention that he was making personal side deals with distributors he knew to get kickbacks. After being confronted, the sales manager left, and shortly thereafter, so did a majority of the firm's sales force. In the end, the company was left with a huge disruption in sales and a lot of angry distributors, because the sales manager had made all kinds of promises and obligations that the company simply could not honor.[xxxix] As always, hiring must be conducted judiciously.

A third disadvantage is that host-country nationals may not understand the international company's culture and ways of doing things. They may not have sufficient knowledge of the firm's policies and culture, particularly the informal decision-making network back at headquarters, which may differ considerably from the official organizational chart. The attitude towards minorities, women, ethics and the environment, or may be very important to the international firm and its stakeholders, but such values may differ significantly in the host country. Attitudes toward bribery and paying taxes may be more lax in the foreign location. A local manager's talk may be consistent with the international firm's culture but their walk (actions) may often reflect their local cultural orientation or training.

TRAINING

A second major HR function is training. Expatriates must be prepared to assimilate into many different cultures and move globally. Foreign language training is important, but the ability to live and work in another country (and culture) requires a cultural flexibility that comes from studying other countries and cultures and understanding that the way you do things at home may not be the way people do things abroad. A corporation-run training program for the expatriate manager pool is important in preparing expatriate executives for a specific region and to help the expat build that cultural flexibility. Teaching about the region's language, recent history, culture, technical shortcomings in the region are all essential. For top managers, foreign-educated lawyers can explain the laws of the specific region and other subtleties not covered in standard expat training.

ETHICS AND BUSINESS REALITIES

A key part of a firm's culture is its ethics. Firms have taken strong ethical stands in recent years on many issues, including the environment. One such firm is General Electric, which has moved to reduce emissions of greenhouse gases in order to reduce global warming. The $163-billion firm seeks to develop new products that help others reduce carbon dioxide emissions. These products include simple things, such as new lightbulbs, and more complex items, such as new emission equipment for coal-fired utilities. GE has also sought to reduce its own energy usage, and has saved over a $100 million a year in reduced energy costs.

Most controversially, GE has received push-back from customers as it has sought to educate them on carbon emissions or encourage them to change the manner in which they do business. Customers have often responded that they simply want to buy the products, not be lectured to, and GE has had high-profile confrontations with individuals in the energy industry. GE also continues to invest in coal-fired utilities even though they are some of the country's major producers of carbon dioxide.

Despite its high profile in promoting the reduction of greenhouse gases and its leadership in seeking to limit global warming, GE also has its own investment needs. The firm spends considerable efforts seeking to balance these two issues, a problem faced by many similar businesses. Having strong environmental values is good, but ultimately the business needs to make a profit. This balancing of interests can be particularly hard for an international firm as it seeks to employ individuals from a host country. The choices faced are typically not profit or environment related. Instead, it is a nuanced balance that is not easily reached by someone who does not have an understanding of the host country's culture and institutions.[xl]

The results of a major study by international HR scholar Professor Rosalie Tung indicated that nearly 60 percent of the international Japanese firms surveyed sponsored formal training programs for their expatriates. The programs, in general, consist of the following components: language training, general training, field training, graduate programs in a foreign country, in-house training programs, and use of external agents to help the expat. Tung also found that American firms doing business internationally did not invest as much as Japanese firms in such programs, because for American firms employment tends to be short-term—if they invest in an employee's development and he or she leaves, the company will not recapture the costs.[xli] Some firms such as Proctor & Gamble have addressed this problem by establishing a mentor program to help the expatriate manage his or her career progression.

This problem of preparation may have improved in recent years, partly because of the attitudes and (self) preparation of expats themselves. For example, in a recent study, Tung noted that many expatriates (including a large number of Americans) were quite successful in navigating their international postings and returning back to their home country with intact career paths. She hypothesized that this stemmed from a more cosmopolitan outlook of the new expatriate class in America and other Western countries. Many had learned one or two additional languages through their own study, and had worked or studied overseas, sometimes multiple times and for extended periods of time. An implication of the research is that including regular language study and exchange programs or extended trips overseas when possible can help you to be better prepared to live and work abroad.[xlii]

APPRAISAL AND COMPENSATION

The third important facet of HR is the appraisal and compensation process. One aspect of compensation was covered in Chapter 7 on motivation. More detail is addressed in this section.

Appraisal

Performance appraisal can be defined as a systematic and periodic review of employee performance, normally on an annual basis. The basic purpose of employee evaluations is to build better-performing organizations and to aid in the professional development of employees. Proper appraisal is an important step to properly motivating and compensating an employee while maintaining a degree of pay equity within the organization. There are several types of performance appraisal. The more common approaches to performance appraisal are summarized below.

The Written Essay This method of employee evaluation involves a manager writing an essay about what he or she considers to be an overall assessment of an employee's performance. It is important to note that nothing obligates the manager to justify anything within the assessment. A second variation has the manager rating an employee using a list of terms such as "above average," "fair," or "poor" on key performance criteria that the firm wants to encourage. This approach is useful because managers subjectively choose evaluation criteria that they think can describe their performance fairly; a certain evaluation criterion can highlight one key aspect of an employee's performance that would have been missed by most other criteria. But this method's subjectivity can deny the firm reliable feedback about employee performance. Evaluations that include further explanation and commentary on performance can help employees to eliminate mistakes and improve their performance.

A second approach is the **trait rating** appraisal. With this method, a list of personality traits and job attitudes important to the job is created and the supervisor must assign a numerical or descriptive rating of the employee's performance. Traits may include items such as cooperation, motivation, flexibility, and attitudes. This approach assumes that one can define and rate traits objectively, and it is often used in conjunction with written feedback or, if available, direct productivity measures. For example, Lincoln Electric has a letter grading system (A, B, C, etc.) of employee traits, behaviors, and attitudes such as teamwork to help form the basis for that employee's annual bonus. A number of banks in East Asia use this approach, including HSBC and Hang Seng Bank in Hong Kong. This system has been successfully implemented in several countries—even those countries thought of as more collective or less production oriented such as Mexico. Some critics argue, however, that, in practice, traits are too broadly defined, as are the criteria for evaluating each trait, or the system is too open to favoritism—perhaps the boss has a favorite trait in mind such as an extraverted or exuberant personality. An introverted person might get a lower evaluation (and raise) at the end of the year based in part on that one trait. One way to combat this problem of fairness is to use **360 degree evaluations**, that is, evaluations by the supervisor, coworkers, subordinates, and even customers or clients outside the immediate work area. This adds a reliability check to see if the manager is treating his or her subordinates well or is pushing them too hard to achieve a performance bonus. If the traits necessary to succeed are well understood in a job, the trait rating approach can work well.

360-degree evaluations
Evaluations of an employee conducted by the supervisor, subordinates, peers, and sometimes customers.

A third approach to appraisal is the **critical incident approach**, which focuses the evaluator's attention on those tasks and behaviors that are key in making the difference between executing a job effectively and executing it ineffectively. The critical incident approach was first popularized in the U.S. and German militaries around World War II with after-action reports describing leaders' and units' behavior under different situations, the successes and failure that occurred, and how problems could be fixed going forward.[xliii] This method was initially used both to transmit knowledge to the rest of the military about what went right and what did not and how an officer in question performed. Critical incidents are important to the military because these are very important to understanding an action's outcome as well as to the overall organizational learning and memory as incidents are recorded and codified into record for future use. For example, salespeople can find out what worked (and what did not) for other salespeople in the past. Marketers can learn about past promotions in an emerging economy such as China and therefore what might be expected to work well in India or Russia, for example.

The critical incident approach to appraisal has since filtered down from the military to organizations in government and the private sector, both large and small.[xliv] A supervisor using this approach will document the employee's on-the-job behaviors in important situations, designating each behavior or incident as either unsatisfactory or satisfactory and then comparing the frequency of satisfactory incidents to unsatisfactory ones. The degree of objectivity can vary depending on the appraiser and what different appraisers view as critical incidents. Managers need to ensure they have sufficient quantity and quality of employee observational opportunities. This can work well with jobs that are otherwise difficult to quantify, and when the supervisor doing the appraising has worked in that particular job and understands what it takes to do well. It is also helpful in that critical incidents are well codified and employee actions debriefed and analyzed.

A fourth approach is called the **behaviorally anchored rating scales (BARS)**. The BARS approach uses the constituents of critical incidents along with graphic rating scales. BARS uses careful job analysis to determine the behaviors required for a particular job. BARS measures behavioral performance factors rather than personality or attitudinal factors on a scale, for example from one to five or from best to worst. For any particular job, BARS involves identifying the complete range of relevant job behaviors and designing appropriate performance dimensions for that job. Southwest Airlines developed a BARS system for its employees based on the most successful and least successful employees in different jobs with the airline. Southwest hires and trains based on these scales and also carries out evaluations guided in part by employee performance on these behaviors. Firms often ask an experienced HR professional to help identify the best performers and worst performers in various jobs in the company, as well as the key behaviors that they are evaluated on. BARS can work well when a job's tasks are well understood and performance can be measured in quantitative terms.

A fifth approach to employee performance appraisal is **managing by objective**, or **MBO**. First popularized by longtime management scholar Peter Drucker, MBO is a process that involves management and employees agreeing to key goals and ways in which they can be reached. MBO was devised as a method of incorporating performance planning into performance appraisal. The manager, or manager and employee together, decides which goals must be achieved by the employee. Consistent with goal-setting theory, goals are connected to a time schedule, are specific and measurable, and become the measure of the employee's performance. Typically, the goals are established at the beginning of an appraisal period and measured at the end of it. Objectives can be set in all domains of activities (production, services, sales, R&D, customer satisfaction, peer review, finance, information systems, and so forth). Objectives can be collective for a whole department or the whole company, or individualized. A system of MBO appraisal can also incorporate other rating systems. MBO employs the principle from goal-setting theory that employees are more likely to accomplish goals that they set themselves or to which they jointly agree. It is argued that MBO-style management and appraisal can trigger employees' unethical behavior by encouraging them to meet goals in any manner possible, such as distorting financial figures to achieve their agreed-upon targets. MBO is also thought to encourage short-term, overly narrow bottom-line mindsets, neglecting innovation and longer-term thinking.[xlv] It is important to remember that, as we saw in Chapter 7, goals work best when they are negotiated with the employee and made public.

Additional Organizational Applications

One of the more novel, though controversial, approaches to appraisal that has appeared in recent years is a variation of the written essay evaluation system. This system of **employee differentiation** was popularized by Jack Welch, the former CEO of General Electric, and it "force ranks" employees into three categories based on what is generically called a vitality curve. In the GE system, there is the top 20 percent, the middle (or "vital") 70 percent, and the bottom 10 percent. This system of appraisal, in which a supervisor typically provides a written evaluation with a ranking, has generated a great deal of debate. Proponents of the forced ranking claim that it is more effective than most qualitative systems for employee appraisal in which employees do not receive honest and specific appraisals because managers are not willing to give them, nor are they incentivized to provide such feedback. They point out that in the most common evaluation systems, managers give most employees a good rating; even low performers receive an "okay." [xlvi] The GE system forces managers to write frank appraisals that can help employees who are not performing well. This system may even reduce lawsuits because the poorly performing employees are fired or transferred after multiple performance warnings. Too often, forced rank proponents argue, poor employees receive acceptable ratings until some critical instance occurs and they are fired without a proper trail of poor evaluations to support such an action.

Opponents of the GE system claim that it hurts teamwork and innovation. They add that it is possible to build teamwork and innovation ratings into performance evaluations to make sure employees are not just stressing personal, individual performance. Others add that such an individual achievement-oriented system would not work well in egalitarian countries such as Sweden or collective societies such as Japan.[xlvii] Welch responds that the differentiation or forced rank system works because mediocre-performing employees improve their performance. Or they move to a different part of the firm and find tasks they can do better and may prefer—something that is very consistent with advice from career scholars as well, that is, try to find work that you enjoy and are good at.[xlviii]

What does the empirical research say about GE's system of employee differentiation or forced ranking? The limited research on forced ranking systems suggests that they produce a short-term improvement in overall division and group performance that fairly quickly levels off, perhaps because the worst performers are removed in a timely fashion. Although former GE boss Welch swears by forced ranking and contends that it has helped GE and other companies considerably in overall performance and management development, others complain about the harmful competition it creates among employees. Some add that forced ranking injects fear into the workplace. When Southwest Airlines began to experiment in ways to develop more accurate metrics for individual employee performance, it found

There are many methods available for evaluating an employee's performance.

the forced ranking system emphasized blame for mistakes for the bottom 10 percent and produced more nonproductive competition. Perhaps while such a model initially may be accurate—10 percent of employees are probably underperforming and need to be replaced or assigned other tasks—after each iteration the average quality of employees will increase, at which point the forced ranking system will start to kick out good performers. These adequately performing managers will be fired or moved to other jobs, and the department or company will lose good employees.

Motorola, Microsoft, and many consulting firms, accounting firms, and law firms use a variation of the force ranking system to eliminate the worst performers. Welch has commented that one of the most asked questions he gets in his talks around the world is about GE's forced rating system. The usual argument is that the forced rating system would not work in a society that is low on individuality (like China), or high on the relational scale (like in Latin America), or even more egalitarian (like Sweden). Welch usually answers by suggesting that the questioner try the method out in part of his or her firm, much like Lincoln Electric's application of their reward system in Mexico (discussed in Chapter 7). Experimenting with the system in a limited way will allow a firm to see how it works without exposing the whole company to major change.

A key question a firm must ask is what is the objective of the review itself. Is it to identify and transfer out poor performers? Is the firm seeking to recognize the best managers and employees? Does the firm want to provide the basis for compensation decisions or promotion? Alternatively, is it a tool to plan for personal development? Perhaps the firm wants some aspect of all of these goals. Too often it is unclear what a firm wants in changing to employee differentiation. But for the system to be effective, the objective needs to be specified by the organization and communicated to employees. As with the old adage "What gets measured is what gets done," it is essential for an organization to give managers direction about the purpose of the performance appraisal, whether or not it's a forced ranking system or a basic verbal feedback.

How often should reviews be conducted? W. Edwards Deming, the famed quality guru introduced earlier in the book, argued that reviews should be held regularly, not just once a year but more often, with feedback provided either in written or verbal form, and that there should be no surprises. Imagine if a football coach waited six months before giving the players feedback! When a player makes a mistake, coaches talk to that player about it right away and explain why it was a mistake. In the same way, for short-term reviews verbal feedback is usually sufficient. For longer-term reviews, written feedback and grading schemes are helpful. Employees can be graded on their production, but also on quality control, checks and balances like teamwork, attention to quality, coaching of other employees, and so forth. Firms can base regular pay on productivity, measuring individual work or team work, but bonuses and other rewards often come from the grading schemes. At Cleveland-based manufacturer Lincoln Electric, straight-A performers in several graded categories of performance (such as teamwork and attendance) can receive sizeable bonuses, often amounting to tens of thousands of dollars. Employees report that the annual bonus is the best and most motivating part of their jobs. Lincoln's incentive and HRM system has led to a history of industry-leading productivity and employee compensation innovations, which have helped to keep Lincoln Electric a worldwide leader in the production of welding equipment and among American leaders in manufacturing productivity.

Compensation

Working hand in hand with the appraisal system is the key human resource function of compensation. We discussed compensation at a general level in Chapter 7 on motivation and go into additional detail here. A central part of the compensation decision an international firm must make is whether to establish an overall policy for all employees or to distinguish among home-country nationals (expatriates), host-country locals, and third-country nationals. It is common for international business to distinguish between expatriates and locals. Thus, an expatriate petroleum engineer may be doing a similar function to the local petroleum engineer in Indonesia, for example, but the expatriate would be paid much more for the work. It is quite common for most firms to also distinguish between types of expatriates. For example, different policies may be set on the basis of length of assignment or on the type of function to be carried out.[xlix] In all cases, the policy should be based on the idea that the expatriate must not suffer a loss because of his or her transfer. Furthermore, the approach selected should not demoralize the foreign subsidiary's staff; for instance, significant and overly visible pay inequity between the expatriate and his or her local peers can create bad feelings and undermine morale, so firms should be careful to consider equity issues carefully.[l]

This does not mean that everyone should be paid the same. Even egalitarian countries expect some pay inequity, and research shows that an optimal amount of pay inequity is when the top earner in a division earns about fifty times the lowest (regular) employee pay.[li] As discussed in Chapter 7, it has sometimes been argued that an aggressive pay-for-performance scheme will be rejected out of hand for cultural reasons by countries with a lower production orientation, such as Mexico or by highly collective cultures, such as China. Years ago a number of books and articles on international business warned business people against introducing such "American systems" into foreign cultures. After nearly 30 years of evidence on appraisal schemes in Mexico, China, and other countries, it has turned out that pay-for-performance appraisal schemes with a heavy variable component were in fact not failures but were well received if implemented carefully, even if they were for individual-based incentive schemes.[lii] One of the most radical piecework systems, developed by manufacturer Lincoln Electric, was never expected to be accepted in Mexico, as noted in Chapter 7. Variations have since been accepted in China and other countries. You will recall that Lincoln did not initially introduce the scheme, instead at first appraising and paying employees with a traditional salary structure. But Lincoln slowly introduced the scheme, giving workers the choice of being included in it. Lincoln's Mexican workers gradually saw that those who got into the piecework scheme were earning more money, and more clamored to join. After only about two years, Lincoln's compensation scheme had been fully implemented in their Mexican plant. The social proof of the successful piecework system, as noted in Chapter 10, had a more powerful impact in influencing Lincoln's Mexican employees than did any cultural propensity toward an egalitarian and relational workplace. The Mexican employees watched a few of their colleagues do the work and make extra money, and they decided they could do the same, opting for pay for performance also. Similarly in China, individual piecework schemes have been widely and successfully implemented in spite of warnings from some culture writers and anthropologists to give only group incentives in this collective culture. Fortunately, theorizing has given way to solid empirical evidence, and firms are introducing individual incentives in jobs where they make the most sense, such as light manufacturing, sales, and marketing. For jobs for which group incentives make more sense, such as an airline crew working together to get a plane off safely and on time, group incentives are often more convenient and effective.[liii] This suggests that the nature of the job is more important in formulating the compensation system than the local culture. It also suggests that people respond to incentives and positive feedback in much the same way all around the world, although the implementation of a compensation system may necessarily be different (and more deliberate) in countries less accustomed to pay for performance and individual rewards.

Compensation policies seek to satisfy numerous objectives.[liv] In the case of expatriates, for example, the compensation policy should be consistent and fair in its treatment of all categories of expatriate employees. The policy must work to attract and retain expatriates in the areas where the corporation has the greatest need. It should also be consistent with the organization's overall strategy and structure, and should serve to motivate employees and provide incentives where needed.

It has been estimated that, on average, expatriates cost employers two to five times as much as corresponding home-country employees, and even more in some lower-wage countries.[lv] There are a number of key aspects to developing the compensation of an expatriate if the firm chooses to place such employees in a foreign environment. These include benefits, base salary, allowances, and tax treatment.

Ineffective expatriate compensation plays a big role in the failure of expatriate assignments. Therefore, international firms need to establish policies for careful and effective management of expatriate compensation. To do so requires that the firm have knowledge of the foreign country's laws, customs, environment, and employment practices, as well as an understanding of the effects of currency exchange fluctuations and inflation on compensation. Within the context of changing political, economic, and social conditions, establishing policy also requires an understanding of why certain allowances are necessary. Recall (from Chapter 7) that pay equity is also a concern. For example, in most of Europe executive pay will be much lower than in the United States. So in asking a U.S. executive to move to a European subsidiary, the executive's pay package will likely be higher than that of their European colleagues. To avoid equity concerns with the European staff, sometimes a portion of the U.S. executive's pay can be in the form of benefits, such as payments for children's schooling, housing benefits, home travel, travel for families, and so forth, which seems to be acceptable to local staff. These sorts of expatriate benefits can be better justified or framed in terms of the expatriate having to work in a foreign country and facing higher expenses, and inequities based on benefits sometimes sit better with the local staff.[lvi]

An assignment in a difficult environment, such as much of Africa, would require greater compensation than an assignment to a more developed environment like Western Europe. A 25 percent hardship allowance is common for more difficult postings. Companies will pay, but only upon completion of the assignment. If the expatriate wants to come home earlier or be transferred, he or she will forfeit the allowance. Figure 12-3 lists the highest and lowest ranking hardship locations for expats.

Base salary
Amount of money that an expatriate normally receives in the home country.

Base Salary International firms tend to use the home-country national's home salary as a base to determine expatriate compensation. **Base salary** is the amount of money that an expatriate normally receives in the home country. In the United States, this has been around $175,000 for upper-level middle managers in recent years, and this

FIGURE 12-3   Hardship Rankings of Cities for Expatriates*

5 Highest in Hardship, Requiring Greater Employee Compensation	5 Lowest in Hardship
1) Moscow, Russia 2) Almaty, Kazakhstan 3) Kinshasa, Zaire 4) Beijing and Shanghai, China 5) New Delhi and Mumbai, India	1) Buenos Aires, Argentina 2) Hong Kong, China 3) Budapest, Hungary 4) Dubai, United Arab Emirates 5) Sao Paulo/Rio de Janeiro, Brazil
	❖ All North American cities tied for sixth.

*Criteria: security, sociopolitical tension, housing, and climate.

Sources: ExpansionManagement.com. (1998). Warning: Living in the U.S. may cause culture shock.http://www.expansionmanagement.com/cmd/articledetail/articleid/14811/default.asp (website accessed December 4, 2008); Bensimon, H. F. (1998). Is it safe to work abroad? *Training & Development* 52(8), 20–24.

rate is similar to that paid to managers in both Japan and Germany. Exchange rates, of course, also affect the real wages. Therefore, a German manager working for a U.S. firm but assigned to Spain would have a base salary that reflects the salary structure in Germany. Expatriates from the United States have salaries tied to U.S. pay levels. Salaries usually are paid in home currency, local currency, or a combination of the two. Base pay also serves as the benchmark against which bonuses and benefits are calculated. Expats posted to countries with volatile currencies should ask the company about getting paid at least partially in the home currency. Firms should be sensitive to the possibility of currency fluctuation and maintaining their expatriate employees' compensation levels in terms of the home currency.

Conditions that force compensation policies to differ from those used for home-country expatriates include inflation and cost of living, housing, security, school costs, and taxation. Furthermore, home-country expatriates often require a salary premium as an inducement to accept the foreign assignment or to endure the hardships of a foreign transfer. In the United States, when an international business enterprise has determined the type of hardship, it can refer to the U.S. State Department's *Hardship Post Differentials Guidelines* to ascertain the appropriate level of premium compensation.

The practice of international businesses paying a higher salary to expatriate managers than to host-country managers (or even managers from a third country) can discourage local managers, especially when they have an equal level of responsibility and workload. International firms must determine how to deal effectively with such inequities, as discussed in Chapter 7. Some believe that international firms should have a standard global policy relating to compensation; that is, regardless of the varying costs of living, all of the corporation's managers in all countries should be compensated on the basis of a standard global salary range based on the level of authority and responsibility. This policy, of course, is debatable and difficult to implement. Most companies will pay based on what the local market will bear, and what managers and professionals expect to be paid.

Allowances and Benefits   As noted earlier in this chapter, international businesses generally pay expatriates certain allowances. These include cost-of-living, housing, education, and relocation allowances. Cost-of-living allowances pay the expatriate for differences in expenses between the home and foreign country. Housing allowances help the expatriate maintain his or her home-country living standards. Education allowances ensure that the expatriate's children will receive at least as good an education as they would receive in the home country. Relocation allowances usually pay for moving, shipping, and storage expenses, temporary living expenses, and other related expenses.[1]

Another important part of an employee's compensation package is the benefits provided. Approximately one-third of compensation for regular employees in the United States consists of benefits. These benefits make up a similar, or even larger, portion of expatriate compensation. Additionally, most international firms provide expatriates with extra vacation and special leaves. The international firm typically will pay the airfare for expatriates and their families to make an annual visit home, for emergency leave, and for expenses when a relative in the home country is sick.

Taxation   For the expatriate, a foreign assignment can mean being double-taxed, by the home-country and the foreign-country governments. This problem is mitigated in the United States by an income exclusion of about $80,000, and by the United States having a reciprocal agreement with some countries whereby an expatriate would pay taxes only in the United States and not the host country. International firms are subject to varying tax rates around the globe. Rates are different from country to country, and they change within countries from time to time. For example, the

TRANSNATIONAL CORPORATIONS AND HRM

The nature of transnational corporations raises many interesting human resource management problems. For example, when a worldwide organization is heavily integrated it can be expected to have managers who will travel extensively. The advent of communications technologies, such as email, has helped firms easily keep in touch, but there is still a critical need to be on location. Conversations between people have a richness that cannot occur through email. Similarly, when there are problems or special projects, people are needed on site.

Transnational corporations are facing increasing problems with monitoring employee tax liability as employees are asked to spend more time abroad. You normally pays taxes in your home country; simply visiting another country for business or pleasure does not create any new tax liability. Most countries, however, now have length-of-stay laws that require expats to pay local taxes if they spend most of your working time within their borders. For example, Britain requires expats to pay taxes if they spend three months or more working there. Transnational corporations with active businesses or a regional headquarters in Britain often have employees who have spent enough time in Britain to be liable for British taxes.

Increasingly, transnational corporations must actively track the countries where their employees are working and how much time they are spending in any given country because it is easy to become liable for taxation. A firm has a duty to help the government obtain the taxes it is owed through withholdings. If a country can prove that a firm or its employees avoided paying taxes required by length-of-stay laws, the firm (and the employee) can be in for some penalties and legal difficulties.[lvii]

current maximum marginal tax rate for those working in Hong Kong is about 16 percent, versus about 35 percent in the United States. In practice this means an American expat in Hong Kong will pay about 16 percent in taxes on about the first $80,000 of income, and then at the higher, U.S. rate above that. A firm's compensation packages must consider how specific compensation practices can be adjusted in each country to provide, within the context of the corporation's overall policy, the most tax-effective, appropriate rewards for expatriate, host-country, and third-country managers.

SOCIALIZATION

The last of the main human resource functions is socialization. This function contains two parts. First is the need to socialize local hires into the company culture. This occurs with careful selection and training. For example, as mentioned earlier, Wal-Mart has emphasized hiring new employees right out of university, before they have the opportunity to learn any other ways of doing business, thereby inculcating their service and cost-control culture in employees who may have never shopped in a Wal-Mart.

The second type of socialization is essentially an acculturation of the expatriate to the local environment. As we have seen before, this can be a difficult process. In recent years, the vast majority (86 percent) of Japanese multinational firms recalled 5 percent or less of their expatriates. In contrast, only a quarter of U.S. international firms recalled expatriates at that same low rate, while another quarter of firms had to recall expats at a much higher rate.[lviii] The Japanese home-country headquarters provides more comprehensive training and employee support than many U.S. firms provide for their expatriates, as well as better guidance from Japanese expatriates who are established in the region already.[lix] U.S. nationals have traditionally been less successful than the nationals of Japanese firms in expatriate assignments, although there is evidence that this is changing as U.S. nationals get more international exposure and American firms gain more experience and benefit from the services of very experienced organizations such as the U.S. State Department.[lx]

ADDITIONAL CHALLENGES FACING EXPATRIATES IN INTERNATIONAL POSTINGS

Some disadvantages of using expatriates were discussed above. In addition, expatriates face many challenges for which they must be prepared. Firms can help, at minimum, by providing some briefing on these problems and by providing training when possible. These include the foreign country's physical and social environments, varying technical sophistication, conflicting objectives and policies between the country and the firm, pitfalls in the human resource planning function, and inadequate repatriation programs.

Physical Environment

Expatriates often encounter adaptation problems caused by both the physical and the sociocultural environments, especially when these environments differ significantly from the expatriate's home environment. For example, geographical distance may result in a type of separation anxiety for expatriates and family members.[lxi] Sometimes the food and weather are much different than in the home country. For example, for someone from southern Europe coming to a Midwestern U.S. state like Michigan or Minnesota, it is important that their preparation include instruction on how to deal with the snow. Otherwise, the first eight-inch snowfall with subfreezing temperatures will be a rude introduction to their new home. Japanese people accustomed to living in very safe cities must be briefed on which neighborhoods of North American cities to stay out of. The first expatriates to China during its early reform period were similarly surprised and ill-prepared by China's lack of basic services, even in the capital of Beijing. For example, accounting people from American Motors's home office could not understand why their expatriate staff in Beijing were spending so much on hotel laundry services, and asked the expatriate staff why they didn't take their clothes to a laundromat. The China expatriates replied that there were no laundromats anywhere in Beijing, and hardly any small professional service businesses of any kind, for that matter.[lxii] The accountants had assumed since there were numerous Chinese-owned laundries in North America, China itself must also have a large number of them, which was not the case.

Social Environment

The social environment can present another major problem for expatriates and their families. The problem can start with language. If an expatriate and his or her family are not capable of communicating in the local language, it can create difficulties. Work difficulties will be most apparent because the expatriate must do everything through interpreters. This makes it harder to build rapport with employees, and translation problems are rife. The expatriate manager may also need to have his or her own interpreter (as opposed to the locally hired one) to be sure that things are being translated accurately. This becomes more challenging if the local language is difficult to read and learn. For example, China and Japan both use a pictograph language that originated in an early Chinese dynasty over 3,000 years ago, although Japan also employs phonetic scripts along with Chinese characters.[lxiii] There are tens of thousands of different Chinese characters, which makes learning these languages rather difficult for most expatriates. These language problems will affect expatriates' ability to deal with individuals and business groups outside the organization, including local partners, bankers, unions, suppliers, and customers, which in turn can hamper the expatriates' effectiveness.[lxiv] Given that the language of international business is now overwhelmingly English, most expatriates do not need to be fluent in the language of the host country. Nevertheless, it is helpful to learn some of the local language, even a difficult language such as Chinese or Thai, and to have translation readily available, especially from translators loyal to the company.[lxv]

Lack of Adequate Training for Foreign Assignments

Many large firms in North America spend little time preparing employees for foreign assignments. Most of the firms that sponsor training programs use environmental briefing programs only. This type of briefing that gives background on the country, its climate, culture, and other basic information, is helpful, but it should be accompanied by contact with individuals familiar with the local environment in the foreign country, preferably other expatriates who have lived there. The adoption of more rigorous training programs could significantly improve the expatriate's performance in an overseas environment, thus minimizing the incidence of failure.[lxvi]

However, changing the behavior of experienced managers could pose a challenging task for a company's training system. First, expatriates without a background in business or psychology, such as more technical staff, generally may not believe in such training. Those conducting the training must bear in mind that the relevance of the training and preparation must be shown to the trainees through specific cases and scenarios; that is, they must not only tell people about the culture but also show how understanding it can help them. If potential expatriates fail to grasp this, the resulting lack of cultural savvy is likely to cause a lot of trouble down the road.[lxvii]

Second, many expatriates believe that the way things are done in their home country is the way to do it and that the HR people and the overseas staff do not know how to handle things properly. If such an expatriate has been highly successful in the past, it may be hard for that person to listen to advice about ways to behave, and the trainer may expect defensive behavior when explaining what to do and how the expatriate may need to change. For instance, consider an executive from the United States who insists on giving his prospective mainland Chinese partners a hug upon greeting them, something that generally makes Chinese people uncomfortable. Or one who calls on the Chinese partners by name during a presentation and insists they answer a question even though they clearly look uncomfortable and do not look able to give an answer. It is important to understand that executives from China and much of Asia typically do not like physical contact, and that gestures such as finger-pointing or singling people out in meetings can be seen overly aggressive or even rude. Expatriates and foreign employees alike should be briefed on cultural differences such as these before the assignment, even if they are initially reluctant and skeptical of such training.

Third, their workload in the midst of preparation for their transfer may not leave expatriates sufficient time for an intensive training program. Even something as basic as language training and communication skills may get neglected. Even if the expatriate does not have time for any language training, the problems of translation must be made clear—mistranslations and miscommunication with locals in foreign assignments are all too common.

Communication Challenges Communication and speaking style is something that firms can coach expatriates on (or any employees dealing extensively with the firm's foreign employees), and it is enormously important to do so. Consider communication problems that have nothing to do with language fluency but concern the use of terms, topics, and expressions. For example, many Americans regularly refer to local events that are familiar and of interest to Americans but are unfamiliar and uninteresting to the rest of the world. Many people in the world have little interest in American politics and do not find repeated references to U.S. politicians, issues, and elections particularly meaningful or interesting. And regardless of what country you may be from, the excessive use of slang and local-interest items in speaking to foreigners can be a problem—a problem that you should try to prevent if you would like to work internationally.

To address this, start with a simple exercise: try listening carefully to the conversations of your friends. Do they use a lot of slang terms? Do they give explanations in terms of local references and stories that would be unfamiliar to foreigners? For example, an American referring to "late in the fourth quarter" (an expression from North American football or basketball meaning near the end of the game) would elicit blank stares from many people from outside of North America. We once heard a Canadian speaker in Hong Kong talk about not arguing with "the ump." He was talking about the umpire in baseball (equivalent to the referee in basketball), but hardly anyone in the room understood what "ump" meant and the point was lost. Try to be aware of those sorts of expressions and remove them from your daily speech when talking to foreigners, unless you have time to explain them as you go along (which means you need to be aware of them in the first place). Removing such expressions from your speech takes a lot of time and effort, and it is helpful to practice doing so before interviewing for an international assignment because firms will be watching for this, especially if your job requires much speaking, presenting, or training in the foreign country. Of course, using home-country references is less of a concern if you speak the local language well, but it is important to remember that many expatriate assignments entail meeting people from many different foreign countries. If you are in a meeting and talking to people from Japan, China, Pakistan, and Malaysia, you will be speaking English, and all the above rules about slang and avoiding overly local (to you) content and references apply.[lxviii] And remember to be patient. If a person from another country does not seem to understand what you are saying the first time, *do not just say the same thing again more loudly.* Explain it or ask your question in a different way. Do not give up too easily; getting your points across clearly and appropriately to foreigners is a key part of the skill set you develop as an expatriate. Figure 12-4 gives some examples of basic communications problems to avoid.

A formal training exercise entails having the expatriate being trained speak to a trainer (or a colleague) who identifies all the slang and potentially unclear expressions being used. It is surprising once you hear yourself speak how much slang and otherwise unclear or ambiguous phrases emerge from your speech. In preparing for an international assignment, practice using more common words

---

FIGURE 12-4   Common Communication Problems to Avoid

1. Use more common words and phrases (i.e., say "Go by bus," not "Take the bus" or "Develop in a different market" not "Incubate in a remote market").
2. If people do not understand the first time, do not just say the same thing again, more loudly. *Explain it a different way.*
3. Use props and common frames of reference when possible (stories the listeners will be aware of), use time words—tenses present a problem in many languages.
4. Try to avoid slang. Do you know what "Do not throw my airplane" means? Probably not, unless you are from Hong Kong. It means "Do not stand me up," but if you are not from North America, you probably do not recognize that expression either, hence the problem with using slang. Both expressions mean the same thing: "Do not miss our meeting (or date) and leave me waiting somewhere." If you use those expressions around people unfamiliar with them, your idea will be missed completely.
5. Avoid sports-related terms and other local references that only people from your country or region would understand.
6. Learn local conversational rituals such as what people say when they greet each other. North Americans commonly say, "How are you?" Chinese will ask, "Have you eaten yet?" These are both simply ways of saying hello.

and phrases. For example, it is probably better to say "go by plane" and not "take the plane" (which sounds to some non-English speakers like you want to carry the plane somewhere), or "develop in a different market" as opposed to "incubate in a remote market." Slang like "to the tune of" or "Does this ring a bell?" or "It's not over till the fat lady sings" are also difficult to understand for foreigners not familiar with English slang. (Think about those expressions and what they mean literally.)

In training for an expatriate assignment or simply in dealing with people who are not fluent speakers of English, it is important to practice critical listening skills: pay attention to the actual words you and others are using and make sure they are appropriate and easily understandable. Expats should be sure to learn local conversational rituals such as what people say when they greet each other. North Americans commonly ask, "How are you?" This is simply a way of saying hello; they are not asking for a medical report. Chinese will ask, "Have you eaten yet?" Sometimes westerners misunderstand that this is a simple greeting, taking it to mean that the Chinese person is asking them to go to lunch or dinner. But like "How are you," it is simply a greeting. Many people from the Philippines will ask, "Where are you going?" To many people this question seems intrusive. But once again, it is just a way of saying hello, and is not to be taken literally. Expats should pay attention to other common conversation rituals such as how to ask for favors, or how to thank people for help, because these rituals help smooth conversations and allow work to get done.[lxix] Though it takes persistence and time to become accustomed to using plain words and terminology, most people can modify their speech simply by paying attention to what they are saying and avoiding certain words or phrases that are likely to be understood. Be patient and make note of the words and expressions that people do not typically understand in the country you are working in, and remove them from your speech.

Technical Sophistication

Expatriates often encounter differences in technical sophistication in the foreign country, a problem that conflicts with their expectations. A key problem for expatriates occurs when they attempt to apply successful home-country managerial and organizational principles in the foreign country. The expatriate may experience considerable frustration because differences in the local culture may make implementation of a new technology or technique more difficult. For example, some countries' firms have shown much reluctance to spend money on indigenizing technology, which occurs after a machine is purchased, when the firm spends additional money on training, maintenance, complementary technologies to make the original one work better, and any modifications to the technology.[lxx] This can prove a source of frustration to an expatriate who may be accustomed to high technology, but it is to be expected when working in developing economies.

Parent Objectives and Policies

Expatriate managers also encounter difficulties because they are responsible for implementing objectives and policies formulated by the home office. Problems can occur when these objectives and policies conflict with the managerial situation experienced by the expatriate manager and with the mandates imposed on him or her by the central government or local officials.[lxxi] That is, the expatriate manager must conduct the foreign operations within constraints imposed by the home office, local laws, and government officials. In many countries there is a great deal of corruption, and officials expect payments to expedite transactions. Much like the Chinese anti-corruption official mentioned in the opening case example, they may expect payments to do their jobs or to speed them up. Most countries, including the United States, now allow for companies to make facilitation payments to speed up a process for which a government official is already legitimately responsible. As noted in Chapter 2 on ethics and corruption, it is important for expatriates to learn what their firm policy and home country laws allow them to do in this regard.[lxxii]

A key problem can occur when a firm centralizes decision making and gives little decision power to the foreign subsidiary. If the expatriate manager's authority is visibly constrained, his or her opportunity to establish and maintain an effective relationship with locals may be reduced. This is especially true in foreign locales where there is high power distance such as in India. If the expatriate manager lacks authority and does not take charge, his or her standing with the host country employees can be harmed.

Family

Another challenge for expatriates is keeping the family happy.[lxxiii] The inability of the expatriate's family to adapt to living and working in the foreign country is a major cause of expatriate failure. Spouses, for example, may not be able to work and can feel isolated, particularly when language and customs are very different. This creates stress for the expatriate's family members, who then create problems for the expatriate, which in turn can result in on-the-job failure. The spouse is the one who has to stay at home and deal with managing the home and dealing with delivery people and repairmen, who in most foreign countries are unlikely to speak much English.

Professor Tung found that the majority of the respondents in a survey of personnel administrators indicated that they recognized the importance of family to successful performance in a foreign assignment, yet few U.S. MNCs actually took it into consideration in the selection decision, and that this problem has persisted over the years.[lxxiv] The U.S. multinationals that interviewed both candidates and spouses to determine suitability for foreign assignments experienced significantly lower incidents of expensive expatriate failure than those that did not. Companies need to be sensitive to these problems and provide some support to help expatriates with the transition. A spouse who does not like the country and demands to leave is a very common reason for the failure of expatriate assignments.

Other Sociocultural Issues in Human Resources Management

Several other sociocultural issues may be present that managers and expatriates must be aware of. These include the societies' power distance, the position of women, and general climate. As we saw in the Chapter 2 discussion on culture, power distance can create a problem for Western expatriates working in high power-distance countries such as East Asia, India, and the Middle East. People are usually addressed more formally in these countries, and titles are important, as is one's position in the organizational hierarchy. To communicate with a colleague high in an organization in a high power-distance society, an expatriate may have to speak through an intermediary, such as that colleague's assistant or secretary, something that might make North Americans or Australians uncomfortable. Another problem is cultural resistance to expatriate female managers. Such cultural bias may show up, particularly in countries with high masculinity scores on Hofstede's cultural values dimension, including Korea, Japan, Latin America, and much of the Middle East. Some locals may worry that a female expatriate will have less influence over decisions at headquarters.[lxxv] It is important that the female expatriate has authority to make decisions, and the firm should make this clear to local employees and other organizational partners. But there is recent evidence to

---

PANDESIC: HIRING TOP MANAGERS WITH THE RIGHT EXPERIENCE

Pandesic, the high-profile joint venture between Intel and SAP, was launched in 1997 to create a low-end disruption selling enterprise resource planning (ERP) software to small businesses that could not afford the full-blown ERP system. Intel and SAP hand-picked some of their most successful, tried-and-true executives to lead the venture.

Pandesic grew to one hundred employees in eight months, and quickly established offices in Europe and Asia. Within a year it had announced forty strategic partnerships with companies such as Compaq, Hewlett-Packard, and Citibank. Pandesic executives boldly announced its first product in advance of launch to warn would-be competitors to stay away from the small business market space. The company signed distribution and implementation agreements with the same IT consulting firms that had served as such capable channel partners for SAP's large-company systems. The product, initially intended to be simple ERP software delivered to small businesses via the Internet, evolved into a completely automated end-to-end solution. Pandesic was a dramatic failure. It sold very few systems and closed its doors in February 2001 after having burned through more than $100 million.

The executives who ran the firm were all experienced senior managers and salespeople. However, they had always run large organizations with a lot of resources and support staff. When it came to running a small entrepreneurial organization, these executives were unprepared. The big organization executives made the product too complicated, staffing was too expensive, and the organization scaled up too fast before gaining enough new clients. It is important to remember that in addition to having international capabilities, international managers still have to be able to operate the businesses they are expected to manage, and previous experience with a similar situation is vital if the executives and their teams are to hit the ground running.[lxxvii]

---

show that even in the masculine countries, foreign women are accepted into authority positions, possibly because the local culture is not threatened because it is not the local women that are leaving their homes to work.[lxxvi] Still, some Middle East countries present a more difficult problem because the rights of women, such as the right to drive, are restricted. Certain other countries in parts of Latin America or Africa may present real safety problems for foreign women executives, and firms must take care to check on local security issues.

Strict Islamic countries may similarly present a problem for expatriates who have trouble acculturating to an environment with little familiar entertainment. Many products and entertainment options from home are less likely to be available. TV programming, sports, and even news magazines such as *The Economist* may be censored and difficult to get. Web sites may be blocked, and even emails and email attachments may be interfered with by local security forces. Alcohol may be difficult to purchase or be very expensive. Such a posting could be particularly uncomfortable for women, as their rights would be limited by local law and customs. Expatriates need to be aware of such issues and prepare for the very different social environment.

Repatriation

Repatriation of the expatriate to his or her home country is often overlooked by the company and the expatriate. Offhand, you might not think of expatriates returning to their home countries as being a problem. But interestingly, this can create a host of problems for the expatriate worker and family. The expatriate may end up returning to the same job at home with no promotion and may thus feel the time on the foreign assignment meant little to his or her career. Sometimes an expatriate will return home only to find that a former colleague got a good promotion, or a former subordinate may now be the expatriate's boss. The returned expatriate is no longer in a central position at work, after having gotten used to giving orders and having quite a bit of help getting things done at work—or even at home. For example, in India, the family may have been able to employ domestic help and the employee provided with a driver. (In China, most international firms will not permit their employees to drive because of security issues on the road.)

Similarly the family may feel out of place back at home, particularly if children spent several formative years in the foreign country. The expatriate's spouse may also miss some of the conveniences that were given to executive expatriates. Another job change may be imminent, because the experience that expatriates acquire in foreign assignments often makes them more marketable outside the home corporation.[lxxvii] As a result, after a lengthy assignment, a home-country national needs up to eighteen months to settle back into a U.S. job.[lxxviii] In part, this is why U.S. firms are typically shortening overseas assignments. Headquarters should have a staff ready to assist any returning expatriate in reestablishing a living situation. The firm should give the returning expat help in reestablishing residence back in the home country. Counseling for the expatriate and his family may be required due to semi-culture-shock.

How do firms prepare expatriates to handle overseas assignments and generally manage their human resources more effectively in foreign locations? They must think strategically about human resources and implement tactics that can reduce expatriate failure and other HR problems in the host country, as in the opening Asimco case example. In particular, because Japanese firms have much experience in managing far-flung subsidiaries and are good at preparing expatriates, they provide some good examples of preparing and managing human resources in the foreign subsidiary.

SUMMARY

This chapter has described the HR function, how it may differ in international firms that have to staff international offices, the questions facing expatriate employees, and when to use expatriates versus host country local employees. International firms have three options for selecting management staff for their foreign operations: send someone from the home country, hire someone in the host country, or hire someone from a third country. The chapter discussed the relative advantages and disadvantages of hiring expatriates and locals, and presented the factors HR managers must consider when deciding whether to use a home-country national, a host-country national, or a third-country national. This chapter also discussed several reasons expatriates fail, including the foreign country's physical and social environments, the expatriate's openness to culture, and communication issues. Other important factors in the expatriate experience were also addressed, such as differences between the home office and the foreign subsidiary, gender and family issues, and the importance of repatriation programs. Also presented were frameworks for selecting and developing effective expatriates, for administrating expatriate programs, and for administering expatriate compensation.

MANAGERIAL GUIDELINES

Managers should remember the following guidelines as they go forward in different environments and seek to move employees to accomplish particular goals and objectives:

1. Strong human resources management leads to greater workforce productivity, improved organizational climate, better employee engagement with the firm and its activities, and other significant benefits. The human resources

department should not be neglected or shunted off to a corner office. Good empirical evidence from both the management and economics fields now strongly shows that excellence in HRM leads to excellent employee and firm performance and superior returns to investors.

2. Given its importance, the human resources function needs to be given support from the firm's top management. Selecting, developing, and rewarding talent is quite important and needs to be seen as part of firm strategy.

3. HR should be explicitly linked with overall strategic planning and should deliver the quality and quantity of leaders the company will need in the future to achieve its goals.

4. Selection is quite important. For firms that need to staff international locations, it is helpful to find employees who have some international experience, preferably experience in living abroad. Multiple interviews and tests for cultural intelligence are helpful in determining a prospective employee's international capabilities. Similar interviews and tests need to be given to foreign employees working for the firm's overseas office.

5. Training is also important for employees going overseas. At a minimum, it is necessary to give briefings on culture and language. Even simple things like when to shake hands, what to say upon on introduction, and what basic language rituals are used each day should be learned.

6. Training is also important in hiring foreign nationals to work in the overseas office. It sometimes takes several months or longer to inculcate the firm's culture, ethics, and values in a foreign national. This is especially important in emerging and transition economies that have much different cultural and commercial traditions, and very little experience with doing business outside of their own regions.

7. There are many appraisal methods, all of which have benefits and drawbacks. It is important for the firm to understand what behaviors and objectives it would like to encourage. It is helpful to try to appraise and reward the behaviors that it thinks will lead to the desired outputs. Remember that what gets measured and rewarded is more likely to get done.

8. Monetary rewards are valued by most employees, but it is important not to neglect non-monetary rewards such as added control over one's job, added tasks that the employee finds interesting, and clear feedback and praise the employee can use to improve at the job and learn more skills.

9. Even if the expatriate is carefully selected and given training, foreign assignments are challenging. Firms can help by giving the expatriate help in settling in, and giving aid to the expat's family with the move and getting settled. Expatriate failure is costly, and a main reason for this is the family's dissatisfaction.

10. Human resources can be used to help the firm achieve its objectives. Top management needs to understand the type of workforce it seeks to build; this is particularly important when going to a new country where the slate is clean and the firm can inculcate its values among new hires.

11. Remember the importance of experience when selecting managers, particularly for a foreign assignment. What type of organization did the candidate work in before? What type of international experience does he or she have, including experiences during school? The work of Professor Morgan McCall on "high fliers" and developing global executives (see Additional Resources section below) provides an excellent guide to the selection and development process for top managers and expatriates.

DOING BUSINESS IN COSTA RICA

Costa Rica is known as the Switzerland of Latin America. It has had a long period of democracy with an active democratic process. The population is principally of European extraction, in contrast to many Latin American countries, such as Guatemala, with populations that have very high percentages of indigenous natives.

Costa Rica differs in many ways from other Latin American countries. For example, Costa Ricans are considered by many to be the most punctual of all Latin Americans. Therefore, it is vital that individuals be on time for appointments. Costa Rica is also different from most Latin American countries in that the power distance is low.[lxxix] Thus, there is less hierarchical organization in business with employees having a far greater desire to have an input into the running of an organization. There is also a greater emphasis on collectivism than is seen in many Latin American countries,[lxxx] so the group and group cohesion is very important.

Costa Rica does, however, have some similarities with its Latin American neighbors. For example, the role of the family is greater in all Latin American countries than in North America.[lxxxi] There is a strong focus on children and spending time with the family, unlike North Americans who tend to focus more on workplace issues. Costa Rica is also strongly Catholic, like most Latin American countries.

In doing business in Costa Rica it should be recognized that most Hispanic people have two surnames: one from their father, which is listed first, followed by one from their mother. Only the father's surname is used when addressing someone. (This can vary around Latin America, so be sure to ask how people are addressed when traveling to those countries.) Using titles is very important, therefore, when conducting business in Costa Rica. Your title should be shown on your business card and you should acknowledge other people's titles when addressing them. Lunch is typically the largest meal of the day and it's not uncommon for it to last a full afternoon, particularly if business is involved.

CULTURE

ADDITIONAL RESOURCES

Axtell, R. E. (Ed.). (1993) *Do's and Taboos Around the World* (3rd ed.). New York: John Wiley & Sons.

Hess, M. B., & Linderman, P. (2002). *Expert Expatriate: Your Guide to Successful Relocation Abroad—Moving, Living, Thriving*. London: Nicholas Brealey Publishing.

Kaplan, R. S., & Norton, D. P. (1996). *The Balanced Scorecard: Translating Strategy into Action*. Boston, MA: Harvard Business School Press.

Lewis, R. D. (2005). *When Cultures Collide: Leading Across Cultures*. London: Nicholas Brealey Publishing.

McCall, M. W. (1997). *High Flyers: Developing the Next Generation of Leaders*. Boston, MA: Harvard Business School Press.

McCall, M. W., & Hollenbeck, G. P. (2002). *Developing Global Executives*. Boston: Harvard Business School Press.

Morrison, T., & Conaway, W. A. (2007). *Kiss, Bow, or Shake Hands* (2nd ed.). Avon, MA: Adams Media.

Peterson, B. (2004). *Cultural Intelligence: A Guide to Working with People from Other Cultures*. Yarmouth, ME: Intercultural Press.

Smith, S., & Maz, R. (2004). *The HR Answer Book: An Indispensable Guide for Managers and Human Resources Professionals*. New York: AMACOM Books.

EXERCISES

Opening Vignette Discussion Questions

1. Could Asimco have done any preparation in terms of human resources to avoid the problems they faced?
2. Do you think this problem is unique to China?

DISCUSSION QUESTIONS

1. How does the international HRM function differ from the domestic HRM function?
2. What selection criteria are most important in choosing people for an overseas assignment? Identify and describe the four that you judge to be of most universal importance, and defend your choices.
3. Building on your answer to Question 2, discuss the theoretical dimensions that may affect anticipatory and in-country adjustment of expatriates. How can these be turned into selection criteria?
4. Why are individuals motivated to accept international assignments? Which of these motivations would you rank as positive reasons? Which would you regard as negative reasons?
5. Discuss the host-country characteristics that might influence the staffing method.

IN-CLASS EXERCISES

1. You are the manager of the international HRM function for a firm whose top management is assigning an executive from the home office to head one of the firm's foreign subsidiaries. Relative to the cultural adaptation phases, what would you advise the top management?
2. Regarding Exercise 1, what questions would you ask the top management in order to be sure that the right expatriate has been selected?
3. What are the international HR implications that can be drawn from the Japanese, European, and U.S. international-expatriate practices? What could U.S. firms do better to prepare someone for an expatriate assignment to mainland China?
4. How could information technologies assist in managing global human resources?
5. Complete the Cultural Intelligence questionnaire below to identify your own cultural intelligence or CQ. The statements reflect different facets of cultural intelligence. For each set, add up your scores and divide by four to produce an average. Our work with large groups of managers shows that for purposes of your own development, it is most useful to think about your scores in comparison to one another. Generally, an average of less than 3 would indicate an area calling for improvement, while an average of greater than 4.5 reflects a true CQ strength.

Cultural Intelligence (CQ)[lxxii]
Rate the extent to which you agree with each statement, using the scale:
1 = Strongly disagree, 2 = Disagree, 3 = Neutral, 4 = Agree, 5 = Strongly agree.

_____ Before I interact with people from a new culture, I ask myself what I hope to achieve.

_____ If I encounter something unexpected while working in a new culture, I use this experience to figure out new ways to approach other cultures in the future.

_____ I plan how I'm going to relate to people from a different culture before I meet them.

_____ When I come into a new cultural situation, I can immediately sense whether something is going well or something is wrong.

TOTAL _____ ÷ 4 = _____ **Cognitive CQ**

_____ It is easy for me to change my body language (for example, eye contact or posture) to suit people from a different culture.

_____ I can alter my expression when a cultural encounter requires it.

_____ I modify my speech style (for example, accent or tone) to suit people from a different culture.

_____ I easily change the way I act when a cross-cultural encounter seems to require it.

TOTAL _____ ÷ 4 = _____ **Physical CQ**

_____ I have confidence that I can deal well with people from a different culture.

_____ I am certain that I can befriend people whose cultural backgrounds are different from mine.

_____ I can adapt to the lifestyle of a different culture with relative ease.

_____ I am confident that I can deal with a cultural situation that's unfamiliar.

TOTAL _____ ÷ 4 = _____ **Emotional / motivational CQ**

TAKE-HOME EXERCISES

1. Expatriates spending extended periods of time in foreign countries are often trained in dinner table etiquette, such as what to eat and drink, and what to talk about during a meal. They are also schooled in proper dress code and in proper protocol for interacting with hosts. The International Business Center Web site (http://www.international-business-center.com) offers information on business etiquette for a variety of countries. Look for information on protocol for an international assignment in South Africa (click on Africa at the left of the webpage). Write down a list of things you should keep in mind as you go abroad to South Africa that may be different from what you are used to.

2. Imagine you are going to work in the Philippines as an HR manager for a North American firm with offices there. After being there for a short time another expatriate from Canada comes to speak to you. Laura tells you that the locals have been quite rude to her. You ask her to describe why she feels this way. She tells you about several minor incidents. For instance while waiting for an elevator at the end of the day a lady she barely knew asked, "Where are you going?" Laura said she just smiled but felt that question was a bit funny, especially since the day before she had been asked by another colleague, "Have you eaten yet?" Write down something you would tell Laura about her Filipino colleagues' communication rituals for basic, polite greetings. (To answer this question look up Professor Deborah Tannen and colleagues, and their work on communication rituals in different countries).

SHORT CASE QUESTIONS

Cultural Sensitivity: How Much Is Too Much? (p. 375)

1. Why do you think Feng Shui works for casinos but did not work well for the Coca-Cola company at its headquarters in Atlanta?
2. Do you think Coke could have done something to make the application of Feng Shui work?
3. Where else would Feng Shui work well for a firm?

Glossary

Acquisition. The outright purchase of a firm or some part of that firm.

Administrative Component. The ratio of support staff (e.g., secretaries and supervisors) to line staff directly engaged in the production and distribution of an organization's products and services.

Agency theory. The recognition that those who own firms and manage them are now separated. Thus, the agents may act in their own best interest rather than that of the firm.

Alderfer's ERG needs hierarchy. A hierarchy-of-needs model comprised of three main needs—existence, relatedness, and growth (ERG).

Anchoring. When a manager relies on one piece of information as the key to his or her decision making.

Attribution error. Occurs when people try to determine cause and effect in their lives and make assumptions about what actions led to this situation.

Authority principle. An influence principle that states people are often influenced by recommendations or requests of an authority or expert.

Availability. The availability heuristic leads to a bias whereby people base their decisions heavily on an example can be easily be brought to mind.

Backward integration. A form of vertical integration that involves the purchase of suppliers of a firm's product.

Balanced reciprocity. Securing a promise of a near-immediate return for a favor done or a gift given; thought to be particularly important in China and in ethnic Chinese communities around the world.

Balanced Scorecard. A system that summarizes an organization's strategic objectives into four main performance metrics: financial, internal processes, customers, and learning and growth. These perspectives provide feedback on the execution of the strategic plan.

Base salary. Amount of money that an expatriate normally receives in the home country.

BATNA. Best alternative to a negotiated agreement.

Behavioral theories. Leadership theories that argue that specific, learned behaviors can differentiate leaders from non-leaders (or successful leaders from unsuccessful leaders), and are behaviors that can be learned.

Big Unit capitalism. A Big Unit economy will be dominated by Big Business, Big Government, and Big Labor. The Big Unit economy generally produced efficient but rigid, pyramidal organizations and government departments that were full of soft niches that relaxed standards and did not demand (and reward) excellence and accountability in work and educational quality.

Born globals. Entrepreneurial firms that are started as international firms.

Bottom billion. The world's poorest billion people who have largely missed the economic progress that has come from globalization over the last 25 years.

Bounded rationality. According to Herbert Simon, people do not have the ability to process all of the information and solutions that face them. This inability leads them to limit their problems and solutions.

Brainstorming. A forecasting method in which a broad topic is set out and a discussion among the participants is utilized to gain insights into what the future may look like.

Bretton Woods system. The Bretton Woods system was a negotiated monetary order after World War II to govern monetary relations and currency exchange rates among independent states.

Business strategy. How the firm will compete in a specific product-market.

Business-level strategy. How a specific business will operate in order to succeed in that specific marketplace.

CAFTA. Central America Free Trade Agreement, a free trade agreement (not a treaty) among the U.S. and several Central American countries and the Dominican Republic. CAFTA is also seen as a stepping stone toward the Free Trade Area of the Americas (FTAA), another, more ambitious free trade agreement, which encompass South American and Caribbean countries. Canada is negotiating a similar trade agreement.

Capabilities. Functional skills that a firm develops and which are the foundation on which a firm builds its strategy.

Charisma. Ability to inspire or influence other individuals.

Civil law. Originated in Ancient Rome and is used on the European continent and to a lesser extent, in China today. This approach to the law uses statutes and comprehensive codes as the primary building blocks, relying heavily on legal scholars to formulate and interpret the laws.

Cognitive dissonance. The negative feeling caused by holding two contradictory ideas simultaneously.

Cognitive diversity. The ability of members of the group to think differently, and to express their opinions and findings.

Cognitive response model of persuasion. A model of persuasion that views the most direct cause of persuasion as the self-talk of the target audience, not the persuasion method itself or its deliverer.

Commercial paper. Bonds that corporations issue directly to the public in order to raise capital.

Common law. Legal systems primarily built on legal precedent established by judges as they resolve individual cases; those case opinions have the force of law and strongly influence future decisions. Common law originated in medieval England and is used in the United Kingdom, the British Commonwealth, and in Britain's former colonies, such as the United States, Singapore, Hong Kong, and India.

Communism. A political system that relies on a dictatorship to govern.

Competitive advantage. Something that a firm does better than any of its nearest competitors, which allows the firm to have an advantage with customers over those competitors.

Competitive scope. The breadth of products a firm will offer, such as the range of customers and/or distributors sold to, and the geographic region the firm will cover.

Compliance. The act of changing one's behavior in response to a direct request.

Conformity. Changing one's behavior to match the responses or actions of others, to fit in with those in proximity.

Confucius. Chinese philosopher who lived from 551 to 479 BCE. He was from eastern China and was a well-known and well-traveled teacher and philosopher.

Consistency. A principle of influence that indicates how people are influenced by showing how their previous statements or stated values fit with a recommendation or request.

Consortia. Where several organizations join together to share expertise and funding for developing, gathering, and distributing new knowledge.

Contingency theory. Theory in which the type of leadership needed is based on the situation being faced.

Control. Actions taken to move a firm to better meet its goals after the evaluation of the firm's gap between goals and achievements.

Copyright. The exclusive right to control reproduction or adaptation of creative works, such as books, movies, music, paintings, photographs, and software. Typically, the copyright holder has the exclusive right to control the product for between 10 and 30 years, depending on jurisdiction.

Core competence. A capability that is most critical to the firm's success.

Corporate entrepreneurship. Mature firms that act more like small startup firms by taking greater risks and reducing bureaucracy.

Corporation strategy. Establishes how diversified the firm is to become and in what domains that diversification will occur.

Cultural intelligence test (CQ). Selection test that evaluates a person's ability in a cross-cultural setting.

Cultural sensitivity. Heightened awareness for the values and frames-of-reference of the host culture.

Cultural-toughness. Selection test that assesses whether a candidate appears able to work in a specific country.

Culture. Acquired knowledge people use to interpret experience and actions. This knowledge then influences values, attitudes, and behaviors.

Delphi method. Experts rank different potential future outcomes and through an iterative process these predictions are refined until a prediction of what the future may hold is reached.

Denominator management. A firm tries to increase its return on investment, or ROI, by simply reducing the denominator, that is, reducing the "I" or amount of invested capital in a new project or division of the firm.

Devil's advocate. Someone who argues against the decision being contemplated, allowing the rationale for the decision to be checked.

Differentiation strategy. Seeks to provide some aspect of a product or service that differs from that of competitors, such as higher quality, to increase the likelihood of customers paying a premium for the product.

Disruptive innovation. A new technological innovation, product, service or business model that overturns the existing dominant innovation or technological standard in the marketplace.

Disruptive technology. Also known as a disruptive innovation, it is a new technology that unexpectedly displaces an established technology, often from the lower end of the market, such as the personal computer's defeat of more powerful minicomputers.

Distributive justice. Asserts that inequality is acceptable if employees have fair access to resources and opportunities such that they recognize any inequality to be the result of their own effort and not because of favoritism by management.

Downstream innovation. The ability to use research and basic product components and to package them together to create a new, salable (sometimes branded) product or service. It is also the indigenization of other technologies into a firm's production and development systems to facilitate creation and delivery of a product.

Economic rent. Profits above what should be the norm of the industry, given its level of risk.

Economies of scale. Average unit costs decline as production quantity increases over a limited period of time.

Economies of scope. Cost savings that result from performing two activities jointly, such as manufacturing one type of car in a plant during the day, and at night, producing a different car that was previously produced somewhere else.

Emergent strategy. Managers see opportunities and shift the organization to that new direction.

Entrepreneurship. Value-creation activities to create new enterprises or build a new business or product line within an existing organization.

Escalation of commitment. The tendency to repeat an apparently bad decision or allocate more resources to a failing course of action. (In poker, this is called "throwing good money after bad.")

Ethnocentrism. The ethnocentric view of culture holds that an individual or a firm will believe that their own way of doing things is the best, and will not seek to adapt to local cultural practices.

European Union (EU). Twenty-seven European countries bound by specific treaty and standard legal and commercial agreements in a large number of areas.

Evaluation. The process of determining a firm's progress toward reaching goals and objectives.

360-degree evaluations. Evaluations of an employee conducted by the supervisor, subordinates, peers, and sometimes customers.

Evidence-based information search. A process of information search and decision-making that does not start with a presumed decision and seeks to evaluate a range of evidence and challenge the emerging solution as it is gradually shaped.

Exit barriers. Barriers that keep firms in an industry and thus can exert downward pressure on industry profits.

Expatriate. A person from one country who is working and residing in another country.

Export. The shipping of a good from the home market to markets outside the home country.

Expropriation. When a government seizes the ownership of a private asset or assets.

Extrinsic motivation. Refers to motivation based on external motivating factors, such as payments, rewards, working conditions, praise or punishment.

Face. Respect of a person's peers; avoiding embarrassment.

Financial controls. Focus on gaps between the desired financial outcomes and the actual outcomes.

Financial panic. Financial panics include a variety of situations in which some banks and financial assets suddenly lose a large part of their value and bad debts multiply quickly.

First mover. The first firm into an area, whether a product or national market. Sometimes multiple firms can enter a product market within the same year and are usually considered multiple first movers.

Foreign Direct Investment (FDI). Investment by foreigners in a nation typically in plant and equipment.

Forward integration. A form of vertical integration whereby a firm's activities are expanded to include the direct distribution of its products and services.

Franchising. A type of alliance where a contract is established between the parent (franchisor) and the individual who actually buys the business unit (franchisee) to sell a given product or conduct business under its trademark.

Functional strategies. Those strategies that direct what occurs in individual functional areas, such as marketing, finance, and accounting.

Gap analysis. Analysis of the gap between what a firm wants to occur and what actually has occurred and is likely to occur.

Giri. Japanese word, which loosely translated means the right way to behave, though in practical terms it refers directly to Japan's complex system of gift-giving and exchange relations in society.

Global strategy. When a firm chooses to compete in the same manner in all countries.

Globalization. Globalization is a modern term used to describe the changes in societies and the world economy that result from dramatically increased international trade, foreign direct investment, and cultural exchange.

Greenfield venture. A firm may choose to establish itself in a given country without the aid of a partner.

Group interviews. Selection tool in which typically there are multiple candidates and multiple interviewers present at the same time.

Groupthink. A mode of thought whereby individuals intentionally conform to what they perceive to be the consensus of the group and preference of the leader.

Hadiths. Several volumes compiled well after the Koran. A major source of Islamic law and moral teachings. Early Muslims used oral traditions regarding the early history and prehistory of Islam and the practice of Muhammad and his first followers, and wrote them down so that they might be preserved.

Harmonization. Efforts between nations to have the same code of standards for products and how they are treated in regards to tariffs.

Horizontal merger and acquisition. Occurs when the acquired and acquiring firms are in the same industry.

Hygiene factors. According to Herzberg's theory, these are factors such as working conditions, salary, and job security that influence a job.

Impasse. When a manager and his or her negotiating partner cannot reach an agreement.

Implicit leadership. Recognizes the process by which persons are perceived as leaders and follows the same basic social-cognitive processes that occur in other contexts of perceptions of persons.

Import substitution. A trade and economic term based on the premise that developing countries should attempt to locally build products that they currently import. Import substitution concomitantly requires high protective tariffs and monetary policy to create an overvalued domestic currency.

Indirect import. Goods may have most of the value added in one country but due to trade barriers the product is shipped to another country where final production on the good occurs, with the good then being listed as an export from that country.

Industrial organization (IO) economics. A branch of economics that focuses on market efficiency and inefficiency.

Influence. Seeking to change people's behaviors.

Intangible assets. Non-monetary, non-physical assets that cannot be physically measured. Intangible assets include copyrights, patents, trademarks, know-how, and collaboration activities.

Internal locus of control. Whether people feel that they can control things themselves or whether forces outside them control their future.

Intrinsic motivation. Motivation based on internal motivating factors. Such intrinsic rewards are internal to the person, such as the satisfaction of meeting a goal or learning a new skill.

Iron Rice Bowl. In China, the concept of the state meeting all worker's needs: not only food, but schools for kids, hospitals, and even vacation locations for workers. These benefits were typically organized around the large state enterprises they served.

Keiretsu. Vertically and horizontally integrated business groups that dominate the Japanese economy.

Key success factors. Things that are important to customers and help determine a business' success in a given industry.

Late entrants. Firms that enter a market after others are clearly there.

Leaders. Individuals who significantly affect the thoughts and behaviors of others, often through persuasion.

Learned needs theory. Proposed by Harvard psychologist David McClelland, this theory suggested there were three basic learned needs: power, affiliation, and achievement.

Licensing agreement. In such an agreement, a firm agrees to pay a firm for the right to either manufacture or sell a product. The firm selling the right to this product typically loses the right to control various aspects of the product when manufactured or sold by the licensee.

Licensing arrangement. One firm agrees to pay another firm for the right to either manufacture or sell a product.

Liking. A principle of influence that holds that people are more likely to be influenced by those who they like or with whom they have similarities.

Low-cost strategy. Where a business seeks to sell a product at or near the lowest possible price in the firm's chosen market segment.

Market for corporate control. The ability to take over a poorly performing firm and turn it around to profitability.

Market power. Occurs when a firm has enough market-share to shape that market's actions. It can be a strategic motivation for a merger or acquisition.

Market-based economic system. Relies on individuals in the society to determine the price of any good.

Maslow's hierarchy of needs. Maslow's theory contends that as people meet basic needs, they seek to satisfy successively higher needs that occupy a set hierarchy.

Mechanistic structures. Structures that are highly inflexible and static, typically in low-technology domains.

Merger. Occurs when two firms combine as relative equals.

Mission. A simple statement of the basic purpose or reason for the business to exist and its activities.

Motivation. The driving force behind an individual's actions that energizes and directs goal-oriented behavior.

Motivators. In Herzberg's motivation-hygiene theory, these are positive influencers, such as job involvement, that are intrinsic to a job and that can push employees to higher levels of performance.

Multi-domestic strategy. A parent company allows each market to adapt to local conditions and pursue the strategy they choose best in that local market.

Multinational enterprise. Large firm that operates in a large number of countries.

NAFTA. The North American Free Trade Agreement, known usually as NAFTA, links Canada, the United States, and Mexico in a free trade sphere. NAFTA went into effect on January 1, 1994.

National champions. A firm that is the only firm producing a certain good in its country, and is protected by high tariffs and favorable monetary policy. Although usually a product of import-substitution policies to reduce imports, most countries intend their national champion firms to become competitive exporters, though few are. (Airbus is one notable exception.)

Nationalize. When a government decides a good or factory will be owned by the national government.

Needs. Represent things or conditions that people would like to have.

Negotiating. A process in which at least two partners with different needs and viewpoints try to reach agreement on matters of mutual interest.

Non-tariff trade barriers. A barrier to free trade that takes a form other than a tariff, for instance quotas or inspection requirements for imported products such as VCRs, automobiles and dairy products.

Normative model of decision making. Decision making using a rational model (i.e., how things ought to be).

Obedience. A special type of compliance that involves changing one's behavior in response to a directive from an authority figure.

OEM. Original equipment manufacturers.

Organic structure. A flexible structure, often decentralized.

Organizational structure. The official manner in which the various parts of a business are to report and coordinate with each other, and at what levels decisions are made.

Outsourcing. Outsourcing (or contracting out) is often defined as the delegation of non-core operations or jobs from internal production to an external entity (such as a subcontractor) that specializes in that operation.

Parkinson's Law. Parkinson's Law states that work expands to fill the time available for its completion. Several corollaries are possible, such as an organization's administrative component grows with time.

Parochialism. Belief that there is no other way of doing things except what is done in one's own culture.

Patent. Granted to a new, useful, and non-obvious invention. It gives the patent holder a right to prevent others from copying the invention without a license for 20 years from the filing date of a patent application.

Persuasion. Seeking to change people's beliefs or attitudes.

Piecework. A type of work in which a worker is paid a fixed "piece rate" for each unit produced or action performed.

Polycentric. The polycentric view of culture holds that multinational enterprises (MNE) should treat each international subsidiary largely as a separate national entity. This means that the subsidiary should do things in a local manner; and MNE subsidiaries may come to differ from each other.

Positions. Bids, offers, and stated objectives for settlement terms.

Positive model of decision making. Actual, day-to-day decision-making model, not idealized.

Price. The exchange ratio for goods and services between what the seller is willing to sell the good for and what the buyer is willing to pay.

Privatize. When government-owned businesses are sold to private individuals or groups.

Problem. Arises when there is a discrepancy between the present situation and the optimal outcome.

Product platform. A package of products that complement each other.

Programmed decision. A decision that follows standard operating procedures. There is no need to explore alternative solutions because the optimal solution has already been identified and documented.

Projection. An unconscious assumption that others share the same or similar beliefs, values, attitudes, or positions on any given subject.

Prospect Theory. Examines risk assessment, loss aversion, and dependence on a reference or starting point. Explains why individuals consistently behave in ways different from what traditional economic and decision theory would predict.

Protocol. Rules for how individuals in a business setting are to interact with each other.

Quality circles. A group of workers who meet on a regular basis to discuss ways of improving the quality of work.

Reactance. When people are told that they cannot have or do something, they tend to want it more.

Reciprocation. A principle of influence that states people are more likely to say yes to a request when the requester has done something for that person in the past.

Red hats. Businesses that the government owns, but which they allow professional managers run.

Reengineering. A radical redesign of an organization's processes so that they can be executed in parallel, and the tasks undertaken by nonspecialists. The job's cycle time to completion is reduced in an effective reengineering.

Renewable energy certificate (REC). Certificate for each 1,000 kilowatts of renewable energy that can be bought or sold. Governments create such certificates for tax purposes and to encourage alternative energy. The production of energy from renewable sources not only generates the energy itself which ultimately consumers use, but for each 1,000 kilowatts of energy generated there is also one REC that can be sold or bought.

Repatriation of profits. The ability of a firm to take the profits it makes in a country out of that country.

Representativeness. The representativeness heuristic is when seeming patterns of data are assumed (incorrectly) to represent something that the data do not warrant.

Reservation Price. A reservation price is the absolute bottom price that is acceptable.

Resources. Tangible and intangible assets that firms possess.

Return on investment (ROI). Return measured by dividing profit by assets or invested capital.

Satisficing. Alternatives that are acceptable or "good enough," rather than the best possible solutions.

Scarcity. A principle of influence that argues that people are more likely to buy a product or want to do something that they perceive as scarce, unique, or dwindling in availability.

Scenario planning. Forecasting method where participants are given potential scenarios and then asked to build likely responses and outcomes for the business.

Second movers. Those that follow the first movers into a market.

Sensitivity analysis. Asks planners to make changes in usually one variable only, to see the likely effect.

Shari'a law. The law system inspired by the Koran, the Sunna, the Hadiths, older Arabic law systems, parallel traditions, and the work of Muslim scholars over the two first centuries of Islam.

Shrinkage. Loss of goods due to stealing or breakage, often in a retail store.

Social proof. A principle of influence that states people are more likely to want to do something if they believe that many others are doing the same thing or buying the same product.

Socialism. An economic policy that can take several forms, in which in its purest form, the state owns all assets of the society. The belief is that if the assets are held by all then all individuals will benefit.

Spin off. To make a separate company of a prior division, for example when Pepsico spun off its restaurant division to form YUM!

Strategic alliance. A partnership of two or more corporations or business units to achieve strategically significant objectives that are mutually beneficial.

Strategic business unit (SBU). A business division within a larger firm that is charged with managing a particular category of product or service.

Strategic controls. Focus on the firm's desired strategic outcomes and the actual outcomes.

Strategic tactics. Strategic actions that help to implement a strategy, such as a new promotion program that would implement a focus on differentiation business strategy.

Strategy. A coordinated set of actions that fulfills the firm's objectives, purposes, and goals.

Stuck in the middle. Where a firm has neither a clear low-cost nor a clear differentiation strategy.

Sustainable competitive advantage. The ability to have a competitive advantage over a period of time.

Tangible assets. Those things that can be touched by an entrepreneur, such as equipment and money.

Tariffs. Taxes on imported (not exported) goods.

Tax neutral. Firms will try to ensure that an expatriate does not pay more tax by being posted abroad.

Technology indigenization. Integrating technologies into a firm's production and development systems (sometimes modifying them in the process) to facilitate the creation and delivery of a product to customers or service to employees.

Township and village enterprises. Unique types of businesses in China that grew out of worker brigades organized by Chairman Mao, the chairman of the Communist Party at the founding of the People's Republic of China.

Trade deficit. A negative balance of trade when a country is importing more than it exports. Usually defined and reported in material trade terms, excluding services and investment.

Trademark. A distinctive symbol used to distinguish the products or services of different businesses.

Trait theory. Argues that people have underlying traits or characteristics that lead to either superior leader or follower performance.

Transfer pricing. Pricing of goods and services within a multi-divisional organization that are supplied to other division or foreign subsidiaries.

Transformational leadership. A combination of learned skills and the ability to transform an organization in new, substantive ways.

Transnational firm. In this type of firm the business assets are highly specialized, but interdependent with the other assets of the firm. The contribution of each nation is integrated with the worldwide network of businesses to provide to the whole the benefits of that nation. Knowledge developed in any unit is shared worldwide within the business.

Transnational strategy. Strategy that combines aspects of multi-domestic and global strategy.

Turnkey operation. One part of the company is responsible for setting up the plant and equipment while another operates the plant.

Turnkey. When a firm can enter the market immediately with a ready-made application that allows the firm to start doing business immediately

Ultimatum. Requiring someone or a group to do specific thing in a specific way in order for negotiations to continue.

Upstream innovation. Scientific research, basic product research and development, and university-company partnerships on developing new products.

USSR. The Union of Soviet Socialist Republics, the communist federation of states headed by Russia.

Valence. The anticipated satisfaction or dissatisfaction that an individual feels about an outcome.

Value chain analysis. Breaks the firm's activities into primary activities and support activities.

Verdict-based information search. A process of information search and decision-making that starts with the presumed answer to the decision and proceeds to only seek out information that confirms the initial verdict or decision.

Vertical integration. When a firm expands its business into areas that are at different points along its production path for a given product.

Vertical merger or acquisition. One where one firm is a supplier to the other or vice versa.

White goods. Goods, such as washer, dryers, and refrigerators.

Wholly owned subsidiary. An organization form where the parent owns the local firm completely; typically the organization would focus only on the country in which it had entered.

World Trade Organization (WTO). An international organization that oversees a large number of agreements defining the rules of trade between its member states.

Bibliography

Chapter 1

i Gilboy, G. F. (2004). The myth behind China's miracle. *Foreign Affairs*, 83(4), 33–48.

ii The *Far Eastern Economic Review* (Sept. 2, 1999).

iii Drezner, D. W. (2004). The outsourcing bogeyman. *Foreign Affairs*, May/June.

iv Drezner, 2004.

v Drezner, 2004.

vi Smith, A. (1776). *The Wealth of Nations*; Bhagwati, J. (2004). *In Defense of Globalization*. Oxford: Oxford University Press.

vii Perhaps the best explanation of the value of globalization is from Jagdish Bhagwati (2004) *In Defense of Globalization*. A single chapter treatment of globalization can be found in World Bank economist Tim Harford's (2006) book *The Undercover Economist: Exposing Why the Rich Are Rich, the Poor Are Poor—and Why You Can Never Buy a Decent Used Car!* (Chapter 9). New York: Oxford University Press.

viii Wessell, D., & Davis, B. (2007, March 28). Pain from free trade spurs second thoughts. *Wall Street Journal*, Col. CCXLIX(72), pp. A1, A14.

ix Hammer, M. (1994). *Understanding Reengineering*. Cambridge, MA: Hammer Videos.

x Landes, D. (1998). *The Wealth and Poverty of Nations: Why Some Are So Rich and Some So Poor*. New York: W.W. Norton.

xi This analogy is drawn from John Kotter's *The New Rules* (1995). New York: Free Press.

xii Bhagwati, J., & Wolf, M. (2004). *Why Globalization Works*. New Haven, CT: Yale University Press.

xiii Central Intelligence Agency. *The World Factbook*. https://www.cia.gov/library/publications/the-world-factbook/index.html (accessed June 24, 2008).

xiv Europa Key figures. http://europa.eu.int/abc/keyfigures/index_en.htm

xv Information from the Office of United States Trade Representative. http://www.ustr.gov/Document_Library/Fact_Sheets/2004/NAFTA_A_Decade_of_Success.html

xvi http://www.cia.gov/cia/publications/factbook/geos/ch.html

xvii Nair, A., Ahlstrom, D., & Filer, L. (2007). Localized advantage in a global economy: The case of Bangalore. *Thunderbird International Business Review*, 49(5), 591–618.

xviii Nair, Ahlstrom, & Filer, 2007.

xix Peng, M. W. (2001). How entrepreneurs create wealth in transaction economies. *Academy of Management Executive*, 15(1), 95–110.

xx ABB case, http://icmrindia.org/casestudies/catalogue/Business%20Ethics/BECG052.htm

xxi Kidder, R. M. (1996). *How Good People Make Tough Choices: Resolving the Dilemmas of Ethical Living*. New York: Harper Paperbacks.

xxii Kidder, 1996.

xxiii A very interesting account of four different subcultures in the United States can be found in Walter Russell Mead's classic article in *The National Interest*, "The Jacksonian Tradition and American Foreign Policy." Winter (1999/2000), pp. 5–29. For a book-length treatment see Mead, W. R. (2001). *Special Providence*. New York: Knopf.

xxiv Halliday, F. (2005). *The Middle East in International Relations*. Cambridge: Cambridge University Press.

Chapter 2

i Readers from large, diverse countries, such as Russia, India, or even the United States will question the proposition that culture is fairly homogeneous in their countries, though other important factors, such as laws or societal institutions that are influenced by national culture, will be fairly uniform.

ii Barone, M. (2005, Winter). *Hard America, Soft America: Competition vs. Coddling and the Battle for the Nation's Future*. New York: Three Rivers Press; Mead, W. R. (1999/2000). The Jacksonian tradition and American foreign policy. *The National Interest*, 56, 5–29.

iii Halliday, F. (2005). *The Middle East in International Relations: Power, Politics and Ideology*. Cambridge: Cambridge University Press; Hofstede, G., & Hofstede, G. J. (2004). *Cultures and Organizations: Software of the Mind*. New York: McGraw-Hill.

iv Hobsbawm, E., & Ranger, T. (Eds.) (1992). *The Invention of Tradition*. Cambridge: Cambridge University Press.

v Hobsbawm & Ranger, 1992; Hofstede & Hofstede, 2004.

vi Harris, M. (1979). *Cultural Materialism: The Struggle for a Science of Culture*. New York: Random House; Halliday, 2005; Hobsbawm & Ranger, 1992.

vii Levine, R. (2003). *The Power of Persuasion: How We're Bought and Sold*. New York: John Wiley & Sons.

viii Levine, 2003.

ix Hofstede & Hofstede, 2004.

x Beech, H. (2005, August 22). The wasted asset. *Time*. http://www.time.com/time/asia/covers/501050829/story.html.

xi Kiegler, P. J. (2003, December). The China puzzle. *Workforce Management*, pp. 28–33; Mahbubani, K. (2001). *Can Asians Think?* Hanover, NH: Steerforth Press; Nisbett, R. (2003). *The Geography of Thought: How Asians and Westerners Think Differently . . . and Why*. New York: Free Press.

xii Kiegler, 2003.

xiii Nisbett, 2003.

xiv Hall, E. T. (1976). *Beyond Culture*. New York: Anchor Press.

xv Ambler, T., & Witzel, M. (2004). *Doing Business in China* (2nd ed.). London: Routledge Curzon.

xvi Hall, E. T., & Hall, M. R. (1960). The silent language of overseas business. *Harvard Business Review*, May–June; Hall, E. T. (1976). *Beyond Culture*. New York: Anchor Press.

xvii Tannen, D. (1995). The power of talk: Who gets heard and why. *Harvard Business Review*, September–October, 138–148.

xviii Perlmutter, H. V. (1969). The tortuous evolution of the multinational corporation. *Columbia Journal of World Business*, IV, January–February, 9–18.

xix Landes, D. S. (1998). *The Wealth and Poverty of Nations: Why Some Are So Rich and Some So Poor*. New York: W.W. Norton; Sowell, T. (1996). *Migrations and Cultures: A World View*. New York: Basic Books.

xx Kluckhohn, F. R., & Strodtbeck. F. L. (1961). *Variations in Value Orientations*. Evanston, IL: Row & Peterson.

xxi Putnam, R. (2000). *Bowling Alone: The Collapse and Revival of American Community*. New York: Simon & Schuster.

xxii Hofstede & Hofstede, 2004.

xxiii Nisbett, 2003.

xxiv Smith, T. C. (1959). *The Agrarian Origins of Modern Japan*. Stanford, CA: Stanford University Press.

xxv Ahlstrom, D., Nair, A., Young, M. N., & Wang, L. C. (2006). China: Competitive myths and realities. *SAM Advanced Management Journal*. 71(3), 4–10; Gilboy, G. (2004). The myth behind China's miracle. *Foreign Affairs*, 83(4), 33–48.

Chapter 3

i Baumol, W. J. (2004). *The Free-Market Innovation Machine: Analyzing the Growth Miracle of Capitalism*. Princeton, NJ: Princeton University Press; Baumol, W. J., Litan, R. E., & Schramm, C. J. (2007). *Good Capitalism, Bad Capitalism*. New Haven, CT: Yale University Press; Friedman, T. L. (2000). *The Lexus and the Olive Tree: Understanding Globalization* (Revised Edition). New York: Farrar, Straus and Giroux; Landes, D. S. (1998). *The Wealth and Poverty of Nations: Why Some Are So Rich and Some So Poor*. New York: W.W. Norton; Sachs, J. D. (2005). *The End of Poverty: Economic Possibilities for Our Time*. New York: Penguin Press.

ii Lott, J. R. (2007). *Freedomnomics: Why the Free Market Works and Other Half-Baked Theories Don't*. Washington, DC: Regnery Publishing; Wolf, M. (2004). *Why Globalization Works*. New Haven, CT: Yale University Press.

iii Bennhold, K. (2006, April 8). Economics, French-style. *International Herald Tribune*.

iv Peng, M. W. (2000). *Business Strategy in Transition Economies*. Thousand Oaks, CA: Sage Publications.

v Bhagwati, J. (2004). *In Defense of Globalization*. Oxford: Oxford University Press.

vi Friedman, 2000.

vii Sachs, 2005, p. 211.

viii James, H. (2003). *Europe Reborn: A History, 1914–2000*. Harlow, UK: Pearson/Longman.

ix Finn's speed fine is a bit rich. (2004, February 10). *BBC News*. http://news.bbc.co.uk/1/hi/business/3477285.stm.

x Gilboy, G. J. (2004). The myth behind China's miracle. *Foreign Affairs*, July–August, 83(4), 33–48.

xi Volkov, V. (2002). *Violent Entrepreneurs: The Use of Force in the Making of Russian Capitalism*. Ithaca, NY: Cornell University Press; Hoffman, D. E. (2002). *The Oligarchs: Wealth and Power in the New Russia*. New York: Public Affairs Books.

xii Heilbroner, R. L. (1999). *The Worldly Philosophers: The Lives, Times and Ideas of the Great Economic Thinkers* (7th ed.). New York: Touchstone.

xiii Case, K. E., & Fair, R. C. (1999). *Principles of Economics* (5th ed.) (p. 822). New York: Prentice Hall.

xiv Braudel, F. (1972). *The Mediterranean and the Mediterranean World in the Age of Philip II, Vol. 1.* (1st U.S. ed.). New York: Harper & Row; Sowell, T. (1994). *Race and Culture: A World View*. New York: Basic Books.

xv Diamond, J. M. (1998). *Guns, Germs, and Steel: The Fates of Human Societies*. New York: W.W. Norton & Co.

xvi Harris, M. (1979). *Cultural Materialism: The Struggle for a Science of Culture*. New York: Random House.

xvii Landes, 1998.

xviii Baumol, W. J., Litan, R. E., & Schramm, C. J. (2007). *Good Capitalism, Bad Capitalism*. New Haven, CT: Yale University Press; Prahalad, C. K. (2004). *The Fortune at the Bottom of the Pyramid: Eradicating Poverty Through Profits*. Philadelphia: Wharton School Publishing.

xix Gwartney, J. D., & Lawson, R. A. (2004). Economic Freedom of the World, 2004 Annual Report. *Frazer Institute Canada Report Economic Freedom*.

xx Solow, R. M. (1956). A contribution to the theory of economic growth. *Quarterly Journal of Economics*, 70, 65–94.

xxi Sachs, J. D. (2001). Tropical underdevelopment. NBER Working Paper W8119 (Feb.). New York: National Bureau of Economic Research.

xxii Olson, M. (1984). *The Rise and Decline of Nations: Economic Growth, Stagflation, and Social Rigidities*. New Haven, CT: Yale University Press; North, D. C. (2005). *Understanding the Process of Economic Change*. Princeton, NJ: Princeton University Press.

xxiii Boisot, M., & Child, J. (1988). The iron law of fiefs: Bureaucratic failure and the problem of governance in the Chinese economic reforms. *Administrative Science Quarterly*, 33, 507–527.

xxiv Harrison, L. E., & Huntington, S. P. (Eds.). (2001). *Culture Matters*. New York: Basic Books.

xxv North, 2005.

xxvi Schumpeter, J. A. (1950). *Capitalism, Socialism and Democracy*. New York: Harper Perennial.

xxvii Porter, M. E. (1990). *The Competitive Advantage of Nations*. New York: Free Press.

xxviii Heckscher, E. F., & Ohlin, (1991). In B., Flam, H., & Flanders, M. J. (Eds.). *Heckscher-Ohlin Trade Theory*. Cambridge, MA: MIT Press.

xxix Johnson, C. (1984). *MITI and the Japanese Miracle: The Growth of Industrial Policy, 1925–1975*. Stanford, CA: Stanford University Press.

xxx Porter, 1990.

xxxi Taylor, A. (2007, August 13). Asian economies near demographic cliff. *Financial Times*, p. 4.

xxxii Pfeffer, J. (1998). *The Human Equation: Building Profits by Putting People First*. Boston: Harvard Business School Press.

xxxiii Hubbard, G. (2006). The productivity riddle. *Strategy+Business*, 45, 1–6.

xxxiv La Porta, R., Lopez-de-Silanes, F., Shleifer, A., & Vishny, R. W. 1998. Law and finance. *The Journal of Political Economy*, 106(6), 1113–1156; La Porta, R., Lopez-de-Silanes, F., Shleifer, A., & Vishny, R. W. (2000). Investor protection and corporate governance. *Journal of Financial Economics*, 58(1,2), 3–27.

xxxv Lubman, S. (1999). *Bird in a Cage: Legal Reform in China after Mao*. Stanford, CA: Stanford University Press.

xxxvi Ahlstrom, D., Bruton, G.D., & Lui, S.Y. (2000). Navigating China's changing economy: Strategies for private firms. *Business Horizons*, 45(6), 49–59.

xxxvii Ahlstrom, D., Young, M. N., & Nair, A. (2002). Deceptive managerial practices in China: Strategies for foreign firms. *Business Horizons*, 43(1), 5–15.

xxxviii Shaw, M. N. (2003). *International Law* (5th ed.). Cambridge: Cambridge University Press.

xxxix Shah, A. (2007). Poverty around the world. *Global Issues*. http://www.globalissues.org/TradeRelated/PovertyAroundTheWorld.asp.

xl Youngers, C. (1999, March 9). U.S. Policy in Latin American and the Caribbean. *Foreign Policy in Focus*, Vol. 3. http://www.fpif.org/progresp/volume3/v3n07_body.html.

xli Ferguson, N. (2008). *The Ascent of Money: A Financial History of the World*. New York: Penguin Press HC.

xlii Transparency International http://www.transparency.org/cpi/2003/cpi2003.en.html.

Chapter 4

i Collis, D. J., & Montgomery, C. A. (1995). Competing on resources: Strategy in the 1990s. *Harvard Business Review*, 118–128.

ii Prahalad, C. K., & Hamel, G. (1990). The core competence of the corporation. *Harvard Business Review*, 66 (May–June), 79–90.

iii Prahalad & Hamel, 1990.

iv Café de Coral Group is the largest Chinese restaurant group selling Chinese fast food. Café de Coral has 120 restaurants worldwide, compared with 150 McDonalds in Hong Kong.

v Porter, M. (1998). *Competitive Advantage: Creating and Sustaining Superior Performance*. New York: Free Press.

vi Holmstrom, B., & Kaplan, S. N. (2001). Corporate governance and merger activity in the U.S.: Making sense of the 1980s and 1990s U.S. *The Journal of Economic Perspectives*, 15(2) (Spring), 121–44; Peng, M. W. (2005). *Global Strategy* (p. 457). Eagan, MN: Thomson South-Western.

vii Dolbeck, A. (2004, July 12). Good news for the M&A market. *Weekly Corporate Growth Report*. http://www.findarticles.com/p/articles/mi_qa3755/is_200407/ai_n9435310.

viii Ip, G., & King, N. Jr. (2006). Engine of globalization runs into big roadblocks. *Asia Wall Street Journal*.

ix Henry, D., & Jesperson, F. (2002, October 14). Why most big deals don't pay off. *BusinessWeek*, 60–70; Sirower, M. L. (1997). *The Synergy Trap*. New York: Free Press.

x Rappaport, A., & Sirower, M. L. 1999. Stock or cash? *Harvard Business Review*, 77(6), 147–158.

xi Walsh, F. (2005, February 9). Booming Reckitt plays it cool on takeover front. *Knight Ridder Tribune Business News*, p. 1.

xii Ledgard, J. (2005). Skoda leaps to market. *Strategy+Business*, Fall, 58–69.

xiii Wright, P., Kroll, M., & Elenkov, D. (2002). Acquisition returns, increase in firm size, and chief executive officer compensation: The moderating role of monitoring. *Academy of Management Journal*, 45(3), 599–608.

xiv Jensen, M. C., & Meckling, W. H. (1976). Theory of the firm: Managerial behavior, agency costs and ownership structure. *Journal of Financial Economics*, 3, 305–360.

xv Wong, G., McGregor, H., Mak, V., & Ng, P. (2002). Social Capital at Work in PCCW's Acquisition of Cable & Wireless HKT. Centre for Asian Business Cases, School of Business, The University of Hong Kong.

xvi Hitt, M.A., Harrison, J. S., & Ireland, R. D. (2001). *Mergers and Acquisitions: A Guide to Creating Value for Shareholders*. New York: Oxford University Press.

xvii http://www.nutraingredients.com/news/ng.asp?id=35419-vertical-integration-the.

xviii Vodaphone posts strong profits. (2000, November 17). *BBC News*. http://news.bbc.co.uk/1/hi/business/1022674.stm.

xix Finkelstein, S. (2003). *Why Smart Executives Fail: And What You Can Learn from Their Mistakes*. New York: Portfolio.

xx Finkelstein, 2003, p. 298.

xxi Kogut, B. (1988). Joint ventures: Theoretical and empirical perspectives. *Strategic Management Journal*, 9, 319–332.

xxii Hitt et al., 2001.

Chapter 5

i Nalebuff, B., & Brandenburger, A. (1997). Co-opetition: Competitive and cooperative business strategies for the digital economy. *Strategy & Leadership*, 25(6), 28–33.

ii Chandler, A. (1994). *Scale and Scope: The Dynamics of Industrial Capitalism* (reprint ed.). Cambridge, MA: Belknap Press.

iii Porter, M. E. (1980). *Competitive Strategy: Techniques for Analyzing Industries and Competitors*. New York: Free Press.

iv Wright, P., Kroll, M., & Tu, H. (1991). Generic strategies and business performance: An empirical study of the screw machine products industry. *British Journal of Management*, 2, 57–66.

v Christensen, C. M. (1997). Making strategy by doing. *Harvard Business Review*, 75(6), 141–156.

vi Ries, A., & Trout, J. (1994). *The 22 Immutable Laws of Marketing*. New York: HarperBusiness.

vii Hamel, G., & Prahalad, C. K. (1994). *Competing for the Future*. Cambridge, MA: Harvard Business School Press.

viii Evans, P., & Wurster, T. S. (1999). *Blown to Bits: How the New Economics of Information Transforms Strategy*. Cambridge, MA: Harvard Business School Press.

ix Kim, E., Nam, D., & Stimpert, J. L. (2004). The applicability of Porter's generic strategies in the digital age: Assumptions, conjectures, and suggestions. *Journal of Management*, 30, 569–589.

x Farris, P. W., & Moore, M. J. (2004). *The Profit Impact of Marketing Strategy Project: Retrospect and Prospects*. Cambridge: Cambridge University Press; also see Tellis & Golder (1996) for a critique of PIMS. Tellis, G., & Golder, P. (1996). First to market, first to fail? The real causes of enduring market leadership. *Sloan Management Review*, 32(2), 65–75.

xi Roth, K. (1992). Implementing international strategy at the business unit level: The role of managerial decision-making characteristics. *Journal of Management*, 18, 769–789.

xii Procter & Gamble making big inroads in Russia. U.K. White Goods. http://www.ukwhitegoods.co.uk/modules.php?name=News&file=print&sid=239

xiii Oyelere, P. B., & Emmanuel, C. R. (1998). International transfer pricing and income shifting: Evidence from the UK. *European Accounting Review*, 7, 623-635.

xiv Pagell, M., & Krausse, D. R. (2002). Strategic consensus in the internal supply chain: Exploring the manufacturing—purchasing link. *International Journal of Production Research*, 40, 3075–3092.

xv Deming, W. E. (1982). *Out of the Crisis*. Cambridge, MA: The MIT Press International.

xvi Peters, T. J., & Waterman, R. H. (1982). *In Search of Excellence: Lessons from America's Best-Run Companies*. New York: Harper & Row.

Chapter 6

i http://www.detnews.com/2005/autoinsider/0504/23/1auto-159177.htm.

ii Tannen, D. (1995). The power of talk: Who gets heard and why. *Harvard Business Review*, September–October, 138–148.

iii Chambers, E.G., Foulon, M., Handfield-Jones, H., Hankin, S.M., & Michaels III, E.G. (1998). The war for talent. *McKinsey Quarterly*, 3, 44–57.

iv Foreign Direct Investment Rose by 34% in 2006. United Nations Conference on Trade and Development (UNCTAD). 2007. http://www.unctad.org/templates/webflyer.asp?docid=7993&intItemID=1528&lang=1 (accessed on October 2, 2007).

v Foreign Direct Investment Rose By 34% in 2006, 2006, UNCTAD press release. http://www.unctad.org/Templates/webflyer.asp?docid=7993&intItemID=1528&lang=1 (accessed October 5, 2008).

vi Viramani, A. (2005, October 2). Bringing down tariffs without hurting. *NewsInsight*. http://www.indiareacts.com/archivespecialreports/nat2.asp?recno=29&ctg=.

vii Nair, A., Ahlstrom, D., & Filer, L. (2007). Localized advantage in a global economy: The case of Bangalore. *Thunderbird International Business Review*, 49(5), 591–618.

viii Yan, A., & Luo, Y. (2001). *International Joint Ventures: Theory and Practice*. Armonk, NY: M.E. Sharpe.

ix Weidenbaum, M., & Hughes, S. (1996). *The Bamboo Network: How Expatriate Chinese Entrepreneurs Are Creating a New Economic Superpower in Asia*. New York: Free Press.

x Purcell, V. (1965). *The Chinese in Southeast Asia* (2nd ed.). London: Oxford University Press.

xi Ahlstrom, D., Young, M. N., Chan, E. S., & Bruton, G. D. (2004). Facing constraints to growth? Overseas Chinese entrepreneurs and traditional business practices in East Asia. *Asia Pacific Journal of Management*, 21(3), 263–285; Seagrave, S. (1995). *Lords of the Rim: The Invisible Empire of the Overseas Chinese*. New York: G.P. Putnam Group.

xii DeFrancis, J. (1986). *The Chinese Language: Fact and Fantasy*. Honolulu: University of Hawaii Press.

xiii Tan, T. W. (Ed.) (1990). *Chinese Dialect Groups: Traits and Trades*. Singapore: Opinion Books.

xiv Seagrave, 1995.

xv Tan, 1990.

xvi Hamel, G., & Prahalad, C. K. (1994). *Competing for the Future*. Boston: Harvard Business School Press.

xvii Yan & Luo, 2001.

xviii Mann, J. (1997). *Beijing Jeep: A Case Study of Western Business in China*. Boulder, CO: Westview Press.

xix Mann, 1997.

xx For a very recent, instructive, and cautionary tale about western firms' odyssey in China, see Tim Clissold's 2006 book *Mr. China: A Memoir*. New York: Collins.

xxi Boulding, W., & Christen, M. (2001). First mover disadvantage. *Harvard Business Review*, October, 20–21.

xxii Levinson, M. (2006). *The Box: How the Shipping Container Made the World Smaller and the World Economy Bigger*. Princeton, NJ: Princeton University Press.

Chapter 7

i Keillor, G. (1985). *Lake Wobegon Days*. New York: Viking Press.

ii Butler, T., & Waldroop, J. (1999). Job sculpting: The art of retaining your best people. *Harvard Business Review*, September–October, 144–152.

iii Trompenaars, F. (1993). *Riding the Waves of Culture*. London: The Economist Books.

iv Trompenaars, 1993, p. 86.

v Semlar, R. (1989). Managing without managers. *Harvard Business Review*, September–October, 2–10.

vi Alderfer, C. P. (1972). *Existence, Relatedness, and Growth: Human Needs in Organizational Settings*. New York: Free Press.

vii Hofstede, G., & Hofstede, G. J. (2005). *Cultures and Organizations: Software of the Mind*. New York: McGraw-Hill; Trompenaars, 1993.

viii Alderfer, 1972.

ix Hofstede & Hofstede, 1993.

x Kovach, K. A. (1987). What motivates employees? Workers and supervisors give different answers. *Business Horizons*, 58–65; Morse, G. (2002). Why we misread motives. *Harvard Business Review*, 81, 1–18.

xi Herzberg, F. (1968). One more time: How do you motivate employees? *Harvard Business Review*, January–February, 54–62.

xii Adler, N. J. (2002). *International Dimensions of Organizational Behavior* (4th ed.) (p. 175). Cincinnati, OH: South-Western College Publishing.

xiii McClelland, D. C., Atkinson, J. W., Clark, R. A., & Lowell, E. L. (1953). *The Achievement Motive*. New York: Appleton-Century-Crofts.

xiv McClelland, D. C. (1961). *The Achieving Society*. Princeton, NJ: Van Nostrand.

xv McCall, M. (1998). *High Fliers*. Boston: Harvard Business School Press.

xvi Bradburn, N. M., & Berlew, D. G. (1961). Need for achievement and English economic growth. *Economic Development and Cultural Change*, 10, 8–20.

xvii DeCharms, R., & Moeller, G. H. (1962). Values expressed in American children's readers: 1800–1950. *Journal of Abnormal and Social Psychology*, 64, 136–142; McClelland, D. C. (1961). *The Achieving Society*. New York: Van Nostrand Reinhold.

xviii Barone, M. (2004). *Hard America, Soft America: Competition vs. Coddling and the Battle for the Nation's Future*. New York: Crown Forum.

xix Kerr, S. (1975). On the folly of rewarding A, while hoping for B. *Academy of Management Journal*, 18, 769–783.

xx McCall, 1998; Butler, T., & Waldroop, J. (1997). *Discovering Your Career in Business*. New York: Perseus Books Group.

xxi Sagie, A., Elizur, D., & Yamauchi, H. (1996). The structure and strength of achievement motivation: A cross-cultural comparison. *Journal of Organizational Behavior*, 17(5), 431–444.

xxii Hundal, P. S. (1971). A study of entrepreneurial motivation: Comparison of fast- and slow-progressing small scale industrial entrepreneurs in Punjab, India. *Journal of Applied Psychology*, 55(4), 317–323.

xxiii Hines, G. H. (1973). Achievement, motivation, occupations and labor turnover in New Zealand. *Journal of Applied Psychology*, 58(3), 313–317.

xxiv Aronoff, J., & Litwin, G. H. (1971). Achievement motivation training and executive advancement. *Journal of Applied Behavioral Science*, 7(2), 215–229; Miron, D., & McClelland, D. C. (1979). The impact of achievement motivation training on small businesses. *California Management Review*, 21(4), 13–28.

xxv Adler, N. J., & Boyacigiller, N. (1995). Global organizational behavior: Going beyond tradition, *Journal of International Management*, 1(3), 73–86; Hofstede, G., & Hofstede, G. R. (2005). *Cultures and Organizations: Software of the Mind*. New York: McGraw-Hill.

xxvi Jaeger, A. M., & Kanungo, R. N. (Eds.). (1990). *Management in Developing Countries*. London: Routledge.

xxvii Kovach, 1987; Kovach, K. A. (1995). Employee motivation: Addressing a crucial factor in your organization's performance. *Employment Relations Today*, Summer, 93–107.

xxviii Vroom, V. H. (1964). *Work and Motivation*. New York: Wiley.

xxix Butler & Waldroop, 1997.

xxx Jaeger & Kanungo, 1990.

xxxi Adams, J. S. (1963). Toward an understanding of inequity. *Journal of Abnormal and Social Psychology*, 67, 422–436.

xxxii Adler, N. J. (2002). *International Dimensions of Organizational Behavior*. Cincinnati, OH: South-Western College Publishing.

xxxiii Akerlof, G. A. (1984). Gift exchange and efficiency—wage theory: Four views. *American Economic Review*, 74, 79–83.

xxxiv Dawson, S. (2000, May 16). Unhappy employees pose greater risk than hackers. *Straits Times* (Singapore), p. 43.

xxxv Friedman, T. L. (2005). *The World Is Flat: A Brief History of the Twentyfirst Century*. New York: Farrar, Straus and Giroux.

xxxvi For discussions on China's industrial organization and management in early republican China, see Fenby, J.

(2004). *Chiang Kai-shek: China's Generalissimo and the Nation He Lost*. New York: Carroll & Graf; Zanasi, M. (2006). *Saving the Nation: Economic Modernity in Republican China*. Chicago: University of Chicago Press.

xxxvii Buck, P. S. (1931). *The Good Earth*. Shanghai: Far Eastern Books.

xxxviii Fok, L. Y., Hartman, S. J., Villere, M. F., & Freibert, R. C. III. (1996). A study of the impact of cross cultural differences on the perceptions of equity and organizational citizenship behavior. *International Journal of Management*, 13, 3–14.

xxxix Pfeffer, J., & Sutton, R. I. (2006). *Hard Facts, Dangerous Half-Truths and Total Nonsense: Profiting From Evidence-Based Management*. Boston: Harvard Business School Press.

xl Ahlstrom, D., Si, S. X., & Kennelly, J. (1999). Free agent performance in major league baseball: Do teams get what they expect. *Journal of Sport Management*, 13(3), 181–196.

xli Locke, E. A., & Latham, G. P. (1990). *A Theory of Goal Setting and Task Performance*. Upper Saddle River, NJ: Prentice Hall; Collins, J. (2005). *Good to Great and the Social Sectors*. Boulder, CO: Jim Collins.

xlii Collins, 2005.

xliii Butler & Waldroop, 1997, 1999.

xliv Kovach, 1987.

Chapter 8

i For a scholarly treatment of Mao's rule in China, particularly during the Cultural Revolution, see MacFarquhar, R., & Schoenhals, M. (2006). *Mao's Last Revolution*. Cambridge, MA: The Belknap Press of Harvard University Press.

ii Yukl, G. (2006). *Leadership in Organizations* (6th ed.) (p. 432). Upper Saddle River, NJ: Pearson Education, Inc.

iii Hofstede, G. (1993). Cultural constraints in management theories. *Academy of Management Executive*, 7(1), 81–94.

iv House, R. J. (1995). Leadership in the 21st century: A speculative enquiry. In A. Howard (Ed.), *The Changing Nature of Work*. San Francisco: Jossey Bass.

v Adler, N. J. (2002). *International Dimensions of Organizational Behavior* (4th ed.). Cincinnati, OH: South-Western.

vi Bass, B. M., & Stogdill, R. M. (1989). *The Handbook of Leadership* (3rd ed.). New York: Free Press.

vii Dorfman, P. W. (1996). International and cross-cultural leadership research. In B. J. Punnett, & O. Shenkar (Eds.), *Handbook for International Management Research* (pp. 267–349). Oxford: Blackwell.

viii MacFarquhar & Schoenhals, 2006.

ix Conger, J. A. (1989). *The Charismatic Leader: Behind the Mystique of Exceptional Leadership*. San Francisco: Jossey-Bass; Howell, J. M. (1988). Two faces of charisma: Socialized and personalized leadership in organizations. In J. A. Conger, & R. N. Kanungo (Eds.), *Charismatic Leadership: The Elusive Factor in Organizational Effectiveness* (pp. 213–236). San Francisco: Jossey-Bass; Khurana, R. (2002). The curse of the superstar CEO. *Harvard Business Review*, September; Collins, J. (2001). *Good to Great*. New York: HarperBusiness.

x Tichy, N. M. & Devanna, M. A. (1986). *The Transformational Leader*. New York: John Wiley & Sons; Bass, B. M. (1985). *Leadership and Performance beyond Expectations*. New York: Free Press.

xi Bass, 1985; Den Hartog, D. N., Van Muijen, J. J., & Koopman, P. L. (1997). Transactional versus transformational leadership: An analysis of the MLQ. *Journal of Occupational and Organizational Psychology*, 70(1), 19–34.

xii Tichy & Devanna, 1986.

xiii Bass, 1985.

xiv Fiol, C. M., Harris, D., & House, R. J. (1999). Charismatic leadership: Strategies for effecting social change. *Leadership Quarterly*, 10(3), 449–482.

xv Lowe, K. B., Kroek, K. G., & Sivasubramanian, N. (1996). Effectiveness correlates of transformational and transactional leadership: A meta-analytic review. *Leadership Quarterly*, 7, 385–425.

xvi Howell, J. M., & Higgins, C. A. (1990). Leadership behaviors, influence tactics, and career experiences of champions of technological innovation. *Leadership Quarterly*, 1, 249–264; Shamir, B., Zakay, E., Breinin, E., & Popper, M. (1998). Correlates of charismatic leader behavior in military units—subordinates attitudes, unit characteristics, and superiors' appraisals of leader performance. *Academy of Management Journal*, 41(4), 387–409; Roberts, N. C. (1985). Transforming leadership: A process of collective action. *Human Relations*, 38, 1023–1046; House, R. J., Spangler, W. D., & Woyke, J. (1991). Personality and charisma in the U.S. presidency: A psychological theory of leadership effectiveness. *Administrative Science Quarterly*, 36, 364–396.

xvii House, R. J., Hanges, P. J., Javidan, M., Dorfman, P. W., & Gupta, V. (Eds.) (2004). *Culture, Leadership, and Organizations: The GLOBE Study of 62 Societies*. Thousand Oaks, CA: Sage Publications.

xviii Dorfman, 1996, p. 271.

xix Graurnan, C. F., & Moscovici, S. (1986). *Changing Conceptions of Leadership* (pp. 241–242). New York: Springer-Verlag.

xx Conger, 1989; Howell, 1988.

xxi Bass, B. M. (1990). *Bass and Stogdill's Handbook of Leadership: Theory, Research and Managerial Applications* (3rd ed.) (p. 196). New York: Free Press.

xxii Bass, B. M. (1997). Does the transactional-transformational paradigm transcend organizational and national boundaries? *American Psychologist*, 52(2), 130–139; Singer, M. S., & Singer, A. E. (1990). Situational constraints on transformational versus transactional leadership behavior, subordinates' leadership preference, and satisfaction. *Journal of Social Psychology*, 130(3), 385–396.

xxiii Dorfman, P. W., Howell, J. P., Hibino, S., Lee, J. K., Tate, U., & Bautista, A. (1997). Leadership in western and Asian countries: Commonalities and differences in effective leadership processes across cultures. *Leadership Quarterly*, 8(3), 233–274.

xxiv Goleman, D., Boyatzis, R., & McKee, A. (2002). *Primal Leadership*. Boston, MA: Harvard Business School Press.

xxv Burns, 1978.

xxvi Bass, 1985.

xxvii Marcoulides, G. A., Yavas, B. F., Bilgin, Z., & Gibson, C. B. (1998). Reconciling culturalist and rationalist approaches: Leadership in the United States and Turkey. *Thunderbird International Business Review*, 40, 563–583.

xxviii Faiola, A. (2005, November 30). U.S. baseball manager's softer style throws Japan's social order a curve. *The Wall Street Journal (Asia)*, p. 32.

xxix Thierry et al., 1999.

xxx Collins, J. (2001). *Good to Great*. New York: HarperBusiness.

xxxi Tung, R. L. (2001). *Learning from World Class Companies*. Florence, KY: Cengage Learning Business Press.

xxxii Jim Collins interview with Charlie Rose. The Charlie Rose Show. Aired June 2002.

xxxiii Frederick, J. (2002, December 9). Going nowhere fast. *Time*, 160(22), 36–41.

xxxiv Goleman et al., 2002.

xxxv Goleman et al., 2002.

xxxvi Fiedler, F. E. (1967). *A Theory of Leadership Effectiveness*. New York: McGraw-Hill.

xxxvii Hersey, P., & Blanchard, K. H. (1993). *Management of Organizational Behavior*. Upper Saddle River, NJ: Prentice Hall.

xxxviii Evans, M. G. (1974). Extensions of a path-goal theory of motivation. *Journal of Applied Psychology*, 59, 172–178; House, R. J. (1971). A path-goal theory of leadership effectiveness. *Administrative Science Quarterly*, 16, 321–338.

xxxix Kagan, R. (2008). *The Return of History and the End of Dreams*. New York: Knopf.

xl Kelner, S. P. Jr., Rivers, C. A., & O'Connell, K. H. (1996). *Managerial Style as a Behavioral Predictor of Organizational Climate*. Boston: McBer & Company; Goleman et al., 2002.

xli Ahlstrom, D., Young, M. N., Chan, E. S., & Bruton, G. D. (2004). Facing constraints to growth? Overseas Chinese entrepreneurs and traditional business practices in East Asia. *Asia Pacific Journal of Management*, 21, 263–285.

xlii Goleman et al., 2002.

xliii Goleman et al., 2002; Sasser, W. E., Schlesinger, L. A., & Heskett, J. L. (1997). *The Service Profit Chain*. New York: Free Press.

xliv Goleman et al., 2002.

xlv Maney, K. (2004, April 21). SAS workers won when greed lost. *USA TODAY*. http://www.usatoday.com/money/industries/technology/2004-04-21-sas-culture_x.htm.

xlvi Goleman et al., 2002.

xlvii Cringley, R. X. (1996). *Accidental Empires* (reprint ed.). New York: Collins Books; Scully, J., & Byrne, J. A. (1987). *Odyssey: Pepsi to Apple. . . A Journey of Adventure, Ideas, and the Future*. New York: HarperCollins.

xlviii Goleman et al., 2002.

xlix Konrad, E. (2000). Implicit leadership theories in Eastern and Western Europe. *Social Science Information*, 39(2), 335–347; Lord, G. R., & Maher, J. K. (1991). *Leadership and Information Processing: Linking Perceptions and Performance*. Boston, MA: Unwin Hyman.

l Lord & Maher, 1991.

li Garten, J. E. (2001). *The Mind of the CEO*. New York: Basic Books.

lii Bass, 1990; Hofstede, G. (1993). Cultural constraints in management theories. *Academy of Management Executive*, 7(1), 81–94.

liii Konrad, 2000; Shama, A. (1993). Management under fire: The transformation of managers in the Soviet Union and Eastern Europe. *Academy of Management Executive*, 7(1), 22–35.

liv Hofstede, G., & Hofstede, G. J. (2005). *Cultures and Organizations: Software of the Mind*. New York: McGraw-Hill.

lv Hofstede, 1993.

lvi Adler, 2002.

Chapter 9

i Von Neumann, J., & Morgenstern, O. (1944). *Theory of Games and Economic Behavior*. Princeton, NJ: Princeton University Press; Dixit, A. K., & Nalebuff, B. J. (1993). *Thinking Strategically: The Competitive Edge in Business, Politics, and Everyday Life*. New York: W.W. Norton & Company.

ii Ayres, I. (2007). *Super Crunchers: Why Thinking-By-Numbers Is the New Way to Be Smart*. Bantam, New York.

iii Cialdini, R. (2008). *Influence: Science and Practice* (8th ed.). New York: Allyn & Bacon; Belsky, G., & Gilovich, T. (2000). *Why Smart People Make Big Money Mistakes and*

How to Correct Them: Lessons from the New Science of Behavioral Economics*. New York: Simon & Schuster; Tversky, A., & Kahneman, D. (1979). Prospect theory: An analysis of decision under risk. *Econometrica*, 47(2), 263–292.

iv Staw, B. M., & Ross, J. (1987). Understanding escalation situations: Antecedents, prototypes, and solutions. In B. M. Staw, & L. L. Cummings (Eds.), *Research in Organizational Behavior*, Vol. 9 (pp. 39–78). Greenwich, CT: JAI Press.

v Kahneman and Tversky originally described this deviation from rational decision making, which they termed the framing effect. See Kahneman, D. & Tversky, A. (2000). *Choices, Values, and Frames*. Cambridge: Cambridge University Press; Belsky & Gilovich, 2000.

vi Simon, H. (1957). *Administrative Behavior: A Study of Decision-making Processes in Administrative Organization*. New York: Free Press.

vii Jung, C. G. (1971). *Psychological Types*. Princeton, NJ: Princeton University Press.

viii Cialdini, 2008.

ix BBC News, September 7, 2007. http://news.bbc.co.uk/1/hi/technology/6981704.stm (accessed October 23, 2007).

x Frey, D. (1982). Different levels of cognitive dissonance, information seeking, and information avoidance. *Journal of Personality and Social Psychology*, 43, 1175–83.

xi Sunstein, C. (2003). *Why Societies Need Dissent*. Boston: Harvard University Press.

xii Janis, I. (1977). *Victims of Groupthink*. Boston: Houghton Mifflin.

xiii Janis, 1977.

xiv Janis, 1977; Surowiecki, J. (2004). *The Wisdom of Crowds*. New York: Anchor Books.

xv Langewiesche, W. (2003). Columbia's last flight. *The Atlantic Monthly*, 292(4), 58–82.

xvi Lomborg, B. (2007). *Cool It: The Skeptical Environmentalist's Guide to Global Warming*. New York: Knopf; Lomborg, B. (Ed.). (2004). *Global Crises, Global Solutions*. Cambridge: Cambridge University Press.

xvii Belsky & Gilovich. 2000; Tversky & Kahneman, 2000; Thaler, R. H. (1994). *The Winner's Curse*. Princeton, NJ: Princeton University Press.

xviii Ahlstrom, D., Nair, A., Young, M. N., & Wang, L. C. (2006). China: Competitive myths and realities. *SAM Advanced Management Journal*, 71, 4–10.

xix Gilboy, G. (2004). The myth behind China's miracle. *Foreign Affairs*, 83(4), 33–48.

xx Levitt, S. D., & Dubner, S. J. (2006). *Freakonomics* [revised and expanded]: *A Rogue Economist Explores the Hidden Side of Everything* (pp. 135–136). New York: William Morrow.

xxi Tversky, A., & Kahneman, D. (1973). Availability: A heuristic for judging frequency and probability. *Cognitive Psychology*, 5, 207–232; Tversky, A., & Kahneman, D. (1974). Judgment under uncertainty: Heuristics and biases. *Science*, 185, 1124–1130.

xxii Belsky & Gilovitch, 2000.

xxiii Milloy, S. (1997). Relax…You might not be doomed. *Public Risk*, February, 2–4.

xxiv ABC News (Australia). Port Headland plant to be demolished. (Accessed January 15, 2008.) http://www.abc.net.au/news/stories/2007/02/15/1848498.htm.

xxv Ng, A. K. (2000). *Why Asians Are Less Creative than Westerners.* Singapore: Prentice Hall.

xxvi Cialdini, 2008.

xxvii Cialdini, 2008.

xxviii Janis, 1977.

xxix Ahlstrom, D., & Wang, L. C. (2008). Groupthink and France's defeat in the 1940 campaign. *Journal of Management History*, in press; Moore, R. (2004). *A Time to Die: The Untold Story of the Kursk Tragedy.* New York: Three Rivers Press; Starbuck, W. H., & Farjoun, M. (Eds.) (2005). *Organization at the Limit: Lessons from the Columbia Disaster.* New York: Wiley-Blackwell.

xxx Janis, 1977.

xxxi Starbuck & Milliken, 1988.

xxxii Starbuck & Milliken, 1988.

xxxiii Doughty, R. A. (1985). *The Seeds of Disaster: The Development of French Army Doctrine, 1919–1939.* New York: Archon Books.

xxxiv Fenby, J. (2005). *Chiang Kai Shek: China's Generalissimo and the Nation He Lost.* New York: Da Capo Press.

xxxv Fenby, J. 2005; Tuchman, B. (2001). *Stilwell and the American Experience in China, 1911–4* (1st Grove Press ed.). New York: Grove Press.

xxxvi Gardner, H. (1993). *Frames of Mind: The Theory of Multiple Intelligences.* New York: Basic Books.

xxxvii Humphries, J., Ingram, K., Kernek, C., & Sadler, T. (2007). The Nez Perce leadership council. *Journal of Management History.* 13(2), 135–152.

xxxviii Surowiecki, 2004.

xxxix Surowiecki, 2004.

xl Drucker, P. F. (1971). What we can learn from Japanese management. *Harvard Business Review.* March–April, 110–122; Pascale, R. T. (1978, March 23). Communication and decision making across cultures: Japanese and American comparisons. *Administrative Science Quarterly*, 23, 91–110.

xli Kakar, S. (1971). Authority patterns and subordinate behavior in Indian organizations. *Administrative Science Quarterly*, 16(3), 298–308.

xlii Gyllenhammer, P. G. (1977). How Volvo adapts work to people. *Harvard Business Review*, 55(4), 102–113.

xliii Christensen, C. M., & Raynor, M. E. (2003). *The Innovator's Solution: Creating and Sustaining Successful Growth* (Chapter 1). Boston: Harvard Business School Press.

Chapter 10

i All managers should take heart from the difficulties that U.S. president Abraham Lincoln had in influencing his generals to do things during the American Civil War, even though they were his subordinates and were supposed to be following his orders. See the classic narrative history about President Lincoln and his generals by historian T. Harry Williams, originally published in 1952 and still in print: Williams, T. H. (1991). *Lincoln and His Generals.* New York: Gramercy.

ii Donald, D. H. (1995). *Lincoln.* New York: Simon & Schuster.

iii Williams, 1991.

iv Cialdini, R. B. (2006). *Influence: The Psychology of Persuasion.* New York: Collins Business Essentials; Cialdini, R. (2009). *Influence: Science and Practice* (5th ed.). New York: Allyn & Bacon; Levine, R. V. (2003). *The Power of Persuasion: How We're Bought and Sold.* New York: John Wiley & Sons.

v Cialdini, 2009.

vi Weick, K. (1979). *The Social Psychology of Organizing* (2nd ed.). New York: McGraw-Hill Humanities/Social Sciences/Languages.

vii McGuire, W. J. (1966). Attitudes and opinions. *Annual Review of Psychology*, 17, 475–514.

viii Greenwald, A. G. (1968). Cognitive learning, cognitive response to persuasion, and attitude change. In A. G. Greenwald, T. C. Brock, & T. M. Ostrom (Eds.), *Psychological Foundations of Attitudes.* New York: Academic Press.

ix Festinger, L. (1957). *A Theory of Cognitive Dissonance.* Stanford, CA: Stanford University Press.

x Goldsten, N. J., Martin, S. J., & Cialdini, R. B. (2007). *Yes! 50 Secrets from the Science of Persuasion.* London: Profile Books Ltd.

xi See the work of innovation scholar Clayton Christensen on this topic of understanding why customers "hired" your product. Christensen, C. M., & Raynor, M. E. (2003). *The Innovator's Solution: Creating and Sustaining Successful Growth* (Ch. 3). Boston: Harvard Business School Press; Eagly, A. H., & Chaiken, S. (1993). *The Psychology of Attitudes.* Fort Worth, TX: Harcourt Brace, Jovanovich.

xii Toshiba format. (2008, February 18). *Financial Times*, p. 1.

xiii Sills, J. (2006). Criticism: Taking the hit. *Psychology Today*, July/August, 61–62.

xiv Hastings, D. (1999). Lincoln Electric's harsh lessons from international expansion. *Harvard Business Review*,

77(3), 162–178; Sullivan, G. R., & Harper, M. V. (1997). *Hope Is Not a Method.* New York: Broadway.

xv Kenrick, D. T., Neuberg, S. L., & Cialdini, R. B. (2006). *Social Psychology: Goals in Interaction.* New York: Allyn & Bacon.

xvi Fritschler, A. L. (1975). *Smoking and Politics.* Englewood Cliffs, NJ: Prentice Hall.

xvii Dunbar, R., & Wasilewski, N. (1985). Regulating external threats: The case of the cigarette industry. *Administrative Science Quarterly,* 30, 540–559.

xviii Kenrick, D. T., Neuberg, S. L., & Cialdini, R. B. (2007). *Social Psychology: Goals in Interaction* (4th ed.). New York: Allyn & Bacon.

xix Kenrick, Neuberg, & Cialdini, 2007.

xx Cialdini, 2009.

xxi Sagarin, B. J., Cialdini, R. B., Rice, W. E., & Serna, S. B. (2002). Dispelling the illusion of invulnerability: The motivations and mechanisms of resistance to persuasion. *Journal of Personality and Social Psychology,* 83, 526–541.

xxii Cialdini, 2008.

xxiii Evans, F. B. (1963). Selling as a dyadic relationship—a new approach. *The American Behavioral Scientist,* 6 (May), 76–79.

xxiv Cialdini, 2009.

xxv Gouldner, A. (1960). The norm of reciprocity: A preliminary statement. *American Sociological Review,* 25(2), 161–178; Fisher, J. D., Nadler, A., & DePaulo, B. M. (Eds.) (1983). *New Directions in Helping. Vol. 1, Recipient Reactions to Aid.* New York: Academic Press.

xxvi Cialdini, 2009.

xxvii Regan, D. T., Williams, M., & Sparling, S. (1972). Voluntary expiation of guilt: A field experiment. *Journal of Personality and Social Psychology,* 24(1), 42–45.

xxviii Cialdini, 2006.

xxix Hastings, 1999; Heath, C., & Heath, D. (2007). *Made to Stick: Why Some Ideas Survive and Others Die.* New York: Random House.

xxx Asch, S. E. (1956). Studies of independence and conformity: A minority of one against a unanimous majority. *Psychological Monographs,* 70(9), 416.

xxxi Berns, G. (2008). *Iconoclast: A Neuroscientist Reveals How to Think Differently.* Jackson, TN: Perseus Distribution Services.

xxxii Cialdini, 2009.

xxxiii Milgram, S. (1974). *Obedience to Authority.* New York: Harper & Row.

xxxiv Milgram, S. (1963). Behavioral study of obedience. *Journal of Abnormal and Social Psychology,* 67, 371–378.

xxxv Milgram, 1963.

xxxvi Milgram, 1963.

xxxvii Blass, T. (2002). The man who shocked the world. *Psychology Today,* 35(2), March/April, 68–74.

xxxviii Bushman, B. J. (1984). Perceived symbols of authority and their influence on compliance. *Journal of Applied Social Psychology,* 14, 501–508; Milgram, 1974.

xxxix Milgram, 1963.

xl Cialdini, 2009.

xli Pye, L. W., & Pye, M. W. (2006). *Asian Power and Politics: The Cultural Dimensions of Authority.* Cambridge, MA: Belknap Press.

xlii Ahlstrom, D., Bruton, G. D., & Yeh, K. S. (2008). Private firms in China: Building legitimacy in an emerging economy. *Journal of World Business,* 43, 385–399.

xliii Cialdini, R. B. (2000). *Influence: Science and Practice* (4th ed.) (Ch. 5). New York: Allyn & Bacon.

xliv Stukas, A. A. Jr., & Snyder, M. (2002). Targets' awareness of expectations and behavioral confirmation in ongoing interactions. *Journal of Experimental Social Psychology,* 38, 31–40.

xlv Cialdini, 2006.

xlvi Berscheid, E., & Walster, E. H. (1978). *Interpersonal Attraction.* New York: Addison-Wesley.

xlvii Carnegie, D. (1998). *How to Win Friends & Influence People.* New York: Pocket Books.

xlviii Carnegie, 1998.

xlix Schwarzwald, J., Bizman, A., & Raz, M. (1983). The foot-in-the-door paradigm: Effects of second request size on donation probability and donor generosity. *Personality and Social Psychology Bulletin,* 9, 443–450.

l Cialdini, 2006.

li Levine, 2003.

lii Cialdini, 2009.

liii Smolowe, J. (1990, November 26). Contents require immediate attention. *Time,* p. 64.

liv Lee, C. (2003). *Cowboys and Dragons.* Chicago: Dearborn Trade Publication.

lv Tsui, A., & Farh, J. L. (1997). Where Guanxi matters: Relational demography and Guanxi in the Chinese context. *Work and Occupations,* 24(1), 56–79; Xin, K., & Pearce, J. (1996). Guanxi: Connections as substitutes for formal institutional support. *Academy of Management Journal,* 39, 1641–1658.

lvi Buchan, N. R., Croson, R. T., & Dawes, R. M. (2002). Swift neighbors and persistent strangers: A cross-cultural investigation of trust and reciprocity in social exchange. *American Journal of Sociology,* 108, 168–220; Gabrenya, W., & Hwang, K. K. (1996). Chinese social interaction: Harmony and hierarchy on the good earth. In M. Bond (Ed.), *The*

Handbook of Chinese Psychology (pp. 309–321). Oxford: Oxford University Press; Xin & Pearce, 1996.

lvii Sahlins, M. (1972). Stone Age Economics. New York: Aldine de Gruyter; Befu, H. (1977). Social exchange. Annual Review of Anthropology, 6, 255–281.

lviii Kenrick, D. T., Neuberg, S. L., & Cialdini, R. B. (2007). Social Psychology: Goals in Interaction (4th ed.). New York: Allyn & Bacon.

lix Brehm, S. S., & Brehm, J. W. (1981). Psychological Reactance: A Theory of Freedom and Control. Oxford: Academic Press.

lx Shelley, M. K. (1994). Individual differences in lottery evaluation models. Organizational Behavior and Human Decision Processes, 60(2), 206–226.

lxi Gouldner, A. (1960). The norm of reciprocity: A preliminary statement. American Sociological Review, 25(2), 161–178; Fisher, J. D., Nadler, A., & DePaulo, B. M. (Eds.). (1983). New Directions in Helping. Vol. I, Recipient Reactions to Aid. New York: Academic Press.

lxii Levine, R. V. (2003). The Power of Persuasion: How We're Bought and Sold. New York: John Wiley & Sons.

lxiii Morris, M., Podolny, J., & Ariel, S. (2001). Culture, norms, and obligations: Cross-national differences in patterns of interpersonal norms and felt obligations toward coworkers. In W. Wosinka, R. B. Cialdini, D. W. Barrett, & J. Reykowski (Eds.). (2001). The Practice of Social Influence in Multiple Cultures. Mahwah, NJ: Lawrence Erlbaum Associates; Levine, 2003.

lxiv Lee, 2003.

lxv Fukuyama, F. (1995). Trust. New York: Free Press.

lxvi See Acuff, F. (2008). How to Negotiate Anything with Anyone Anywhere Around the World (3rd ed.). New York: AMACOM.

lxvii Lee, 2003.

lxviii Hammond, J. S., Keeney, R. L., & Raiffa, H. (1998). The hidden traps in decision making. Harvard Business Review, 76(5), 47–54.

lxix Teach, E. (2004, June 2). Avoiding decision traps. CFO.com. http://www.cfo.com/printable/article.cfm/3014027?f=options (accessed November 8, 2008).

lxx Donald, D. H. (1995). Lincoln. New York: Simon & Schuster.

lxxi Williams, 1993.

lxxii Michaelson, G. A. (2001). Sun Tzu: The Art of War for Managers; 50 Strategic Rules. New York: Adams Media.

lxxiii Lee, 2003; Zeng, M., & Williamson, P. J. (2007). Dragons at Your Door: How Chinese Cost Innovation Is Disrupting Global Competition. Boston: Harvard Business School Press.

lxxiv Fisher, R., & Ury, W. L. (1992). Getting to Yes: Negotiating Agreement Without Giving In. New York: Penguin.

lxxv Goldsten, Martin, & Cialdini, 2007.

lxxvi Fisher & Ury, 1992; Cialdini, 2009.

lxxvii Henrich, J., Boyd, R., Bowles, S., Camerer, C., Fehr, E., & Gintis, H. (2004). Foundations of Human Sociality: Economic Experiments and Ethnographic Evidence from Fifteen Small-Scale Societies. Oxford: Oxford University Press.

lxxviii Henrich et al., 2004.

lxxix Lee, 2003.

lxxx Cialdini, 2009; Fisher et al., 1983.

lxxxi Lerner, J. S., Small, D. A., & Lowenstein, G. (2004). Heart strings and purse strings: Carryover effects of emotions on economic decisions. Psychological Science, 15, 337–341.

lxxxii Lerner et al., 2004.

lxxxiii Acuff, 2008; Tinsley, C. R., & Weiss, S. E. (1999). Examining international business negotiations and directions for the future. International Negotiation, 4(1), 95–97; Weiss, S. E. (1996). International negotiations: Bricks, mortar, and prospects. In B. J. Punnett, & O. Shenkar (Eds.), Handbook for International Management Research (pp. 209–265). Cambridge, MA: Blackwell.

lxxxiv Weiss, S. E. (1994). Negotiating with 'Romans'— Part 1. Sloan Management Review, Winter, 51–62; Weiss, S. E. (1994). Negotiating with 'Romans'—Part 2. Sloan Management Review, Spring, 85–100.

lxxxv Tung, R. L. (1982). U.S.–China trade negotiations: Practices, procedures and outcomes. Journal of International Business Studies, 13, 25–38; Tinsley, C. H. (1998). Models of conflict resolution in Japanese, German and American cultures. Journal of Applied Psychology, 83, 316–323; Tung, R. L. (1984). How to negotiate with the Japanese. California Management Review, 26(4), 62–77.

lxxxvi Wright, P. (1981). Doing business in Islamic markets. Harvard Business Review, 59(1), 34–41.

lxxxvii Acuff, F. (2008). How to Negotiate Anything with Anyone Anywhere Around the World. (3rd ed.). New York: AMACOM; Tinsley, 1998.

lxxxviii Acuff, 2008.

lxxxix Glenn, E. S., Witmeyer, D., & Stevenson, K. A. (1977). Cultural styles of persuasion, International Journal of Intercultural Relations, 1(3), 52–66.

xc Hofstede, G, & Hofstede, G. J. (2005). Cultures and Organizations: Software of the Mind. New York: McGraw-Hill.

xci Hofstede & Hofstede, 2005.

xcii Lee, 2003.

xciii Chan, J. L. (2003). China Streetsmart: What You MUST Know to Be Effective and Profitable in China. Singapore: Pearson Education Asia Pte Ltd.; Lee, 2003.

xciv Graham, J. (1985). The influence of culture on the negotiation process. Journal of International Business Studies,

16(1), 81–96; Pye, L. W., & Pye, M. W. (2006). *Asian Power and Politics: The Cultural Dimension of Authority.* Cambridge, MA: Belknap Press.

xcv Kassin, S., & Kiechel, K. (1996). The social psychology of false confessions: Compliance, internalization, and confabulation. *Psychological Science*, 16(6), 481–486; Pye, L. (1982). *Chinese Commercial Negotiating Style.* Cambridge, MA: Oelgeschlager, Gunn and Hain.

xcvi Lee, 2003.

xcvii Pye, 1982.

Chapter 11

i Leeson, N., & Whitley, E. (1996). *Rogue Trader: How I Brought Down Baring's Bank and Shook the Financial World* (p. 141). New York: Little Brown and Company.

ii Hamel, G., & Prahalad, C. K. (1994). *Competing for the Future.* Boston, MA: Harvard Business School Publishing.

iii Christensen, C. M. (1997). *The Innovator's Dilemma.* Boston, MA: Harvard Business School Publishing.

iv Gilboy, G. J. (2004). The myth behind China's miracle. *Foreign Affairs*, 83(4), 33–48; Ahlstrom, D., Nair, A., Young, M. N., & Wang, L. C. (2006). China: Competitive myths and realities. *SAM Advanced Management Journal*, 71, 4–10.

v Christensen, 1997.

vi Christensen, C. M., & Raynor, M. E. 2003. *The Innovator's Solution.* Boston, MA: Harvard Business School Publishing.

vii Christensen, 1997.

viii For more detail on how to identify disruptive innovation and respond to it, see Christensen, C. M., Johnson, M. W., & Rigby, D. K. (2002). Foundations for growth: How to identify and build disruptive new businesses. *MIT Sloan Management Review*, Spring, 22–31; Zeng, M., & Williamson, P. J. (2007). *Dragons at Your Door: How Chinese Cost Innovation Is Disrupting Global Competition.* Boston, MA: Harvard Business School Publishing.

ix Hammer, M., & Champy, J. (1993). *Reengineering the Corporation: A Manifesto for Business Revolution.* New York: HarperBusiness.

x mySAP™ Supplier Relationship Management At Xerox Europe, www.sap.com/solutions/business-suite/srm/pdf/CCS_Xerox.pdf

xi Hamel & Prahalad, 1994.

xii Hamel, G. (2002). *Leading the Revolution: How to Thrive in Turbulent Times by Making Innovation a Way of Life* (revised ed.). Boston, MA: Harvard Business School Publishing.

xiii Fahey, L., & Randall, R. M. (1998). *Learning from the Future.* New York: John Wiley & Sons.

xiv Colchester, M. (2007, August 24). Can wine in a sippy box lure back French drinkers? *Wall Street Journal.,* http://online.wsj.com/article/SB118791573049507305.html?mod=dist_smartbrief

xv Mintzberg, H., Quinn, J. B., & Ghoshal, S. (1998). *The Strategy Process.* New York: Prentice Hall.

xvi Hamel & Prahalad, 1994.

xvii Gerstner, L. (2002). *Who Says Elephants Can't Dance? Inside IBM's Historic Turnaround.* New York: HarperCollins.

xviii Key to success: People, people, people. (1997, October 27). *Fortune*, p. 232; Collins, J. (2001). *Good to Great: Why Some Companies Make the Leap—and Others Don't.* New York: HarperBusiness; Pfeffer, J. (1998). *The Human Equation: Building Profits by Putting People First.* Boston, MA: Harvard Business School Publishing.

xix McCall, M. (1998). *High Fliers.* Boston, MA: Harvard Business School Publishing.

xx Pfeffer, 1998.

xxi Welsh, J., & Welsh, S. (2007). *Winning.* New York: HarperBusiness.

xxii Sullivan, J. J., Suzuki, T., & Kondo, Y. (1983). Managerial theories and the performance control process in Japanese and American work groups. *Academy of Management Proceedings*, 98–102.

xxiii Adler, N. J. (2004). *International Dimensions of Organizational Behavior.* Cincinnati, OH: South-Western/Thomson Learning; Sullivan et al., 1985.

xxiv Smith, T. C. (1959). *The Agrarian Origins of Modern Japan.* Stanford, CA: Stanford University Press.

xxv McShane, S. L., & Travaglione, T. (2006). *Organizational Behavior on the Pacific Rim* (Chapter 1). Singapore: McGraw-Hill.

xxvi Pfeffer, 1998.

xxvii Hamel, 2002.

xxviii O'Reilly, C. 2000; Heskett, J. L., Sasser, W. E., & Schlesinger, L. A. (1997). *The Service Profit Chain.* New York: Free Press.

xxix Collins, J. 2001; Pfeffer, 1998.

xxx Garvin, D. (1984). Japanese quality management. *Columbia Journal of World Business*, Fall, 3–12.

xxxi Garvin, 1984.

xxxii Sullivan, J. J. (1992). Japanese management philosophies: From the vacuous to the brilliant. *California Management Review*, Winter, 34(2), 66–87.

xxxiii Young, M. N., Ahlstrom, D., & Bruton, G. D. (2004). The globalization of corporate governance in East Asia: The transnational solution. *Management International Review*, 44(2), 31–50.

xxxiv Young, M. N., Buchholtz, A. K., & Ahlstrom, D. (2003). How can board members be empowered if they are spread too thin? *SAM Advanced Management Journal*, 68(4), 4–11.

xxxv Young et al., 2004.

xxxvi Young, M. N., Peng, M. W., Ahlstrom, D., Bruton, G. D., & Jiang, Y. (2008). Corporate governance in emerging economies: A review of the principal–principal perspective. *Journal of Management Studies*, 45(1), 196–220.

xxxvii Young, Peng, Ahlstrom, Bruton & Jiang, 2008.

xxxviii Young, Peng, Ahlstrom, Bruton & Jiang, 2008.

xxxix Hastings, D. (1999). Lincoln Electric's harsh lessons from international expansion. *Harvard Business Review*. May/June, 162–178.

xl Collins, 2001.

xli See Collins, 2001, especially Chapter 4, "Confront the Brutal Facts (Yet Never Lose Faith)".

xlii For a cautionary tale about investing in China see Clissold, T. (2006). *Mr. China: A Memoir*. New York: Collins. Also see McGregor, J. (2005). *One Billion Customers: Lessons from the Front Lines of Doing Business in China*. New York: Simon & Schuster.

xliii Ahlstrom, D., Young, M. N., & Nair, A. (2002). Deceptive managerial practices in China: Strategies for foreign firms. *Business Horizons*, 45(6), 49–59; Ahlstrom, D., Young, M. N., & Nair, A. (2003). Navigating China's feudal governance structures: Guidelines for foreign enterprises. *SAM Advanced Management Journal*, 68(1), 4–14.

xliv Kaplan, R. S., & Norton, D. P. (1996). *The Balanced Scorecard: Translating Strategy into Action*. Boston, MA: Harvard Business School Publishing.

xlv Kaplan, R. S., & Norton, D. P. (2008). *The Execution Premium*. Boston, MA: Harvard Business School Publishing.

xlvi For an excellent discussion on firm mission and focus, see Collins, J., & Porras, J. I. (1994). *Built to Last: Successful Habits of Visionary Companies*. New York: HarperBusiness.

xlvii Hamel & Prahalad, 1994.

xlviii Ahlstrom, D., Bruton, G. D., & Yeh, K. S. (2008). Private firms in China: Building legitimacy in an emerging economy. *Journal of World Business*, 43, 385–399.

xlix For more information on additional firm performance measures, see Kaplan & Norton, 1996, 2008, and Niven, P. S. (2006). *Balanced Scorecard Step-by-Step: Maximizing Performance and Maintaining Results* (2nd ed.). Hoboken, NJ: John Wiley & Sons.

l Kindleberger, C., & Aliber, R. (2005). *Manias, Panics, and Crashes: A History of Financial Crises* (5th ed.). Hoboken, NJ: John Wiley & Sons; Krugman, P. R. (1994). The myth of Asia's miracle. *Foreign Affairs*, 73 (6), 62–78; Porter, M. E., Takeuchi, H., & Sakakibara, M. (2000). *Can Japan Compete?* New York: Basic Books; Radelet, S., & Sachs, J. (1998). The East-Asian financial crisis: Diagnosis, remedies, prospects. *Brookings Papers on Economic Activity*, 1, 1–90.

Chapter 12

i Clissold, T. (2004). *Mr. China*. London: Robinson; Chan, J. L. (2003). *China Streetsmart: What You MUST Know to Be Effective and Profitable in China*. Singapore: Pearson Education Asia.

ii Hastings, D. F. (1999). Lincoln Electric's harsh lessons from international expansion. *Harvard Business Review*, 77(3), 162–178.

iii Harzing, A. K. (1995). The persistent myth of high expatriate failure rate. *The International Journal of Human Resources Management*, 6(2), 457–474.

iv Hastings, D. F. (1999). Lincoln Electric's harsh lessons from international expansion. *Harvard Business Review*, 77(3), 162–178.

vi Tung, R. L. (1982). Selection and training procedures of U.S., European, and Japanese multinationals. *California Management Review*, 25(1), 57–71.

vii Robbins, S. P. (2003). *The Truth About Managing People . . . And Nothing But the Truth*. London: FT Press.

viii Carlton, J. (1998). *Apple: The Inside Story of Intrigue, Egomania, and Business Blunders*. New York: Times Business/Random House.

ix Cohen, A., Watkinson J., & Boone, J. (2005). Southwest Airlines CEO grounded in real world by professor. Babson Insight, special to SearchCIO.com. Accessed March 25, 2006. http://searchcio.techtarget.com/originalContent/0,289142,sid19_gci1071837,00.html

x Mendenhall, M., & Oddou, G. (1985). The dimensions of expatriate acculturation: A review. *Academy of Management Review*, 10(1), 39–47.

xi Early, C., & Mosakowski, E. (2005). Cultural intelligence. *Harvard Business Review*, 82(10), 139–146.

xii Bjorkman, I., & Lu, Y. (1999). A corporate perspective on the management of human resources in China. *Journal of World Business*, 34(1), 16–25.

xiii Hoecklin, L. (1994). *Managing Cultural Differences* (p. 124). Wokingham, UK: Addison-Wesley.

xiv Ryan, A. M., McFarland, L., Baron, H., & Page, R. (1999). An international look at selection practices: Nation and culture as explanations for variability in practice. *Personnel Psychology*, 52(2), 359–391.

xv Levy-Leboyer, C. (1994). Selection and assessment in Europe. In H. C. Triandis, M. D. Dunnette, & L. M. Hough (Eds.), *Handbook of Industrial and Organizational Psychology*, Vol. 4 (pp. 173–190). Palo Alto, CA: Consulting Psychologists Press.

xvi Selmer, J. (1997). Effects of coping strategies on sociocultural and psychological adjustment of Western expatriate managers in the PRC. *Journal of World Business*, 34(1), 41–51.

xvii Hays, C. (2004). *Pop: Truth and Power at the Coca-Cola Company*. London: Hutchison.

xviii Hofstede, G., & Hofstede, G. J. (2005). *Cultures and Organizations: Software of the Mind*. New York: McGraw-Hill.

xix Hastings, 1999.

xx Hastings, 1999.

xxi For more problems expatriates face, see Thornton, R. L., & Thornton, M. K. (1995). Personnel problems in "carry the flag" missions in foreign assignments. *Business Horizons*, January/February, 59–65.

xxii Christensen, C. M., Roth, E. A., & Anthony, S. D. (2004). *Seeing What's Next: Using Theories of Innovation to Predict Industry Change*. Boston, MA: Harvard Business School Press.

xxiii Ahlstrom, D., Bruton, G. D., & Yeh, K. (2008). Private firms in China: Building legitimacy in an emerging economy. *Journal of World Business*, 43(4), 385–399.

xxiv Miller E. L., & Cheng J. L. (1978). A closer look at the decision to accept an overseas position. *Management International Review*, 18(1), 25–27.

xxv Prahalad, C. K., & Lieberthal K. (1998). The end of corporate imperialism. *Harvard Business Review*, 76(4), 68–79.

xxvi Butler, C. (1999). A world of trouble. *Sales and Marketing Management*, 151(9), 44–50.

xxvii Black J. S., & Gregersen, H. B. (1999). The right way to manage expatriates. *Harvard Business Review*, 77(2), 52–63.

xxviii Butler, 1999.

xxix Butler, 1999.

xxx Miller, E. L. (1972). The selection decision for an international assignment: A study of decision makers' behavior. *Journal of International Business Studies*, 3(2), 49–65.

xxxi Tung, R. L. (1981). Selection and training of personnel. *Columbia Journal of World Business*, 16(1), 68–78; McCall, M. W. (1998). *High Fliers: Developing the Next Generation of Leaders*. Boston, MA: Harvard Business School Press.

xxxii Tung, 1982.

xxxiii Black & Gregersen, 1999.

xxxiv McCall, 1998.

xxxv Troy, M. (2004). Overseas reputation diligently guarded to avoid repeating domestic disputes. *DSN Retailing Today*, 43(23), 33.

xxxvi Farrel, D., & Grant, A. J. (2005). China's looming talent shortage. *McKinsey Quarterly*, 4, 70–79.

xxxvii Farrel & Grant, 2005.

xxxviii Prasad, S. B., & Shetty, Y. K. (1976). *Introduction to Multinational Management*. New York: Prentice Hall.

xxxix Chan, J. L. (2003). *China Streetsmart: What You MUST Know to Be Effective and Profitable in China*. Singapore: Pearson Education Asia.

xl Kranhold, K. (2007, September 14). GE's environmental push hits business realities. *Wall Street Journal*, CCL(88), pp. A1, A10.

xli Tung, 1982.

xlii Tung, R. (1998). American expatriates abroad: From neophytes to cosmopolitans. *Journal of World Business*, 33(2), 125–144.

xliii Murray, W. (1986). Clausewitz: Some thoughts on what the Germans got right. *Journal of Strategic Studies*, 9(2–3), 267–286.

xliv Sullivan, G., & Harper, M. V. (1997). *Hope is Not a Method*. New York: Broadway.

xlv Castellano, J. F., Rosenzweig, K., & Roehm, H. A. (2004). How corporate culture impacts unethical distortion of financial numbers. *Management Accounting Quarterly*, 5(4), 37–41.

xlvi Welsh, J., & Welsh, S. (2005). *Winning*. New York: HarperBusiness.

xlvii Welsh, J., & Welsh, S. (2006). *Winning: The Answers*. New Delhi: HarperCollins.

xlviii Butler, T., & Waldroop, J. (1996). *Discovering Your Career in Business*. New York: Basic Books; Welsh & Welsh, 2006.

xlix Tung, 1982.

l Frazee, V. (1998, September 9). Is the balance sheet right for your expatriates? *Workforce*, 77(9), 19.

li Pfeffer, J. & Sutton, R. I. (2006). *Hard Facts, Dangerous Half-truths, and Total Nonsense: Profiting from Evidence-based Management*. Boston, MA: Harvard Business School Press.

lii E.g. see Hastings, 1999.

liii Bethune, G., & Huler, S. (1999). *From Worst to First: Behind the Scenes of Continental's Remarkable Comeback*. New York: John Wiley & Sons.

liv Dowling, P., Schuler, R. S., & Welch, D. E. (1993). *International Dimensions of Human Resource Management* (p. 117). Cincinnati, OH: Thomson South-Western.

lv Reynolds, C. (1997). Expatriate compensation in historical perspective. *Journal of World Business*, 32(2), 118–132.

lvi Fryer, B., Milkovich, G. T., Thinnes, J. A., Yaffe, J., & Kokott, D. (2003). In a world of pay. *Harvard Business Review*, (81)11, 31–40.

lvii In search of stealth: Expatriate workers (The rise of the stealth expat). (2005, April 23). *The Economist*, pp. 62–64.

lviii Tung, 1982.

lix Baker, J. C., Ryans, K., & Howard, G. (1988). *International Business Classics* (pp. 283–295). Lexington, MA: D.C. Heath and Co.

lx Reynolds, 1997; Tung, R. L. (1988). *The New Expatriates: Managing Human Resources Abroad*. Cambridge, MA: Ballinger; Tung, 1998.

lxi Heenan, D. A. (1970). The corporate expatriate: Assignment to ambiguity. *Columbia Journal of World Business*, 5(3), 49–54.

lxii Mann, J. (1997). *Beijing Jeep: A Case Study of Western Business in China*. Boulder, CO: Westview Press.

lxiii Ostler, N. (2005). *Empires of the Word: A Language History of the World*. New York: HarperCollins.

lxiv Rahim, A. (1983, April). A model for developing key expatriate executives. *Personnel Journal*, pp. 312–317.

lxv Skapinker, M. (2007, November 9). Whose language? *Financial Times*, p. 9.

lxvi Tung, 1982.

lxvii See the excellent article by former National University of Singapore Business School Dean Christopher Early and colleague in *Harvard Business Review* on cultural intelligence (Early & Mosakowski, 2005).

lxviii Lewis, R. D. (2005). *When Cultures Collide: Leading Across Cultures*. London: Nicholas Brealey Publishing.

lxix Tannen, D. (1996). *Talking from 9 to 5: Women and Men at Work*. Lancaster Place, U.K.: Virago Press.

lxx Gilboy, G. (2004). The myth behind China's miracle. *Foreign Affairs*, 83(4), 33–48.

lxxi Bruton, G. D., Ahlstrom, D., & Chan, E. S. (2001). Foreign firms in China: Facing human resources challenges in a transitional economy. *SAM Advanced Management Journal*, 65(4), Autumn, 4–11.

lxxii Rahim, 1983.

lxxiii Butler, 1999.

lxxiv Adler, N. J. (2004). *International Dimensions of Organizational Behavior* (5th ed.). Cincinnati, OH: South-Western/Thomson Learning; Tung, 1982, 1988.

lxxv Israeli, D. N., Banai, M., & Zeira, Y. (1980). Women executives in MNC subsidiaries. *California Management Review*, 23(1), 53–63.

lxxvi McCall, M. W. (1998). *High Fliers: Developing the Next Generation of Leaders*. Boston, MA: Harvard Business School Press.

lxxvii Adler, 2004.

lxxviii Hofstede & Hofstede, 2005.

lxxix Hofstede & Hofstede, 2005.

lxxx Fukuyama, F. (1995). *Trust: The Social Virtues and the Creation of Prosperity*. New York: Free Press.

lxxxi Clague, L., & Krupp, N. B. (1978). International personnel: The repatriation problem, *The Personnel Administrator*, April, p. 32.

lxxxii Butler, 1999.

Chapter 13

i Chandler, A. D. (1969). *Strategy and Structure: Chapters in the History of American Industrial Enterprise* (paperback ed.). Cambridge, MA: MIT Press; Chandler, A. D. (1990). *Scale and Scope*. Cambridge, MA: Belknap Press.

ii Scott, W. R. (2003). *Organizations: Rational, Natural, and Open Systems*. Upper Saddle River, NJ: Prentice Hall; Donaldson, L. (1995). *American Anti-Management Theories of Organization: A Critique of Paradigm Proliferation*. Cambridge: Cambridge University Press.

iii Parkinson, C. N. (1993). *Parkinson's Law*. Cutchogue, NY: Buccaneer Books.

iv Parkinson, 1993.

v Kemenade, W. V. (1998). *China, Hong Kong, Taiwan, Inc.: The Dynamics of a New Empire*. New York: Vintage Books.

vi Backman, M. (1995). *Overseas Chinese Business Networks in Asia*. Canberra: Australian Government.

vii Ahlstrom, D., Young, M. N., Chan, E. S., & Bruton, G. D. (2004). Facing constraints to growth? Overseas Chinese entrepreneurs and traditional business practices in East Asia. *Asia Pacific Journal of Management*, 21, 263–285.

viii Ahlstrom et al., 2004.

ix Weidenbaum, M., & Hughes, M. (1996). *Bamboo Network: How Expatriate Chinese Entrepreneurs Are Creating a New Economic Superpower in Asia*. New York: Free Press.

x Chandler, A. D. (1990). The enduring logic of industrial success. *Harvard Business Review*, 68(2), 130–140.

xi Trout, Jack. (1995). *The New Positioning*. New York: McGraw-Hill.

xii Trout, 1995, pp. 52–53.

xiii Trout, 1995, pp. 52–53.

xiv Rugman, A. M., & Girod, S. (2003). Retail multinationals & globalization: The evidence is regional. *European Management Journal*, 21(1), 24–45.

xv Prewitt, E. (2003, September 1). GM's matrix reloaded. *CIO Magazine*. http://www.cio.com/archive/090103/hs_reload.html

xvi Donaldson, 1995.

xvii Donaldson, 1995.

xviii Senge, P. M. (1990). *The Fifth Discipline: The Art and Practice of the Learning Organization* (p. 3). New York: Doubleday/Currency.

xix Christensen, C. M., & Raynor, M. E. (2003). *The Innovator's Solution: Creating and Sustaining Successful Growth*. Boston: Harvard Business School Press.

xx Hammer, M. (1990, July/August) Reengineering work: Don't automate, obliterate. *Harvard Business Review*, pp. 70–91.

xxi Heathfield, S. M. (2005). Consequences and employee involvement during change. http://humanresources.about.com/od/changemanagement/a/change_wisdom.htm.

xxii Friedman, T. L. (2000). *The Lexus and the Olive Tree: Understanding Globalization*. New York: Anchor Books.

xxiii Enterprise modeling and simulation in reengineering. (1994, December). *Hewlett Packard Journal*. http://www.hpl.hp.com/hpjournal/94dec/dec94a10b.pdf

xxiv Heathfield, S. M. (2005). Executive support and leadership for change management. http://humanresources.about.com/od/changemanagement/a/change_lessons_2.htm

xxv Stephenson, K. (2006). *The Quantum Theory of Trust: The Secret of Mapping and Managing Human Relationships*. Upper Saddle River, NJ: Prentice Hall.

xxvi Ahlstrom, Young, Chan, & Bruton, 2004.

xxvii Prahalad, C. K., & Hamel, G. (1990). The core competence of the corporation. *Harvard Business Review*, 65(3), 79–90; Lieberthal, K., & Lieberthal, G. (2003). The great transition. *Harvard Business Review*, 81(10), 70–79.

xxviii Senge, 1990; Hamel, G. (2002). *Leading the Revolution: How to Thrive in Turbulent Times by Making Innovation a Way of Life* (revised ed.). Boston: Harvard Business School Press.

Chapter 14

i Damels, J. D., Ogram, E. W., & Radebaugh, L. H. (1982). *International Business Environments and Operations* (3rd ed.). Reading, MA: Addison-Wesley.

ii The CIA World Factbook. List of Countries by Exports. http://en.wikipedia.org/wiki/List_of_countries_by_exports, accessed November 11, 2008; WTO reports. 2007. WTO: 2007 PRESS RELEASES. http://www.wto.org/english/news_e/pres07_e/pr472_e.htm (accessed January 17, 2008).

iii Shapiro, A. C. (1992). *Multicultural Financial Management* (4th ed.) (p. 5). Needham Heights, MA: Allyn & Bacon.

iv The challengers. (2007). *The Economist*, 386(8562), 61–63.

v Hambrick, D. C., Korn, L. B., Frederickson, J. W., & Feny, R.M. (1989). *21st Century Report: Reinventing the CEO* (pp. 1–94). New York: Korn-Feny and Columbia University's Graduate School of Business.

vi Hambrick, Korn, Frederickson, & Feny, 1989.

vii Baumol, W. J. (2004). *The Free-Market Innovation Machine: Analyzing the Growth Miracle of Capitalism*. Princeton, NJ: Princeton University Press; Christensen, C. M., Roth, E. A., & Anthony, S. D. (2004). *Seeing What's Next: Using Theories of Innovation to Predict Industry Change*. Boston: Harvard Business School Press.

viii Bhide, A. V. (2000). *The Origin and Evolution of New Businesses*. New York: Oxford University Press; Baumol, 2004.

ix Acs, Z. (2006). How is entrepreneurship good for economic growth? *Innovations*, Winter, 97–107.

x Timmons, J. A., & Spinelli, S. (2008). *New Venture Creation: Entrepreneurship for the 21st Century* (8th ed.). Boston: McGraw-Hill/Irwin.

xi Acs, 2006.

xii Barone, M. (2005). *Hard America, Soft America: Competition vs. Coddling and the Battle for the Nation's Future*. New York: Three Rivers Press.

xiii James, H. (2006). *Family Capitalism: Wendels, Haniels, Falcks, and the Continental European Model*. Cambridge, MA: Belknap Press.

xiv Barone, 2005.

xv Yergin, D., & Stanislaw, J. (2002). *The Commanding Heights: The Battle for the World Economy* (revised updated 2nd ed.). New York: Free Press.

xvi Hastings, D. F. (1999). Lincoln Electric's harsh lessons from international expansion. *Harvard Business Review*, May/June, 3–11.

xvii Christensen, C. M., Craig, T., & Hart, S. (2001). The great disruption. *Foreign Affairs*, March/April, 80–95; Timmons & Spinelli, 2008.

xviii Schumpeter, J. (2008). *Capitalism, Socialism and Democracy*. New York: Harper Perennial Modern Classics.

xix Baumol, W. J., Litan, R. E., & Schramm, C. J. (2007). *Good Capitalism, Bad Capitalism, and the Economics of Growth and Prosperity*. New Haven, CT: Yale University Press; Timmons & Spinelli, 2008.

xx Baumol, 2004.

xxi Timmons & Spinelli, 2008.

xxii Christensen, Craig, & Hart, 2001; Christensen & Raynor, 2003.

xxiii Porter, M. E. (1980). *Competitive Strategy: Techniques for Analyzing Industries and Competitors*. New York: Free Press; Johnson, C. A. (1983). *MITI and the Japanese Miracle: The Growth of Industrial Policy 1925–1975*. Stanford, CA: Stanford University Press.

xxiv Porter, M. E. (1990). *The Competitive Advantage of Nations*. New York: Free Press.

xxv Acs, 2006.

xxvi Christensen, C., & Hart, 2001; Studwell, J. (2007). *Asian Godfathers: Money and Power in Hong Kong and Southeast Asia*. New York: Atlantic Monthly Press.

xxvii Christensen et al., 2001; Porter et al., 2000.

xxviii Fallows, J. (1995). *Looking at the Sun: The Rise of the New East Asian Economic and Political System*. New York: Vintage; Johnson, 1983.

xxix Vogel, E. F. (1979). *Japan as Number One: Lessons for America*. Cambridge: Harvard University Press.

xxx Johnson, 1983; Vogel, 1979.

xxxi Christensen, Craig, & Hart, 2001.

xxxii Christensen, Craig, & Hart, 2001.

xxxiii Christensen, Craig, & Hart, 2001; Porter, M. E., Takeuchi, H., & Sakakibara, M. (2000). *Can Japan Compete?* Basingstoke, UK: Macmillan.

xxxiv Johnson, C. A. (1983). *MITI and the Japanese Miracle: The Growth of Industrial Policy 1925–1975.* Stanford, CA: Stanford University Press; Vogel, E. F. (1979). *Japan as Number One: Lessons for America.* Cambridge, MA: Harvard University Press.

xxxv Porter, M. E., Takeuchi, H., & Sakakibara, M. (2000). *Can Japan Compete?* Basingstoke, UK: Macmillan.

xxxvi Christensen, C. M., Craig, T., & Hart, S. (1002). The great disruption. *Foreign Affairs*, March/April, 80–95; Porter, M. E. (1990). *The Competitive Advantage of Nations.* New York: The Free Press.

xxxvii Studwell, 2007.

xxxviii Baumol et al., 2007.

xxxix Acs, 2006.

xl McDougall, P. P., & Oviatt, B. M. (1996). New venture internationalization, strategic change, and performance: A follow-up study. *Journal of Business Venturing*, 11(1), 23–40.

xli McDougall & Oviatt, 1996.

xlii McDougall & Oviatt, 1996.

xliii Khanna, T. (2008). *Billions of Entrepreneurs: How China and India Are Reshaping Their Futures—and Yours.* Boston: Harvard Business School Press.

xliv Khanna, 2008; Zeng, M., & Williamson, P. J. (2007). *Dragons at Your Door: How Chinese Cost Innovation Is Disrupting Global Competition.* Boston: Harvard Business School Press.

xlv Ahlstrom, D., Young, M. N., Nair, A., & Wang, L. C. (2006). China: Competitive myths and realities. *SAM Advanced Management Journal*, 71(4), 4–10; Gilboy, G. J. (2004). The myth behind China's miracle. *Foreign Affairs*, 83(4), 33–48.

xlvi Gilboy, 2004.

xlvii Porter, 1990.

xlviii Nelson, R. R. (1993). *National Innovation Systems: A Comparative Analysis.* New York: Oxford University Press; Nelson, R. R., & Wright, G. (1992). The rise and fall of American technological leadership: The postwar era in historical perspective. *Journal of Economic Literature*, 30 (December), 1931–1964.

xlix Porter, 1990.

l Bhidé, A. (2006). *Venturesome consumption, innovation and globalization.* Paper presented at the Joint Conference of CESifo and the Center on Capitalism and Society—Perspectives on the Performance of the Continent's Economies. Venice, July 21–22; Gilboy, 2004.

li Gilboy, 2004.

lii Gilboy, 2004.

liii Bhidé, 2006.

liv Von Hippel, E. (2006). *Democratizing Innovation.* Cambridge, MA: The MIT Press.

lv Elgin, B. (2007, October 29). Little green lies. *BusinessWeek*, 45–52.

lvi Easterly, W. (2006). *The White Man's Burden: Why the West's Efforts to Aid the Rest Have Done So Much Ill and So Little Good.* New York: Penguin Press HC.

lvii Ferguson, N. (2008). *The Ascent of Money.* New York: Penguin Press.

lviii Kindleberger, C. P., & Aliber, R. (2005). *Manias, Panics, and Crashes: A History of Financial Crises* (5th ed.). New York: John Wiley & Sons.

lix Ferguson, 2008.

lx Ferguson, 2008; Kindleberger & Aliber, 2005.

lxi Kindleberger & Aliber, 2005.

lxii Bhagwati, J. (2004). *In Defense of Globalization.* Oxford: Oxford University Press.

lxiii U.S. Department of Labor. (1998). *Hourly Compensation Costs in U.S. Dollars. Table 1.* (September). Washington, DC: U.S. Department of Labor, Bureau of Labor Statistics.

lxiv Friedman, T. L. (2007). *The World Is Flat 3.0: A Brief History of the Twenty-first Century.* New York: Picador.

lxv Wolf, M. (2004). *Why Globalization Works.* New Haven: Yale University Press.

lxvi Bhagwati, 2004; Wolf, 2004.

lxvii Bhidé, 2007.

lxviii Studwell, J. (2007). *Asian Godfathers.* London: Profile Books.

lxix *Economic Outlook* 1998. International Monetary Fund (October). Washington, DC.

Name Index

Subject Index

Case Name	Case Authors	Pages	Source	Topics	Chapters
South African Breweries International: Devising a China Market Strategy	Dawar, N.; Everatt, D.	23	Richard Ivey School of Business	Market Strategy, Emerging Markets, Brand Positioning, Corporate Strategy.	1, 2, 5,
Eskom South African Electrification Program A-E	Gorman, M.; Werhane, P.; Cunningham, B.	15 (A); 2 (B); 2 (C); 3 (D); 4 (E)	Darden	Financing; Business and society; Business Ethics; Planning; Business/Government Relations; Capital Investment; Corporate Responsibility; Developing Countries; Distribution; Ethics; IB; MBO; Personal Values; R&D; Public Policy; Risk Analysis; Strategic Planning & Implementation.	2, 3, 7, 8, 10
Privatizing Poland's Telecom Industry: Opportunities & Challenges In The New Economy & E-Business	Conklin, D.W.; Siwak, M.; Cadieux, D.	25 (A); 4 (B)	Richard Ivey School of Business	General Business Environment, Strategy, Privatization, Entrepreneurship and Innovation.	3, 6, 14
Komia And The 3g Wireless Phone Auction In Poland A&B	Bonardi, J.P.; Siwak, M.	24 (A) 3 (B)	Richard Ivey School of Business	Bidding, Deregulation, Political Environment, Uncertainty.	1, 3, 10, 14
Vincor International Inc.	Fry, J.N./ Roberts, D.	25	Richard Ivey School of Business	Industry Analysis, Initial Public Offerings, Strategic Planning.	5, 6, 12
An International Project Manager's Day	Lane, H.W.; Wright, L.	5 (A); 17 (B); 5 (C); 21 (D)	Richard Ivey School of Business	Project Management, Intercultural Relations, International Business, Construction.	2, 9, 10
Asimco International Casting Company (A)	Klassen, R.; Lui, S.	18	Richard Ivey School of Business	Operations Management, Process Design/Change, International Business, Technology.	5, 6, 9
FirstCaribbean International Bank: The Marketing & Branding Challenges of a Startup	Chen, G.; Deslandes, D.	20	Richard Ivey School of Business	Brand Management, Brand Positioning, Market Strategy, Marketing Planning.	1, 6, 14
Meridco Magnesium: International Technology Transfer	Bansal, P.; Cole, K.	14	Richard Ivey School of Business	Technology Transfer, International Business, Knowledge Management, Strategy Implementation.	8, 9, 11
Manulife Financial: Adjusting International Strategies In Response to the Asian Crisis	Conklin, D.W.; Tsai, T.; Everatt, D.; Hunter, T.	33	Richard Ivey School of Business	Growth Strategy, Developing Countries, Strategic Planning, Management in a Global Environment.	1, 3, 4, 10

Case Name	Case Authors	Pages	Source	Topics	Chapters
International Bank of Malaysia Limited	DiStefano, J.J.	10	Richard Ivey School of Business	International Business, Government Regulation, Interdepartmental Relations, Intercultural Relations.	3, 10, 12, 13
L.L. Bean Latin America	Cardona, Pablo; Araiza, Eduardo.	19	IESE	Clothing; Cross Cultural Relations; International Business; Retailing.	2, 11, 12, 13
Worldwide Equipment (China) LTD: A Sales Performance Dilemma	Cotte, J.; Yang, A.	19	Richard Ivey School of Business	Sales Management, Sales Organization, Performance Evaluation, Organizational Behaviour.	4, 7, 8, 12
Tricon Logistics China	Lanfranconi, C.P.; Wang, M.	12	Richard Ivey School of Business	Control Systems, Cost Systems, Cost Control	4, 11
Technosoft Russia	Erskine, J.A.; Suzdalev, F.	15	Richard Ivey School of Business	Performance Evaluation, Leadership, Contracting, Human Resources Management.	6, 8, 12
Harmonization Of Compensation And Benefits For FirstCaribbean International Bank	Corbin, E.; Punnett, B.	10	Richard Ivey School of Business	Benefits Policy, Change Management, Compensation, Consolidations and Mergers.	7, 12
Hazelton International Limited	Lane, H.W.; Wright, L	12	Richard Ivey School of Business	Project Management, International Business, Third World	9, 10, 11

MAKE IT YOURS

Make It Yours, add business cases to your text. Your course is unique, create a text that reflects it. Let us help you put together a quality International Management casebook simply, quickly, and affordably. We have aligned best-selling business cases from leading case providers such Darden and Ivey at the chapter level for this text. Create a comprehensive learning solution by adding cases into your text, or simply select cases to create a casebook. To review and select your cases please visit us online at: www.cengage.com/custom/makeityours/AhlstromBruton1

GLOBAL ECONOMIC CRISIS RESOURCE CENTER

Global Economic Crisis Resource Center— the new online web portal features the solutions you want in an easy-to-use teachable format, including:

* A global issues database
* A thorough overview and timeline of events leading up to the global economic crisis
* Links to the latest news and resources
* Discussion and testing content
* Text specific content
* A built-in instructor feedback forum so we can hear your suggestions to make this cutting-edge resource even stronger!

For more information on how you can access this resource, please visit www.cengage.com/rc/gec.